本书由中央财政支持地方高校发展专项资金提供资助

AN INTRODUCTION TO FOREIGN EXCHANGE MARKET INSTRUMENTS

外汇市场交易工具入门

主编　陶庆梅

重庆大学出版社

内容简介

本书首先从汇率制度和国际货币体系入手，介绍了外汇市场的规则和行业惯例。进而具体解释了外汇市场最基本的五个交易工具，即期、远期、交换、期货、期权。另外还介绍了交易场所、交易平台、交易规则、交易术语等。其中运用了少量数学公式进一步说明了外汇市场的各种价格。

本书可作为普通高等院校金融专业的教材，也可作为外汇爱好者的入门读物。本书每一章后安排了案例分析、习题和答案以及拓展阅读。案例分析主要是围绕中国的外汇市场展开；习题和答案的设计目标是对章节内容进行巩固；拓展阅读给出的资料是为了学生对外汇做进一步学习，授课者可以根据学生的学习情况酌情安排阅读。

图书在版编目(CIP)数据

外汇市场交易工具入门 = An Introduction to Foreign Exchange Market Instruments：英文 / 陶庆梅主编. -- 重庆：重庆大学出版社，2023.7
ISBN 978-7-5689-2707-9

Ⅰ.①外… Ⅱ.①陶… Ⅲ.①外汇市场—英文②外汇交易—英文 Ⅳ.①F830.92

中国版本图书馆 CIP 数据核字(2021)第 095502 号

外汇市场交易工具入门
主　编　陶庆梅
策划编辑：尚东亮　　特邀编辑：张雨竹
责任编辑：尚东亮　　版式设计：尚东亮
责任校对：邹　忌　　责任印制：张　策
*
重庆大学出版社出版发行
出版人：饶帮华
社址：重庆市沙坪坝区大学城西路 21 号
邮编：401331
电话：(023) 88617190　88617185(中小学)
传真：(023) 88617186　88617166
网址：http://www.cqup.com.cn
邮箱：fxk@cqup.com.cn (营销中心)
全国新华书店经销
POD：重庆新生代彩印技术有限公司
*
开本：787mm×1092mm　1/16　印张：23.25　字数：683千
2023 年 7 月第 1 版　2023 年 7 月第 1 次印刷
ISBN 978-7-5689-2707-9　定价：78.00 元

PREFACE

Intended Audience

An Introduction to Foreign Exchange Market Instruments is specially designed for students of finance who plan to study foreign exchange market. As foreign exchange market is originated from the UK, financial centers of foreign exchange are located mainly in the UK and the US, and English is the language applied in software and program for quantitative analysis, English is essential for a better understanding of foreign exchange market. To meet the bilingual teaching's call and to fulfill the gap between job demand and current education supply, this book is written in English. It can be used in advanced undergraduate in the major of finance, international finance, international monetary economics, and international financial management. It is also an ideal textbook for English-speaking readers.

Presentation

Grew from the lecture notes for undergraduate students at Chongqing Technology and Business Unversity, the text has proved to be successful. As an introduction book, lacking necessary expertise in foreign exchange is assumed from readers. Mathematically sophisticated undergraduates should be able to read it on their own. Numerical techniques are presented and the underlying financial theory is covered. Each chapter is followed by case studies, exercises and further readings. Case studies are mainly about foreign exchange practice. An integral part of the text is exercises placed after the relevant materials with answers provided in the end.

Organization

An Introduction to Foreign Exchange Market Instruments offers a concise yet comprehensive overview of international currency markets, financial products in foreign exchange market, and fundamental applications of quantitative models. By introducing cases and examples, this book presents basic knowledge in international monetary theory, foreign exchange market, and investment analysis.

With the application of the basic principles on real world problems, especially with China's cases, the book provides guidance on how to solve exchange rate trade issues as well as practical foreign exchange products management.

This book is composed by the following 7 chapters:

Chapter 1 surveys the exchange rate regimes and introduces international monetary systems.

Chapter 2 illustrates the evolution of worldwide foreign exchange market and introduces the foreign exchange market in China.

Chapter 3 states the conventions of foreign exchange spot. Algorithm expressing is outlined.

Chapter 4 contains foreign exchange forward and probes deeper into interest rate parity that links forward, spot and interest rates.

Chapter 5 covers foreign exchange swap and introduces fundamental algorithm analysis about swap.

Chapter 6 is about foreign exchange futures and investigates basic foreign exchange futures trade conventions.

Chapter 7 discusses the fundamental theory and practice of foreign exchange option.

CONTENTS

Chapter 1
Exchange Rate Regimes and International Monetary Systems

Since the foundation of the People's Republic of China, the annual exchange rate between the U.S. dollar and Chinese yuan as shown in Figure 1-1 below has gone through 4 main stages. It is not only interesting but also necessary to analyze these exchange rate changes given both China and the U.S. are the top economies in the world.

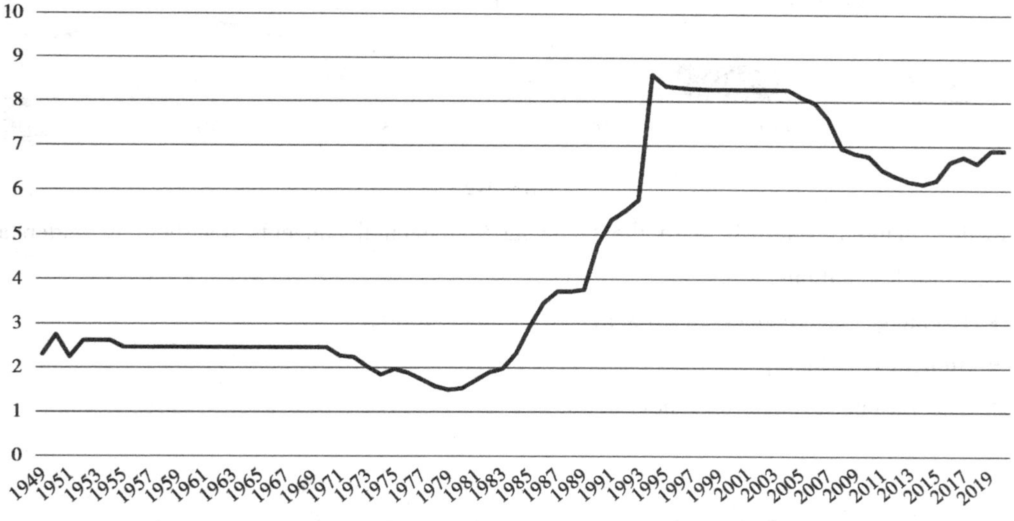

Figure 1-1 Annual Average USD/CNY 1949—2019

Figure 1-2 provides a closer look into the daily exchange rate since the end of year 2019, one may find that the exchange rate has been quite active since Jan. 2020.

Lots of reasons led to these fluctuations: COVID-19 pandemic, Sino-US trade conflict, the U.S. election, etc.

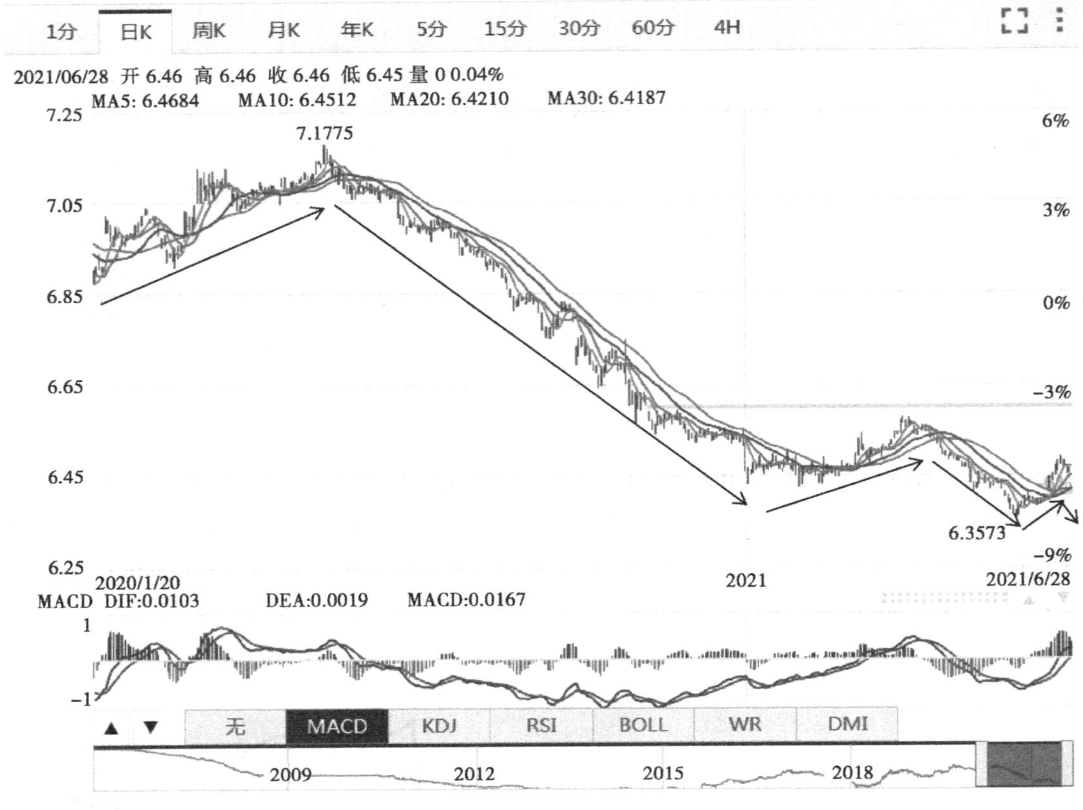

Figure 1-2

In this chapter, you will learn the following fundamental concepts that help to understand exchange rate fluctuations.

- Exchange rate regimes and practice in the real world;
- Monetary systems;
- The European single currency.

§1 Exchange Rate Regimes

1.1 Definition

Globalization makes countries and economies interact more frequently in many aspects, including in money market. Every economy should choose how to manage its currency in relation to other currencies. The way an economy manages its currency in relation to other currencies and the foreign exchange market is called the exchange rate regime (exchange rate system/exchange rate arrangement). The Exchange rate regime can affect one country's macroeconomic performance (inflation, economic growth, susceptibility to crises) and it contributes to the stability of the international monetary system. Common exchange rate regimes include floating, fixed and pegged rates.

Most countries nowadays choose exchange rate regime that is between floating exchange and fixed exchange rate.

The exchange rate regime is highly related with monetary policy, which is main factor for money price determination. Specifically, money has two prices: interest rate and exchange rate. The changes of economy can affect both prices. As one of the key macroeconomic policies, monetary policy can affect interest rate hence exchange rate regime.

1.2 Contents of Exchange Rate Regimes

It is believed that the world economy has experienced several exchange rate regimes. The International Monetary Fund (IMF) has initially classified the exchange rate regimes into 8 categories according to the degree of flexibility of the arrangement①. They are:

(1) exchange arrangements with no separate legal tender.

(2) currency board arrangements.

(3) conventional fixed peg arrangements.

(4) pegged exchange rates within horizontal bands.

(5) crawling pegs.

(6) exchange rates within crawling bands.

(7) managed floating with no predetermined path for the exchange rates.

(8) independent floating.

In 2009, IMF has revised the above classification and has put the exchange rate regimes into 4 main categories: hard pegs, soft pegs, floating, and residual. Under each category, there are more detailed types as shown below:

1) Hard Pegs

(1) Exchange Arrangement with No Separate Legal Tender

Under this arrangement, one country puts it in law that it chooses another country's currency as its national currency. Ecuador in Jan. 2000, for example, officially replaced its national currency, the Ecuadorian sucre, with the US dollar (a policy called dollarization). By adopting such an arrangement, Ecuador can benefit from the currency issuing country's (the U.S.) economic stability but with the cost of monetary sovereignty. This arrangement is not always beneficial though, Argentina's hard peg turned out to be a failure and has collapsed in 2002.

---

① www.imf.com

(2) Currency Board Arrangement

A currency board arrangement is a monetary arrangement based on an explicit legislative commitment to exchange domestic currency for a specified foreign currency at a fixed exchange rate, combined with restrictions on the issuing authority to ensure the fulfillment of its legal obligation. This implies that domestic currency will be issued only against foreign exchange and that it remains fully backed by foreign assets, eliminating traditional central bank functions such as monetary control and lender-of-last-resort, and leaving little scope for discretionary monetary policy. Initiated by the UK since 1849, currency board arrangement once was adopted by more than 70 countries in 1940's. Nowadays, some flexibility may be afforded, depending on the strictness of the banking rules of the currency board arrangement.

2) **Soft Pegs**

(1) Conventional Pegged Arrangement

For classification as a conventional pegged arrangement, the country formally pegs its currency at a fixed rate to another currency or a basket of currencies, where the basket is formed, for example, from the currencies of major trading or financial partners, and weights reflect the geographic distribution of trade, services, or capital flows. The anchor currency or basket weights are publicly notified. The country authorities stand ready to maintain the fixed parity through direct intervention (i.e., via sale or purchase of foreign exchange in the market) or indirect intervention (e.g., via exchange rate related use of interest rate policy, imposition of foreign exchange regulations, exercise of moral suasion that constrains foreign exchange activity, or intervention by other public institutions). There is no commitment to irrevocably keep the parity, but the formal arrangement must be confirmed empirically: the exchange rate may fluctuate within narrow margins of less than ±1% around a central rate—or the maximum and minimum value of the spot market exchange rate must remain within a narrow margin of 2%—for at least 6 months.

(2) Stabilized Arrangement

Classification as a stabilized arrangement entails a spot market exchange rate that remains within a margin of 2% for 6 months or more (with the exception of a specified number of outliers or step adjustments), and is not floating. The required margin of stability can be met either with respect to a single currency or a basket of currencies, where the anchor currency or the basket is ascertained or confirmed using statistical techniques. Classification as a stabilized arrangement requires that the statistical criteria are met, and that the exchange rate remains stable as a result of official action (including structural market rigidities). The classification does not imply a policy commitment on the part of the country authorities.

(3) Crawling Peg

Classification as a crawling peg involves the confirmation of the country authorities' de jure exchange rate arrangement. The currency is adjusted in small amounts at a fixed rate or in response to changes in selected quantitative indicators, such as past inflation differentials vis-à-vis major trading partners or differentials between the inflation target and expected inflation in major trading partners. The rate of crawl can be set to generate inflation-adjusted changes in the exchange rate (backward looking) or set at a predetermined fixed rate and/or below the projected inflation differentials (forward looking). The rules and parameters of the arrangement are public.

(4) Crawl-like Arrangement

For classification as a crawl-like arrangement, the exchange rate must remain within a narrow margin of 2% relative to a statistically identified trend for 6 months or more (with the exception of a specified number of outliers), and the exchange rate arrangement cannot be considered as floating. Normally, a minimum rate of change greater than allowed under a stabilized (peg-like) arrangement is required. However, an arrangement will be considered crawl-like with an annualized rate of change of at least 1%, provided that the exchange rate appreciates or depreciates in a sufficiently monotonic and continuous manner.

(5) Pegged Exchange Rate within Horizontal Bands

Classification as a pegged exchange rate within horizontal bands involves the confirmation of the country authorities' de jure exchange rate arrangement. The value of the currency is maintained within certain margins of fluctuation of at least ±1% around a fixed central rate, or the margin between the maximum and minimum value of the exchange rate exceeds 2%. It includes arrangements of countries in the Exchange Rate Mechanism (ERM) of the European Monetary System (EMS), which was replaced with the ERM Ⅱ on 1st Jan. 1999, for those countries with margins of fluctuation wider than ±1%. The central rate and width of the band are public.

3) Floating Arrangements

(1) Floating

A floating exchange rate is largely market determined, without an ascertainable or predictable path for the rate. In particular, an exchange rate that satisfies the statistical criteria for a peg-like or a crawl-like arrangement will be classified as such unless it is clear that the stability of the exchange rate is not the result of official actions. Foreign exchange market intervention may be either direct or indirect, and serves to moderate the rate of change and prevent undue fluctuations in the exchange rate. But policies targeting a specific level of the exchange rate are incompatible with floating. Indicators for managing the rate are broadly judgmental (e.g., balance of payments position, international reserves, parallel market developments). Floating arrangements may exhibit more or less exchange rate volatility, depending on the size of the shocks affecting the economy.

(2) Free Floating

A floating exchange rate can be classified as free floating if intervention occurs only exceptionally, aims to address disorderly market conditions, and if the authorities have provided information or data confirming that intervention has been limited to at most three instances in the previous 6 months, each lasting no more than 3 business days. If the information or data required are not available, the arrangement is not free floating, but floating.

4) Residual

When the exchange rate arrangement does not meet the criteria for any of the other categories, it is classified as residual. Arrangements characterized by frequent shifts in policies may fall into this category.

1.3 Practice Situation

The given exchange rate regimes have many subtle varieties in between, and thus countries with the same exchange rate regime may differ widely if central banks have different international reserves and interest rates. This explains why in reality there are no two countries have exactly the same exchange rate regime, nor is there any exchange rate regime that is suitable for all countries or at all times. Central banks need to find the most suitable one for their countries by balancing between the monetary autonomy and exchange rate stability due to the impossible trinity.

Very few countries apply absolute floating exchange rate. Even the most frequently traded currencies are not 100% pure floating, as central banks intervene to avoid excessive fluctuation of the exchange rate. The most common exchange rate regime today is called a managed float or a dirty float. For example, the dollar, Euro, British pound and Japanese yen all are managed floating currencies.

Pegged floating currencies are relatively fixed to some currencies or one currency, only periodically adjusted. The well-known case is that after World War Ⅱ the United States pegged the dollar to gold ($35.00 was equal to one ounce of gold), and most other countries had pegged their currencies to the US dollar. China has also gone through pegged floating (1955–1970 and 1995–2005) as Figure 1-1 indicates.

Meanwhile, the choice of foreign exchange rate regimes can influence or determine how the exchange rate between two currencies moves and fluctuates in foreign exchange market. For example, there is little sense to study the market force for the sake of exchange rate determination under pegged floating exchange rate regime.

1.4 Evolution of Exchange Rate Regime

Evolution of exchange rate regime is generally summed into 4 stages:

1) Exchange Rate Regimes when Money Is Based on a Metallic Standard

If money has an intrinsic value, i.e. money value is based on a precious metal, it leads to a fixed exchange rate system. For most of human history, money was based on some variation of a metallic standard. The last period with such a standard (called reserve currency standard) ended in 1971. One of the challenges of a metallic standard is that it does not allow countries to conduct independent monetary policies. It is a kind of fixed exchange rate.

2) Exchange Rate Regimes when Money Is Fiat

Fiat currency has no intrinsic value and does not lead to a specific exchange rate regime. Under countries have autonomy to choose their exchange rate regime. When the last metallic standard period ended in 1971, money in all countries was fiat money. Nowadays, many developed countries choose flexible exchange rate regimes where the value of currencies is decided in foreign exchange markets with minimum interventions based on the demand for and supply of currencies.

3) Pegged Regimes and Their Purposes in a Fiat Currency System

Since 1971, most developing countries have adopted a variety of pegged exchange rate regimes. One of the important factors that affect the type of the pegged regime is the extent to which the pegged regime can exercise control over monetary policy. Hard pegs such as currency board and dollarization do not provide as much monetary autonomy as soft pegs do. While hard pegs are used to signal stability, soft pegs can serve to make exports or imports cheaper or to attract foreign investors. Although pegged regimes provide a balance between fixed and free floats, they are susceptible to exchange rate overvaluation, which hurts competitiveness and undermines growth performance.

4) Optimum Currency Area

The concept of the optimum currency area shows that under certain circumstances it would be more efficient to have a common currency in a region. The term optimum implies the requirements for an efficiency-enhancing common currency. Countries in the common-currency region should experience similar economic shocks and have labor mobility among them. Despite benefits, a common currency requires a strong monetary policy coordination as well as fiscal policy coordination.

So far, there is no optimum area. Euro Zone is not an optimum area yet.

1.5 Tradeoffs Associated with Various Exchange Rate Regimes

All exchange rate regimes offer benefits with cost. The table below provides a summary of the cost and benefit associated with various exchange rate regimes.

Table 1-1 Comparison of Exchange Rate Regimes

exchange rate regimes	pros	cons
fixed (commodity money)	• No sudden changes in exchange rates • No need to forecast future exchange rates	• Importing other countries' domestic economic problems, such as inflation and unemployment • Monetary policy cannot be used as stabilization policy
flexible (fiat money)	• Insulation of countries from other countries' economic problems, such as inflation and unemployment • A monetary autonomy	• Excessive volatility in exchange rates
pegged (fiat money)	• Stability provided by a nominal anchor • Aiding economic development through adjusting the price of exports or imports	• Efficiency cost of keeping prices of exports or imports • Prone to speculative attack (hot money leaving the country fast if investors doubt the credibility of the peg)

The exchange-rate regime is often seen as constrained by the monetary policy trilemma, which imposes a tradeoff among exchange stability, monetary independence, and capital market openness①. It is necessary to know more about international monetary systems for a country in order to choose the most suitable exchange rate regime.

§2 China's Exchange Rate Regime

On 21st Jul. 2005 China announced that its currency RMB no longer be pegged to the U.S. dollar②. A gradual reform on exchange rate regime has been implemented in order to absorb external shocks and maintain policy authority. China then launched a managed exchange rate regime and planned to transit towards greater exchange rate flexibility step by step.

From 2005 onwards, China's exchange rate regime has been evolving in a smooth way to a more flexible exchange rate arrangement. So far, China has gone through the following five distinct regimes regarding its exchange rate regime reform.

① Obstfeld M, Shambaugh J C, Taylor A M. The Trilemma in History: Tradeoffs among Exchange Rates, Monetary Policies, and Capital Mobility[J]. Review of Economics & Statistics, 2005, 87(3): 423-438.

② www.pbc.gov.cn/english/130721/2831438/index.html

2.1 Jul. 2005-Jul. 2015

After two decades' economic reform, pegged currency arrangement was found not helping China's economic growth any more. It became unsustainable and undesirable for responding to real-side shocks as well as to secular changes in the economy such as real appreciation. China moved into a managed floating exchange rate regime based on market supply and demand with reference to a basket of currencies. To increase exchange rate flexibility over time, a daily rate of Chinese yuan against a basket of currencies was announced before the start of the trading day. This rate acted as an anchor to form the midpoint of the band within which the USD/CNY rate① could fluctuate on that day. The previous day's close was applied as the central parity. A daily band of 0.3% around this central parity was allowed for USD/CNY rate. Other foreign currencies against Chinese yuan were granted an extra 1.5% fluctuation comparing with USD/CNY rate. The People's Bank of China as the central bank, would make adjustment of the exchange rate band when necessary according to market development as well as the economic and financial situation.

The Jul. 2005 reform was accompanied by a 2.1% step revaluation of Chinese yuan. As one can find from Figure 1-3 below, the Chinese yuan was managed to appreciate gradually against the U.S. dollar, except for during the global financial crises when the rate was kept fixed again at around 6.8 yuan per dollar.

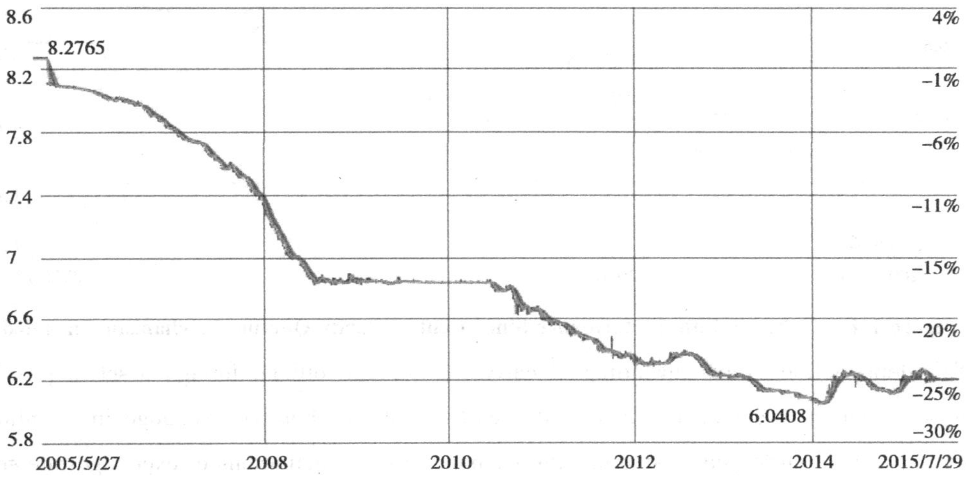

Figure 1-3 Managed Appreciation of Chinese yuan against U.S. dollar

As stated by the People's Bank of China, the central parity and band mechanism have been adjusted consistently. In May 2007, for example, daily band of USD/CNY has be released to 0.5%. Then the formation of central parity has been changed. Before the opening of the market on

① Exchange rate, means the quantity of Chinese yuan for each U.S. dollar, where CNY stands for Chinese yuan.

each business day, all market makers report their prices to China Foreign Exchange Trading System (CFETS). The highest and lowest offers being excluded, and then the weighted average of the remaining prices in the sample is the central parity of USD/CNY for the day.

Markets for forward, swap and option have been established during that period of time. With reserves increasing from 733 billion dollars in Jul. 2005 to 3.99 trillion dollars in Jun. 2014, China was able to moderate its currency appreciation from Jul. 2005 to Jul. 2015 (appreciated by 26% against U.S. dollar).

2.2 Aug. 2015–Dec. 2016

On 11th Aug. 2015, central parity quoting mechanism was amended accompanied by a depreciation of Chinese yuan as shown in Figure 1-4. Market makers in China's foreign exchange market offer their prices referring to the closing rate of the inter-bank foreign exchange market on the previous day and in conjunction with demand and supply condition in the foreign exchange market and exchange rate movement of the major currencies.

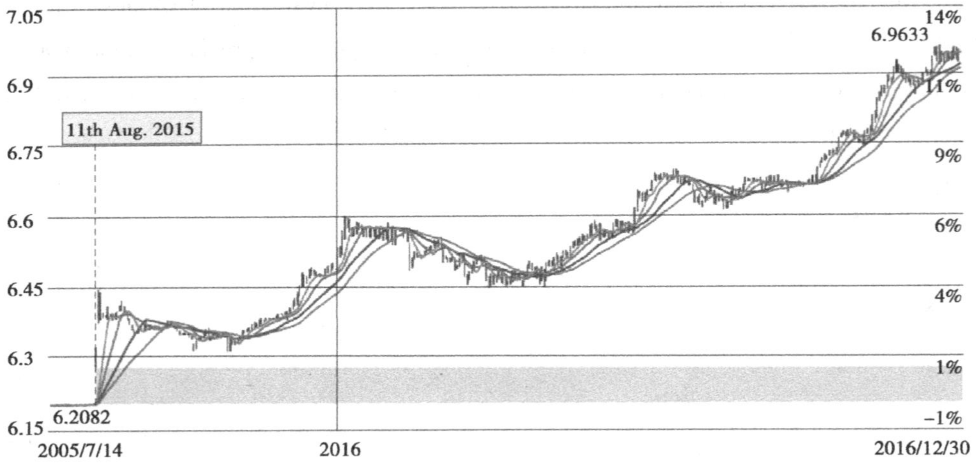

Figure 1-4 Exchange Rate Performance Since Central Parity Quoting Mechanism Amended

This depreciation, plus unwinding of carry trades, and official foreign asset acquisition as well as some capital flight have accelerated a capital outflow. Foreign exchange intervention and moral suasion were employed to stabilize the exchange rate. Fluctuations of exchange rate serve to adjust trade and investment activities with multiple trading partners, the bilateral USD/CNY exchange rate alone is not enough to serve as a good indicator of the international parity of tradable goods. The China Foreign Exchange Trade System thus has published CFETS exchange rate index on its website on 11th Dec. 2015. Market makers were instructed to both consider the CFETS currency basket and refer to the Bank for International Settlements (BIS) and Special Drawing Rights (SDR) baskets in a bid to remove the noise among the changes in the currency basket.

2.3 Jun. 2016–Dec. 2017

With capital flow management and foreign exchange intervention as well as guidance on the central parity mechanism, Chinese yuan has been stable against the CFETS basket during this period of time and foreign reserves began to increase in Feb. 2017. The transition to an adjustable basket peg that was announced in 2005 has been accomplished. In order to curb irrational depreciation sentiment and pro-cyclical herding behavior, the CFETS had adjusted its guidance to market-making banks on their central parity quotes on 26th May 2017 by introducing counter-cyclical adjustment factor to the existing pricing model of the yuan's central parity rate against the U.S. dollar. Pass-through from the previous day's closing rate to the current day's USD/CNY central parity rate was reduced as shown in Figure 1-5.

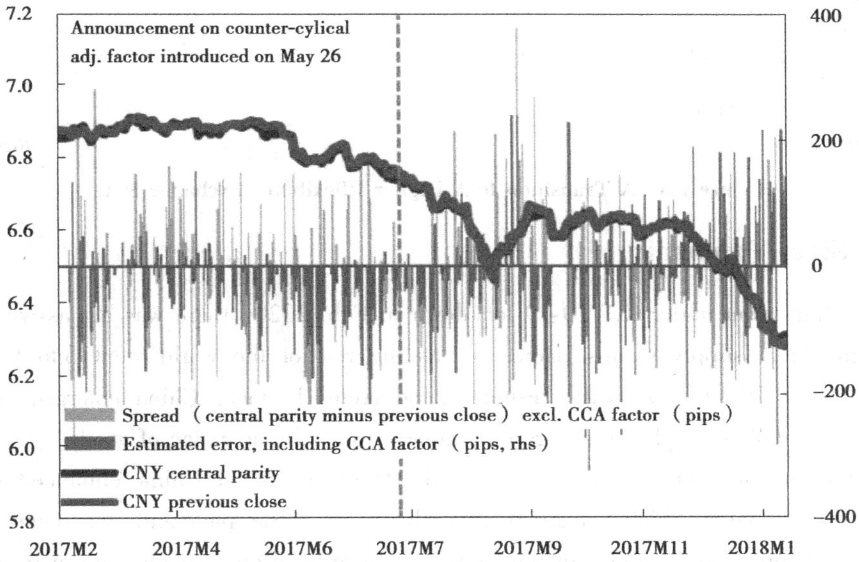

Figure 1-5 USD/CNY Central Parity

Source: bloomberg and IMF staff estimations

Market-making banks during that period of time employed different parameters to reflect their assessment of economic fundamentals, and foreign exchange intervention played a more important role in exchange rate stabilization than the central parity mechanism did.

As capital flows were quenched, the counter-cyclical adjustment factor was then set to neutral but not dropped in early 2018.

2.4 Jan. 2018–Dec. 2019

In the first half of 2018, progress towards a floating exchange rate was continued till the rising trade tensions and initial signs of slowdown in the economy across the world. A significant depreciation of Chinese yuan arose but the volatility was reduced by measures such as re-instituted the reserve requirement, re-activated the counter-cyclical adjustment factor and some indirect interventions. A continued gradual transition to a higher flexibility exchange rate was in progress till the world economy was hit by COVID-19.

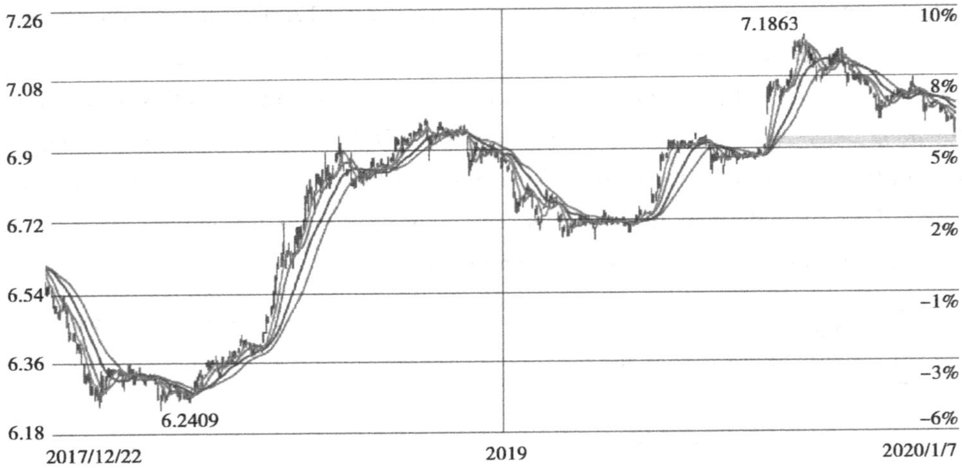

Figure 1-6 A Transition to A Higher Rflexibility Exchange Rate

2.5 Since Pandemic

When China went under COVID-19 lockdown in Feb. 2020, there was a massive short-term disruption to global supply chains. However, as the rest of the world went into lockdown in Mar. and Apr. 2020, China swiftly resumed production. In fact, China emerged as a highly productive and reliable supplier for large quantities across a broad range of goods.

Robust economic recovery from the COVID-19 pandemic in China enhanced confidence further in Chinese yuan which remained generally stable. The pandemic has been effectively controlled and China's social and economic activities have been on a steady path of recovery since the second quarter of 2020. China eventually turned out to be the only major economy to have a positive GDP growth rate in year 2020. Positive prospects for China's exports and increased holding of CNY-denominated assets by overseas investors have led to a relatively mild appreciation of Chinese yuan, which was still in line with the performance of other major international currencies and also in line with China's goal of increased exchange rate flexibility. Shanghai's lockdown in April 2020 has led a dramatic depreciation, which has rallied back as the COVID-19 curb be lifted.

By Oct. 2020 market-making banks have phased out the use of the counter-cyclical adjustment factor in the pricing mechanism of Chinese yuan's central parity rate against the U.S. dollar. They have made the move on their own initiative based on their judgment of economic fundamentals and market situations. The transparency and effectiveness of Chinese yuan's existing pricing model has been improved by this adjustment. Chinese yuan pricing is more market-based.

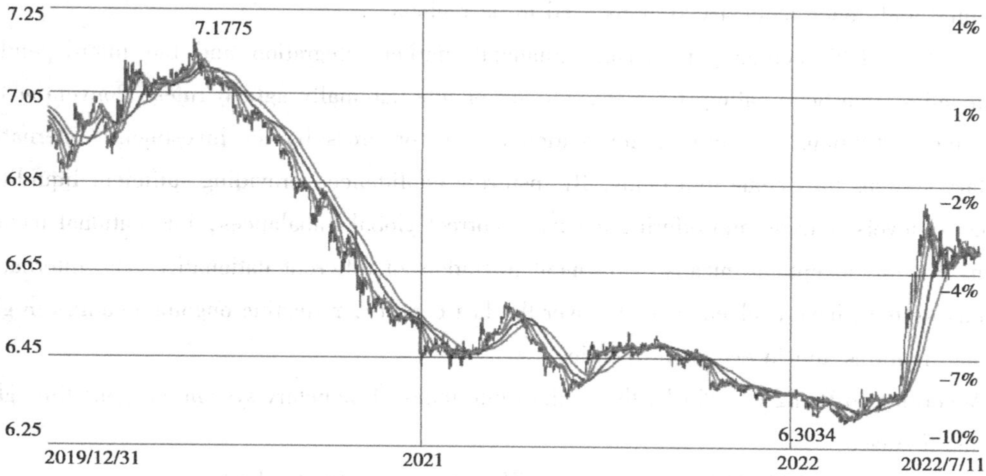

Figure 1-7 Exchange Rate Fluctuates with Economy Performance

Zero-COVID policy has kept service imports by Chinese tourists low and China's exports jumped to a record $325.5 billion in Nov. 2021 and the current-account surplus in the first three quarters of year 2021 reached the equivalent of $203 billion, the highest since 2015, according to State Administration of Foreign Exchange data. With long-term goal of promoting more balanced two-way capital flows and maintaining the general stability of the Chinese yuan, the short-term appreciation momentum has been keenly supervised. The expanded Qualified Domestic Institutional Investor (QDII) quotas facilitated more outbound investment and helped balance the influx of money, thus easing pressure for Chinese yuan appreciation.

Before COVID-19, invoicing in CNY provided advantages such as hedging risk and advantages in price negotiations. CNY has evolved increasingly relevant to international settlement. A stable Chinese yuan encourages an even higher portion of CNY invoicing, which contributes to internationalization of Chinese yuan. Since the offshore RMB (Chinese yuan) market established in Hong Kong Special Administrative Region in 2010, other offshore centers have developed in several countries enhancing the degree of internationalization of China's financial sector.

§ 3 International Monetary System

3.1 An Overview

The international monetary system is a way to conduct international business. The system covers types of currency from different countries and the resulting exchange rates as well as the characteristics of various exchange rate regimes. The global monetary system initially was quite segmented and hence monetary systems used to be regional.

Until the 19th century, increasing financial market integration and the interdependence of economies have been calling for a feasible set of internationally agreed rules, conventions and supporting institutions to facilitate international trade or cross border investment. International monetary systems thus come into being. By inspiring confidence, providing sufficient liquidity for fluctuating levels of trade and offering means to correct global imbalances, international monetary systems provide acceptable means of payment to traders of different nationality. The international monetary systems have evolved specially over the last century, reflecting ongoing changes in global economic realities and in economic theories.

According to Wang (2005)①, the modern international monetary system has gone through the following 5 stages:

1821–1914	The classical gold standard
1914–1943	Interim instability
1944–1971	The Bretton Woods system
1971–1973	The collapse of the Bretton Woods system
1973–present	The recent float

After the collapse of the Bretton Woods system, the prevailing international monetary system is characterized by floating exchange rates, free capital flows and independent monetary policy in the main developed economies. The monetary policy framework also transitioned from a monetary targeting regime in the 1970s and the 1980s to inflation targeting frameworks. Financial sector regulation then moved from an intrusive framework to a light-touch framework.

3.2 Definition of International Monetary System

"International monetary system" is often used interchangeably with terms such as "international monetary and financial system" and "international financial architecture". Dorrucci and McKay (2015)② defined international monetary system as: (i) the set of conventions, rules and policy instruments as well as (ii) the economic, institutional and political environment which determine the delivery of two fundamental global public goods: an international currency (or currencies) and external stability.

International monetary systems can either be constructed by a single architectural vision such as Bretton Woods System or arise from numerous individual agreements.

In order to contribute to stable and high global economic growth, while fostering price and financial stability, the international monetary system comprises the set of official arrangements that

① Wang P. The Economics of Foreign Exchange and Global Finance[M]. Springer, 2005.

② Dorrucci E, McKay J. The International Monetary System after the Financial Crisis[J]. Open Economies Review, 2015, 9(1 Supplement): 701-708.

regulate key dimensions of the balance of payments. It thus consists of 4 elements:

① exchange rate regimes;

② international payments and transfers relating to current international transactions;

③ international capital movements;

④ international reserves.

3.3 The Performance of Modern International Monetary System

The main strength of today's international monetary system is its flexibility and adaptability. This strength can also become its weakness, as it may contribute to unsustainable growth models and imbalances. International monetary system is like a public goods. When it is functioning smoothly, all countries gain from international flows of goods, services, and capital. But when it breaks down or is poorly organized, nations are unable to sustain high levels of trade and investment.

International monetary system has collapsed 3 times in the past hundred years: in 1914, 1939 and 1971. Each collapse was followed by tumults: war, civil unrest, or significant damage to the stability of the global economy.

The modern international monetary system unfortunately has not fully met the essential purpose yet, which is to facilitate the exchange of goods, services and capital among countries.

1) Exchange Rate Regimes

It is desirable that exchange rates should move stably in reflection of economic fundamentals. As discussed in last section, the floating exchange rates introduced by recent international monetary system has brought great volatility since the collapse of the Bretton Woods system. This volatility failed exchange rates to reflect fundamentals between countries.

2) International Payment and Transfer

According to recent data, increased free flow of capital has not brought the expected benefits to the global economy. On the contrary, it enlarged the volatility of exchange rates, destabilized the economies' growth and encouraged speculations.

3) International Capital Movements

As financial markets get more integrated and cross border financial transactions become freer, capital flows are enhanced and their volatilities become more active. Financial crises are more contagious and fatal since the rise of shadow banking system.

4) International Reserves

The birth of Euro has challenged the role of the U.S. dollar as the global economy's reserve currency. However, the currency composition of allocated reserves is still concentrated in the U.S. dollars.

Emerging economies have dominated the surge of reserve accumulation, especially Asian's share that accounts for more than half of the reserve as shown in Figure 1-8, which is a significant imbalance. It confirms that international monetary system has not succeeded in its key objective of growth with stability in the global economy in the post-Bretton Woods regime.

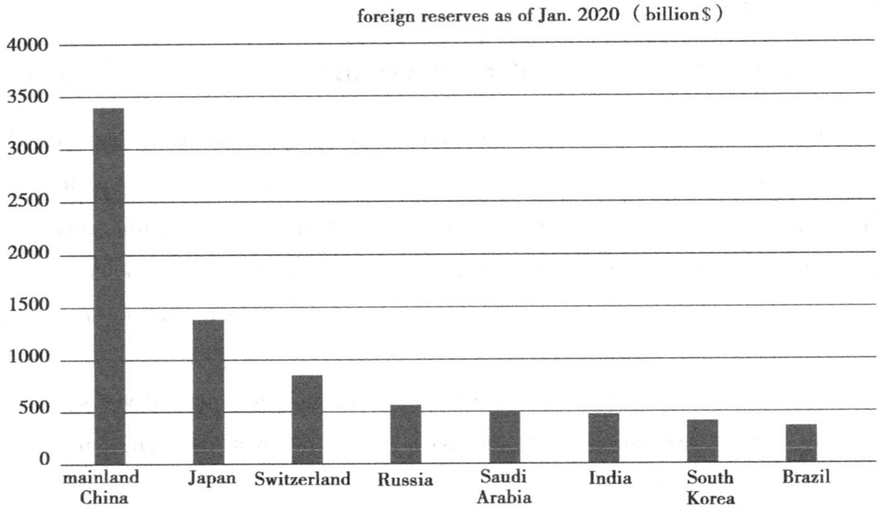

Figure 1-8 Top 8 Countries with the Largest Foreign Currency Reserve Assets as of Jan. 2020

Generally, most industrialized countries are now adopted independent floating, but the present international monetary system is a mixture of several kinds of exchange rate arrangements operating in parallel at the same time. Given the emerging markets gain more shares in the world, the global financial crisis of 2008 – 2009, the follow-on Great Recession and the Euro area sovereign debt crisis and the hit caused by COVID-19, the reforming of the international monetary system has been urgently called for.

This dollar-dominated reserve situation granted the U. S. an effective way to impose the U.S. power without spending money or sending troops: financial sanctions on undesirable foreigners, with tough enforcement through the banking system. Several alternatives to the U.S. dollar payments system have suggested to avoid the U.S. power over dollars, such as gold standard or decentralization digital cash. But the principal banks in the Euro area, the UK or Switzerland are so intertwined with the dollar clearing system that they and the U.S. will be the main obstacles to alternative currency.

A transitional framework for the Chinese yuan as a dollar alternative has been suggested. China has been working on it's currency globalization through a set-up called Cross-Border Interbank Payments System, or CIPS, and bilateral "clearing accounts" with several central banks. But there is a long way to use Chinese yuan on a large scale under capital accounts in terms of saving funds, attracting participants, and others.

§ 4 The European Single Currency

4.1 The History of Euro

After World War Ⅱ, most western economies adopted Bretton Woods System of fixed exchange rates, which brought many internal balance and external balance problems. In order to achieve a stability and an environment for higher growth and employment, the European Monetary Cooperation Fund was set up in 1973. It then was taken over by the European Monetary Institute, which was dissolved on 1st Jun., 1998 with the creation of the European Central Bank and the European System of Central Banks.

The move toward a common market revealed a need for monetary coordination. Euro area then has gone through 4 phases to come into being:

1) 1957–1970: from the Treaty of Rome to the Werner Report

The international currency stability that reigned in the immediate post-war period did not last. International currency market turmoils between 1968 and 1969 threatened the common price system of the agricultural policy, a main pillar of what was then the European Economic Community. In response to this troubling background, Europe's leaders set up a high-level group led by Pierre Werner, the Luxembourg Prime Minister at the time, to report on how European Monetary Union (EMU) could be achieved by 1980.

2) 1970–1979: from the Werner Report to the European Monetary System

The Werner group set out a three-stage process to achieve EMU within ten years, including the possibility of a single currency. The member states agreed in principle in 1971 and began the first stage—narrowing currency fluctuations. However, a wave of currency instability on international markets squashed hopes of tying the community's currencies closer together. Subsequent attempts at achieving stable exchange rates were hit by oil crises and other shocks until, in 1979, the European Monetary System was launched.

3) 1979–1991: from the Start of European Monetary System to Maastricht

The European Monetary System was built on exchange rates defined with reference to a newly created European Currency Unit, a weighted average of European Monetary System currencies. An exchange rate mechanism was used to keep participating currencies within a narrow band. The European Monetary System represented a new and unprecedented coordination of monetary policies between the member states, and operated successfully for over a decade.

This success provided the impetus for further discussions between the member states on achieving economic and monetary union. At the request of the European leaders, the European Commission President, Jacques Delors, and the central bank governors of the EU member states produced the "Delors Report", which is a basis for reflection and debate about what choices should be made in formulating policies, on how EMU could be achieved.

4) 1991–2002: from Maastricht to Euro and the Euro Area

The Delors Report proposed a three-stage preparatory period for economic and monetary union and the Euro area, spanning the period 1990 to 1999. Preparations involved:

- Completing the internal market (1990–1994), namely through the introduction of the free movement of capital;
- Preparing for the European Central Bank and the European System of Central Banks, and achieving economic convergence (1994–1999);
- Fixing exchange rates and launching Euro (1999 onwards);
- European leaders accepted the recommendations in the Delors Report. The new Treaty on European Union, which contained the provisions needed to implement EMU, was agreed at the European Council held at Maastricht, the Netherlands, in Dec. 1991. This council also agreed the "Maastricht convergence criteria" that each member state would have to meet to participate in the Euro area.

After a decade of preparations, Euro was launched on 1st Jan., 1999. At the same time, the Euro area came into operation, and monetary policy passed to the European Central Bank, established a few months previously—1st Jun., 1998—in preparation for the third stage of EMU. After three years of working with the Euro as "book money" alongside national currencies, euro coins and banknotes were launched on 1st Jan., 2002 and the biggest cash changeover in history took place in 12 EU countries (Austria, Belgium, Finland, France, Germany, Greece, Ireland, Italy, Luxembourg, the Netherlands, Portugal and Spain). More countries have joined Euro zone as shown in Figure 1-9.

The introduction of Euro banknotes and coins in 2002 was the largest-ever currency changeover. In preparation for it, around 14 billion notes and 52 billion coins were produced, of which some 7.8 billion notes and 40 billion coins were distributed at the beginning of Jan. 2002 to 218,000 banks and post offices, 2.8 million sales outlets, and 302 million individuals in the 12 participating countries. In parallel, a large proportion of the 9 billion national notes and 107 billion national coins in circulation were withdrawn.

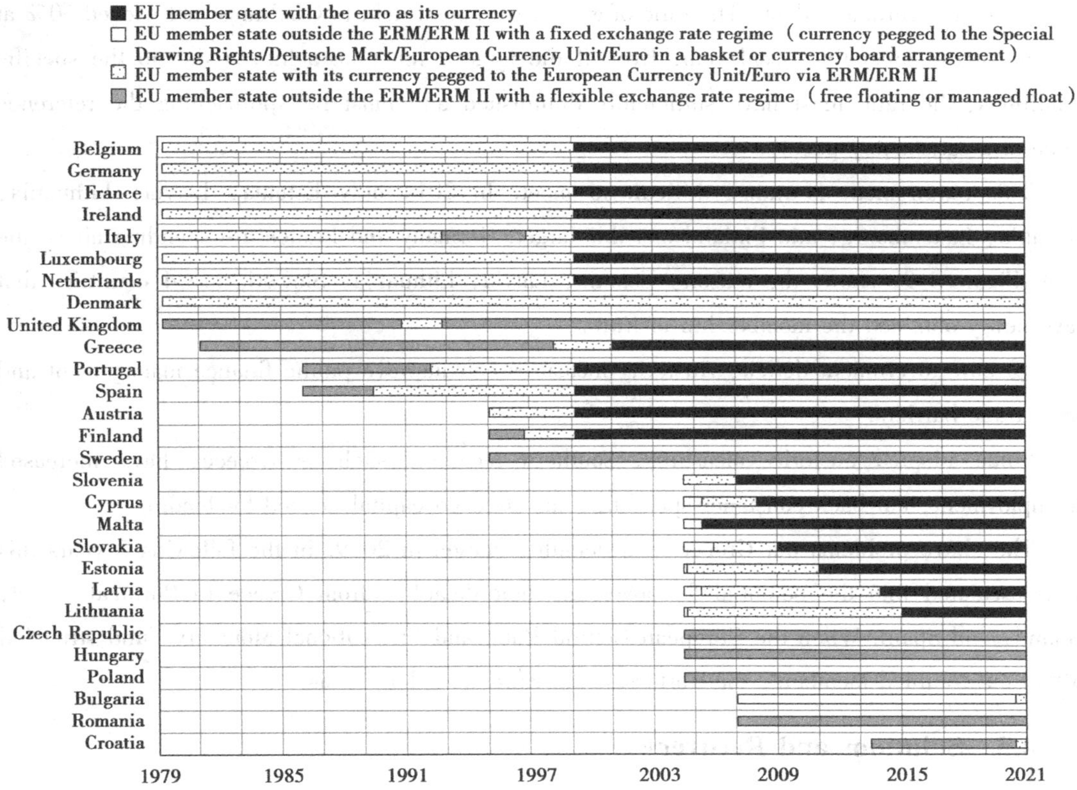

Figure 1-9 Exchange Rate Regimes of EU Member States

4.2 Problems the European Monetary Union Need to Solve

Europe's single currency has promoted European political and economic integration, yet it still needs to be improved.

Some EU members, for instance, have violated the Maastricht Treaty, and they fell into serious debt crisis. The Maastricht Treaty specifies the macroeconomic convergence criteria that EU member countries must satisfy, among which 3 criteria are essential: long-term interest rate, government deficit and government debt.

① Low interest rate: To maintain price stability within the Euro zone, the nominal long-term interest rate must not be more than 2 percentage points higher than in the three lowest inflation member states.

This requirement increased investment capital, most of which was from Germany and France to the southern members. But with the inflow of capital, wages and prices increased in southern nations as well, worsened their current account. Southern members cannot use monetary policy, raise interest rates or cut money supply, so their current account and inflation are getting worse hence less tax revenues.

② Low government debt: The ratio of gross government debt to GDP must not exceed 60% at the end of the preceding fiscal year. Even if the target cannot be achieved due to the specific conditions, the ratio must have sufficiently diminished and must be approaching the reference value at a satisfactory pace.

This requirement is rather difficult to meet. In 2014 only Estonia, Latvia, Lithuania, Slovakia, Luxembourg, and Finland met this target. Germany and France are spending above the limit. Figure 1-9, shows the reason: Estonia, Latvia, Lithuania, Slovakia are 4 countries that have newly obtained the membership of Euro.

③ Low government deficit: Austerity measures can improve public finance management and lower trade barriers.

Since adopted austerity measures, southern members such as Greece, have increased unemployment, cut back consumer spending, and reduced capital needed for lending.

The above problems put Greece in a default situation in 2009. In the following 3 years this crisis escalated into the potential for sovereign debt defaults, from Greece to Portugal, Italy, Ireland, and Spain. When the European Central Bank and International Monetary Fund struggled to bail out troubled members, the world saw the Euro zone debt crisis.

4.3 Solutions and Recovery

Learned from the experience of integrating east Germany, former German Chancellor Merkel developed a plan to rescue Euro zone. In 2011, EU leaders agreed to a German-backed fiscal union that allows Brussels to dictate national budgets, and 2012 began the process of creating a Euro zone-wide banking union. More specifically, the solutions are as follows:

① Launch quick-start programs to facilitate business start-ups;

② Relax protections against wrongful dismissal;

③ Introduce "mini-jobs" with lower taxes;

④ Combine apprenticeship with vocational education targeted toward youth unemployment;

⑤ Create special funds and tax benefits to privatize state-owned businesses;

⑥ Establish special economic zones, like those in China;

⑦ Invest in renewable energy.

With this plan and an intergovernmental treaty, the EU leaders agreed to create a fiscal unity parallel to the monetary union that already exists.

On May 9th, 2010, the 27 EU member states agreed to create the European Financial Stability Facility. This institution was set up to preserve financial stability in Europe by providing financial assistance to Euro zone states in difficulty.

On 5th Jan. 2011, the European Union created the European Financial Stabilization

Mechanism (EFSM), an emergency funding programme reliant upon funds raised on the financial markets and guaranteed by the European Commission using the budget of the European Union as collateral.

A total sum of 720 billion Euro' bailout restored faith in Euro, followed by the intervention from other countries as well as interest cut by European Central Bank. By 2014, Ireland, Spain and Portugal had completed their bailout programs.

More than 10 years has passed yet deep structural problems persist, including high unemployment, weak banking systems, huge debt, and rigid labor markets. Further reforms are needed to improve governance and coordinate economic policy.

Case Studies

Case 1 The Chinese Yuan and Exchange Rate Regimes

(1) Evolution in Chinese yuan Exchange Rate Regime

① 1949–1972 Peg to the U.S. Dollar

After liberalization, Chinese economy was in urgent need of restore. Foreign exchange resources were scarce and the authority enforced control on foreign exchange by a series of reforms. The exchange rate was officially determined. Chinese Yuan was pegged to the U.S. dollar.

② 1973–1985 Peg to a Basket of Currencies

China has gone through currencies and weights adjustments 7 times, and Chinese Yuan was then officially converted into a basket of currencies.

In 1985, only official rate published by the State Administration for Exchange Control prevailed.

In 1986, a swap center was established to associate exchange rate determination converting to managed floating. But the exchange rate determined in swap center went array from the official rate. As the gap between official rate and swap rate enlarged, China started to unify exchange rates.

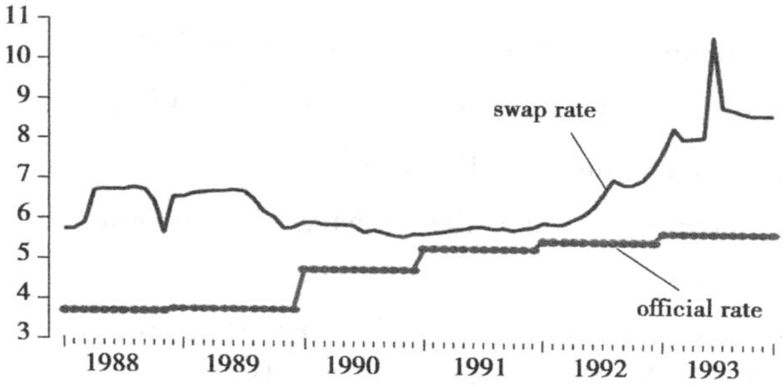

③ 1994—2005 Market-Based Managed Floating Exchange Rate

On 1st Dec. 1996, China accepted the obligations of Article VIII of the IMF Articles of Agreement on current account convertibility. After conditional current account convertibility was introduced, the exchange market was unified.

China adopted market-based managed floating exchange rate by setting up China Foreign Exchange Trading Center where inter-bank foreign exchange is traded. This center is electronically linked with major foreign exchange trading centers.

④ 2005—2010 Closing Rate against Major Currencies

Since 2005, China launched reforms on foreign exchange regime. The U.S. dollar is no long the only currency in Chinese Yuan exchange rate determination. On July 22, 2005, China started to announce the Chinese Yuan closing rate against major currencies, the data is collected from the inter-bank foreign exchange market by the end of each trading day.

China then started direct trading between Chinese Yuan and other currencies①.

⑤ 2010—Present Chinese Yuan Internationalization

On 15th Dec. 2010, the first overseas market of Chinese Yuan was established, the yuan started trading in Russia.

On 13th Jan. 2011, qualified domestic enterprises were proved to invest in foreign countries directly using Chinese yuan.

On 1st Dec. 2016, Chinese Yuan has been officially included in SDR basket.

(2) A Chronicle of Major Reform on Exchange Rate Formation Mechanism: 2005—2015

- 21st Jul. 2005: China initiated the reforms by de-pegging the yuan from the U. S. dollar. The PBOC said it had shifted to "a managed floating exchange rate based on market supply and demand with reference to a basket of weighted currencies." The yuan against the U.S. dollar appreciated by 2% to 8.11 on that day.
- 22nd Jul. 2005: The PBOC began announcing the yuan's closing rate against major currencies on the inter-bank foreign exchange market each trading day.
- 11th Jan. 2007: The central parity rate of the yuan against the U.S. dollar topped 7.8. The yuan's value exceeded the Hong Kong dollar for the first time in 13 years.
- 21st May. 2007: The yuan's value was allowed to rise or fall by 0.5% from the central parity rate each trading day, from a previous limit of 0.3%.
- 8th Apr. 2009: Cross-border trade was allowed to be settled in the Chinese yuan on a trial basis in Shanghai and Guangdong Province.
- 21st Jul. 2009: Four years since the exchange rate reform, the yuan against the U.S.

① By the end of 2016, China has direct trading with 21 currencies: MYR, RUB, JPY, AUD, NZD, GBP, EUR, SGD, CHF, ZAR, KRW, SAR, AED, CAD, MXI, TRY, PLN, DKK, HUF, NOK, SEK.

dollar had appreciated by 21%.

- 19th Aug. 2010: China started direct trading between the yuan and the Malaysian ringgit.
- 15th Sep. 2010: The U.S. lawmakers at a Congress hearing pressured China to appreciate its currency. China's Foreign Ministry said the yuan's appreciation would not help the Sino-US trade deficit.
- 22nd Nov. 2010: China started direct trading between the yuan and the Russian ruble on the inter-bank foreign exchange market.
- 15th Dec. 2010: The yuan started trading in Russia, the first overseas market of the Chinese yuan.
- 13th Jan. 2011: The PBOC allowed qualified domestic enterprises to invest in foreign countries directly using the yuan.
- 16th Apr. 2012: The yuan's value was allowed to rise or fall by 1% from the central parity rate each trading day, from the previous limit of 0.5%.
- 1st Jun. 2012: China started direct trading between the Chinese yuan and the Japanese yen on the inter-bank foreign exchange market.
- 9th Apr. 2013: China started direct trading between the yuan and the Australian dollar on the inter-bank foreign exchange market.
- 17th Mar. 2014: The yuan's value was allowed to rise or fall by 2% from the central parity rate each trading day, from the previous limit of 1%.
- 18th Mar. 2014: China started direct trading between the yuan and the New Zealand dollar on the inter-bank foreign exchange market.
- 18th Jun. 2014: China started direct trading between the yuan and the British pound on the inter-bank foreign exchange market.
- 30th Sep. 2014: China started direct trading between the yuan and Euro on the inter-bank foreign exchange market.
- 27th Nov. 2014: The vice PBOC governor at the time said the bank had "largely" withdrawn from intervention in daily foreign exchange business.
- 26th May. 2015: David Lipton, first deputy managing director of the International Monetary Fund (IMF), said Chinese Yuan was no longer undervalued.
- 27th Jun. 2015: The PBOC said it would continue to push ahead with reforms in the exchange rate formation mechanism.
- 11th Aug. 2015: The PBOC said daily central parity quotes reported to the China Foreign Exchange Trade System before the market opens should be based on the closing rate of the inter-bank foreign exchange market on the previous day, supply and demand in the market, and price movement of major currencies. The central parity rate of the yuan

against the U.S. dollar weakened sharply to 6.2298.

➢ 12th Aug. 2015: The IMF described Tuesday's policy change as "a welcome step" that allows market forces to have a greater role in determining the exchange rate. The USD-CNY rate declined to 6.3306.

(3) RMB (Chinese yuan) Internationalization

In order to lower exchange costs, facilitate use of the two currencies in trade settlement and boost bilateral investment, direct on shore trade is allowed in a number of currencies, including the Malaysian ringgit, Russian ruble, Japanese yen, Australian dollar, New Zealand dollar, British Pound, Euro, Singapore dollar, South Korean won, South African rand, the riyal of Saudi Arabia and the dirham of the United Arab. (Sep. 2016)

RMB has passed the assessment on the use of RMB in commercial banks' liabilities, its share in global foreign exchange and derivatives transactions, its ranking in international reserves, RMB capital account convertibility and its proportion in the global bond market, then has been officially included in SDR basket on 1st Dec., 2016.

Since the handover of Hongkong in 1997, China has been expanding use of the yuan in Hong Kong—a process that will eventually cement the decline of the U. S. dollar as the primary international settlement currency. There is a long way for the Chinese yuan to replace the U.S. dollar as a global settlement currency for international trade.

① Chinese Yuan availability is limited;

② China's bond market, which central banks and international companies would access to borrow yuan for payment transactions, is small to facilitate global trade, compared to the U.S. bond market;

③ the Chinese banking system is not yet sophisticated enough to effectively manage the fund stream of a bond market of a depth, breadth and scale required for international trade;

④ the Chinese markets are not totally open to outside investors.

(4) Further Reforms for RMB Internationalization

More reforms are expected to be unveiled to accelerate the internationalization of the yuan, or the RMB.

The RMB's inclusion into the SDR basket came after a series of reforms, including the exchange rate formation mechanism and cross-border interbank payment.

After the IMF 's SDR inclusion of the RMB on 30th Nov. 2015

The People's Bank of China (PBOC) approved RMB convertibility on the capital account within a prescribed limit of $10 million for the Tianjin, Guangdong and Fujian free trade zones on 11th Dec. 2015, a historic step by China to open up its capital accounts.

China allowed RMB convertibility on the trade accounts nearly two decades ago, but almost all capital account transactions in the mainland remain under varying degrees of control.

On 11th Dec. 2015, the central bank released the yuan exchange rate composite index measuring the currency's strength relative to a basket of other currencies to better reflect the market.

It helped bring about a shift in how the public and the market observe RMB exchange rate movements, as the CFETS exchange rate composite index measures the yuan's strength relative to a basket of 13 foreign currencies, including the U.S. dollar, Euro and Japanese yen, weighted according to their trade volume with China.

Compared with just one currency, a basket of currencies can better capture the competitiveness of a country's goods and services and better enable the exchange rate to adjust imports, exports, and investment activities and the balance of payments position.

However, valuing against a basket of currencies does not mean a peg to the basket. Market demand and supply will also play a key role in formulating the rate.

The establishment of the China-initiated Asian Infrastructure Investment Bank on 25th Dec. 2015 in Beijing also helped the internationalization of the RMB, as it created more possibilities for the international use of the currency.

China will seek to optimize the interest rate transmission mechanism and exchange rate formation mechanism as well as improve transparency of monetary policies.

Case 2 China Largely Succeeds in RMB Exchange Rate Reform over Past Year①

Updated: Aug 15, 2016 7:16 AM

WASHINGTON (Xinhua)—China's authorities have largely succeeded in its objective of revamping the foreign exchange mechanism to make the currency RMB more market-oriented and relatively stable to a basket of currencies over the past year, thanks to improved policy communication, US experts have said.

On Aug 11, 2015, the People's Bank of China (PBOC), the central bank, announced a major improvement to the formation of the RMB's central parity rate against the US dollar, by taking into consideration the closing rate on the inter-bank FX market of the previous day.

The move was described by the PBOC as a "one-time correction" to bridge previously accumulated differences between the central parity rate and the spot market rate, which would make the central parity rate more consistent with the needs of market development.

The central parity rate is the starting point for daily FX trading, and the RMB is allowed to rise or fall by 2 percent from the central parity rate each trading day from March 2014.

Think tank and the International Monetary Fund (IMF) experts agreed that the central bank's move was very much in the direction to increase the role of market forces in the determination

① http://Chinadaily.com.cn

of the RMB exchange rate.

But some market participants at that time misinterpreted it as an effort to prop up the economic growth by currency devaluation and incorrectly jumped to the conclusion that China's economy was probably worse than stated. The RMB fell sharply in value in the following days after the reform of the central parity system.

"I think initially when they started changing the system a year ago, they were not good at communication, and there was a lot of confusion in the market about what their intention was," said David Dollar, a senior fellow with the Brookings Institution and former official of the World Bank and the US Treasury Department.

However, Chinese authorities provided "pretty good and clear communication" about its exchange rate policy over the next few weeks and months, Dollar said, citing authorities' arguments that they wanted to have more market forces involved and there was no need for large depreciation of the currency.

Chinese officials have also repeatedly said that China has no intention of devaluating the RMB to gain an advantage in global trade. China has successfully moved up the value chain into higher value-added products and its share of global exports continued to expand in recent years despite the significant appreciation of the RMB, according to Nicholas Lardy, a senior fellow at the Peterson Institute for International Economics and a leading expert on China's economy.

China's current account surplus was about 300 billion dollars last year, which was the largest in the world in absolute terms, indicating that China didn't need to devalue its currency to boost the economic growth, Lardy said.

"China has a large trade surplus, and it's a rapidly growing economy, there's not really the basis for depreciation," echoed Dollar.

But capital outflows from China increased significantly in September and December as market participants expected that the US Federal Reserve would start raising interest rates by the end of the year and the dollar would rise more rapidly against other currencies.

On December 11, China introduced a RMB exchange rate composite index to help guide market participants to shift their focus from the bilateral RMB/USD exchange rate to the effective exchange rate based on a basket of currencies.

The new index, released by China Foreign Exchange Trade System (CFETS), is calculated by comparing RMB to the average value of the 13 foreign currencies, including the US dollar, EURO and Japanese yen, weighted according to the trade volume with China.

The PBOC noted that valuing against a basket of currencies does not mean a peg to the basket, but it "will contribute to maintaining the RMB exchange rate basically stable at an adaptive and equilibrium level."

The PBOC also took several other steps, including selling FX reserves, implementing macro prudential regulations and strengthening checks on capital outflows, to help stabilize market expectations for the RMB exchange rate, according to Guan Tao, a senior fellow at the China Finance 40 Forum and former official at China's central bank.

But the large decline in China's FX reserves and rumors about tightening of capital control measures seemed to further fuel market expectations of a weakening RMB at the beginning of this year. China's FX reserves shrank by $ 512.7 billion in 2015, the largest annual decline on record.

"I think the argument that the decline in reserves is because of panic mainlanders trying to get their money offshore is somewhat misleading," Lardy said. "I think it largely reflects actions of investors and corporations in response to change in exchange rate expectations and interest rate differentials."

The Institute of International Finance (IIF), a global association representing about 500 financial institutions, also estimated that a large part of capital outflows from China last year were repayments of dollar-denominated debts by Chinese companies, in order to mitigate the impact of the dollar appreciation.

In an interview with Chinese magazine Caixin in February, Zhou Xiaochuan, governor of the PBOC, chose a critical moment to clarify China's exchange rate policy, as Chinese financial markets prepared to reopen after the week-long Lunar New Year holiday.

Zhou reiterated that China will "rely further on the market to decide the level of the currency and to achieve a more flexible foreign exchange rate". He signaled that China will keep the RMB broadly stable versus a basket of currencies while allowing greater volatility against the dollar.

Zhou dismissed speculation that China plans to tighten capital controls and said there's no need to worry about a short-term decline in FX reserves. He reassured investors that there is no basis for the continued depreciation of the RMB and that China would not let market sentiment be dominated by speculative forces.

Zhou's comments helped ease the RMB's depreciation pressures and received praise from IMF chief Christine Lagarde. "We have been delighted to see the communication efforts undertaken by policymakers, particularly Governor Zhou," Lagarde said in February, adding that it was "a good example of how communication can actually clear the uncertainties and trepidations."

At the same month, the PBOC clarified that the central parity rate formation system would be based on the closing rate of the previous trading day and movements of a basket of currencies. Such exchange rate regime reflects a balance among market supply and demand, relative stability against a basket of currencies and stable market expectations, the central bank said.

Since then the RMB has seemed to enter a more stable period, as the Fed signaled slower pace of interest rate hikes this year and market participants gradually got used to two-way fluctuations of the RMB exchange rate. Speculators have also learnt that it's not wise to battle against the PBOC.

Charles Collyns, managing director and chief economist at the IIF, said China's central bank has been "much more successful" in currency management over the past six months, compared to the period from last August to this February.

"I think it finally convinced markets that it wanted to avoid an abrupt depreciation of the RMB once keeping market conditions broadly stable," Collyns told Xinhua, adding that "it has also shown it's possible for the RMB to fluctuate in response to short-term shifts of market conditions without destabilizing markets".

He hoped that China's central bank would keep good communication and let the exchange rate move in line with market conditions going forward, noting that the central bank could reduce the risk of instability "by communicating more openly with markets".

"We learned a very important lesson about the importance of communication," Dollar said, believing that Chinese authorities have "largely succeeded" in their objective of the market-oriented exchange rate reform over the past year with improved communication.

"The currency has been relatively stable. It has appreciated a little bit against the basket, but not very much, and then depreciated a little bit more against the dollar, because the dollar has been strengthening against other currencies," he said.

"The RMB remains broadly in line with fundamentals," the IMF said in a report after concluding its annual economic health check on the Chinese economy, expecting the volume of capital outflows from China to moderate this year.

"The large outflow seen in 2015: Q3–2016: Q1 will gradually moderate as the pressure from external debt repayment peters out. The secular trend of residents' acquisition of foreign assets to balance their investment portfolio is expected to continue, but not materially accelerate from current levels." the report said.

The IMF welcomed China's steps toward an effectively floating exchange rate regime and supported a cautious approach to capital account liberalization "that is carefully sequenced with the progress on exchange rate flexibility and financial sector reforms".

The IMF last year approved the inclusion of the RMB into its Special Drawing Rights (SDR) basket as a fifth currency, along with the US dollar, EURO, the Japanese yen and the British pound, marking a milestone in the RMB global march. The new SDR basket will be effective from Oct 1, 2016.

Dollar said China has done financial reforms needed for the RMB to be officially included into the new SDR basket. He encouraged China to move ahead with structural reforms in the real economy, dealing with excessive capacity, zombie firms and bad debts, which would make China's financial system more robust and underpin the RMB's reserve currency status.

Case 3 China's Evolving Exchange Rate Regime (1MF working papers)

Exercises

Ⅰ. *For the following questions, consider each of the choices separately and select all that apply.*

1. IMF has put the exchange rate regimes into (   ).
   A. hard pegs B. soft pegs C. floating D. residual
2. Hard pegs exchange rate regime arrangement includes (   ).
   A. conventional pegged arrangement
   B. exchange arrangement with no separate legal tender
   C. stabilized arrangement
   D. currency board arrangement
3. Exchange rate regime has gone through stages as (   ).
   A. money is based on a metallic standard B. money is fiat
   C. pegged regimes D. optimum currency area
4. The international monetary system consists of (   ).
   A. exchange rate regimes
   B. international payments and transfers relating to current international transactions
   C. international capital movements
   D. international reserves
5. The Maastricht Treaty specifies (   ), the macroeconomic convergence criteria that EU member countries must satisfy.
   A. government tax revenue B. government debt
   C. government deficit D. interest rate

Ⅱ. *Short answer questions.*

1. *Why in reality there are no two countries have exactly the same exchange rate regime?*

2. *How do international monetary systems fulfill the transaction function?*

3. *Has the modern international monetary system successfully facilitated the exchange of goods, services and capital among countries?*

Chapter 2
The Foreign Exchange Market

On 30th Nov. 2011, when the Euro debt crisis was in its worst time, the European Central Bank, the U.S. Federal Reserve, the central banks of Canada, Japan, Britain and the Swiss National Bank provided global financial markets with additional liquidity to support the real economy. The central banks agreed to lower the cost of dollar currency swaps by 50 basis points to come into effect on 5th December 2011. They also agreed to provide each other with abundant liquidity to make sure that commercial banks stay liquid in other currencies.

The above support took effect in the foreign exchange market, through which the money of one country is exchanged for that of another country, the rate of exchange between currencies is determined and foreign exchange transactions are physically completed.

This chapter is going to

- Give an overview of the foreign exchange market by explaining its concept, analyzing its features, and introducing basic mechanics of currency trading;
- Provide some suggestions for individuals to participate in the foreign exchange market;
- Introduce China's foreign exchange market and its evolution.

§ 1 Overview

1.1 Definition

The foreign exchange market (FX) or currency market, is where foreign exchange be traded. It is by far the world's largest financial market, in which there is no bear market. Currencies are constantly traded, regardless of prices of stocks or bonds. FX trader's profit or loss stems only from changes in the relative value of the currencies being traded, not the value of stocks, bonds or other commodities.

The foreign exchange market was initially designed for firms or banks to buy and sell foreign currencies for international trade and investment purposes, individuals usually take part in the market through brokers or banks. The foreign exchange market is generally a worldwide Over-the-Counter (OTC) financial market, that is, the foreign exchange market could be a decentralized market without a central physical location where market participants trade with each other through various communication modes and with advanced technologies such as liquidity aggregation and algorithmic trading techniques. All the traders and the market participants worldwide deal directly with each other, there could be no central exchange at the foreign exchange market. Financial centers around the world function as anchors of trading between buyers and sellers. According to Bank for International Settlement (BIS) report, the top 5 trading centers in year 2022 are London, New York City, Singapore, HongKong SAR, and Tokyo, among which London is by far the biggest foreign exchange trading centre①. It is more cost-effective to centralise counter party and credit relationships, or technical and legal infrastructures, in a handful of hubs than to spread them across many countries. FX trading has been increasingly concentrated in financial centres.

1.2 Features

Foreign exchange market has dynamic market participants, high daily transaction volume, worldwide around the clock of the trade, little regulation and shows a trend of consolidation.

1) Dynamic Market Participants

The foreign exchange market is one of the largest and liquid financial markets in the world. The main market participants in foreign exchange market are international commercial banks, central banks, large investment firms, multinational commercial companies, hedge funds, mutual funds, insurance companies and retail foreign exchange brokers, etc.

Foreign exchange market is divided into levels of access that are determined by the size of the "line" (the amount of money with which they are trading). The top-tier access is the interbank market, which accounts for more than half of all transactions. Central banks, commercial banks and large investment banks are market makers in the top-tier, and they stand ready to make a market in FX. In the interbank market, the standard size trade is 10 million U.S. dollars, and the stakes are high.

At the next level there are smaller investment banks, followed by large multi-national corporations, large hedge funds, pension funds, and some of the retail foreign exchange brokers.

Although some activity in foreign exchange market is driven by real commercial needs, most of the FX participators get involved in FX for hedging, speculative and arbitrage transactions.

The following table shows the top 10 foreign exchange dealers in 2020, where large commercial banks dominate FX trading.

---

① Triennial Central Bank Survey 2022: Foreign exchange and derivatives market activity in 2022. www.bis.org/statistics/rpfx22_fx.htm

Table 2-1 Top 10 Foreign Exchange Traders

% of overall volume, May 2020

rank in 2020	rank in 2019	dealer	market share %
1	3	Deutsche Bank	13.96
2	2	UBS	13.32
3	1	JPMorgan	12.13
4	4	Citi	6.52
5	5	Bank of America	6.40
6	7	HSBC	5.12
7	6	Goldman Sachs	4.73
8	8	XTX Markets	4.55
9	9	Barclays	4.42
10	13	BNP Paribas	3.12

Source: https://www.euromoney.com/article/b1lp3zhln6vv9p/fx-survey-2020-market-share-by-institution-type

The above table provided by Euromoney survey shows a very competitive market. Ranks change year after year, although Deutsche Bank, UBS and JPMorgan dominate the foreign exchange market for now.

Part of the interbank trading among international banks involves adjusting the inventory position banks hold in various foreign currencies. However, most interbank trades are speculative or arbitrage transactions, where participants attempt to judge the future direction of exchange rate movement.

FX brokers match buy and sell orders and charge commission fees, but they do not carry inventory. The international banks serve the bank customers, in the conduct of international commerce. The bank customers include multinational companies, money managers, and private speculators.

In order to maintain exchange rate regime, the central bank intervenes in the FX market in an attempt to influence the price of its currency against that of a major trading partner or a country that it fixes or pegs its currency against. The central bank is the only market participant who is not driven exclusively by profit.

Although interbank trade dominates foreign exchange market, widespread use of high technology provides easier access for more market participants to get involved in this market. The availability of new dealing technologies has redefined the roles of each of the major foreign exchange market players. Electronic trading in general and retail-oriented trading platforms in particular have provided FX market access to a broader range of end users and favor a more active participation of non-dealer traders.

2) Large Size and High Liquid

Foreign exchange market is the biggest market in terms of trade volume. It is also one of the fastest growing segments in the financial world because that the currency trading has become more influential as an asset class and the fund management assets as hedge and pension funds increase. Up to 90% of the daily volume of trading activity in the foreign exchange market is a result of speculator activity, with the balance primarily made up of commercial hedging transactions.

Trading in foreign exchange market averaged $6.6 trillion per day in Apr. 2019. It reached to $7.5 trillion pey day in Apr. 2022 according to Triennial Central Bank Survey 2022 by BIS among which the U.S. dollar remained the dominant vehicle currency.

Table 2-2 Top 10 Currency Distribution of OTC Foreign Exchange Turnover

Net-net basis, percentage shares of average daily turnover in April 2004—2022

currency ISOcode	2004		2007		2010		2013		2016		2019		2022	
	share	rank	share	rank	share	rank	share	rank	share	rank	share	rank	share	rank
USD	88	1	85.6	1	84.9	1	87	1	87.6	1	88.3	1	88.5	1
EUR	37.4	2	37	2	39	2	33.4	2	31.4	2	32.3	2	30.5	2
JPY	20.8	3	17.2	3	19	3	23	3	21.6	3	16.8	3	16.7	3
GBP	16.5	4	14.9	4	12.9	4	11.8	4	12.8	4	12.8	4	12.9	4
AUD	6	6	6.6	6	7.6	5	8.6	5	6.9	5	6.8	5	6.4	6
CAD	4.2	7	4.3	7	5.3	7	4.6	7	5.1	6	5	6	6.2	7
CHF	6	5	6.8	5	6.3	6	5.2	6	4.8	7	5	7	5.2	8
CNY	**0.1**	**29**	**0.5**	**20**	**0.9**	**17**	**2.2**	**9**	**4**	**8**	**4.3**	**8**	**7**	**5**
HKD	1.8	9	2.7	8	2.4	8	1.4	13	1.7	13	3.5	9	2.6	9
NZD	1.1	13	1.9	11	1.6	10	2	10	2.1	10	2.1	10	1.7	14

Source: BIS Triennial Central Bank Survey

The above summary table shows that foreign exchange activity is concentrated in 3 "major" currencies in trades against the USD: EUR, JPY, and GBP.

This concentration of liquidity in a few currency pairs reflects the importance of the underlying financial and physical product markets denominated in those currencies.

(1) The U.S. Dollar (USD)

The USD is the world's dominant currency, being on one side of 88.5% of all FX trades. The economic and political significance of the U.S. makes the dollar the world's most heavily traded currency.

The scale, diversity and sophistication of financial instruments available in U.S. markets attract foreign investors. The USD is the most widely used currency for global investors so far. Generally, for any country has its currency be widely used, it must meet 7 conditions:

① The currency should be prudently managed;

② A robust legal system is required to safe-guard contracts;

③ The Treasury bill market is deep and liquid;

④ Money markets are readily tapped for borrowing purposes and are safe for investment;

⑤ The government bond market is deep and liquid;

⑥ Private sector bonds and equities provide a wide range of investment opportunities;

⑦ Each cash market is mirrored by deep, liquid derivatives markets which offer efficient hedging tools and speculative position-plays.

The U.S. has met the above conditions and attracts the central banks to hold the majority of foreign currency reserves in U.S. T-bills. It also attracts the entire range of private investors, from the risk-averse, holding U.S. Treasury bonds, to the most speculative players looking for high returns from growth stocks, high-yield bonds and open futures and options positions.

According to BIS survey, in Apr. 2022 88.5% of the transactions in foreign exchange markets involve the dollar. It took a long way for USD to obtain the achievement. Before the establishment of the Federal Reserve System in 1913, various currencies were issued in the U.S.

In the late 18th century and during the American Revolution, the Continental Congress printed its first paper money, known as continentals. But inflation was rapidly increasing and continentals were becoming worthless quickly.

The First Bank of the United States established in 1791 was the first attempt to central banking, which was not well-received by agrarian electorates. When the bank's 20-year charter expired in 1811, votes in Congress were not enough to renew it.

The Second Bank of the United States of 1816 had a similar story. The Free Banking Era (1836–1865) had state-chartered banks and unchartered "free banks," issuing their own notes, redeemable in gold or specie. Following the financial panics of the late 19th and early 20th century, the American public was ready for a central bank. In 1913, President Woodrow Wilson signed the Federal Reserve Act into law. The U.S. dollar came into being.

(2) Euro (EUR)

Euro takes over from the German Deutschmark (DEM) as the world's second largest trading currency.

Before the advent of the Euro, the DEM accounted for 25% of all FX transactions, with USD/DEM being the most liquid and traded pair. Euro has expanded on this. Not only does Euro also take in the German Deutschmark and 18 other European currencies, it is also expected to stimulate the growth of the EMU's Euro-denominated debt and equity markets, that have the potential to rival U.S. financial markets in terms of depth and liquidity.

Introduced in 1999, as stated in Chapter 1 section 4, Euro became the second highest-traded currency in the world with a 30.5% share in daily transactions. Introducing a new common currency and a central bank that oversees this currency was not an easy task. Since the early 1960s, the central banks of the European Economic Community (EEC) had been trying to coordinate their monetary policies and promote price stability. The Maastricht Treaty of 1992 put a long-contemplated idea on paper: a common currency. In 1998, the European Central Bank was established.

(3) The Japanese Yen (JPY)

With a share of over 16.7% of the daily currency transactions, the Japanese Yen ranks No. 3 in spot market. This third most traded currency is primarily active against USD and EUR. Liquidity is substantially reduced against other currencies. The Japanese demand USD for investment purposes, to service USD debt and to import oil, gas and commodities.

Japan's domestic financial markets are difficult for foreign players to access. As such, demand for JPY is predominantly from Japanese companies repatriating trade profits, investment returns and debt capital. The Japanese yen is particularly sensitive to the profitability of these companies and to the domestic property market.

The history of the Japanese yen goes back to 1871 when it was adopted officially as the Japanese currency by Japan's Meiji government. In 1882, the Bank of Japan was established under the Bank of Japan Act as the country's central bank.

The Bank of Japan was reorganized in 1942 according to the new Bank of Japan Act. The Act of 1942 states the objectives of the Bank of Japan as regulating the currency as well as controlling and facilitating credit and finance to enhance the country's general economic performance.

The Act of 1942 was amended several times after World War II and was completely revised in 1997 to reflect the modern principles of central banking: transparency and independence from fiscal authority.

(4) British Pound (GBP)

The British pound has a share of 12.9% in daily currency trades according to BIS Triennial Central Bank Survey. It is most heavily traded against USD and EUR and over half of these trades are through London, the major FX center.

The city of London and the GBP were at the center of all FX activity before the rise of the USD. Britain and the U.S. maintain a historic two-way investment relationship, with many U.S. companies investing and operating in the UK and vice versa.

As the British economy is now far smaller and has been far less fundamentally stable over time than the U.S. and Germany, it has made for highly volatile currency pairings with the USD and EUR, giving London dealers in particular, many opportunities for speculative position plays.

The official name of the currency is pound sterling which is mainly issued by the Bank of England. As one of the oldest central banks in the world, the Bank of England was founded in 1694 to act as the government's banker and debt-manager. It began issuing notes the same year, where notes had a few lines of engraved text, promising to pay a specified sum at the bank's premises with spaces for a handwritten date, number, signature, and the name of the payee. In 1734, the Bank of England moved to Threadneedle Street in London and is still located there today.

(5) the Australian Dollar (AUD)

This currency has 6.4% share in daily currency transactions. Prior to 1911, private trading banks were issuing currency in Australia.

In 1911, legislation established the Commonwealth Bank of Australia. However, at that time the bank was just like a commercial bank and did not assume the responsibilities of a central bank. Then, the Australian Department of the Treasury was in charge of issuing notes. In 1924, the Commonwealth Bank Act was amended and the bank was given control over the note issue. From this time until 1945, the Commonwealth Bank of Australia gradually evolved its central banking activities.

In 1959, part of the Commonwealth Bank of Australia was renamed as the Reserve Bank of Australia (RBA) to fulfill the functions of a central bank. The commercial banking functions were kept by the Commonwealth Bank of Australia.

(6) The Canadian Dollar (CAD)

The Canadian dollar ranks as the No. 7 currency with 6.2% share in daily currency transactions in the world. Until the early 19th century, a number of different currencies, British, French, and local currencies, were used in the Canadian provinces. In the years leading up to the Confederation, most of the country was organized as small rural settlements spread over a large area, which made branch banking a practical approach.

During the 18th and early 19th century, the branch banking worked well. Then, bank runs reduced confidence in the system, and the idea that government should issue currency started gaining support. In 1871, the dominion government passed the Uniform Currency Act.

The Great Depression of the early 1930s convinced policy makers to establish a central bank. In March 1935, the Bank of Canada (Banque du Canada) opened its doors as the central bank.

(7) the Swiss Franc (CHF)

With 5.2% of daily currency transactions, the Swiss franc takes the 8th spot. Until the mid-19th century, cantons (states or provinces is Swiss) and other entities were producing their own currency. After the first Federal Constitution went into effect in 1848, the Federal Coinage Act was passed in 1850.

Between 1876 and 1901, three agreements were passed to ensure and facilitate the reciprocal conversion of banknotes without any charges. While several attempts were made to establish a central bank, either the motion didn't pass in the parliament or, if it did, it was rejected by voters.

Finally, the Swiss National Bank was established after the introduction of the Federal Act on the Swiss National Bank in 1905. In 1910, the Swiss National Bank received its monopoly position in issuing money.

(8) Chinese RMB (CNY)

From the above Table 2-2 one can find that in 2022 the RMB share rose to 7%, making it the 5th most traded currency (ω_p from 8th place in 2019 with a 4% share). CNY trading increased in line with aggregate market growth. To become a truly international currency, Chinese currency still need to remove impediments such as the low liquidity outside the CNY/USD pair, capital controls, the wedge between the offshore and onshore exchange rates. etc.

FX contracts trade similarly to stock markets and most technical analysis methods work with currency markets exactly the same as with other stocks and commodity markets. There's only one exception: currency contracts tend to trend substantially more than most stocks and commodity markets. Currency contracts trend about 55% of the time, while other financial markets such as stock indexes, precious metals and bonds only trend about 30% on the average.

3) Worldwide and Around the Clock

The legacy of Britain's historic dominance of international trade has placed the City of London① at the center of the world's time zones. Since the 1960s, the big American banks have moved into the City of London to operate offshore USD business, reinforcing London's historic dominance. Nowadays London is still the world's biggest FX center. New York, as the center of domestic U.S. finance, ranks the second biggest FX trading hub.

Geographically, the FX market spans the globe with prices moving and currencies trading every hour of every business day. As shown in Figure 2-1, major world trading starts each morning in Sydney and Tokyo, then moves west to China's Hong Kong and Singapore, continuing to Europe and finishing on the West Coast of the U.S. Most active trading takes place when European and Asian centers overlap or American and European centers overlap.

① Should not be confused with the metropolis of London. The City of London is a city and county within London. While the metropolis of London was founded in the 1st century AD.

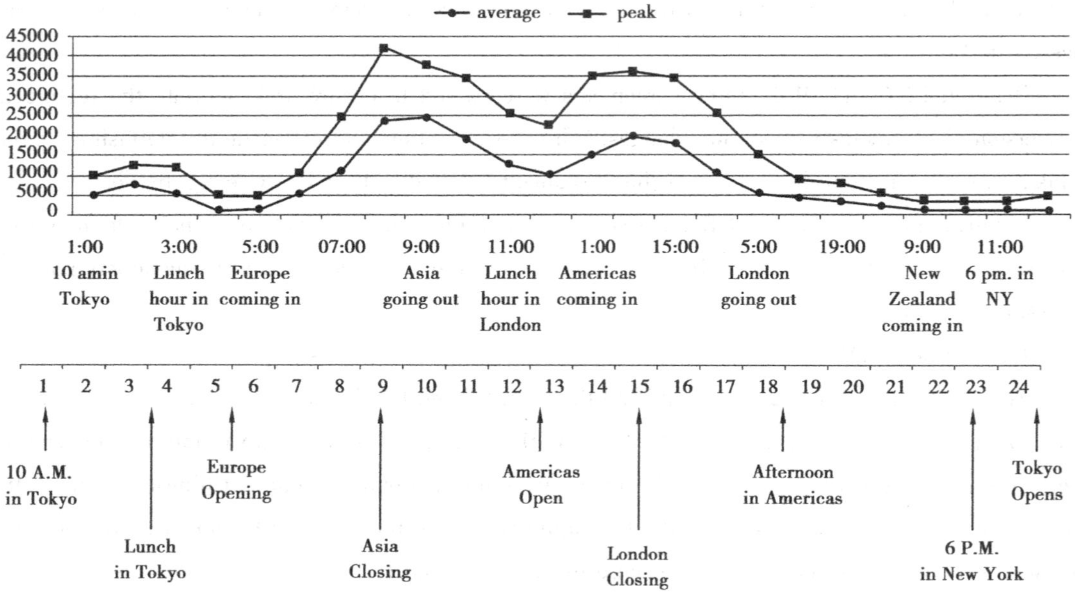

Figure 2-1 Electronic Conversations per Hour

Markets fully closed from Friday New York Closing to Monday Auckland Open, but still some trade on Saturday and Sunday in middle-east.

4) Few Regulation

Because of the sovereignty issue, when involving two currencies, FX market has little (if any) supervisory entity regulating its actions. Some countries do regulate FX brokers through governmental and independent supervisory bodies. For example, the National Futures Association (NFA) and the Commodity Futures Trading Commission (CFTC) in the U.S., and the Financial Conduct Authority (FCA) in the UK act as watchdogs for their respective markets and provide financial licenses to organizations that comply with local regulations.

Other supervisory institutions are listed in Table 2-3 for reference.

Table 2-3 FX Market Supervisors

supervisory institution	country
Australian Securities and Investments Commission (ASIC)	Australia
Federal Financial Supervisory Authority (FFSA)	Germany
Swiss Financial Market Supervisory Authority (SFMSA)	Switzerland
Financial Services Agency (FSA)	Japan
State Administration of Foreign Exchange (SAFE)	China

5) General Trend of Consolidation

Foreign exchange dealing has become steadily more concentrated among a handful of powerful dealing banks as the development of electronic trading has materially altered the nature of the foreign exchange market. Although trading in foreign exchange has been growing, the number of banks doing large-scale foreign exchange trading has been shrinking. The growth rate of reporting dealers is not high comparing with that of other financial institutions as one can find from Figure 2-2. Electronic trading has resulted in reporting dealers now trading less with other reporting dealers and more with other financial institutions.

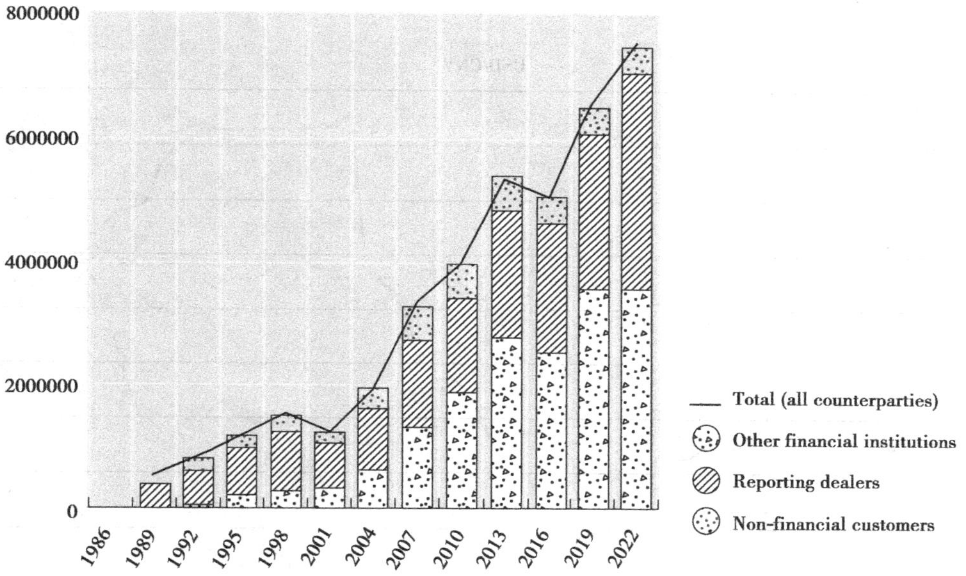

Figure 2-2 FX Market Turnover by Counterparty Daily Averages in Apr. 2022

1.3 Currency Intervention

Because of its huge trading volume, high liquidity, geographical dispersion, continuous operation and low margin of profit, FX market has been referred to as the market closest to the ideal of perfect competition if not for currency intervention by central banks.

Currency intervention, also known as foreign exchange market intervention, is a monetary policy operation. It occurs when a government or central bank buys or sells foreign currency in exchange for domestic currency, generally with the intention of influencing the exchange rate.

Policy makers may intervene in FX market in order to advance a variety of economic objectives: controlling inflation, maintaining competitiveness, or maintaining financial stability.

Nowadays FX market intervention is largely used by the central banks of developing countries, and less so by developed countries. Generally, there are four groups that stand out as frequent currency manipulators: longstanding advanced and developed economies, such as Japan and Switzerland, newly industrialized economies such as Singapore, developing economies, and oil exporters.

Since 1989, China's central bank has devalued CNY by buying USD with CNY, which caused higher supply of the CNY in the foreign exchange market, thus increasing the price of USD. In 1994 China began its currency intervention. By the end of 2014, China's foreign exchange reserve holds more than $3.8 trillion, making it the highest foreign exchange reserve in the world. 58% of this reserve was composed of U.S. government bonds and debentures as shown in Figure 2-3.

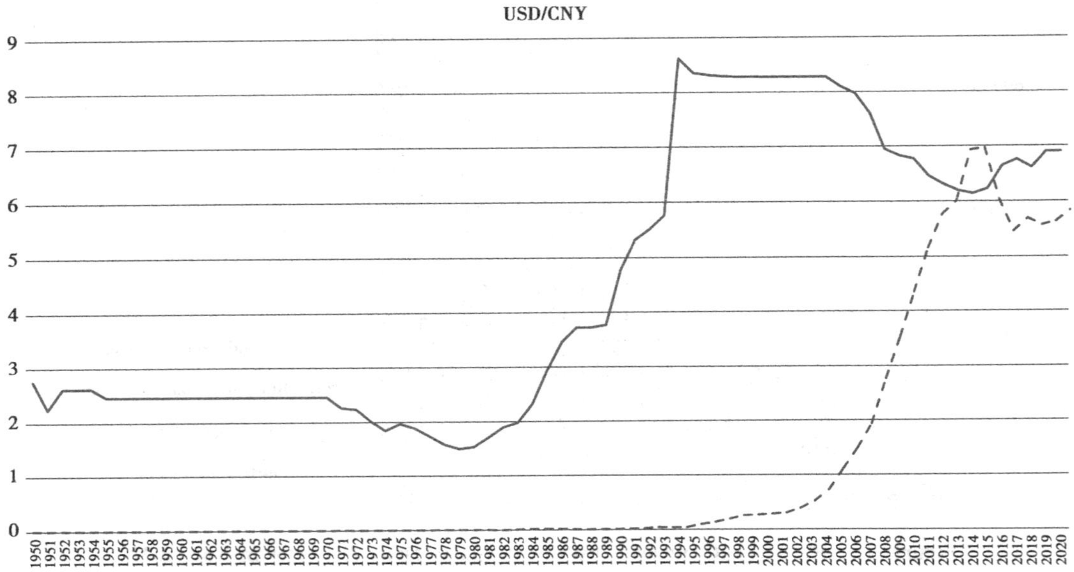

Figure 2-3 Exchange Rate and Reserves (dash line is China's foreign reserves, solid line is annual exchange rate USD/CNY)

Scholars have different opinions on China's currency intervention.

Paul Krugman argued in 2010 that Chinese currency devaluation helps China by boosting its exports, and hurts the U.S. by widening its trade deficit. The U.S. was suggested to impose tariffs on Chinese goods. Greg Mankiw, on the other hand, asserted in 2010 the U.S. protectionism via tariffs will hurt the U.S. economy far more than Chinese devaluation. Jin and Choi (2014) have computed the annual and cumulative accounting profits since 1994 when China began its currency intervention, and have found that profits initially were positive but China has suffered a massive loss from the currency market since 2007①.

Another typical currency intervention is the Swiss franc. CHF has good reputation of stability. As a safe-heaven currency with nearly zero inflation rate and strong gold reserves, CHF had been getting even stronger since 2008 financial crisis. Its central bank, the Swiss National Bank (SNB), devotes itself into exchange rate management. When a sharp appreciation of the Swiss franc arose in 2011 due to European Debt Crisis, SNB quickly introduced a minimum exchange rate of 1.20 CHF per EUR. This minimum exchange rate supported Swiss exporting with a cost: by purchasing large amount of Euros its foreign exchange reserve rocketed to 495 billion by the end of year 2014 almost 3 quarters of Swiss national output.

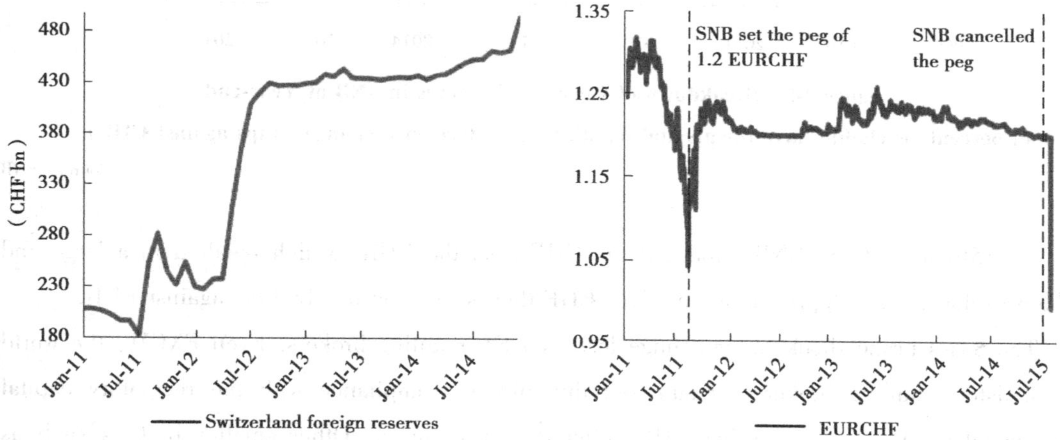

Figure 2-4 Switzerland Foreign Reserves and EUR/CHF

Source: SNB

As one can find in Figure 2-5 Switzerland holds large amount of EUR. The the European Central Bank signaled a quantitative easing program which would depreciate SNB's euro-denominated reserve even more. To relieve the appreciation pressure on CHF, SNB set a negative key interest rate, as −0.25%. But it did not effect much. Bringing more depreciating euros into its reserve is not a sustainable way to maintain the minimum exchange rate of EUR/CHF. Besides, CHF would over-depreciate against USD with the peg to EUR, and would be listed on the U.S. Treasury Department's Monitoring List as the foreign exchange polices bear close monitoring.

① Jin H, Choi E K. China's Profits and Losses from Currency Intervention, 1994—2011[J]. Pacific Economic Review, 2014, 19(2):170-183.

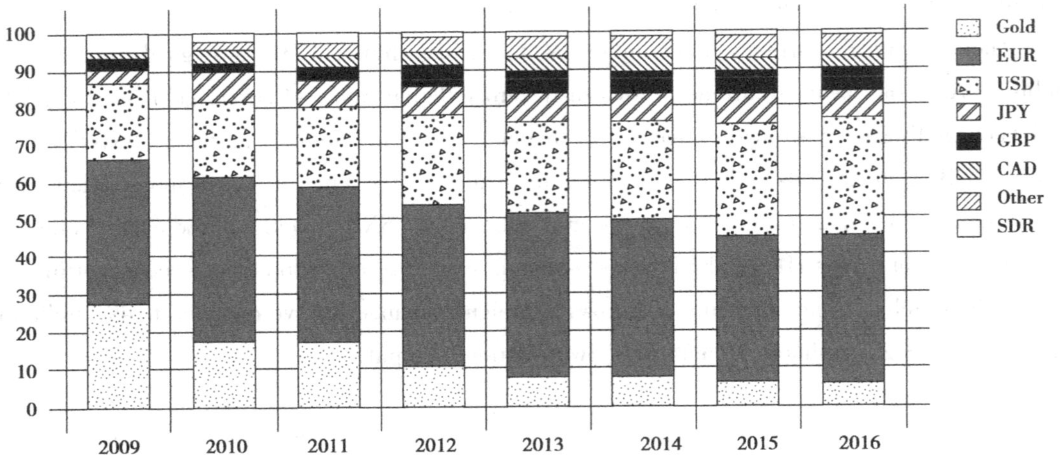

Figure 2-5 Breakdown of Currency Reserves in SNB at Year-end

(in percent, excluding investments and liabilities from foreign exchange swaps against CHF)

Source: SNB

On 15th Jan. 2015, SNB unpegged the CHF from the EUR, which resulted in a large and sudden exchange rate appreciation on CHF. CHF then soared by nearly 30% against EUR.

The Swiss Franc shock brought huge losses to FX retailing brokers. Even FXCM, the world largest listed retailing broker, encountered difficulty in compliance with the regulatory capital requirement as its clients shorting CHF suffered equity shrink. Other smaller brokers such as Alpari, a British-based broker, simply filed for bankruptcy right after the SBN announcement. The Swiss Franc shock addressed issues about capital buffer and leverage regulations on FX brokers.

§ 2 The Market Structure

2.1 FX Trading Platforms' Evolution

Although foreign exchange trading could be sourced back to ancient Babylon, globalized FX trading officially started in 80's last century when Britain moved away from fixed exchange rate releasing capital control. Floating exchange rate arrangement and capital control release gave rise to current foreign exchange trading.

Trading practices have changed dramatically over recent decades as electronification advanced the fastest in FX trading. Telephone lines used to be employed in FX trading last century have now largely been replaced by electronic trading platforms and traders were gaining access to faster and more transparent transactions according to the 2019 survey of Banking of International Settlement in Figure 2-6. The relative shares of voice and electronic execution in the FX market have not changed since 2019, and around 60% of trades continue to be executed electronically.

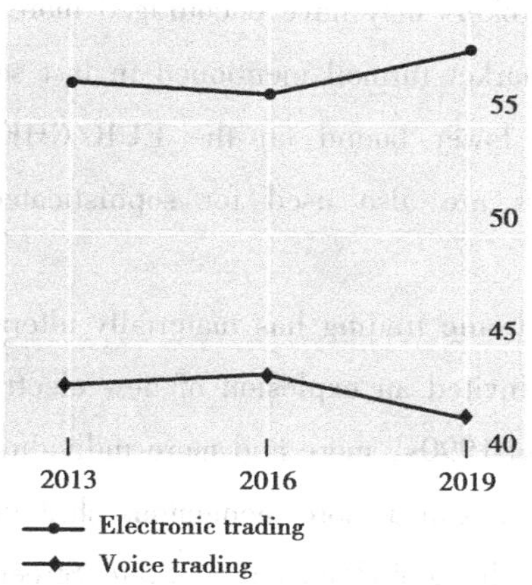

Figure 2-6 Share of Execution Methods in FX Trading

Sources: BIS Triennial Central Bank Survey

Since late 1980s the electronic trading platforms have transformed FX trading practices. Starting from inter-bank wholesale market, this advanced trading methods eventually reached the retail market in the 1990s. Electronic Communication Network brokers such as Reuters, EBS, FastMatch are the brokerages in FX. Reuters has been the leading force in FX trading practices evolution. It first launched a system for bilateral trades between dealers replacing telephone conversations with typed messages. Reuters then offered a computer page called FXFX which provides dealers' indicative quotes for liquid currencies in real time. Thomson Reuters Matching, introduced in 1992 pioneered the electronic limit-order market to foreign exchange. One year later, in 1993, other banks were forced to form a consortium and brought the Electronic Broking Service (EBS) to compete with Reuters. In 2002, Continuous Linked Settlement was constructed. By settling both legs of every trade simultaneously and multilateral netting, this electronic trading system has soon become an integral part of FX market.

Foreign exchange dealing has become steadily more concentrated among a handful of powerful dealers due to the network externalities. The trading volume in foreign exchange has been growing while the number of dealers doing large-scale foreign exchange trading has been shrinking. Meanwhile, trading platforms survived from competition have gained speciality in some specific currencies. For example, Reuters dominates currencies of Commonwealth of Nations and the

Scandinavian currencies, while EBS provides better liquidity for the EUR, JPY, and CHF.

Although the voice brokers and direct interdealer trading through telephone gave way to electronic trading platforms in the liquid currencies, some emerging-market currencies that are relatively not liquid are traded by telephone lines. Voice brokers have not been completely mopped up yet. In fact, the electronic brokers may have encouraged more speculative trading. They were said to be liable for the 2015 market turmoil mentioned in last section when the Swiss National Bank's (SNB) eliminated the lower bound on the EUR/CHF exchange rate on 15th Jan. 2015. Nowadays, voice brokers are also used for sophisticated foreign exchange derivative trading.

As the development of electronic trading has materially altered the nature of the inter-bank market, intensified competition invited an explosion of new electronic trading platforms targeting the retail market. Since middle of 1990s, more and more individual traders were able to take part in FX trading as non-bank firms began a more momentous shift in FX market. FX Connect, the electronic platform launched by the global custodian State Street in 1996, provided electronic trading for end-customers. By the end of last centenary, electronic trading platforms such as Currenex, Hotspot FX, Lava were mushroomed. Major banks responded to competition from these new entrants by offering new system and acquiring independent platforms. More multibank trading systems for end-customers were available. Even the famous inter-bank brokers, Thomson Reuters Matching and EBS, were opened for customers via prime brokerage.

2.2 Electronic Communications Networks (ECNs) for Individual Traders

Market makers usually trade either by dealing directly with each other or trading through electronic communications network brokers. Individual traders take part in the foreign exchange trading through two types of brokers: markets makers and electronic communications networks (ECNs). One retail trader can easily collect information, charting software and news feeds, through the user-friendly trading platforms provided by market makers.

When a dealer puts a price at a foreign exchange broker or via some internet trading platforms, it is called brokered dealing. Like a silent auction, the buyers and sellers in a brokered dealing are unaware of each other's identity until the deal is done, and the trading process may not be accepted if the price offered is not satisfying.

The vast majority of interbank trades flows over Electronic Broking Service (EBS) and Thomson Reuters Forex Capital Markets (FXCM) platforms. They are main electronic communications network brokers.

ECNs pass on prices from multiple market participants, such as banks and market makers, as well as other traders, and display the best quotes on their trading platforms based on these prices. ECN-type brokers also serve as counterparties to FX transactions, but they operate on a settlement, rather than pricing basis. Unlike fixed spreads, which are offered by some market makers, spreads of currency pairs vary on ECNs, depending on the pair's trading activities. During very active trading periods, there can be no ECN spread at all, particularly in very liquid currency pairs such as the majors (EUR/USD, USD/JPY, GBP/USD and USD/CHF) and some currency crosses.

Electronic networks make money by charging customers a fixed commission for each transaction. Authentic ECNs do not play any role in making or setting prices, therefore, the risks of price manipulation are reduced for retail traders.

There are two main types of ECNs: retail and institutional. Institutional ECNs relay the best bid/ask from many institutional market makers such as banks, to other banks and institutions such as hedge funds or large corporations. Retail ECNs, on the other hand, offer quotes from a few banks and other traders on the ECN to the retail trader.

1) Electronic Broking System (EBS)

EBS BrokerTec is a market-leading e-trading technology and solutions web-based provider. It is part of Inter Capital (ICAP), a leading markets operator. ICAP has a long history of excellence in broking foreign exchange and is well established as one of the leading global brokers for spot foreign exchange. A daily average spot trade of 82.3 billion dollar was recorded on EBS in Apr. 2016. On 1st Feb. 2017, EBS BrokerTec enhanced its EBS Live Ultra data feed, providing spot foreign exchange data at 5 millisecond intervals and launching the fastest FX live streaming data feed available from a primary FX market venue. In 2008, China's state news agency, Xinhua, integrated ICAP's global market data into its financial service platform. This collaboration gave birth to CFETS-NEX. (www.cfets-nex.com.cn)

2) Thomson Reuters (including matching and FXall)

As the competitor to EBS, Thomson Reuters gained the champion in 2016 with daily average spot trade of 97 billion dollar recorded in Apr. 2016. Founded in 1851, Thomson Reuters has been at the forefront of a thriving and dynamic FX marketplace. In foreign exchange market, Thomson Reuters created the first community (Thomson Reuters Dealing), the first video terminal for trading currencies, and the first global electronic matching service. In 2014, a foreign trade desktop was launched to deliver the value of all FX offering to the global professional community, for all stages of the trading life cycle and featuring single sign-on with FXall Treasury Center, Electronic Trading and Thomson Reuters Eikon™. In addition to the FX Trading desktop, Electronic Trading was introduced to provide banks with a FX rate engine and white-labelecommerce capability.

Nowadays, there are various brokers for individual traders to choose. The following table gives some suggestions.

Table 2-4 Summary of Brokers for Individual Traders

Broker	Type	Since	Leverage	Commission	Spread	$ Minimum①	Contract size	Regulator
CMS	MM	1999	100 : 1	NONE	2-5	200	10K	CFTC, NFA
FXBTG	ECN	2002	400 : 1	NONE	FLOAT	300	0.01K	FSA, NFA, ASIC
FX Club	MM	2005	100 : 1	NONE	3-5	10	1K	CFTC, NFA
FX Solutions	MM	2001	400 : 1	NONE	3-4	250	1K	CFTC, NFA
FXCM	ECN	1999	200 : 1	NONE	3-5	300	10K	CFTC, NFA
GCG	MM	1999	200 : 1	NONE	1-2	250	10K	CFTC, NFA
Hotspot	ECN	2004	50 : 1	$ 3/100k	1-3	7500	100K	CFTC, NFA
IFX Markets	MM	1995	400 : 1	NONE	2-3	250	1K	CFTC, NFA, ASIC, FSA
Interactive	ECN	1994	50 : 1	$ 2/100k	0.5-3	10000	25K	CFTC, NFA
MB Trading	ECN	2002	100 : 1	$ 5/100k	0.5-3	400	10K	CFTC, NFA
MG FX	MM	1992	100 : 1	NONE	3-5	500	10K	CFTC, NFA
Oanda	MM	2002	50 : 1	NONE	1.5-3.5	1	1K	CFTC, NFA
IBFX	ECN	2001	400 : 1	NONE	2-4	1	0.1K	CFTC, NFA

2.3 FX Market Structure

1) Market Makers

To simplify analysis, the participants of foreign exchange market could be classified into two tiers: the interbank or wholesale market, and the client or retail market. Those large banks in Table 2-1 form the wholesale market (interbank market), where most foreign exchange trading activities take place. Since large transactions may affect the prices, the basic prices in foreign exchange market are determined in wholesale market, where market makers in the major money center banks around the world deal in two-way prices for both buying and selling. Table 2-1 proves

① the minimum deposit required and to open an account.

that the interbank market is an exclusive club of large banks, and that their expectations and actions are decisive on day-to-day exchange rate movements, thus they are called market makers. Market makers deal with each other, they keep the market liquid and help keep the prices announced from diverging greatly. Market makers "make" or set both the selling and the buying prices on their systems and display them publicly on their quote screens. They stand prepared to make transactions at these prices with their customers. Because the foreign exchange market is a continuous auction market, buy and sell orders do not match at all points in time, market makers enable the immediate execution of orders from ultimate traders by willing to take the other side of the transaction, they therefore provide liquidity to the foreign exchange market.

There are usually more than one market maker in foreign exchange market, all of whom simultaneously announce buying and selling prices, the same underlying currency trades may take place at different exchange rates. As the technology develops and as the stiff competition between numerous market makers, this exchange rate difference is narrowed down squishing out any possible arbitrage opportunity. Still, there normally exits a dispersion of buying and selling prices throughout the foreign exchange market, hence no "overall equilibrium" prevailing in foreign exchange market.

2) Participants diversified and market structure

Long characterized by a two-tier structure, electronification in FX market advanced most rapidly in dealer-to-customer trading. Financial innovations brought many trading venues and more choices in FX trade execution. With more non-bank financial institutions such as prime brokerage offering inter-mediation functions, FX market structure has become quite fragmented. Many principal trading firms were established. By employing the prime brokerage services, these principal trading firms have made their stand in the realm that previously was exclusive to inter-banks. Different FX venues are available for a diverse set of market participants with diverse trading interests. The changing composition of market participants contributed a fast growth of tier 2.

When FX trading be fragmented across many venues, the structure of FX market became multilayered as shown in Figure 2-7. Execution methods are now classified into two types: direct trading and indirect trading. Direct trading is dealt with a chatting system, via a proprietary single-bank platform, or a direct electronic price stream. Indirect trading involves a third party for matching. It could be a traditional voice broker, an electronic broker platform or a multi-bank platform.

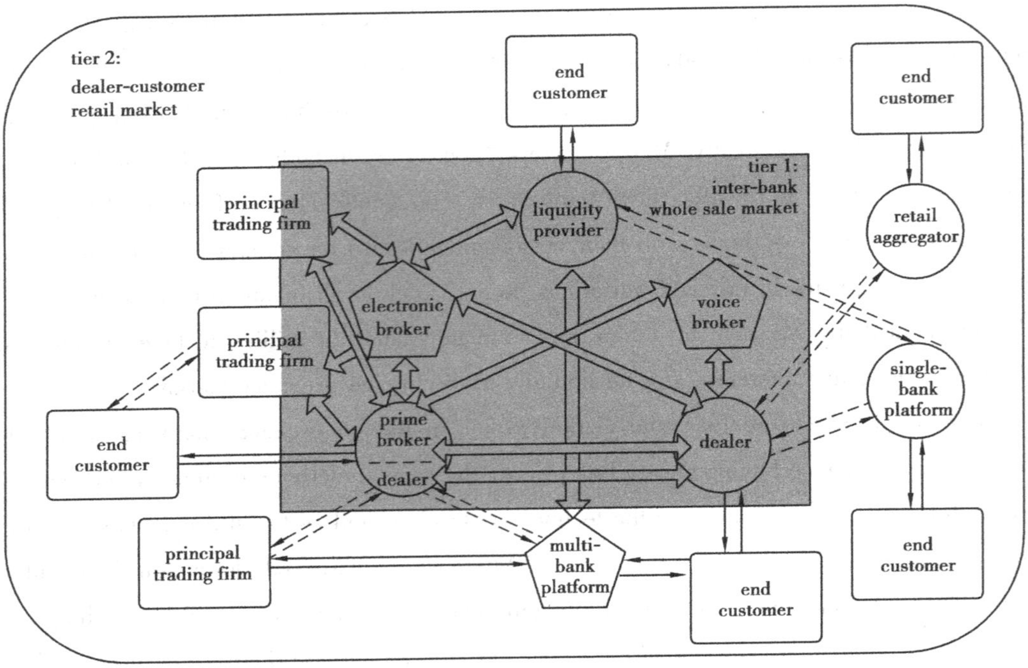

Figure 2-7　FX Market Structure

§ 3　How Individual Traders Participate in FX

FX trading platforms provide service for individual traders to trade small amounts online. FX trading has become more and more popular because of the internet and online retail FX trading platforms.

3.1　Choosing Broker

For retail trading, there are 4 types of FX brokers through whom. Individual traders could participate FX trading: market-making, no-dealing desk, straight through processing brokers (STP) and ECN brokers. If chosen market maker as broker, individual traders may confront a conflict interest when market maker trade against them. ECN brokers, on the contrary, pass on one's orders to a bank or another customer on the opposite side of the transaction reducing the risk of price manipulation. For each transaction taken through ECN broker, individual traders are required a fixed commission. This commission fee varies among ECN brokers. It is important, as an individual trader, to choose ECN broker carefully, because broker services affect the trade significantly through commission fees, execution efficiency and trading platforms.

There are 4 basic aspects one individual trader needs to consider when choosing the FX broker:

① Internet connection: if a broker does not execute trade in a timely fashion with the price the individual trader orders, one trading opportunity can quickly turn into a loss.

② Information service: individual traders can get well-informed through free charting software and news provided by brokers. User-friendly trading platform may facilitate trade well.

③ Option to open a miniforeign exchange account: for those are fresh in foreign exchange market, it is necessary to start with a small sum of money.

④ The rules and regulations: different brokers may have different rules when dealing with foreign exchange trade. Individual trader can choose the one that offers best quotation and commission fees.

Most foreign exchange dealing brokers choose Java-based software dealing programs because they are not easy to acquire viruses and to be hacked by unauthorized individuals during the downloading and installation procedure.

A lot have changed since the first platforms for online retail FX trading were launched, and today's platforms tend to have a lot of tools for the trader to make use of providing statistical analysis, receive tailor-made news feeds, utilize automated orders, etc. Some platforms are downloadable programs that need to be installed on computers, but there are also platforms available where traders carry out transactions directly in browser window. Recently, special trading apps has been launched for mobile touch screen devices using iOS, Android or Windows Mobile.

In China, individual FX Traders can choose charted bank as broker and all FX trading should be firm offer.

3.2 Placing an Order

The instruction that traders give brokers to buy or sell currencies is called placing an order. Those orders are usually issued directly to the broker through the trading platform. It is as easy as a click of the mouse for traders. As every foreign exchange trade includes one currency X exchanged for another Y, there is both a buy and a sell in every FX trade.

If the amount of currency held in a portfolio is positive, the investor is said to hold a long position; otherwise, a short position is taken or the currency is shorted. More specifically, to buy currency X with currency Y, is said to be taking a long position in X. Just like any buying, if the underlying currency X appreciates against the other one Y, the long position generates profit. Similarly, one who sells a currency X for another one Y is said to be going short in X. That trader will profit if the underlying currency X depreciates against currency Y.

The buy and sell in every trade currencies are called currency pair. When a currency pair

X/Y is purchased, the trader is purchasing the base currency X and selling the quote currency Y. When a currency pair is sold, the trader is selling the base currency X and buying the quote currency Y.

Various types of orders are used in foreign exchange market, among which 4 common types of orders are the Market Order, the Limit Order, the Stop Order, and the Stop Close Only Orders.

① The Market Order instructs the broker to buy at the current market rate. This order type is usually executed immediately, at the price displayed in the trading platform at the time the order is placed.

② The Limit Order instructs the broker to execute a trade to enter a trade at a specific price. The trade could be either to buy currency when it reaches a specific price below the present market price; or to sell the currency when it reaches a specific price above the present market price. Because the Limit Order automates the process, traders save a lot of time from waiting for their target entry price. But this kind of order is only effective at the price input before, it cannot meet much flexibility requirement.

③ The Stop Order is used to exit an existing trade by liquidating a position when the market price changes against the expectations of the trader. This order is thus used to limit losses.

④ The Stop Close Only Orders (SCO) are the orders in foreign exchange with an important twist associated with them. The twist is that to enter long, the market must close above a price that have been pre-selected. For a sell, the market must close below the pre-selected price. Here is an example which will better explain the situation:

Suppose that a trader buys a contract on the close at 990.50 USD/JPY stop close only orders. This means that the USD closes at or above 990.50 JPY. The idea is that with an SCO order, this trader has placed an important restriction on the market order, making it a viable entry. This forces the strategy developer to find a price that the market must close above (or below) before the strategy takes a position. This restriction turns a market order into a valid type of entry.

In foreign exchange market, the trader can trade with leverage, that is to place an order to sell a currency that she does not "own". She needs to borrow this currency and pay the interest to the owner. To exit that "short trade", the trader simply places an order to buy the currency later on. A trader thus exits a position when she executes the opposite trade by which she started. Margin trading is not allowed in China.

Most platforms automatically calculate profit or loss. Profit or loss is the difference between the value of the currency when the trade was entered, and when it was exited.

3.3 Exchange-Traded vs. Over the Counter (OTC)

Many financial markets around the world, such as stock markets and FX futures as well as some FX options, do their trading through exchanges, while FX spot, FX forward, FX swap and some FX options trade as "Over-The-Counter" markets (OTC).

In a market that operates with exchange trading, transactions are completed through a centralized source. In other words, one party acts as the mediator connecting buyers and sellers. There is a specified number of traders that will trade on that single centralized system. This situation places great power on the mediator, and this is a key disadvantage to this type of trading. The positive aspect to this is that it allows for better transaction enforcement, and stricter security. The NYSE is a typical example of an exchange-traded market. In such a market, products could be standardized, and it could also be guaranteed that tradings are in compliance with the terms of trade.

On the other hand, OTC markets are generally decentralized. There are many mediators who compete to link buyers to sellers. The advantage is that costs for intermediary services are ensured as low as possible. The downside is that these markets are not 100% regulated, and prone to untrustworthy and fraudulent mediators. OTC markets have overtaken exchange markets in terms of volumes traded daily, mainly due to the increase in electronic trading and the rise in alternative investing.

The differences also demonstrate that there is more counter party risk in OTC traded markets than in exchange-traded ones, because the "exchange" acts as the regulatory, and is a counter-part to each transaction thus ensuring the delivery.

Also, exchange-traded markets have less chances of price manipulation by mediators, since trading is on a centralized system. However, in OTC markets, it will largely be determined by how many dealers are trading in a particular security at a given time.

3.4 Main Factors Affect Exchange Rate

Among dynamic prices prevailing in FX market there is one fundamental price: exchange rate. Many other prices are financial derivatives, such as forward, futures, swap, options, that are priced according to exchange rate. FX market participators are mainly trading against exchange rates.

Among many influnce factors there are 8 factors that can significantly affect the fluctuation of foreign exchange rates. People who engage in money transfer internationally stay updated on these 8 factors so that to be able to decide the best times when they can carry out their money transfer.

1) Inflation Rates

Market inflation causes change in currency rates. The value of currency appreciates when a country is experiencing low inflation rates. When the inflation rate is low, good and services price will increase at a low rate. When a country is experiencing high inflation rates, the currency value depreciates.

2) Interest Rates

Varying interest rates affect the value of a currency according to Interest Rate Parity. When a country has high interest rates, its currency value appreciates because lenders make more profit, this results to increased foreign capital and high exchange rates.

3) Country's Balance of Payments

When a country has loss on its current account because of earning less money from its exports and spending more on imports, this leads to depreciation. Balance of payments can lead to unstable domestic currency rates.

4) Government Debts

When a country has a lot of debts, it cannot acquire cheap foreign capital for financial sustainability. If a certain country suffers a serious debts issue, panic selling will depreciate its currency.

5) Terms of Trade

Terms of trade (TOT) are the ratio between a country's export prices and its import prices. One country with greater TOT experiences a high revenue, high currency demand and increased currency value.

6) Political Stability and Performance

Political and economic stability of a country determines the strength of its currency. Foreign investors are always attracted to countries that are stable both economically and politically. Countries that experience political and economic turmoils often miss a lot of investment from foreign investors. High inflow of foreign capital causes a country's currency value to appreciate while currencies of countries with political and economic crisis go depreciation.

7) Recession

When countries experience recession, their interest rates fall drastically making it impossible to attract foreign investors. The currency values of such countries become weak leading to depreciation.

8) Speculation

Foreign investor will invest more in countries that have a possibility of experiencing high currency values in future. This leads to a high demand on that currency and the currency value rises up even faster. When speculators sense any hint of depreciation, they would compete to dump that currency, worsening the depreciation.

We come to the conclusion that exchange rates are never constant in the global market. They keep changing from time to time. In fact, they are constantly changing every minute as viewed in the stock market graphs. The FX brokers and the foreign exchange experts always keep their eyes on the constant changes. This may help them to know when to make purchases and sales of the money. The factors that affect the behavior of currencies in the international market mainly are the supply and demand. The factors that determine the supply and demand can be political stability in a country, the economic stability in a country and the security that exists within the borders of a particular country.

Exchange rate determination is a huge topic, the above listed factors just touch the surface. Interested reader may try conducting a web search under "exchange rate" and can have access to numbers of publications on this exciting subject.

§4 China's Foreign Exchange Market and Regulations

4.1 Overview of China's Financial Market

China has a relatively long history in FX compared to many developing markets and regions. The sheer size of China attract brokers from far and wide to this booming market.

In Aug. 2010 China overtook Japan to be the world's second-largest economy. The general economy and fundamentals have been pushing the nation to economic glory. China is now the largest trading and industrial nation in the world. It is the largest trading pratner to about 130 countries. New cash for the public means new investment opportunities; China's vibrant financial markets have been growing to match with its economy.

China has two developed stock exchanges (Shanghai and Shenzhen) with over 3800 listed companies between them. Shanghai Stock exchange is the world's 3rd largest in terms of volumes.

FX trading first started in China as people were increasing their international usage and looking for investment opportunities with low capital entry levels and high growth returns.

Hong Kong-based brokers followed by more overseas brokers were the first to open up offices in Shanghai with local representative. The office would complete the account opening and trade life cycle for more clients.

Foreign brokers caught on to the large opportunities China offers; Forex Capital Markets (FXCM) set up a regulated entity in Hong Kong. UK-based CMC Markets followed FXCM by getting authorized by the China Banking and Insurance Regulatory Commission (CBIRC) to offer "non-business" related services to mainland China residents. CMC Markets already had an established client base trading FX, stock indices and major commodities via its London head office.

China has been hosting numerous finance and investment related expositions, including FX Expo and World Money Show China which were FX and derivatives based.

In addition to brokers, software vendors or resellers of platforms including Metaquotes and Vertex FX (from Hybrid Solutions) are active. Chinese-origin brokers who are acting as market makers have been increasing. Other noteworthy Chinese origin brokers include Hantec (Australia/UK), City Credit Capital (UK) and HenYep Markets.

China has recently allowed local futures brokers to trade in global futures contracts. FX as an asset class will continue to gain attraction from investors. The next phase of liberalization will be eagerly awaited by the market at large.

4.2 FX Evolution in China

As Deng Xiaoping initiated open-door policy, international trade mushroomed between China and rest of the world. International settlement from trades as well as foreign direct investment in special economic zone have been calling for more frequent exchange between Chinese yuan and other currency. Foreign exchange derivatives operations arose since 1980, by which, the government matched the buying and selling orders.

In 1985, a foreign exchange market substituted foreign exchange operations. The prevailing foreign exchange, the official rate, in the market was determined by government, which was higher than the rates caused the boom of black market at that time.

In 1989, an open foreign exchange market was introduced. Because of the overvalued official rates, many Chinese companies invested overseas, and there were serious capital flights. Therefore, the official CNY devalued by 33% on 1st Jan. 1994, and an interbank trading system, China Foreign Exchange Trade System (CFETS) has been set up to achieve a more market-oriented exchange rate. This system, then, linked 24 cities in China through satellite and ground communications with daily trading turnover of 270 million dollars. It is a sub-department of People's Bank of China (PBOC), and is also regulated by the State Administration of Foreign Exchange (SAFE).

In 2005, Chinese authorities announced a switch to a new exchange rate regime innitiated Chinese yuan's liberalization as shown in figure 2-8. The exchange rate would be set with reference to a basket of other currencies allowing a movement of up to +/−0.3% within any given day. China thus has moved into a managed floating exchange rate regime based on market supply and demand with reference of a basket of currencies.

In 2005 the State Administration of Foreign Exchange decided to introduce the market maker system into the inter-bank foreign exchange market. The products being traded on CFETS include spot trading, deliverable forward contracts between CNY and USD, and currency swaps between CNY and other foreign currencies.

In the spot market, China imposed transfer restriction to control capital. Foreign transaction must be a current account transaction, i.e. linked to trading needs, otherwise, the trading party must prove that this capital account transaction is in line with capital control policies. In Oct. 2005, China established onshore interbank foreign exchange forward market. China then introduced foreign exchange option trade in 2011.

On 11th Aug. 2015, the People's Bank of China (PBOC), the central bank, announced that daily central parity quotes reported to the China Foreign Exchange Trade System before the market opens should be based on the closing rate of the inter-bank foreign exchange market on the previous day, supply and demand in the market, and price movement of major currencies. This change exchange rate regime could marketize the exchange rate, comply with IMF conditions to get CNY included in the SDR basket. China then continues in improving the market-based CNY exchange rate formation mechanism and speeds up the marketization of interest rates. The level of convertibility in cross-border capital and banking transactions is further enhanced.

In 2015, According to the initial foreign exchange rules, the People's Bank of China, set a midpoint for the USD/CNY exchange rate from which the currency could float up or down by a maximum of 2%. If quotes exceeds the limit, trading stops automatically. The new mechanism has the PBOC still setting the midpoint, but is supposedly based on the market movements of the previous day.

Since 4th Jan. 2015, the foreign exchange market trading time was extended from 9:30 a.m. to 23:30 p.m. for CNY and other currencies exchange, and 7:00—23:30 for other currencies' exchange①.

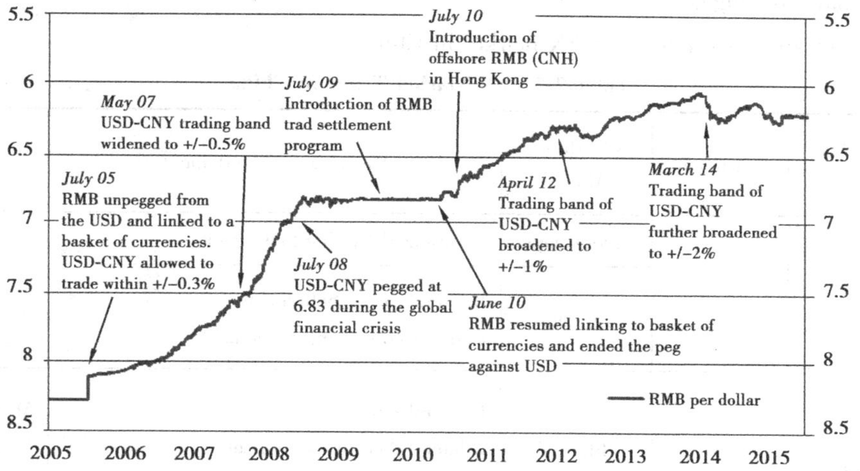

Figure 2-8 Major RMB's Liberalization Steps Since 2005

source: Natixis Research

① Trading hours for CNY/KZT and CNY/THB are 10:30 am— 4:30 pm and 9:30 am— 4:30 pm respectively, excluding Chinese statutory holidays.

4.3 Interbank FX Market in China

China now has platform for FX trade among banks and companies.

The interbank FX market, consisting of the RMB/FX market, the foreign currency pairs market and foreign currency lending market, is the marketplace in which institutions conduct FX trading. The interbank FX market works on a membership and market-making system, and its participants include FX-designated banks, qualified non-banking financial institutions and non-financial enterprises.

China Foreign Exchange Trade System (CFETS) founded on 18th Apr. 1994 is responsible for offering an integrated and efficient e-trading system for the interbank FX market. The system provides two trading modes, exchange trading and bilateral OTC trading, as well as functions such as single-bank platforms, trading analyses, market making interfaces and live communication tools.

CFETS supports:

① Spot trading facilities for CNY against 28 currencies;

② Forwards and swaps for CNY against 25 currencies;

③ Cross-Currency swaps for CNY against 7 currencies;

④ Foreign currency lending for 12 currencies;

⑤ Interbank OTC gold spot trading, and forwards and swaps with the cooperation of the Shanghai Gold Exchange.

Table 2-5 gives a summary of FX market in China.

Table 2-5 FX Market Trade in China

Interbank FX Market	Instrument	Trading Model	Clearing and Settlement	Trading Hour
Interbank RMB/FX Market	Spot	Anonymous	Centralized Netting Settlement	
		Bilatera	Bilateral Gross Settlement Centralized Netting Settlement*	
Interbank RMB/FX Market	Forward	Bilateral	Bilateral Gross Settlement Bilateral Netting Settlement Centralized Netting Settlement*	Monday-Friday (excluding national holidays) Beijing Time 9:30– 23:30
		Matching	Bilateral Gross Settlement Centralized Netting Settlement*	

Continued

Interbank FX Market	Instrument	Trading Model	Clearing and Settlement	Trading Hour
Interbank RMB/FX Market	Swap	Bilatera	Bilateral Gross Settlement Centralized Netting Settlement *	Monday-Friday (excluding national holidays) Beijing Time 9:30—23:30
		Matching	Bilateral Gross Settlement Centralized Netting Settlement *	
	Currency Swap	Bilateral	Bilateral Gross Settlement	
	Option	Bilateral	Option Premium: Bilateral Settlement	
			Spot transaction generated from exercising full amount delivery options: Bilateral Gross Settlement	
			Netting amount by exercising netting delivery options: Bilateral Netting Settlement	
Interbank Foreign Currency Market	Spot	Anonymous	Centralized Netting Settlement	Monday-Friday (excluding national holidays) Beijing Time 7:00—23:30
		Bilatera	Bilateral Gross Settlement	
	Forward	Bilatera	Bilateral Gross Settlement	
	Swap	Bilatera	Bilateral Gross Settlement	
Foreign Currency Lending Market	/	Bilatera	Bilateral Settlement	

source: http://www.chinamoney.com.cn

4.4 Interbank FX Market Performance

1) Gap between onshore and offshore exchange rates

As China began to open up its economy, its currency has been frequently used in the international market to settle trade and financial transactions.

Hong Kong, which has served as an international hub for mainland China, is a great place for an offshore (CNH) market. Singapore, Taiwan China and London have since developed offshore CNH markets.

It began with the development of personal Chinese yuan banking business in 2004 when RMB deposits were allowed in Hong Kong. Bank of China (Hong Kong) was designated as the sole offshore CNH clearing bank in 2004. RMB deposits continued to climb, especially once the bond market was established in 2007. Bonds issued in RMB outside the mainland were dubbed dim sum bonds. RMB deposits continued to pick up with the launch of the trade settlement scheme in 2009–2010.

The offshore CNH doesn't fluctuate within a tight band like the onshore CNY.

And borrowing costs are much cheaper in the CNH bond market than in mainland China. In settling trade, many companies accept CNY payments from Chinese importers and change that into USD at the more attractive offshore rate.

2) Trading volume is growing

Table 2-6 shows a summary of foreign exchange market products traded in China from 2011 till 2020. Every aspect has been growing greathy and the pace of market openness has accelerated significantly.

Table 2-6 A Summary of FX Traded in China's Interbank Market (100 million US$)

year	turnover	spot	forward	swap	option
2011	86400	62500	6017	17842	10
2012	91800	61400	4507	25290	318
2013	112000	70900	6045	34800	732
2014	127600	72500	5979	47200	1928
2015	135488.9486	82601.68561	4949.601979	86033.11906	4046.749078
2016	168498.1072	88354.47164	3783.136086	101296.6186	9549.667421
2017	203365.3201	94893.89891	4258.949679	135671.7796	6020.534959
2018	248453.7478	110646.8431	5418.818321	166171.2828	8473.81924
2019	250078.9636	113561.2303	3806.413204	165328.6228	8500.215068
2020	253956.6855	119430.1503	5643.153372	165859.8102	8412.373284
2021	313457.0569	142223.3134	9309.043688	204762.6962	12380.854670
2022	287363.8195	125923.7484	10574.075275	195085.8974	13417.204637

Besides, the FX market members are enriched. Till Jul. 2021 the RMB/FX market had 725 members among which there are 25 market makers, 20 institutions were market makers for trial.

3) The FX Market Construction

The quotation mechanism of CNY central parity was improved and market's transition from fundamental role to decisive role achieved gradually.

The pace of FX market openness accelerated by expanding eligible overseas participants. Based on the sustained openness of the interbank FX market to CNH clearing banks, the overseas central banks and similar institutions were granted multi-channel and multi-way access into China's interbank FX market. By 2021, 44 foreign banks and financial institutions have acquired membership and officially entered China Interbank FX Market①, plus 22 overseas clearing banks.

The mechanism innovation such as C-Swap and e-transaction in the FX market have associated FX market to moved forward continuously. The queue of CNY direct trading expanded. By the end of 2016, RMB established direct trading with 21 currencies, see Table 2-7 for details.

Table 2-7 Direct Trading Currencies

Currency	ISO Code	Direct Trading Since
Malaysian Ringgit	MYR	18 Aug. 10
Russian Ruble	RUB	22 Nov. 10
Japanese Yen	JPY	29 May 12
Australian Dollar	AUD	9 Apr. 13
New Zealand Dollar	NZD	18 Mar. 14
The Great Britain Pound	GBP	18 Jun. 14
EURO	EUR	29 Sep. 14
Singapore Dollar	SGD	27 Oct. 14
Swiss Franc	CHF	9 Nov. 15
South African Rand	ZAR	17 Jun. 16
Korean Won	KRW	24 Jun. 16
Asudi Riyal	SAR	23 Sep. 16
United Arab Emirates Dirham	AED	23 Sep. 16

① according to the statistic published by National Interbank Funding Center.

Continued

Currency	ISO Code	Direct Trading Since
Canadian Dollar	CAD	11 Nov. 16
Mexican Peso	MXN	9 Dec. 16
Turkish Lira	TRY	9 Dec. 16
Polish Zloty	PLN	9 Dec. 16
Danish Krone	DKK	9 Dec. 16
Hungarian Forint	HUF	9 Dec. 16
Norwegian Krone	NOK	9 Dec. 16
Swedish Krona	SEK	9 Dec. 16

source: State Administration of Foreign Exchange

So far China has signed Currency Reciprocal Agreement with 39 countries' central banks.

4) FX Reform

China first announced Tentative Provisions on the Administration of Inter-bank Foreign Exchange market in 1996 and in 2008 published Regulations of the People's Republic of China on Foreign Exchange Administration.

By the end of 2010 China has published its first set of formal guidelines, governing market-makers trading the Chinese yuan against foreign currencies. The guideline divides market makers into three types: yuan foreign exchange spot trading market makers, those for forwards and swap trading, and those for all business. It also requires a trial period before getting such status. The guideline took effect on 1st Jan. 2011. Only banks can assume the role of market makers.

To minimize the risk of the extended foreign currency reserve, the Chinese central government began foreign exchange administrative reforms. The main areas of these reforms are:

① Foreign exchange in trade;

② Foreign exchange in external guarantees;

③ Foreign exchange in capital investments;

④ Foreign exchange law amendment.

After years' reform, despite the complex and volatile environment, China's foreign exchange market was generally stable. The CNY exchange rate remained stable, cross-border capital flows were in a reasonably and orderly manner, and the balance of payments was basically balanced. China's foreign exchange market now presents 3 characteristics:

① the exchange rate of CNY is expected to be relatively stable

The spot exchange rate of the CNY against USD rose and fell and maintained two-way fluctuations in different stages. The two-way fluctuations of exchange rate were affected by various factors, including mainly the international financial environment as well as the supply and demand of the domestic foreign exchange market. Professional indicators, such as foreign exchange forwards and options, have shown signs of reasonable divergence and relative stability in the market expectations for exchange rates.

② real economic activities promoted cross-border capital inflows

China's import and export of goods continued to maintain a relatively high surplus since 2019. It demonstrated the advantages of China's industrial and supply chains in the face of the pandemic. According to the data from the Ministry of Commerce, the actual use of foreign investment in China in 2021 stood at US $ 173.5 billion, a year-on-year increase of 20%, which reached a historical high. It reflected China's good economic development prospects have strong attraction for overseas long-term capital. In addition, in 2021, foreign investors increased their holdings of domestic bonds by US $ 166.6 billion, and CNY assets have become an important choice for foreign capital allocation. Real economic activities such as trade and investment have become the main driving force for cross-border capital inflows.

③ the external assets of China's private sector increased significantly

According to the balance of international payments (BOP), China's outbound investment, especially that of the private sector, increased correspondingly under the background of current account surplus and overall inflow of overseas capital. In general, China's private sector including enterprises and financial institutions had cross-border capital flows in and out, forming a pattern of independent balance of international payments.

Case Studies

Case 1 China FX Regulator Aims to Loosen Controls in FX Market

March 2, 2017, 10:11:00 PM EDT By Reuters Elias Glenn and Winni Zhou

China will create an open, competitive domestic currency market and should let a flexible exchange rate mechanism regulate the impact of capital flows and balance international payments, a deputy head of its foreign exchange regulator has said. Writing in a State Administration of Foreign Exchange (SAFE) publication on Thursday, Fang Shangpu said a so-called "negative list" would be established, based on prudential assessment. Analysts believe such a list would specify sectors of the foreign exchange market that would remain subject to controls. According to

Fang, foreign exchange conversion limits would be gradually phased out for "microscopic areas", a term interpreted by analysts as meaning transactions by individuals and companies. China's foreign exchange reserves unexpectedly fell below the closely watched $3 trillion level in January for the first time in nearly six years, though tighter regulatory controls appeared to making some progress in slowing capital outflows.

China has long committed that it would push forward with market-oriented exchange rate reform that allows for two-way flexibility in the Chinese currency, though the yuan remains tightly controlled. And some analysts fear a heavy and sustained drain on reserves could prompt Beijing to devalue the yuan as it did in 2015.

Fang said SAFE will "strengthen checks on authenticity and compliance of banks' foreign exchange businesses". He reiterated SAFE's call for tighter controls of capital outflows, which have contributed to a weakening yuan and the drawdown of FX reserves. The authority will also continue to "combat illegal activities and wrongdoings in order to keep order in the FX market", and it will "strictly deter arbitrage that circumvents policies," Fang said. SAFE said this week that it would let foreign investors trade FX derivatives in its interbank bond market for the first time.

"(China should) increase the depth of the foreign exchange market, increase the number of trading tools and market participants, and establish a multi-tiered and inclusive trading platform," Fang said. He also said China would work on including cross-border capital flow management in its macro prudential risk assessment framework for banks and would improve policy tools for counter-cyclical management of cross-border flows. Analysts and market participants said they did not expect any relaxation of the domestic foreign exchange market soon, and were unclear over the extent of the plans for liberalization.

China will tighten foreign exchange market regulations in 2017 and crack down on relevant legal violations in order to maintain a healthy balance of international payments for the country, according to China's foreign exchange authority.

The Chinese State Administration of Foreign Exchange also said that it will make policy more transparent to further open China's financial market to the outside world.

"We will continue to push forward and support the two-way opening of China's financial market, and further promote the facilitation of cross-border trade and investment so that the financial market can better serve the real economy," said Pan Gongsheng, head of the Chinese State Administration of Foreign Exchange.

Pan said that China's foreign exchange market is currently stable, and cross-border capital flows remain balanced. Several companies, however, were found using false documents and fictitious trade records to evade foreign exchange control in the recent crackdown, with many individuals held suspect for money laundering and illegal assets transfer.

The administration has recently cracked down on several cases related to China's foreign exchange laws and regulations, including an illegal private bank, which involved nearly 50 billion yuan (about 7.3 billion US dollars).

Case 2 The Following Case Explains Broker Failure and the Consequences

FXCM to Pay $650000 CFTC Fine Over Capital Shortfall

by Reuters 14th Feb. 2017

NEW YORK, Feb 13 (Reuters)—FXCM Inc (FXCM.O) agreed to pay a $650000 civil fine to settle US Commodity Futures Trading Commission charges that the currencies broker was undercapitalized in January 2015 and was too slow to report the shortfall.

A consent order describing the settlement was filed on Monday with the federal court in Manhattan and approved by U.S. District Judge Katherine Forrest.

The settlement also resolved a claim that FXCM violated CFTC rules by representing to customers that it would limit their losses, through a policy of "zeroing out" negative balances.

FXCM did not admit or deny wrongdoing. A spokeswoman did not immediately respond to requests for comment.

The settlement was disclosed one week after New York-based FXCM said it intended to pull out of US retail foreign exchange, and sell its customer accounts to Gain Capital Holdings Inc (GCAP.N).

That announcement accompanied a $7 million CFTC fine against FXCM and founding partners Dror "Drew" Niv and William Ahdout to resolve charges that over five years they concealed FXCM's close ties to a market maker that received favored treatment.

FXCM, Niv and Ahdout were also barred from markets overseen by the CFTC.

Monday's settlement stemmed from the Swiss National Bank's decision on Jan. 15, 2015 to eliminate a cap on the Swiss franc's value relative to the euro.

That decision caused EURO to plunge, and led FXCM a day later to report having lost more than $200 million as a result.

Case 3 UK Becomes Second-Largest Offshore RMB Clearing Centre

28th Apr. 2016

The UK unseated the southeast Asian financial hub as the largest clearing centre for the RMB outside of greater China in March, according to SWIFT's RMB tracker. The financial transaction system's data showed the value of UK RMB payments rose 21% year-on-year last month.

That reflects the growing dominance of China's currency in payments between the UK and China, which now accounts for 40% of all payments in the corridor, followed by the Hong Kong dollar (24%).

London is the world's largest single FX-trading centre, with $2.15tn traded daily, according to the latest data from the Bank of England. The RMB has climbed to be the eighth most-traded currency in the city, involved in 1.8% of transactions—equivalent to about $ 39bn of deals, compared with $1.9tn for the dollar and $837bn for the euro.

With the UK accounting for 6.3% of all offshore transactions using the Chinese currency at last count, Singapore has been bumped to third place at 4.6%. But both are still leagues behind Hong Kong, which processes 72.5% of all RMB payments.

Stephen Gilderdale, managing director for UK, Ireland and Nordics at SWIFT, attributed the rise to steady growth in RMB clearance at China Construction Bank's UK branch, which opened in June 2014.

Case 4 Foreign Exchange could be Weapon

In 2018 the US reactivated a slew of sanctions on Iran's financial and industrial sectors beginning on 7th Aug. 2018.

The action, followed by another set of sanctions brought U.S. sanctions against Iran to the level on par with those prior to a major multilateral nuclear deal reached in 2015.

The first batch of sanctions target Tehran's purchase of U.S. banknotes, trade in gold and other precious metals, as well as the use of graphite, coal, aluminum and steel in industrial processes.

Another round of sanctions reinstalled were on Iran's port, energy and shipping sectors, its petroleum-related transactions, and foreign transactions with the Central Bank of Iran. Furthermore, the U.S. administration has chosen to kick Russia out of SWIFT and confiscate its assets. The U.S. dollar has been weaponised with the cost of degrading the world's trust in the U.S. over time. Investors and countries are actively looking to lessen the dominance of the U.S. dollar in international finance.

Exercises

Ⅰ. *For the following questions, consider each of the choices seperatly and select all that apply.*

1. Foreign exchange market has featured by (　　).

A. dynamic market participants

B. high daily transaction volume

C. worldwide

D. around the clock of the trade

2. Foreign exchange activity is concentrated in "major" currencies such as ( ) against the USD.

A. GBP B. CNY

C. EUR D. JPY

3. Policymakers may intervene in foreign exchange markets in order to ( ).

A. make profit

B. controll inflation

C. maintain currency competitiveness

D. maintain financial stability.

4. Individual traders should consider ( ) of one broker before deciding which broker to trade through.

A. internet connection B. information service

C. account size D. rules and regulations

5. The products being traded on CFETS currently include ( ).

A. spot B. forward

C. swap D. option

Ⅱ. ***Short answer questions.***

1. *What are orders that commonly used in foreign exchange market?*

2. *What is short position and short selling?*

3. *What are factors that can significantly affect the fluctuation of foreign exchange rates?*

Chapter 3
Foreign Exchange Spots

A foreign exchange spot transaction, also known as FX spot, is an agreement between two parties to buy one currency against selling another currency at an agreed price for settlement on the spot date. The exchange rate at which the transaction is done is called the spot exchange rate, it is to price one currency with the other currency. Chapter 2 states that foreign exchange market is by far the largest financial market on which the spot exchange rate is determined. Spot rate is the fundation to construct the whole foreigh exchange market. It is the core element with which rest of the FX derivatives are built. This chapter shares knowledge on:

- Some basic principles of FX spot;
- The quotation conventions in foreign exchange market;
- Bid-Ask spread;
- Arbitrages in FX spot.

§ 1 Currency Code and Currency Symbol

1.1 International Organization for Standardization (ISO)

Given the size and dynamic participants, there originally has no absolute rule nor unified regulation in the foreign exchange market. Over time, many standards have been developed to bring in uniformity. One institution focuses on uniformity is the International Organization for Standardization. In short, it is called ISO. It is an independent, non-governmental international organization with a membership of 168 national standards bodies. Through its members, ISO brings together experts to share knowledge and develop voluntary, consensus-based, market relevant International Standards that support innovation and provide solutions to global challenges.

1.2 Currency Code

ISO has over 24770 International Standards covering almost all aspects of technology and business, among which, ISO 4217 deals with standardization of currency codes. Currency code is a three-letter ISO 4217 abbreviation. ISO 4217 specifies a 3-letter alphabetic code as well as 3-digit numeric code. Currencies can be represented in the code in two ways: a three-letter alphabetic code and a three-digit numeric code. This book applies a three-letter alphabetic code.

Take the Special Drawing Rights currency basket for instance, it is composed by USD, EUR, CNY, GBP and JPY① as shown in Figure 3-1. USD is for U.S. dollar, EUR for Euro, CNY for Chinese yuan, GBP for British pound and JPY for Jananese Yen.

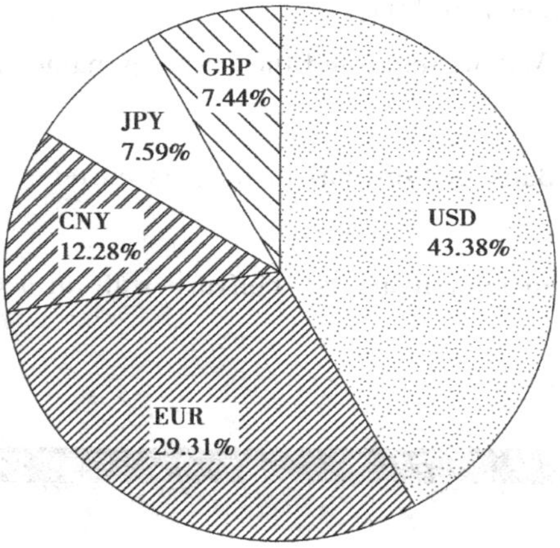

Figure 3-1 SDR Currency Basket

source: BIS

More specifically, the first two letters of each currency code represent the abbreviation of country name while the last letter indicates the currency name. In CNY, "CN" stand for China, and "Y" for Chinese currency unit "yuan".

Table 3-1 gives a detailed explanation for these five currencies.

Table 3-1 SDR Currency Basket

Country or Economy	Currency	Alphabetic Code	Numeric Code	Minor Unit
UNITED STATES OF AMERICA (THE)	US Dollar	USD	840	2
EURO ZONE	Euro	EUR	978	2
CHINA	Yuan Renminbi	CNY	156	2

① Composition of the SDR currency basket as of May 2022 by IMF.

Continued

Country or Economy	Currency	Alphabetic Code	Numeric Code	Minor Unit
UNITED KINGDOM OF GREAT BRITAIN AND NORTHERN IRELAND (THE)	Pound Sterling	GBP	826	2
JAPAN	Yen	JPY	392	0

source: ISO

"ISO 4217: 2015" is the 8th edition standard. The 7th edition ("ISO:4217:2008") was canceled in Aug. 2015. Changes to the currency codes lists occur if a currency is created, withdrawn or amended from time to time. Figure 3-2 for example, shows that on 24th Feb. 2016, three amendments were announced by ISO:

① The Reserve Bank of Malawi requested the currency name change from Kwacha to Malawi Kwacha;

② The Central Reserve Bank of Peru has change its currency name from Nuevo Sol to Sol, effective Dec. 15, 2015;

③ Venezuela amended currency name as "bolívar" with an accent on the letter i.

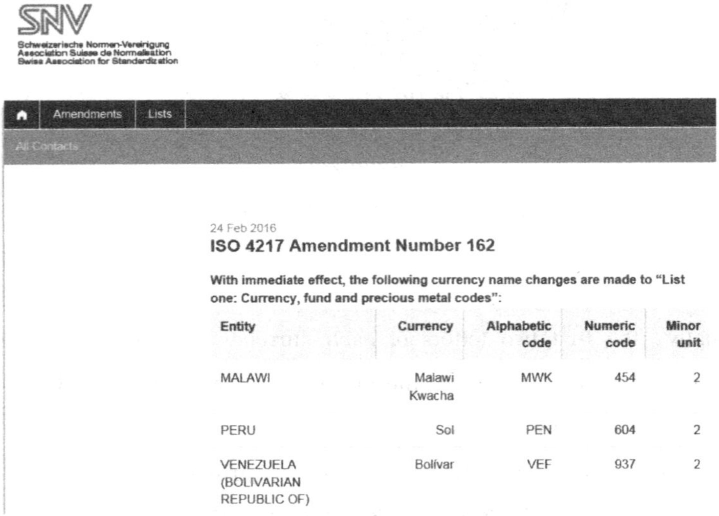
SNV
Schweizerische Normen-Vereinigung
Association Suisse de Normalisation
Swiss Association for Standardization

Amendments | Lists

All Contacts

24 Feb 2016

ISO 4217 Amendment Number 162

With immediate effect, the following currency name changes are made to "List one: Currency, fund and precious metal codes":

Entity	Currency	Alphabetic code	Numeric code	Minor unit
MALAWI	Malawi Kwacha	MWK	454	2
PERU	Sol	PEN	604	2
VENEZUELA (BOLIVARIAN REPUBLIC OF)	Bolívar	VEF	937	2

Figure 3-2　ISO 4217 Amendment

source: ISO

1.3　Currency Symbol

A currency symbol is a graphic symbol used as a shorthand for a currency's name, especially in reference to amounts of money. The placement of currency symbols with respect to the amount of money varies among currencies. Latin American and English-speaking countries typically place money symbols before the amount ($100[①] or £100) while many European countries place the symbol after the amount (100 €). The Cape Verdean places its symbol in the decimal separator position (20$00).

All currencies in the world have currency codes, still most have no specific currency symbol. There are countries share the same currency symbol. For example, ¥ are used both in China and in Japan. The ISO 4217 set of currency abbreviations are a method of representation that passes unchanged and without difficulty in all of these media. It has been long used by the international banking community. Table 3-2 lists frequently traded currency symbols. One can find that some currencies share the same symbol while their ISO codes are unique.

Table 3-2 Frequently Traded Currency Symbols

Rank	Currency	ISO 4271 Code	currency symbol
1	United States Dollar	USD	$
2	EURO	EUR	€
3	Japanese Yen	JPY	¥
4	Pound Sterling	GBP	£
5	Australian Dollar	AUD	$
6	Canadian Dollar	CAD	$
7	Swiss Franc	CHF	Fr
8	Chinese Yuan	CNY	¥
9	Hong Kong dollar	HKD	HK$
10	New zealand dollar	NZD	NZ$

§2 Spot Quotations

Among all market trading critera the price is essential for trader's profit or loss. The price prevailing in foreign exchange market is exchange rate. It is the price of one currency expressed in terms of another currency. Just as the interest rate is determined by money supply and money demand in the domestic money market, money value in relation to foreign currencies is mostly

① $ is the currency symbol of many countries in South America: Argentina, Chile, Colombia, Ecuador, Guyana, Suriname.

determined by supply and demand in foreign exchange market. A statement of willingness to buy or sell at an announced rate is called a foreign exchange quotation or quote. For most currencies in foreign exchange markets, all trades take place using one convention.

In FX market, currencies are traded in the form of currency pairs. In practice, FX pip is used to associate trading. Pip stands for "price interest point". A FX pip is one unit utilized to denote value changes for currency pairs. It refers to the smallest incremental price move of a currency. One pip is 0.0001 in case of all the currencies excluding Japanese Yen. That is, 1 pip is one unit of the 4th decimal point. Most major currencies on the FX market are priced in four decimal places, with 1 pip being one unit of the 4th decimal point. An important exception is the Japanese Yen (JPY) which is priced in second decimal place, with 1 pip being one unit of the 2nd decimal point. That is, for JPY one pip is 0.01. As currency rates do not change a lot the changes are brought out in pips.

The quantity of FX trades among banks are usually very large and because of that investors may profit even from only small price movements.

In 2005, Barclays Capital broke convention by quoting spot exchange rates with six decimal places on their electronic dealing platform. The contraction of spreads (the difference between the buy and sell prices) necessitated finer pricing and gave the banks the ability to win transactions on multibank trading platforms where all banks may otherwise have been quoting the same price. A number of other banks have now followed this system. Tick size (0.00001) is thus applied to stand for the smallest possible change in price.

2.1 Direct Quotation vs. Indirect Quotation

The participants of foreign exchange market could be classified into two tiers: the interbank (or wholesale market), and the client (or retail market). Quotations are expressed 5 or 6 decimal places in interbank quotations while usually expressed in 4 decimal places in retail market. In the retail market, quotes are most often given as the home currency price of the foreign currency. It is called direct quotation. An indirect quote is foreign currency price of one unit of domestic currency. When one buys foreign currency from a bank, she usually gets direct quotation, i.e., how much domestic currency she needs to pay for each unit of foreign currency. A quotation becomes direct/indirect quotations depending on who is using this quote. For example, if one Chinese goes to a local bank to buy some US dollars, bank offers 7.0626 yuan for each dollar. 1 USD = 7.0626 CNY is direct quotation for this Chinese. With the same quote the bank offers, however, it is an indirect quotation for any customer from the United States. When foreign exchange trade does not involve in any domestic currency, direct/indirection quotation does not apply.

In retail market of China, banks previously had to price the over-the-counter yuan-dollar rate within 3% of the central bank's midpoint. Since July 2014, banks in China could freely set exchange rates for over-the-counter transactions. Different banks may offer different prices. One could find current exchange rates banks offer by checking their websites, for example, the following links provide offers of top market markers in China's interbank market.

2.2 European Quotation vs. American Quotation

Direct/indirection quotation can be very confusing because it changes depending on which country the trader is from. The professional interbank market, instead, has standardized its quotation system: European style and American.

2.3 Currency Pairs

Because that a foreign exchange rate is the price of one currency expressed in terms of another currency, the value of a currency is determined by its comparison to another currency. All foreign exchange trades involve the simultaneous buying of one currency and selling of another, thus quotes are given as currency pairs. Currency pair means the quotation and pricing structure of the currencies traded in the foreign exchange market. One currency pair shows how many units of quote currency (variable currency or reference currency) for one unit of base currency (fixed currency). Currency pairs normally have the base currency as the first currency to be listed and is equal to one. The second currency is the quote currency. It is usual to take the "heavier" currency as the base. For example, in currency pair USD/CNY = 6.8659, USD is the base currency while CNY is the quote currency. It means one USD costs 6.8659 CNY, or the Chinese quoted price of each dollar is 6.8659. Most major currencies on the FX market are priced in four decimal places (pip) while some FX trading platforms online display changes as small as 1/10 pip (tickle). Some currency pairs such as EUR/USD is displayed down to the 5th decimal, while some such as EUR/JPY is displayed down to the 3rd decimal.

Traders in foreign exchange market always purchase and sell a fixed amount of the base currency in exchange of the amount of the quote currency. When the quoted price increases, the base currency is appreciating against the quote currency, or, the quote currency is depreciating against the base currency. But the percentage appreciation of base currency is not equal to percentage depreciation of quote currency.

Take USD/CNY for instance, the magnitude of percentage appreciation or depreciation for the base currency USD is measured as follows:

Given that on 3rd Jan. 2007, USD/CNY = 7.8160; and on 3rd Jan. 2017, USD/CNY = 6.6915. Percentage change in USD exchange rate is $(6.6915 - 7.8160) \div 7.8160 \times 100\% \approx -14.39\%$. The negative value indicates USD depreciation. One can say that for the past 10 years, USD has depreciated against CNY by 14.39%. It also means that for the past 10 years, CNY has appreciated against USD. The appreciation percentage can be found out by first converting the existing quotations so that CNY becomes the base currency. Hence, on 3rd Jan. 2007, CNY/USD = $1\div7.8160\approx0.1279$; and on 3rd Jan. 2017, CNY/USD $=1\div6.6915\approx0.1494$. Percentage is calculated as $(0.1494-0.1279)\div0.1279\times100\%\approx16.84\%$. For the past 10 years, CNY has appreciated against USD by 16.84%. In this case, the percentage depreciation of USD is 14.39%; while the percentage appreciation of CNY is 16.84%.

2.4 Cross Currency and Cross Currency Arbitrage

1) Dollar and Cross Currency

According to BIS statistics, more than 80% of foreign exchange trading is conducted against USD. U.S. dollar by far is the world's most actively traded currency due to the size and the strength of the United States economy. This convention facilitates trading. For a set of N currencies, there are potentially $C_N^2=\frac{N!}{2!\,(N-2)!}=\frac{N^2-N}{2}$ combinations. Applying the USD quotation reduces possible combination from $\frac{N^2-N}{2}$ to $(N-1)$.

Because that only the most economically and politically stable and liquid currencies are demanded in sufficient quantities, there are many official currencies that are used all over the world. But there only a handful of currencies that are traded actively in the foreign exchange market. the 7 most traded currencies (in the order for base currency in currency pair) are USD, EUR, JPY, GBP, AUD, CAD, CHF①. As currencies must be traded in pairs, 7 currencies mathematically make $C_7^2=\frac{7!}{2!\,(7-2)!}=21$ currency pairs. Using only the USD quotation reduces possible combination to $7-1=6$.

Currency vendor provides quotes for only the most liquid currencies, exchange rate between currencies other than USD is normally calculated as the cross rates using the quotes for major currencies. A cross currency is when a currency quote that is without USD as one of its components. The most conventionally quoted cross currency pairs are the EUR/GBP, EUR/CAD and EUR/AUD according to the overall liquidity record of foreign exchange market makers.

Cross currency pairs are not as actively traded as pairs that include USD and cross rate is a bilateral exchange rate calculated from two other bilateral exchange rates.

For example, there is not much exchange between Cambodia and Georgia, one can hardly

---

① according to BIS statistics of 2019.

find any market maker offer direct exchange rate between these two currencies. If one Cambodian plans to travel to Georgia, she needs to spend Cambodian Riels to buy some U.S. dollars and then with these dollars, she further exchanges for Georgian Lari. The exchange rate between Cambodian Riel (KHR) and Georgian Lari (GEL) could then be derived from actual exchange rate between KHR and USD and between USD and GEL. Given USD/KHR = 4022 and USD/GEL = 2.6354, the cross rate between Cambodian Riel (KHR) and Georgian Lari (GEL) is GEL/KHR = USD/KHR ÷ USD/GEL = 4022 ÷ 2.6354 = 1526.14. Each Georgian Lari thus costs 1526.14 Cambodian Riels at this given time. In practice, if one Georgian plans to travel Siem Reap in Cambodia, she does not need to go all the way to exchange for Cambodian Riel, because U.S. dollars is widely used in tourism fields in Cambodia.

2) Cross Currency Arbitrage

As exchange rates offered by different banks are not always agree with each other, one may find some arbitrage opportunity. The act of exploiting an arbitrage opportunity resulting from a pricing discrepancy among three different currencies in the foreign exchange market is called cross currency arbitrage. (also referred to as triangular arbitrage or three-point arbitrage.) Cross currency arbitrage eventually keeps exchange rates in line with each other and with risk-free interest rates.

As stated in Chapter 2, foreign exchange market is dominated by large commercial banks. Each bank offers exchange rate according to its liquidity and inventory need. It is therefore possible that banks may offer different exchange rates. Market participants may take advantage of this pricing discrepancy by carrying out the 3-step strategy as shown in Figure 3-3.

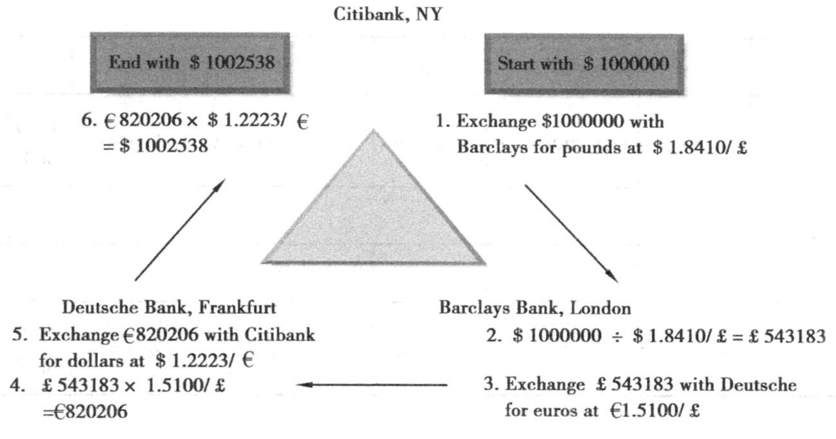

Figure 3-3 An Example of Triangular Arbitrage

Suppose that Citibank in New York offers EUR/USD = 1.2223; Barclays Bank in London offers GBP/USD = 1.8410; Dresdner Bank in Frankfurt offers GBP/EUR = 1.5100. Once the market participant spots the above information, she could execute 3 trades demonstrated in Figure 3-3 to realize the arbitrage opportunity. She first borrows dollars from Citibank and exchanges dollars for pounds with Barclays bank; then she sells pounds to Dresdner bank for euros; at last, she converts euros into dollars and repays her debt to Citibank. This arbitrage renders her 2538 dollars if starts with 1 million dollars. $\left(1000000\times\left(\frac{1.51\times1.2223}{1.841}-1\right)\approx2538.29\right)$.

Generally, a triangular arbitrage strategy involves 3 exchanges:

① Exchange the initial currency for a second,

② Exchange the second currency for a third,

③ Convert the third currency into the initial currency.

During the second trade, the arbitrageur locks in a zero-risk profit from the discrepancy that exists when the market cross exchange rate is not aligned with the implicit cross exchange rate.

Rule of thumb: given 3 currencies pairs, $X/Y=\alpha$, $Z/Y=\beta$, $Z/X=\gamma$, there are 3! = 3×2×1 = 6 possible transactions. Should $\alpha\times\gamma\neq\beta$, Table 3-3 gives arbitrage strategy as:

Table 3-3 Triangular Arbitrage

If $\alpha\times\gamma>\beta$, then						
X	→	Y	→	Z	→	X
borrow 1 unit of X	$X/Y=\alpha$	α units of Y	$Z/Y=\beta$	α/β units of Z	$Z/X=\gamma$	$\alpha\gamma/\beta>1$ units of X, repay
or						
Y	→	Z	→	X	→	Y
borrow 1 unit of Y	$Z/Y=\beta$	$1/\beta$ units of Z	$Z/X=\gamma$	γ/β units of X	$X/Y=\alpha$	$\alpha\gamma/\beta>1$ units of Y, repay
or						
Z	→	X	→	Y	→	Z
borrow 1 unit of Z	$Z/X=\gamma$	γ units of X	$X/Y=\alpha$	$\alpha\gamma$ units of Y	$Z/Y=\beta$	$\alpha\gamma/\beta>1$ units of Z, repay

Continued

All 3 above arbitrages provide the same positive rate of return.								
If $\alpha\times\gamma<\beta$, then								
X	$\rightarrow$	Z	$\rightarrow$	Y	$\rightarrow$	X		
borrow 1 unit of X	$Z/X=\gamma$	$1/\gamma$ units of Z	$Z/Y=\beta$	β/γ units of Y	$X/Y=\alpha$	$\beta/\alpha\gamma>1$ units of X, repay		
or								
Y	$\rightarrow$	X	$\rightarrow$	Z	$\rightarrow$	Y		
borrow 1 unit of Y	$X/Y=\alpha$	$1/\alpha$ units of X	$Z/X=\gamma$	$1/\alpha\gamma$ units of Z	$Z/Y=\beta$	$\beta/\alpha\gamma>1$ units of Y, repay		
or								
Z	$\rightarrow$	Y	$\rightarrow$	X	$\rightarrow$	Z		
borrow 1 unit of Z	$Z/Y=\beta$	β units of Y	$X/Y=\alpha$	β/α units of X	$Z/X=\gamma$	$\beta/\alpha\gamma>1$ units of Z, repay		
All 3 above arbitrages provide the same positive rate of return.								

If put into figure arbitrage strategy is summed as follows:

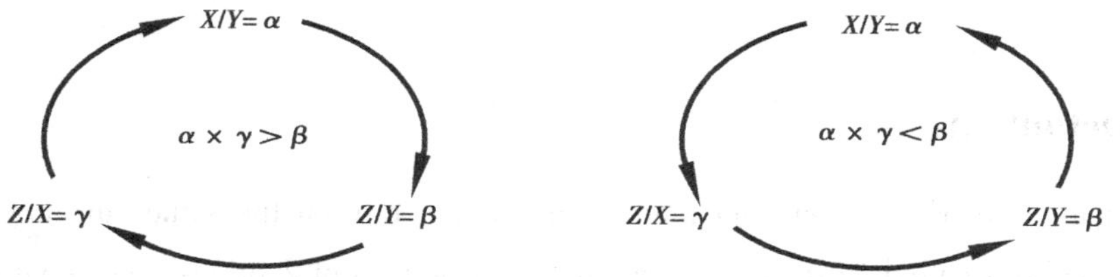

Figure 3-4 Triangular Arbitrage Strategies

Although arbitrage opportunities in FX market is less frequent than some other profit-making opportunities, it is a key element in maintaining liquidity of market whenever arbitrageurs bring prices across markets into balance. "According to the law of one price-a foundation of modern finance-arbitrage activity should ensure that prices of identical assets converge, lest unlimited risk-free profits may arise," economist Paolo Pasquariello noted in a study on financial market dislocations[①].

The use of triangular arbitrage can be an efficient way to profit whenever the parity law is

① Pasquariello P. Financial Market Dislocations[J]. Scorn Electronic Journal, 2012, 27(6):1868-1914.

violent. But the fierce competition in FX market can correct price discrepancies very rapidly leaving few arbitrage opportunities, small and very short-lived (as short as seconds or milliseconds). Adopting arbitrage strategies nowadays need artificial systems to monitor the market closely to spot the opportunities.

As technology improved, asymmetric information may be reduced. Market participants are better informed by various media. Once different exchange rates are offered, almost every trader can sense the discrepancy. Take Figure 3-3 for instance, when dealers all rush into the first step, there is increased demand for pounds and increased supply of dollars, pounds would cost more dollars, it will rise from GBP/USD = 1.8410 to a higher level. In the second step, when many traders give up pounds for euros, the demand and supply analysis suggests that each pound cost less euros, exchange rate will drop down, lower than GBP/EUR = 1.5100. At last, when many traders use euros to buy dollars, dollar appreciates against euro, EUR/USD = 1.2223 cannot hold any more. The whole dynamic process indicates that the size of the arbitrage profit will soon be reduced $\left(\frac{1.5\downarrow \times 1.2223\downarrow}{1.841\uparrow}\right)$. The process, however, does not always stop whenever the arbitrage profit is eliminated due to the over-react, which may push exchange rate to the over direction away from equilibrium and new arbitrage opportunities arise. Thus, there are trades all the time.

§3 Bid Price and Ask Price

3.1 Definitions

Market makers in FX market offer buying and selling rate on the same currency pair. A full quotation, sometimes called "two way quotation", is made up of 2 prices: the buying rate "bid" and the selling rate "ask" (or offer). Market makers quote to their advantage and to their trading party's disadvantage. For example, one bank, as a market maker, usually offers exchange rate as EUR/USD = 1.3261/63, where the bid price, 1.3261, is the dollar price (in quote currency) this bank offers to buy one unit of the base currency Euro; the ask price, 1.3263, is the price (in quote currency) this bank requires to sell one unit of the base currency. The quote before the slash, 1.3261, is the bid price, and the two digits after the slash represent the ask price (only the last two digits of the full price are typically quoted). A quote on USD/JPY of 89.89/90.00, for example, is said to be 11 pips wide (ask 90.00-bid 89.89). Because market makers buy with low price and sell with higher price, the bid price is always smaller than the ask price (bid low, ask high).

In practice, exchange rates are usually quoted only the last two numbers for simplicity. It is presumed that anyone trading in FX already knows the big figure (the first 3 figures in the quotation). For example, instead of EUR/USD = 1.2329/31, the market maker would quote "29/31" assuming the other party knows the rest of the price 1.23 (in this case, 1.23 is called "the big figure"). In an example of GBP/USD being quoted 1.4298−1.4301, the big figure are 1.42 and 1.43. The market maker would say: "98-01, around 1.43." If the GBP/USD bid is given as 1.8493 and the ask is 1.8502, the dealer would say: "93-02, around 1.85".

The difference between bid and ask is referred to as the "spread". The spread (the transaction cost) is essentially the profit of FX market makers. The wider the spread the more expensive to trade.

Midpoint is ofter used for academic analysis. Midpoint = spread ÷ 2 = (ask − bid) ÷ 2.

In general, bid and ask quotation could be summarized as the following example in Table 3-4.

Table 3-4 Quotation

EUR/USD = 1.0721/25	Meaning	in this EUR/USD case
Base Currency	currency to the left	Euro, EUR, €
Quote Currency	currency to the right	dollar, USD, $
Bid	price for which the market maker will buy the base currency	1.0721 dollars for each euro
Ask	price for which the market maker will sell the base currency	1.0725 dollars for each euro
Pip	one point move, in EUR/USD it is 0.0001	1 point change would be from 1.0721 to 1.0722 or 1.0720
Spread	difference between bid and ask price	1.0725−1.0721 = 4 pips

3.2 Two Currency Arbitrage

Suppose that dealer A in New York offers GBP/USD = 1.4034 to buy British pounds, while dealer B in London sells British pounds at GBP/USD = 1.4032. An investor with no initial capital could realize a risk free profit from their offers. This dealer could borrow £ 1 from A, and sell this £ 1 to A for $1.4034; then sell $1.4034 to B, for £ 1.4034/1.4032, in the end repay 1 £ to A, gaining a positive profit £(1.4034/1.4032−1).

Or, she could borrow $1 from B, and exchange this $1 with B for £ 1/1.4032; then exchange £ 1/1.4032 with A for $ 1.4034/1.4032, and repay $ 1 to B, gaining a positive profit $(1.4034/1.4032−1).

Both ways provide a positive rate of return 0.02%.

But the arbitrage activities would compel both A and B to adjust the exchange rates so that this profitable opportunity could not last long.

Any offers showing a negative spread, (that is one seller's ask price is lower than another buyer's bid price), a 2-currency arbitrage arises.

More generally, for currency pair X/Y, Bank A offers bid_A/ask_A, Bank B offers bid_B/ask_B. If $ask_A < bid_B$, one can first borrow currency Y and exchange Y with A for X (long X), secondly exchange X with B for Y (short X), and in the end she could repay Y gaining $(bid_B/ask_A - 1)$ Y as profit.

borrow Y	Y→X A	X→Y B	end with	repay and gain positive rate of return
1 unit of Y	$\div ask_A$	$bid_B \div ask_A$	bid_B/ask_A unit of Y	$bid_B/ask_A - 1 > 0$

Or first borrow currency X and exchange X with B for Y (short X), secondly exchange Y with A for X (long X), and in the end she could repay X gaining $(bid_B/ask_A - 1)$ X as profit.

borrow X	X→Y B	Y→X A	end with	repay and gain positive rate of return
1 unit of X	$\times bid_B$	$bid_B \div ask_A$	bid_B/ask_A unit of X	$bid_B/ask_A - 1 > 0$

Both arbitrages provide the same positive rate of return. $\frac{bid_B}{ask_A} - 1$ as demenstrated in the following figure.

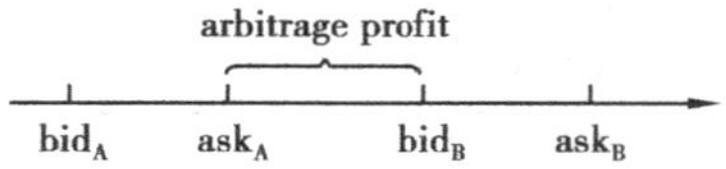

Two currency arbitrage occurs on occasion when there is high volatility or thin liquidity. It has become more rare in recent years due to high-frequency trading, where computer algorithms have made pricing more efficient and reduced the time windows for such trading to occur.

As technology improved, arbitrage is rarely possible because when such opportunities arise, trades that take advantage of the imperfections are executed immediately and prices adjust up or down until the opportunity disappears. The low risk profit-seeking motive pushes exchange rates into alignment with each other. The arbitrage opportunities thus rarely exist or are rarely exploitable for two primary reasons:

① Arbitrage trading kills arbitrage opportunities;

② The arbitrage profit in buying low and selling high can hardly cover commission fee.

3.3 Triangular Arbitrage with Bid-Ask Spread

The triangular arbitrage case in Section 2.4 disappears, given the bid and ask prices as GBP/USD = 1.8404/33, GBP/EUR = 1.5091/105, EUR/USD = 1.2213/29. With the same strategy, a trader first borrows one million dollars from Citibank, when exchanges dollars for pounds with Barclays bank, she should spend 1.8433 dollars for each pounds; then she sells pounds to Dresdner bank for Euros, with the price of 1.5091 Euro for each pound; at last, the price she can get for dollar is 1.2213 dollars each Euro. When bid-ask spread is considered, the previous strategy turned out to be a loss:

$$1000000\times\left(\frac{1.2213\times1.5091}{1.8433}-1\right)\approx-236.17 \text{ dollars.}$$

No profit can be achieved in the other 2 strategies.

Is there any arbitrage opportunity if banks (A, B, and C) provide the following exchange rates.

A: GBP/USD = 1.9712/17

B: EUR/USD = 1.4738/42

C: GBP/EUR = 1.3310/17

The arbitrage opportunity can be realized by longing pounds from C for € 1.3317 and shorting those pounds for € 1.3371, then go through A and B:

Borrow	€→£ C	£→$ A	$→€ B	Obtain	Repay and Profit
€ 1.3317	÷1.3317	×1.9712	÷1.4742	=€ 1.3371	1.3371−1.3317=€ 0.005

or borrow some pounds and exchange for dollar from A, then go through B and C:

Borrow	£→$ A	$→€ B	€→£ C	Obtain	Repay and Profit
£ 1	×1.9712	÷1.4742	÷1.3317	=£ 1.004	1.004−1=£ 0.004

or borrow dollar and exchange for Euro from B, then go through C to A:

Borrow	$→€ B	€→£ C	£→$ A	Obtain	Repay and Profit
$ 1.4742	÷1.4742	÷1.3317	×1.9712	=$ 1.4802	1.4802−1.4742=$ 0.006

The following senario provides another triangular arbitrage example.

Investors can exploit risk free profits with no initial investment if three banks (A, B, and C) provide the following exchange rates.

A: USD/EUR = 0.8171/75

B: EUR/GBP = 1.1906/10

C: USD/GBP = 1.4650/56

One can catch triangular arbitrage by

Borrow	\$→€ A	€→£ B	£→\$ C	Obtain	Repay and Profit
\$1	×0.8171	÷1.1910	×1.4650	=\$1.0051	1.005 1−1=\$0.0051

or

Borrow	€→£ B	£→\$ C	\$→€ A	Obtain	Repay and Profit
€ 1.1910	÷1.1910	×1.4650	×0.8171	=€ 1.7929	1.7929−1.1910=€ 0.6019

or

Borrow	£→\$ C	\$→€ A	€→£ B	Obtain	Repay and Profit
£ 1	×1.4650	×0.8171	÷1.1910	=£ 1.0051	1.0051−1=£ 0.0051

If $ask_B \times ask_C < bid_A$, the arbitrage transactions should use 3 prices: ask_B, ask_C, and bid_A. More specifically, to make a triangular arbitrage one investor need a portfolio composed of two long positions (use ask_B and ask_C) and one short position (use bid_A):

Borrow Z: from C ⇒long X ⇒long Y(bid_A)⇒long Z ⇒repay and profit.

Borrow	Z→X C	X→Y A	Y→Z B	Repay and Gain Positive Rate of Return
1Z	$(1 \div ask_C)$X	$(bid_A \div ask_C)$Y	$(bid_A \div ask_B \div ask_C)$Z	$(bid_A \div ask_B \div ask_C)-1$

Borrow X: from A ⇒long Y(bid_A)⇒long Z ⇒long X ⇒repay and profit.

Borrow	X→Y A	Y→Z B	Z→X C	Repay and Gain Positive Rate of Return
1X	(bid_A)Y	$(bid_A \div ask_B)$Z	$(bid_A \div ask_B \div ask_C)$X	$(bid_A \div ask_B \div ask_C)-1$

Borrow Y: from B ⇒long Z ⇒long X ⇒long Y(bid_A)⇒repay and profit.

Borrow	Y→Z B	Z→X C	X→Y A	Repay and Gain Positive Rate of Return
1Y	$(1 \div ask_B)Z$	$(1 \div ask_B \div ask_C)X$	$(bid_A \div ask_B \div ask_C)Y$	$(bid_A \div ask_B \div ask_C)-1$

If $bid_B \times bid_C > ask_A$, the arbitrage transactions should use 3 prices: bid_B, bid_C, and ask_A. More specifically, to make a triangular arbitrage one investor needs a portfolio composed of two short positions (use bid_B and bid_C) and one long position (use ask_A):

Borrow X: from C⇒short X ⇒short Z ⇒short Y(ask_A)⇒repay and profit.

Borrow	X→Z C	Z→Y B	Y→X A	Repay and Gain Positive Rate of Return
1X	$(bid_C)Z$	$(bid_B \times bid_C)Y$	$(bid_B \times bid_C \div ask_A)X$	$(bid_B \times bid_C \div ask_A)-1$

Borrow Y: from A ⇒short Y(ask_A)⇒short X ⇒short Z ⇒repay and profit.

Borrow	Y→X A	X→Z C	Z→Y B	Repay and Gain Positive Rate of Return
1Y	$(1 \div ask_A)X$	$(bid_C \div ask_A)Z$	$(bid_B \times bid_C \div ask_A)Y$	$(bid_B \times bid_C \div ask_A)-1$

Borrow Z: from B ⇒short Z ⇒short Y(ask_A)⇒short X ⇒repay and profit.

Borrow	Z→Y B	Y→X A	X→Z C	Repay and Gain Positive Rate of Return
1Z	$(bid_B)Y$	$(bid_B \div ask_A)X$	$(bid_B \times bid_C \div ask_A)Z$	$(bid_B \times bid_C \div ask_A)-1$

Figure 3-5 gives the rule of thumb: It does not matter which bank offers which currency pair, as long as one bank's bid is greater than the product of the other two banks' ask (clockwise trade) or one bank's ask is less than the product of the other two banks' bid (anti-clockwise trade).

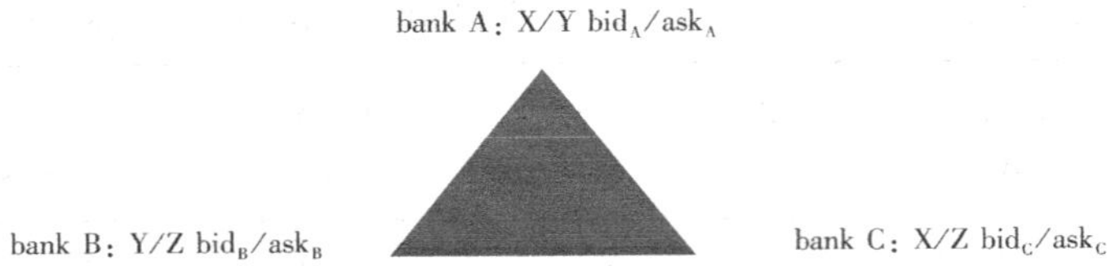

A	X→Y→Z→X anti-clockwise	$bid_A \times bid_B \div ask_C > 1$	$bid_A \times bid_B > ask_C$	bid_A/ask_A
	Y→X→Z→Y clockwise	$1 \div ask_A \times bid_C \div ask_B > 1$	$bid_C > ask_A\, ask_B$	
B	Y→Z→X→Y anti-clockwise	$bid_B \div ask_C \times bid_A > 1$	$bid_A \times bid_B > ask_C$	bid_B/ask_B
	Z→Y→X→Z clockwise	$1 \div ask_B \div ask_A \times bid_C > 1$	$bid_C > ask_A \times ask_B$	
C	Z→X→Y→Z anti-clockwise	$1 \div ask_C \times bid_A \times bid_B > 1$	$bid_A \times bid_B > ask_C$	bid_C/ask_C
	X→Z→Y→X clockwise	$bid_C \div ask_B \div ask_A > 1$	$bid_C > ask_A \times ask_B$	

Figure 3-5 Triangular Arbitrage Rule

3.4 Deriving Cross Rate under Bid-Ask Quotation

If bid and ask were taken into account to derive cross rates for currency pair that does not include USD, there are 3 situations.

1) Both Currency Pairs Have USD as Base Currency (European Terms)

To derive cross rate from two European term currency pairs one should divide the quote currency by the base currency on the opposite side. The new bid rate is obtained through dividing the quote currency bid with the base currency ask; while the new ask rate is obtained by dividing the quote currency ask with the base currency bid.

For example, Given USD/JPY = 113.85/99 and USD/CAD = 1.3368/79, solve for bid and ask of CAD/JPY.

In new currency pair CAD/JPY, base currency is CAD, quote currency is JPY, then the $CAD/JPY_{bid} = 113.85 \div 1.3379 = 85.096$, which is the rate market maker buys CAD and sells JPY; the $CAD/JPY_{ask} = 113.99 \div 1.3368 = 85.271$, which is the rate market maker sells CAD and buys JPY.

If generalized into currency X, Y, and USD, given USD/X = bid_X/ask_X and USD/Y = bid_Y/ask_Y, to achieve bid and ask of X/Y, trader should go through the following process:

Bid price of X/Y is the price that bank (market maker) buys currency X from this individual trader, i.e. the price with which this individual trader sells currency X to bank. She first needs to sell X to bank for USD, the price she could get is ask_X. For each X she sells, she gets $1 \div ask_X$ dollars. She then uses dollar to buy Y from bank. The price she could have is bid_Y. Eventually, each X this individual trader sells to bank, i.e. each X bank buys from individual trader gives the rate as bid price of $X/Y = bid_Y \div ask_X$.

If start with $1X \rightarrow \$ (1 \div ask_X) \rightarrow$ end with $(bid_Y \div ask_X)Y$, then $1X = (bid_Y \div ask_X)Y$ is the bid price of currency pair X/Y.

Ask price of X/Y is the price that bank sells currency X to this individual trader, i.e. the price with which this individual trader buys currency X from bank. She first needs to sell Y for USD, the price she could get is ask_Y, that is for each Y she sells, she gets $1 \div ask_Y$ dollars. She then uses dollar to buy X from bank. The price she could have is bid_X. In conclusion, she starts with 1 unit of Y and ends with $bid_X \div ask_Y$ units of X. Each X this individual trader buys from bank, i.e. each X bank sells to this individual trader is the ask price of $X/Y = 1 \div (bid_X \div ask_Y) = ask_Y \div bid_X$.

If start with $1Y \rightarrow \$ (1 \div ask_Y) \rightarrow$ end with $(bid_X \div ask_Y)X$, then $1X = 1 \div (bid_X \div ask_Y)Y = (ask_Y \div bid_X)Y$ is the ask price.

The following figure gives a summary of the method to calculate the cross-rate for two sided quotes when both currencies are quoted in European terms. The deriving process form as heart shape.

Heart Shape Divid

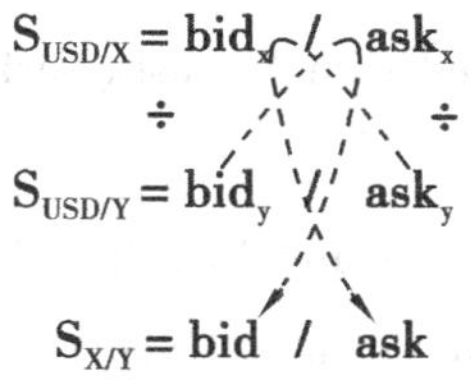

2) One of the Pairs Has USD as Quote Currency

To derive cross rate from currency pairs with one has USD as quote currency is to multiply on the same side. The new bid rate is calculated by multiplying the quote currency bid by the base currency bid; and the new ask rate is calculated by multiplying the quote currency ask by the base currency ask.

(1) Given X/USD (American term) and USD/Y (European term), solve for X/Y

For example, GBP/USD = 1.2285/96 and USD/MXN = 19.487/93, solve for bid and ask of GBP/MNX.

In new currency pair GBP/MNX, base currency is GBP, quote currency is MNX. The bid price $GBP/MNX_{bid} = 19.487 \times 1.2285 = 23.94$, is the rate bank (as the market maker) buys GBP and sells MNX; the $GBP/MNX_{ask} = 19.493 \times 1.2296 = 23.97$, is the rate bank sells GBP and buys MNX.

To generalized the above calculation, suppose that quotations of X, Y and USD are given as $X/USD = bid_X/ask_X$ and $USD/Y = bid_Y/ask_Y$, to achieve bid and ask for X/Y, an individual trader goes through the following process:

Bid price of X/Y is the price that bank buys currency X from this individual trader, i.e. the price with which this individual trader sells currency X to bank. She first needs to sell X for USD, the price she could get is bid_X. For each X she sells, she gets bid_X units of dollars. She then use dollar to buy Y from bank. The price she could have is bid_Y. Each X this individual trader sells to bank, i.e. each X bank buys from individual trader follows the rate as bid price of $X/Y = bid_X \times bid_Y$.

If start with $1X \to \$\, bid_X \to$ end with $(bid_X \times bid_Y)\,Y$, then $1X = (bid_X \times bid_Y)\,Y$ is the bid price.

Ask price of X/Y is the price that bank sells currency X to this individual trader, i.e. the price with which this individual trader buys currency X from bank. She first needs to sell Y for USD, the price she could get is ask_Y. For each Y she sells, she gets $1 \div ask_Y$ dollars. She then uses dollar to buy X from bank. The price she could have is ask_X. She starts with 1 unit of Y and ends with $1 \div (ask_X \times ask_Y)$ units of X; each X this individual trader buys from bank, i.e. each X bank sells to this individual trader is ask price of $X/Y = ask_X \times ask_Y$.

If start with $1Y \to \$\,(1 \div ask_Y) \to$ end with $1 \div (ask_X \times ask_Y)\,X$, then $1X = (ask_X \times ask_Y)\,Y$ is the ask price.

(2) Given USD/X (European term) and Y/USD (American term), solve for X/Y

If quotations of X, Y and USD are given as $USD/X = bid_X/ask_X$ and $Y/USD = bid_Y/ask_Y$, to achieve bid and ask for X/Y, an individual trader goes through the following process:

Bid price of X/Y is the price that bank buys currency X from this individual trader, i.e. the price with which this individual trader sells currency X to bank. She first needs to sell X for USD, the price she could get is ask_X, that is for each X she sells, she gets $1 \div ask_X$ dollars. She then uses dollar to buy Y from bank. The price she could have is ask_Y. Each X this individual trader sells to bank, i.e. each X bank buys from individual trader follows the rate as bid price of $X/Y = 1 \div (ask_X \times ask_Y)$.

If start with $1X \to \$\,(1 \div ask_X) \to$ end with $1 \div (ask_X \times ask_Y)\,Y$, then $1X = 1 \div (ask_X \times ask_Y)\,Y$ is the bid price.

Ask price of X/Y is the price that bank sells currency X to this individual trader, i.e. the price with which this individual trader buys currency X from bank. She first needs to sell Y for USD, the price she could get is bid_Y, that is, for each Y she sells, she gets bid_Y dollars. She then uses dollar to buy X from bank. The price she could have is bid_X. She starts with 1 unit of Y and ends with $bid_X \times bid_Y$ units of X; each X this individual trader buys from bank, i.e. each X bank sells to this individual trader follows the rate as ask price of $X/Y = 1 \div (bid_X \times bid_Y)$.

If start with $1Y \rightarrow \$ bid_Y \rightarrow$ end with $(bid_X \times bid_Y) X$, then $1X = 1 \div (bid_X \times bid_Y) Y$ is the ask price.

It is usually to quote cross-currency exchange rates using the "heavier" currency as the base, for example, the number of yen per dollar. For currencies like the euro and sterling, it is market practice to multiply the respective currencies against each other. For example, consider the following:

USD/JPY = 107.32/37

GBP/USD = 1.4231/38

Between sterling and yen, the heavier currency is sterling, then the sterling against yen spot cross rate calculation will be GBP/JPY = 107.32×1.4231/107.37×1.4238 = 152.73/87.

For two currencies as demenstrated in the following figure, one quoted in European terms and the other in American terms, the bid rate of the cross-rate is the product of the two spot bids, and the cross-rate ask is the product of the two spot asks, with the American-quoted currency as the unit of account.

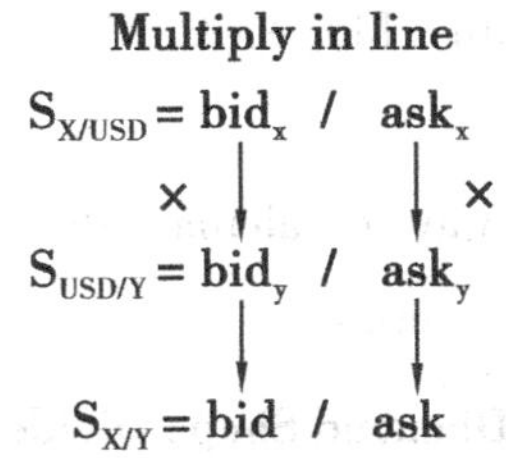

3) Both Pairs Have USD as Quote Currency (American Term)

To achieve the cross rate from two American term currency pairs one should divide the base currency by the quote currency on opposite side. The new bid rate is achieved by dividing the base currency bid by the quote currency ask; while the new ask rate is obtained by dividing the base currency ask by the quote currency bid.

For example, given GBP/USD = 1.2285/96 and EUR/USD = 1.0615/21, solve for bid and ask of EUR/GBP.

In new currency pair EUR/GBP, base currency is EUR, quote currency is GBP, then the $EUR/GBP_{bid} = 1.0615 \div 1.2296 = 0.8633$, which is the rate bank buys EUR and sells GBP; the $EUR/GBP_{ask} = 1.0621 \div 1.2285 = 0.8646$, which is the rate bank sells EUR and buys GBP.

If generalized into currency X, Y, and USD, given $X/USD = bid_X/ask_X$ and $Y/USD = bid_Y/ask_Y$, to achieve bid and ask for X/Y, an individual trader goes through the following process:

Bid price of X/Y is the price that bank buys currency X from this individual trader, i.e. the price with which this individual trader sells currency X to bank. She first needs to sell X for USD, the price she could get is bid_X; that is, for each X she sells, she gets bid_X dollars. She then uses dollar to buy Y from bank. The price she could have is ask_Y. Each X this individual trader sells to bank, i.e. each X bank buys from individual trader follows the rate as bid price of $X/Y = bid_X \div ask_Y$.

If start with $1X \rightarrow \$ bid_X \rightarrow$ end with $(bid_X \div ask_Y)Y$, then $1X = (bid_X \div ask_Y)Y$ is the bid price.

Ask price of X/Y is the price that bank sells currency X to this individual trader, i.e. the price with which this individual trader buys currency X from bank. She first needs to sell Y for USD, the price she could get is bid_Y; i.e, for each Y she sells, she gets bid_Y dollars. She then uses dollar to buy X from bank. The price she could have is ask_X. She starts with 1 unit of Y and ends with $bid_Y \div ask_X$ units of X; each X this individual trader buys from bank, i.e. each X bank sells to this individual trader follows the rate as ask price of $X/Y = 1 \div (bid_Y \div ask_X) = ask_X \div bid_Y$.

If start with $1Y \rightarrow \$ bid_Y \rightarrow$ end with $(bid_Y \div ask_X)X$, then $1X = 1 \div (bid_Y \div ask_X)Y = (ask_X \div bid_Y)Y$ is the ask price.

The following figure pictures the way to calculate the cross rate with two sided quotes when both currencies are quoted in American terms.

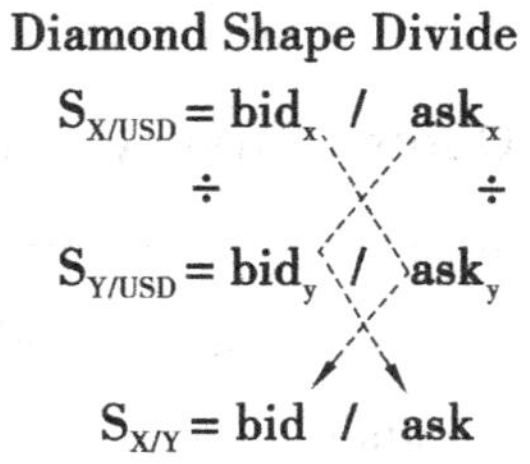

A summary about rules to derive spot cross rate is provided as follows:

Table 3-5 Cross Rate

	Bid	Ask		Bid	Ask
USD/X=	bid_X	ask_X	X/USD=	bid_X	ask_X
USD/Y=	bid_Y	ask_Y	Y/USD=	bid_Y	ask_Y
X/Y=	$\frac{bid_Y}{ask_X}$	$\frac{ask_Y}{bid_X}$	X/Y=	$\frac{bid_X}{ask_Y}$	$\frac{ask_X}{bid_Y}$
	Bid	Ask		Bid	Ask
USD/X=	bid_X	ask_X	X/USD=	bid_X	ask_X
Y/USD=	bid_Y	ask_Y	USD/Y=	bid_Y	ask_Y
X/Y=	$\frac{1}{ask_X ask_Y}$	$\frac{1}{bid_X bid_Y}$	X/Y=	$bid_X bid_Y$	$ask_X ask_Y$

3.5 Bid-Ask Spread Determinations

The difference between bid and ask prices is referred to as the "spread". Market makers usually quote bid-ask spread in percentage terms. It is customarily calculated as a percentage of ask price: spread $=\frac{ask-bid}{ask}\times 100\%$.

Individual traders in FX market may have many choices for the same currency pair, and can choose the offer with the most beneficial spreads. They shop around for the best spreads, choosing the highest bid rate and the lowest ask rate. Generally, the wider the spread the more expensive it is for an individual trader, whereas the thinner the spread the cheaper.

Market makers consider the following 4 main factors to offer bid-ask prices:

- Inventory holding costs;
- Currency pair's liquidity or trading volume;
- Exchange rate volatility (market uncertainty);
- Number of dealers (market competition).

1) Inventory Holding Cost

Bid-ask spread must cover market makers' costs, such as phone bills, internet charges, employees' salary and bookkeeping charges, as well as their potential profit.

The inventory holding cost is to compensate the opportunity cost a dealer has to forgo for holding one specific currency or the potential loss that the inventory currency value will change adversely.

Take currency pair GBP/USD for instance, if a dealer forecasts that GBP will depreciate against USD, it will enlarge bid-ask spread to compensate the opportunity cost for holding GBP instead of holding USD. Particularly, it would increase spread by lowering bid price down, which would discourage traders to sell GBP to this dealer and reduce GBP inventory.

If a dealer has an overly large position in a currency relative to the desired net position, the dealer will alter the midpoint of the spread rather than adjust the spread. If one dealer has a serious shortage of one currency, she will move the midpoint of the direct quote up; if one intends to reduce one currency inventory, she cuts the midpoint of the direct quote down.

2) Currency Pair's Liquidity or Trading Volume

Market makers' costs are largely fixed, therefore their contribution to the size of the bid-ask spread fall with trading volume, i. e. the higher the trading volume, the lower the bid-ask spread. Large and frequently traded currencies usually offer a small bid-ask spread while small and infrequently used currencies have a large bid-ask spread.

The most frequently traded currency pairs generally have the narrowest spreads, as long as no major fluctuations are seen in a country's supply and demand. High liquidity narrows the spread. It is because most frequently traded currency pairs have lower volume-adjusted transaction costs; while least frequently traded currency pairs incur higher volume-adjusted transaction costs. If there is an imbalance in the supply and demand of a country's currency then the bid-ask spread will widen. The higher the volume, the lower the bid-ask spread; or the more active a market, the lower the bid-ask spread.

3) Exchange Rate Volatility (Market Uncertainty)

Risks such as political instability, high inflation and changing economic conditions would contribute to uncertainty. One of criteria to measure the risks is the exchange rate volatility. The higher the uncertainty, the higher volatility. In order to cover risks, currency dealers or market makers increase the spread①.

4) Number of Dealers (Market Competition)

Market makers or exchange dealers gain market share by narrowing spread down. The more fierce the competition is, the narrower the bid-ask spread is②. If there is barriers to entry in the market, spread would be wider; when competition increases, the bid-ask spread approaches the expected marginal cost of supplying liquidity.

The before mentioned factors are main bid-ask spread determinations. Besides those, spreads

---

① Bollerslev T, Melvin M. Bid—ask spreads and volatility in the foreign exchange market: An empirical analysis[J]. Journal of International Economics,1994, 36(3-4): 355-372.

② Huang R D, Masulis R W. FX Spreads and Dealer Competition across the 24-Hour Trading Day[J]. Social Science Electronic Publishing, 1999, 12(1):61-93.

are also affected by the size of the transaction①, time of the trading in the day②, order placement strategy③, adverse selection④, etc.

3.6　CNY Central Parity Rates and Reference Rate

When analysis exchange rate movements, mid-rate is applied. Mid-rate is the sum of bid and ask divided by 2: $\text{mid-rate}=\frac{\text{bid}+\text{ask}}{2}$.

A very important mid-rate in China's foreign exchange market is CNY central parity rate.

The China Foreign Exchange Trade System (CFETS), authorized by the People's Bank of China, calculates and publishes the central parity of CNY against USD and other 23 major foreign currencies on each business day.

One can check CNY central parity rates through http://www.chinamoney.com.cn/english/.

Since Jan. 4, 2006, the People's Bank of China has authorized the CFETS to announce the daily central parity of the CNY exchange rate against USD, EUR, JPY and the Hong Kong dollar HKD on each trading day, which is considered the central parity of the exchange rate for the interbank foreign exchange spot market (including OTC transactions and auto-matching transactions) and for retail market on that day.

The exchange rate of the CNY against GBP announced on 1st Aug. 2006.

The exchange rate of the CNY against MYR announced on 19th Aug. 2010.

The exchange rate of the CNY against the RUB announced on 22ed Nov. 2010.

The exchange rate of the CNY against the AUD and the CAD announced on 28th Nov. 2011.

The exchange rate of the CNY against the NZD announced on 19th Mar. 2014.

The exchange rate of the CNY against the SGD announced on 28th Oct. 2014.

The exchange rate of the CNY against the CHF announced on 10th Nov. 2015.

The exchange rate of the CNY against the ZAR announced on 20th Jun. 2016.

The exchange rate of the CNY against the KRW announced on 27th Jun. 2016.

---

① Liang D. Bid-ask spread and order size in the foreign exchange market: an empirical investigation[J]. International Journal of Finance & Economics, 2009, 14(1):98-105.

② Pasquariello P. The Microstructure of Currency Markets: An Empirical Model of Intra-day Return and Bid-Ask Spread Behavior[J]. Social Science Electronic Publishing, 2000.

③ Cohen K J, Maier S F, Schwartz R A, et al. Transaction Costs, Order Placement Strategy, and Existence of the Bid-Ask Spread[J]. Journal of Political Economy, 1981, 89(2): 287-305.

④ Osler C, Wang X. The Microstructure of Currency Markets[M]//H K Baker, H Kiymaz. Market Microstructure in Emerging and Developed Markets, Hoboken, New Jersey: Niley, 2013:79-97.

The exchange rate of the CNY against the AED, SAR announced on 26th Sep. 2016.

The exchange rate of the CNY against the HUF、PLN、DKK、SEK、NOK、TRY、MXN announced on 12th Dec. 2016.

On 5th Feb. 2018 the exchange rate of CNY against THB was announced.

The CNY extended its slide on 12th Sep. 2017 after China's central bank lowered the mid-rate around which the currency can trade against USD since Jan. 2017.

The decline followed the Chinese currency's challenging day in three months on 11th Sep. 2017 after the People's Bank of China on 8th Sep. 2017 dropped a requirement raising the cost of betting on CNY depreciation, and scrapped a requirement that banks hold reserves against CNY deposits held in Hong Kong and other offshore centers.

On 12th Sep. 2017 the PBOC set the daily fix—the mid-rate around which the CNY can trade 2% in either direction against the dollar—at CNY 6.5277, which was 0.4% softer than the previous day and the most significant weakening since 9th Jan. 2017.

That prompted the onshore exchange rate for the CNY to weaken as much as 0.3% to CNY 6.548 against the dollar, bringing it down a cumulative 1.7% from 8th Sep. 2017's peak.

The offshore rate, which is not bound by the PBOC band, eased as much as 0.2% to CNY 6.5518 per dollar.

The central parity of CNY against USD is determined in the following way: The CFETS first inquires prices from all market makers before the opening of the market on each business day. Market makers should refer to the closing rate of the inter-bank foreign exchange market on the previous day, in conjunction with demand and supply condition in the foreign exchange market and exchange rate movement of the major currencies. CFETS excludes the highest and lowest offers, and then calculates the weighted average of the remaining prices in the sample as the central parity of CNY against USD for the day. The weights are determined by the CFETS in line with the transaction volumes of the respective market makers in the market as well as other indicators such as the performance of market-making.

The central parity of CNY against HKD and CAD are calculated by counting the cross rates between the CNY central parity and the exchange rates of USD against HKD and CAD quoted at international FX market at 9:00 am, respectively.

The central parity of CNY against EUR, JPY, GBP, AUD, NZD, SGD, CHF, MYR, RUB, ZAR and KRW are determined in the following way: the CFETS inquires prices from market makers for EUR, JPY, GBP, AUD, NZD, SGD, CHF, MYR, RUB, ZAR and KRW respectively before the opening of the foreign exchange market on each business day, and calculates the average of the prices as the central parity of CNY against EUR, JPY, GBP, AUD, NZD, SGD, CHF, MYR, RUB, ZAR and KRW for the day.

In total, there are 23 CNY central parity rates provided, including 21 direct trading currencies and HKD and USD.

Because the inclusion of the Chinese currency in the Special Drawing Right (SDR) basket would require a market-based CNY/USD "reference" rate, which will serve as the pricing standard for the SDR, as well as in order to better facilitate CNY/FX pricing and trading and provide more market-based exchange rate references for the market players, CFETS has started to publish the reference rates of CNY against USD and other major foreign currencies according to market requirements on each trading day since 24th Aug. 2015 on www.chinamoney.com.cn. The adopted calculation method is by taking the weighted average of the market dealt prices within 30 seconds before each time point respectively. The reference rates of all the time points are based on the domestic interbank FX market dealt prices and are a comprehensive reflection of FX market supply and demand on the due trading day. The USD/CNY reference rates is updated 5 time each day: 10:00, 11:00, 14:00, 15:00, 16:00. Following USD/CNY pair, CFETS published seven more reference rates at 17:00, 18:00, 19:00, 20:00, 21:00, 22:00 and 23:00 since the extension of trading time of China interbank FX market on Jan. 1, 2016.

CFETS has started to publish the EUR/CNY, JPY/CNY and GBP/CNY reference rates since 25th Aug. 2016, including reference rates at 11:00 and 15:00.

§4 FX Spot Contract Specifications

FX spot contract specifiations are essential to understand trading. The following figure gives a screenshot of FX spot contracts.

Spread betting | **Forex** | Indices | Energy | Metals

Symbol	EUR/USD	USD/JPY	GBP/USD	USD/CHF	AUD/CAD	AUD/CHF
Currency Pair:	Euro vs. US Dollar	US Dollar vs. Japanese Yen	British Pound vs. US Dollar	US Dollar vs. Swiss Franc	Australian Dollar vs Canadian Dollar	Australian Dollar vs Swiss Franc
Lot Size (Volume 1.0):	100,000	100,000	100,000	100,000	100,000	100,000
Minimum Trade Size:	0.01	0.01	0.01	0.01	0.01	0.01
Maximum Trade Size:	100	100	100	100	100	100
Pip Increment:	0.0001	0.01	0.0001	0.0001	0.0001	0.0001
Minimum Increment:	0.00001	0.001	0.00001	0.00001	0.00001	0.00001
Min. Standard Spread:	0.8	1	1.2	1	2	2
Min. Pro/Premium Spread:	0.0	0.2	0.4	0.2	1.2	1.2
Max Leverage:	500:1	500:1	500:1	500:1	500:1	500:1

Important Note: Upon expiration all open CFD positions will be automatically closed at the listed expiration date and time. Closed positions will not automatically roll-over into the new contract.

Margin Call Policy: The forced liquidation level is 50% Please review the ThinkForex Margin Call Policy for complete details.

Figure 3-6 A Screenshot of FX Spot Contract

4.1 Pip Value

In the FX market, pip stands for "percentage in point" and is the fourth decimal point, which is 1/100th of 1%. A pip used to be the smallest unit of price change in currency trading. Every 100 pips are usually 1%. Among the major currencies, the only exception to that quoting rule is currency pairs including the Japanese Yen. The quotation is only taken out to two decimal points (i.e. to 1/100th of yen). For example, a change from 114.05 to 114.06 for the USD/JPY is called "a 1 pip difference".

The value of a pip is always denominated in USD and is determined by the quote currency.

When USD is the quote currency, each pip is worth one dollar when trading in lots of 10000 and ten dollars with lots of 100000. However, when USD is the base currency, the price per pip varies, depending on the quote currency.

4.2 Spot Contract Size

Contract size for most of the equity option contracts is 100 shares, while the size of contract for financial instruments and commodities like interest rate futures and currencies generally varies widely.

For individual traders, there is a minimum money to start with. The smallest size of currency in a standard account is called "one lot". It is important to note that the size of lot varies for different currencies, and it is never the same for all currencies. In case of USD with the lot size as 100000, whenever the traders enter a trade with their margin account, the smallest amount they can sell or buy is of 100000, irrespective the size of the margin.

At a retail level, FX trading usually offers to the small investors 4 lot sizes:

① Standard lot = 100000 units of base currency;

② Mini lot = 10000 units of base currency, for every 1 pip change, the trader can earn 10% of profit and will lose 10% of amount for the loss of 1 pip by the FX;

③ Micro lot = 1000 units of base currency;

④ Nano lot = 100 units of base currency;

1 standard lot = 10 mini lot = 100 micro lot = 1000 nano lot.

Each lot size accounts for a different measure of units of the base currency, which in turn presents a different pip value. Below is a table to show the differences in lot sizes, measured in units, volume for the major pairs where the quote currency is USD.

Table 3-6 Pip Value for Different Lot

Lot Size	Unit of Base Currency	Volume	Pip Value in USD
1 standard lot	100000	1	10

Continued

Lot Size	Unit of Base Currency	Volume	Pip Value in USD
1 mini lot	10000	0.1	1
1 micro lot	1000	0.01	0.1
1 nano lot	100	0.001	0.01

Pips are the basis for FX trading calculating. When trade through brokers, the calculation of the dollar pip value is done by the broker automatically. In FX, the tick size and pip are almost synonymous. Pip is the smallest incremental price move of a currency and tick size is the smallest possible change in price. The minimum possible amount that a price can move is also the market's tick size. With 4 digit brokers, the EUR/USD has a tick size of 0.0001, which means that the smallest increment that the price can move from 1.3840 would be up to 1.3841 or down to 1.3839.

The following screenshot is a FX spot contract specification provided by a broker.

Forex Currency Pairs[1] (Online Trading Platform Symbol)[2]	Contract Size (Standard Lot)	Minimum Price Fluctuation		Pip Value (Standard Lot)	Spread on Orders from Market Price
		Tick / Point	Value		
Australian Dollar / Canadian Dollar (AUDCAD# / AUDCAD')	AUD 100,000	0.00001	CAD 1	CAD 10	15 pips
Australian Dollar / Swiss Franc (AUDCHF# / AUDCHF')	AUD 100,000	0.00001	CHF 1	CHF 10	10 pips
Australian Dollar / Japanese Yen (AUDJPY# / AUDJPY')	AUD 100,000	0.001	JPY 100	JPY 1,000	10 pips
Australian Dollar / New Zealand Dollar (AUDNZD# / AUDNZD')	AUD 100,000	0.00001	NZD 1	NZD 10	20 pips
Australian Dollar / US Dollar (AUDUSD# / AUDUSD')	AUD 100,000	0.00001	US$ 1	US$ 10	5 pips
Canadian Dollar / Swiss Franc (CADCHF# / CADCHF')	CAD 100,000	0.00001	CHF 1	CHF 10	10 pips
Canadian Dollar / Japanese Yen (CADJPY# / CADJPY')	CAD 100,000	0.001	JPY 100	JPY 1,000	10 pips
Swiss Franc / Japanese Yen (CHFJPY# / CHFJPY')	CHF 100,000	0.001	JPY 100	JPY 1,000	10 pips
Euro / Australian Dollar (EURAUD# / EURAUD')	EURO 100,000	0.00001	AUD 1	AUD 10	15 pips
Euro / Canadian Dollar (EURCAD#/EURCAD')	EURO 100,000	0.00001	CAD 1	CAD 10	10 pips
Euro / Swiss Franc (EURCHF# / EURCHF')	EURO 100,000	0.00001	CHF 1	CHF 10	5 pips
Euro / British Pound Sterling (EURGBP# /EURGBP')	EURO 100,000	0.00001	GBP 1	GBP 10	5 pips
Euro / Japanese Yen (EURJPY# / EURJPY')	EURO 100,000	0.001	JPY 100	JPY 1,000	5 pips
Euro / US Dollar (EURUSD# / EURUSD')	EURO 100,000	0.00001	US$ 1	US$ 10	5 pips
Euro / New Zealand Dollar (EURNZD#/EURNZD')	EURO 100,000	0.00001	NZD 1	NZD 10	15 pips
British Pound Sterling / Australian Dollar (GBPAUD# / GBPAUD')	GBP 100,000	0.00001	AUD 1	AUD 10	15 pips
British Pound Sterling / Canadian Dollar (GBPCAD# / GBPCAD')	GBP 100,000	0.00001	CAD 1	CAD 10	12 pips
British Pound Sterling / Swiss Franc (GBPCHF# / GBPCHF')	GBP 100,000	0.00001	CHF 1	CHF 10	10 pips
British Pound Sterling / Japanese Yen (GBPJPY# / GBPJPY')	GBP 100,000	0.001	JPY 100	JPY 1,000	10 pips
British Pound Sterling / New Zealand Dollar (GBPNZD# / GBPNZD')	GBP 100,000	0.00001	NZD 1	NZD 10	35 pips
British Pound Sterling / US Dollar (GBPUSD# / GBPUSD')	GBP 100,000	0.00001	US$ 1	US$ 10	5 pips
New Zealand Dollar / Canadian Dollar (NZDCAD# / NZDCAD')	NZD 100,000	0.00001	CAD 1	CAD 10	12 pips
New Zealand Dollar / Swiss Franc (NZDCHF# / NZDCHF')	NZD 100,000	0.00001	CHF 1	CHF 10	12 pips
New Zealand Dollar / Japanese Yen (NZDJPY# / NZDJPY')	NZD 100,000	0.001	JPY 100	JPY 1,000	10 pips
New Zealand Dollar / US Dollar (NZDUSD# / NZDUSD')	NZD 100,000	0.00001	US$ 1	US$ 10	5 pips
US Dollar / Canadian Dollar (USDCAD# / USDCAD')	USD 100,000	0.00001	CAD 1	CAD 10	5 pips
US Dollar / Swiss Franc (USDCHF# / USDCHF')	USD 100,000	0.00001	CHF 1	CHF 10	5 pips
US Dollar / Japanese Yen (USDJPY# / USDJPY')	USD 100,000	0.001	JPY 100	JPY 1,000	5 pips

Margin Requirement based on 1:500 Leverage[3] (Standard Lot)	Transaction Size (Standard Lot)		Automated Transaction Size (Standard Lot)		Local Trading Time (CY)[4]	
	Min	Max	Min	Max	Open	Close
US$ 200	0.01	2	0.01	2	Mon 00:00	Fri 23:45

[1] All Forex Currency Pairs are traded as Market/"One-Click"Execution

Symbol on the Online Trading Platform for Dynamic Fixed Spread trading account; example: EURUSD'

[4] GMT +3 summer time; GMT +2 winter time

Contract Specification should be read in conjunction with the Trading Mechanism for specific type of trading account

All information is subject to change without prior notice

[2] Symbol on the Online Trading Platform for Dynamic STP trading account; example: EURUSD#

[3] As agreed between Client and Windsor

Note: Regarding public holidays, Clients will be informed via Windsor's website

Forex Currency Pairs[1] (Online Trading Platform Symbol)[2]	Contract Size (Standard Lot)	Minimum Price Fluctuation		Pip Value (Standard Lot)	Spread on Orders from Market Price
		Tick / Point	Value		
US Dollar / Singapore Dollar (USDSGD# / USDSGD')	USD 100,000	0.00001	SGD 1	SGD 10	8 pips
Euro / Singapore Dollar (EURSGD# / EURSGD')	EUR 100,000	0.00001	SGD 1	SGD 10	8 pips
British Pound Sterling / Singapore Dollar (GBPSGD# / GBPSGD')	GBP 100,000	0.00001	SGD 1	SGD 10	12 pips
Singapore Dollar / Japanese Yen (SGDJPY# / SGDJPY')	SGD 100,000	0.001	JPY 100	JPY 1,000	8 pips
US Dollar / South African Rand (USDZAR# / USDZAR')	USD 100,000	0.0001	ZAR 1	ZAR 10	70 pips
US Dollar / Swedish Krona (USDSEK# / USDSEK')	USD 100,000	0.00001	SEK 1	SEK 10	40 pips

Margin Requirement based on 1:500 Leverage[3] (Standard Lot)	Transaction Size (Standard Lot)		Automated Transaction Size (Standard Lot)		Local Trading Time (CY)[4]	
	Min	Max	Min	Max	Open	Close
US$ 400	0.01	2	0.01	2	Mon 00:00	Fri 23:45

Forex Currency Pairs[1] (Online Trading Platform Symbol)[2]	Contract Size (Standard Lot)	Minimum Price Fluctuation		Pip Value (Standard Lot)	Spread on Orders from Market Price
		Tick / Point	Value		
US Dollar / Turkish Lira (USDTRY# / USDTRY')	USD 100,000	0.00001	TRY 1	TRY 10	7 pips
Euro / Turkish Lira (EURTRY# / EURTRY')	EUR 100,000	0.00001	TRY 1	TRY 10	8 pips
US Dollar/Polish Zloty (USDPLN#)	USD 100,000	0.00001	PLN 1	PLN 10	25 pips

Margin Requirement based on 1:500 Leverage[3] (Standard Lot)	Transaction Size (Standard Lot)		Automated Transaction Size (Standard Lot)		Local Trading Time (CY)[4]	
	Min	Max	Min	Max	Open	Close
US$ 400	0.01	2	0.01	2	Mon 00:00	Fri 23:30

[1] All Forex Currency Pairs are traded as Market/"One-Click"Execution

[2] Symbol on the Online Trading Platform for Dynamic STP trading account; example: EURUSD#

Symbol on the Online Trading Platform for Dynamic Fixed Spread trading account; example: EURUSD'

[3] As agreed between Client and Windsor

[4] GMT +3 summer time; GMT +2 winter time

Note: Regarding public holidays, Clients will be informed via Windsor's website

Contract Specification should be read in conjunction with the Trading Mechanism for specific type of trading account

All information is subject to change without prior notice

Figure 3-7 Contract Specification

4.3 Leverage and Margin

1) Leverage

Leverage is like a loan offered by the broker, to help the traders to trade larger amounts of securities by having a smaller account balance. Without leverage, many individual traders are still not able to afford contract size. Each and every standard lot traded in the FX market is at least equivalent to 100000 units of base currency. In any firm trade trading one lot in a standard account, 100000 units of base currency is required to be placed in the FX market. Many brokers or dealers provide leverage to traders to place the same lot. For example, a leverage of 100 for a mini lot of $10000 trade requires client to keep at least $100 in her account. Of course this client could put more than $ 100 in her account (in the following figure the individual trader has put $1000 in her account).

Leverage provides investor the ability to control a large amount of money using little of her own money and borrowing the rest. For example, to control a standard $ 100000 position, the broker will set aside $ 1000 from an investor's account. The leverage is 100. This investor is controlling $100000 with $1000. If the $100000 investment rises in value to $101000 should this investor come up with the entire $100000 capital herself, her return would be a 1% ($1000 ÷ $100000). This is called 1 : 1 leverage. The broker only had to put aside $ 1000 of investor's money for a leverage of 100, so the return becomes 100% ($1000÷$1000). What if this investor lost $1000 with leverage of 100? She would suffer a negative rate of return, −100%.

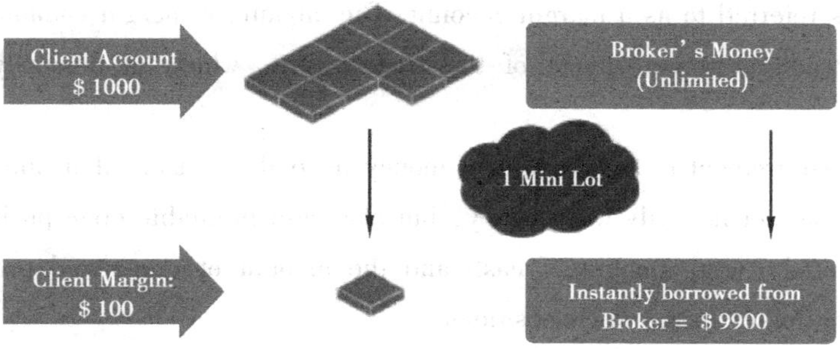

Figure 3-8 A Leverage of 100 for a Mini Lot

Although leverage offered by broker can enable a trader to trade large amounts with a small amount of money in account, it is a double-edged sword. Significant leverage can just as easily result in great losses as it can in great gains, leverage therefore should be used with prudence and caution. Before 2010, most brokers allowed substantial leverage, sometimes up to 400, where a $100 deposit would allow a trader to trade up to $ 40000 worth of currency. But in 2010, U.S. regulations limited to 100. Since then, the allowed leverage for U.S. customers has been reduced even further, to 50, even if the broker is located in other countries than the U.S. So a trader with a $100 deposit can only trade up to $5000 worth of currencies. Japan restricts leverage to 25. In China, leverage trading in FX spot is not allowed.

Because that leverage is kind of financing provided by brokers, each night the investor should pay a small financing charge on the exposure of the FX trade including the amount that has been effectively borrowed in order to trade the full position. In this sense, leverage works in a very similar way to how one might buy a house on a mortgage.

2) Margin

(1) Margin Calculation

In FX, for a leverage of 100, to control a $100000 position, broker will set aside $1000 from one investor's account. The $1000 deposit is "margin" this investor has to give in order to use leverage. Margin is the amount of money one investor needed as a "good faith deposit" to open a position with a broker.

As margin is the amount required to open a new FX position, it serves to ensure that individual traders have a sufficient account balance relative to the size of their positions. Brokers basically collect margin deposits and pool them together, and use this one "super margin deposit" to be able to place trades within the interbank network. The margin in a FX account is often referred to as a performance bond, because it is not borrowed money but only the amount of equity needed to ensure that one can cover the losses. In most FX transactions, nothing is actually being bought or sold, only the agreements to buy or sell are exchanged. In order to enter and maintain a leverage trading, the trader must commit some of the trading account and the trading account itself is sometimes referred to as a margin account. The amount of margin committed by the trader for any specific trade is a percentage of the trade value, which is inversely proportional to leverage.

The margin requirement is the amount of money needed to ensure that one trader can cover her losses. It can be met not only with money, but also with profitable open positions. The money in one's account is the total amount of cash and the amount of unrealized profits in her open positions minus the losses in the open positions.

The table below illustrates the leverage type, percentage on margin needed to open up one lot, and resulting dollar amount required to open one lot (standard, mini, micro and nano).

Table 3-7 Matching Lots with Leverages

Leverage/Margin Requirement Table for Various Lot Sizes					
Leverage	% of margin needed to open 1 lot	$ Amount (Margin) Required for 1 standard lot ($ 100000)	$ Amount (Margin) Required for 1 mini lot ($ 10000)	$ Amount (Margin) Required for 1 micro lot ($ 1000)	$ Amount (Margin) Required for 1 Nano lot ($ 100)
25	4%	$ 4000	$ 400	$ 40	$ 4
50	2%	$ 2000	$ 200	$ 20	$ 2
100	1%	$ 1000	$ 100	$ 10	$ 1
200	0.50%	$ 500	$ 50	$ 5	$ 0.50
400	0.25%	$ 250	$ 25	$ 2.50	$ 0.25

With a leverage of 100 only $ 10 is required for each ($ 1000) micro lot. This means that if one had just $ 200 in her account, she would have the capacity to trade up to up to 20 micro lot positions, if she so desires.

The minimum amount of this account is also set by the brokerage terms. In addition to the established minimum, the account also has a very practical use for margin. USD usually is the currency for booking, thus it is necessary to convert margin requirement into U.S. dollars:

① When USD is Base Currency: margin = lot size × number of lot ÷ leverage.

For example, consider the trader who enters one full size trade for USD/JPY, which has a value of $ 100000. If the leverage offered by the broker is 50, the trader must maintain and commit $ 2000 = 100000 × 1 ÷ 50 in her margin account. If the USD/JPY trade gains in value, the trader's account balance will increase by the amount of the profit, providing additional funds that the trader might use to enter additional trades.

However, if the trade loses funds, even temporarily, the trader must commit additional margin funds to the trade, reducing the amount in the margin account that would otherwise be available to commit to other trades. If losses in the trade exceed the balance available in the trader's account, the trading platform usually exits the position automatically.

② USD as Quote Currency: margin = ask price×lot size×number of lot÷leverage.

Suppose that one trader buys a mini GBP at $S_{GBP/USD} = 1.2469/72$ with a leverage of 25, she must maintain and commit $\$498.88 = 1.2472 \times 10000 \times 1 \div 25$.

③ cross rate margin = ask price of base currency against USD × lot size × number of lot ÷ leverage.

Suppose that one trader buys a mini GBP/JPY with a leverage of 25, given $S_{GBP/USD} = 1.2469/72$, she must maintain and commit $\$498.88 = 1.2472 \times 10000 \times 1 \div 25$. It is exactly the same as margin requirement of GBP/USD in the above example.

(2) Used Margin and Free Margin

Suppose that one client inputs \$1000 in her account and has a leverage of 100 for USD/JPY account, then in order to trade one mini lot she needs to take \$100 from her account and borrow the rest \$9900 from the broker. The money she takes from her account (\$100) is the margin or used margin, which is being used to maintain the open trade position. There is now \$900 in her account that is not being traded. The capacity to make another trade is determined by the free margin, that is the equity from which the current used margin is subtracted. (free margin = equity−used margin)

If the open positions make money, the more they go to profit, the greater the equity is, and the higher free margin will be.

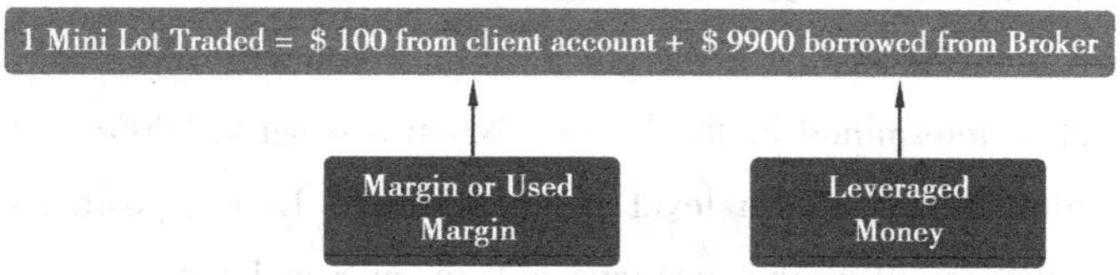

For example, with one mini lot and a leverage of 100, given current exchange rate as EUR/USD = 1.0665, the used margin for EUR/USD is:

used margin = (current exchange rate×lots) ÷leverage = $1.0665 \times 10000 \div 100 = \$106.65$

In order to open and retain the trade, at least \$106.65 of the available equity is needed to remain on the account.

(3) Margin Call, Margin Level and Stop Out Level

① Margin Call.

Margin call is literally a warning from a broker that the trader's account has slipped past the required margin in percent, and that there is not enough equity on the account to support open trades any further. To protect themselves from losing the money, brokers who had granted retail traders via margin and leverage use an automatic full or partial liquidation of retail traders' positions when the account falls below the minimum margin, which is required to be maintained at all times. If a margin call occurs, some or all open positions will be closed by the broker at the market price. Margin call can be described as an event where a trader faced severe losses in her trading that put her on the verge of entering a negative balance in her trading account. This is where margin call will occur in order to prevent the trader's account from turning into negative balance and thus preventing the trader from losing all her capital. This is a very important safety features which prevent traders from greater risks as they made their trading with large leverage in a greatly fluctuate environment.

② Margin Level.

Margin level is the ratio of equity to margin. For example, when the equity is $1000 and the margin is also $1000, margin level will be $1000÷$1000 = 1 or 100%. If the equity grows to $2000 and the margin is $1000, then the margin level would be 200%. Brokers use margin level to determine whether the traders can take any new positions or not. 100% margin call level means if the account margin level reaches 100%, the trader can still close her open positions, but she cannot take any new positions. It happens when trader has losing position/positions and the market keeps on going against her and when her account equity equals the margin, she will not be able to take any new positions anymore. Once margin level is 100%, a margin call liquidation is triggered. (with maybe an email or phone call warning beforehand) Soon after the retail trader's positions will be closed out (usually one by one, starting from the least profitable until the minimum margin requirement is met). While a 100% margin level requirement makes a risk of margin call much closer, it does save more money when further losses are inevitable.

Margin call level is the level that if margin level goes below it, no new position is allowed to take. Margin call level is determined by the broker. When it is set to 100%, trader will not be able to take any new position if her margin level reaches 100%. Losing positions push margin level down to the margin call level. Winning positions pull up margin level.

③ Stop Out Level.

While some FX brokers operate only with margin calls, others operate with stop out levels. Stop out level is defined as the level that if the margin level goes below it, the system starts closing the losing positions. Stop out level is also a certain required margin level in percentage, at which a trading platform will start to automatically close trading positions in order to prevent further account losses. It will close the biggest losing position first. If this helps the margin level go above the stop out level, no more position will be closed. Then if there are other losing positions keep on losing and the margin level goes below the stop out level again, the system closes another losing position which is the biggest one.

For example, if some broker offers "margin call level 70% and stop out 30%", this means that when the account equity becomes equal 70% of the required margin, broker will give a warning either as a highlight on the platform or a certain message or an email etc. saying that the equity is now insufficient to continue trading and maintaining currently active positions. The trader under this circumstance either need to close some of the positions or add more funds to the account to meet the minimum margin requirements. If this trader did not do anything in a timely manner and the market still does not cut any slack to the losing trades, this trader will be approaching the stop out level, which is 30% of the required margin in this case. The system will perform an automated closure of the unprofitable trades starting from the least profitable and until the minimum margin requirements are met. Closing one losing position may take the margin level higher than 30%, because it will release the margin of that position, and so the total used margin will go lower and therefore the margin level will go higher. The system takes the margin level higher than 30% by closing the biggest losing position first. However, if other losing positions keep on losing and the margin level reaches 30% again, the system will close another losing position.

If broker states a 100% margin call, this means that margin call = stop out level = 100 required margin. When the equity slops below 100% of the required margin, trader will get a margin call and the positions will be liquidized starting from the biggest losing ones. In the 100% margin call, the warning stage is omitted.

By having the margin call level set at lower levels, trader's risk of having a margin call are pushed further away (which can be good if traders are trading with grid or martingale systems). However, if traders are not careful enough, these more generous margin call brokers can leave retail traders with very little left in the account if the market moves in the opposite direction of trader's forecast. The opportunity of the two staged process does not keep the broker from closing trades without prior notice even if it is only a margin call stage. Both margin call level and stop out level are set by brokers to avoid any loss more than the money deposited in clients' account. That is, brokers provide leverage to encourage FX trading under the condition of baring no loss.

3) Balance and Equity

Balance is the amount of the money in the account when there is no open position yet. It is the total amount of the money one trader put in her account before taking any position. When a position is opened and its profit/loss goes up and down as the market moves, the account balance is still the same as it was before taking the position. If the position is closed, the profit/loss of the position will be added/subtracted to the account balance and the new account balance will be displayed.

For example, when one trader has a $ 6000 account and she has no open position, her account balance is $6000.

Equity is the sum of account balance and the floating profit/loss of the open positions. (equity=balance+p/l) When there is no open position, and so no floating profit/loss, then the account equity and balance are the same.

For example when one has an open position which is \$500 in profit while her account balance is \$5000, then her account equity is \$5500. If this position is closed, the \$500 profit will be added to account balance and so the account balance will become \$5500. If it was a losing position with -\$500 loss, then while it was opened, the account equity would be \$4500 and if it was closed, \$500 will be deducted from the account balance and so the account balance will be \$4500. When no position is opened, the account equity will be the same as the account balance.

When there is no open position, no money from the account is used as the margin. Therefore the account equity and free margin are the same as the account balance.

The screenshot below shows that there is no trade taken place yet therefore no open position. Thus free margin = equity = balance = \$100000.

Figure 3-9 Trade Platform of FX Spot

The following screenshot gives a summary of above said FX spot contract specifications.

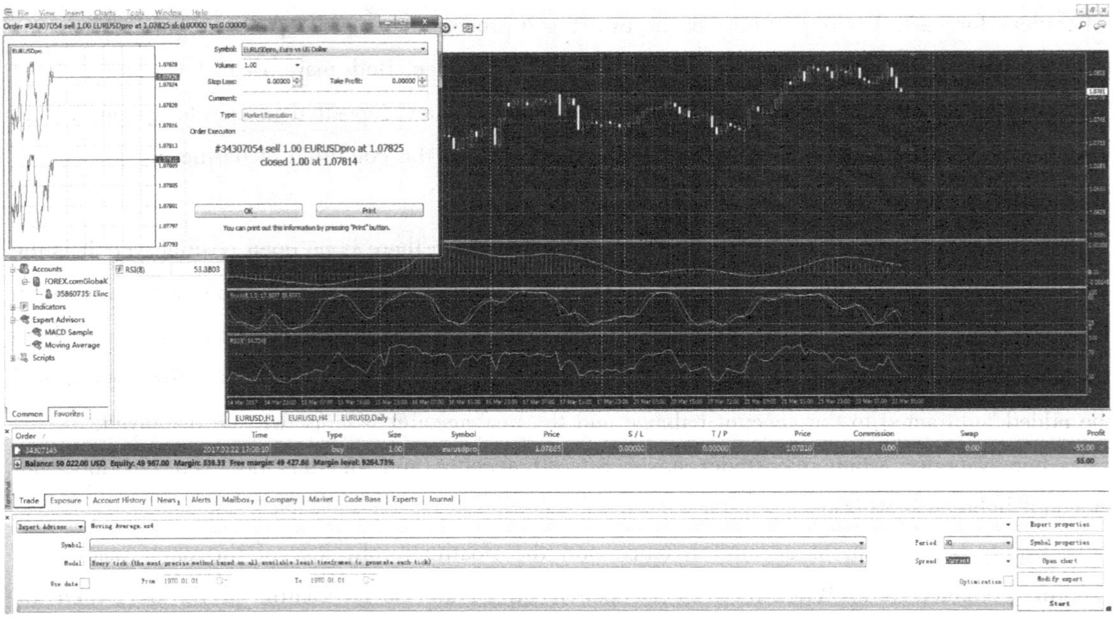

Figure 3-10 FX Spot Contract

balance = \$ 50022, this trader initially put \$ 50000 in her account, she has gone through several trades and has gained \$22 in total as profit, which is added to her initial account.

equity = balance + p/l = 50022 + (1.07810 − 1.07865) × 100000 = \$ 49967, there is a potential loss of \$55 in her open position, which shown at the end of the line. She could either wait to see if EUR will appreciate as she expected or she could close this open position by selling one standard lot of EUR/USD, which will realize this \$55 potential loss, i.e. \$55 will be deducted from her balance.

margin $= S_{EUR/USD} \times lots \div leverage = 1.07865 \times 100000 \div 200 = 539.325 \approx \$539.33$. This trader is granted a leverage of 200, she has chosen one standard lot, thus her margin is \$ 539.33 as calculated. Margin is usually rounded up to the second decimal point.

$$free\ margin = equity - used\ margin = 49967 - 539.325 = 49427.675 \approx \$49427.68$$

This trader has \$49427.68 free margin available for additional trades. Suppose that exchange rate ran against her expectation causing loss consumed up all her free margin, for a 100% margin call broker, this trader will receive a margin call liquidation once the equity falls below \$539.33 (100% margin level).

$$margin\ level = equity \div margin = 49967 \div 539.325 \approx 9264.73\%$$

Margin level percentage gives a quick visual of the level of margin, particularly how close the trader is to reach 100% margin level, the typical level that once reached for many brokers will result in a margin call liquidation.

An another example for better understanding the above key terms applied in trades on FX market.

If one trader owns a trading account of 1068.11 dollars and is granted a leverage of 500, she has bought a EUR with 1.12571, and now the exchange rate is 1.12583.

Order	Time	Type	Size	Symbol	Price	S/L	T/P	Price	commission	swap	profit
22359485	2021.12.15 13:41:23	buy	1.00	eurusd	1.12571	0.00000	0.00000	1.12583	0.00	0.00	12.00
Balance: 1068.11 USD Equity: 1080.11 Margin: 225.166 Free margin: 854.944 Margin level: 479.69%											12

Balance, 1068.11 USD, shows the amount of deposited money in trading account. The profit/loss of orders will be added or deducted to/from trading account balance when orders are closed.

Balance and Equity show the same values as long as there is no open order. When orders are opened, the balance will not change and it will stay fixed. The equity, however, will be floated according to the profit/loss of current orders.

Given EUR has appreciated from 1.12571 to 1.12583, bringing 0.00012 profit to the trader, her current equity is $1068.11 + 0.00012 \times 100000 = 1080.11$. Of course, this number is subject to exchange rate fluctuation and is changing every now and then.

Given margin is the amount of the money that is used to open a position or trade, it is calculated based on the leverage. In other words, it is the amount of the money that gets involved in a position as collateral. This money is locked until the position is closed.

$$\text{margin} = \text{current rate} \times \text{contract size} \div \text{leverage} = 1.12583 \times 100000 \div 500 = 225.166$$

Free margin is the difference of account equity and margin used for the open positions. When there is no positions then no money from trading account is used for margin, therefore all the money in the account is free for trading.

$$\text{free margin} = \text{equity} - \text{margin} = 1080.11 - 225.166 = 854.944$$

Margin level is the ratio of the equity to the margin. Margin level is very important since brokers use it to determine whether the traders can take any new positions when they already have some positions.

$$\text{margin level} = \text{equity} \div \text{margin} \times 100\% = 1080.11 \div 225.166 \times 100\% = 479.69\%$$

Different brokers have different limits for the margin level, but this limit, margin call level, is usually 100% with most of the brokers. 100% margin call level means if one account margin level reaches 100%, open positions can still be closed, but no new position can be opened. 100% margin call level happens when account equity equals the required margin.

4) Advantage and Disadvantage of Leverage Trade

Advantages of leverage FX trading are that leverage enables large trades without tying up a lot of capital. One can make a € 100 trade and end up with a € 1 profit (1% profit). If one had made a € 50000 trade with the same profit 1%, her gain would have been € 500. With a broker that offers a leverage of 50, only € 1000 deposit is needed to make a € 50000 trade.

The downside of leverage trading is that it is possible to end up in a situation where one owns the broker large amounts of money and finds it difficult to repay her debt since she has been trading with money that she never owned in the first place.

Most FX broker that offer leverage will have a safety feature installed that automatically closes the position when it loses more than a certain percentage. Exactly where the stop loss is placed varies, so trader should always check up on this beforehand.

A stop loss might sound like a wonderful idea for individual traders. But a stop loss is automatically triggered based on math, and will automatically close the position even in situations where the human would believe that it will be much better to keep the position open and ride out the market turbulence.

Once a position has been closed, the loss has been realized. Even if the exchange rate in question starts to favor the trader the loss is not revocable because the position has already been closed.

Even an extremely short-lived and understandable dip in currency price will trigger a stop loss, creating a permanent loss in a situation where the position, had it been left open, would have bounced back in no time and maybe even yielded a profit before it was closed manually.

The combination of automatic stop loss and leverage can be very risky for the trader, since the position may be closed automatically and leave trader heavily in debt. Of course, one does not have to take full advantage of the leverage. For example, given a leverage of 100, one can just use the leverage to double the trade amount: deposit € 100 and use the leverage to make a € 200 trade. Traders need decide where the right balance point is.

For example, Jeff opens a micro account with \$1000 at a leverage of 100. He analyzes the EUR/USD and decides to go short, entering 4 mini lots on EUR/USD at the price of 1.3200. According to the margin formula, (current exchange rate×lots)÷leverage, Jeff would be using (1.3200×40000)÷100=\$520 margin. Before entering, Jeff's free margin was \$1000, and after entering, his free margin is \$1000−\$520=\$480.

Disaster strikes and Jeff's trades go against him: EUR/USD jumps up 100 pips, and since every pip with 4 mini lots equals \$4, his loss is 100 × 4 = \$400 and equity drops down to 1000−400=\$600. Now Jeff sees that his Margin Level is Equity÷Margin=\$600÷\$520=115%, dangerously close to his 100% max margin level. At this point his margin bar has turned red as a warning. When the EUR/USD jumps up another 25 pips, his account is suffered with another loss of 25× \$4=\$100 and equity becomes \$500. Now he has reached below 100% max margin level (equity÷margin=500÷520) and the system automatically closes trades at a loss to recover more margin.

When margin level gets close to 100%, a number of things can happen, depending on the margin policy of the broker. Since Jeff has a 100% margin call level policy with his broker with partial liquidation procedure, his broker starts to auto-liquidate positions (largest loses first) till his account moves back above the 100% margin call level. At first he might see that one of his four positions be stopped out at 125 pips loss, lowering his margin requirement down to \$390 (for a \$500 equity), which resets his margin level to 128%.

But if the market falls by an additional 25 pips, he would see his account go down by 25× \$3=\$75 to \$375 equity, which again pushes him beneath the 100% max margin level, and he would end up losing a second position at 150 pips loss. This would in turn lower his margin requirement down to \$260, and with \$375 equity, his margin level would be reset to 144%. Perhaps then, seeing that he has lost over 60% of his original, Jeff would call it quits and close out the last two positions with −150 pips loss each, for a grand total loss of \$625.

4.4 Profit Loss Calculation

1) An Example

All trades are profit-driven. In foreign exchange market, if a trader buys one currency pair, it means she uses quote currency to buy base currency. It is usually called a long trade on a currency pair.

In a long trade on a currency pair, profit/loss of one individual trader is the difference between the ask price when the trade is entered, and the bid price when the trade is exited. Conversely, in a short trade, profit/loss is calculated as the difference between the bid price at the time of entry, and the ask at the time the trade is exited. An example will help to clarify the calculation.

Assume that a trader believes that EUR will appreciate against USD. This trader places a long trade on EUR/USD, and the order is executed at 1.3490/93. Since the trader must buy at the ask price, given a full size account $ 100000, the purchase is for 100000 EUR at the price of 134930 USD.

As the trader hoped, the value of EUR does increase relative to USD. The trader closes the trade by selling EUR/USD, at the market price of 1.3505/08. Since the trader must sell at the bid price, she sells the EUR/USD for 135050 USD. The profit on this trade is 80 USD (135050—1354930).

If the exchange rate does not work out as the trader hoped, the trade will be exited below the entry price, and this trader will suffer from a loss. Suppose that the trade is closed by selling the EUR/USD position when the price dropped at 1.3484/87. The 100000 EUR are sold for 134840 USD. The trade results in a loss of 90USD(134840−134930). The detailed P/L calculations are classified into the following 3 types:

2) P/L Pip Value when USD is Quote Currency

Because the pip value does not divide with the current rate, it remains the same value between the pairs when calculate, bare into mind the pip value of a micro lot (1000 units) is $0.1 (10 cents), the pip value of a mini lot (10000 units) is $1, and the pip value of a standard lot (100000 units) is $10.

The following table gives an example of pip value calculation of a bank as the market maker.

Table 3-8 Pip Value Calculation: EUR/USD Lot Size 200000

Type	Calculation	Quotation: 1.4204/378
Pip Value	lot size × tick size	200000 × 0.0001=$20
P/L in Pips	sell-buy	1.4378−1.4204=0.0174(174profit)
P/L in $	p/l in pips × pip value	174 × $20=$3480

An individual trader, for example, if bought 100000 GBP/USD at 1.3242 then sold at 1.3238

P/L in pips is 1.3238−1.3242=−0.0004(4 loss)

lot size is 100000

tick size is 0.0001

Her P/L= P/L in pips × lot size × tick size = (−4) ×100000×0.0001=−40 USD

3) P/L Pip Value when USD is Base Currency

When USD is the heavier currency, American terms are applied.

According to Table 3-9, the only difference in pip value calculation between European and American terms is the division with the ask rate (lot size×tick size÷ask rate). This division takes away from the more fixed rate of the American term. It makes all the pip values between the European term pairs differ, and all the pip values will dynamically change relative to the current rate that changes constantly.

Table 3-9 Pip Value Calculation: USD/JPY Lot Size 100000

Type	Calculation	Quotation: 81.34/2.12
Pip Value	lot size×tick size÷ask rate	100000×0.01÷82.12=$12.17
P/L in Pips	sell-buy	82.12−81.34=0.78(78 profit)
P/L in $	p/l in pips × pip value	78×$12.17=$949

Another example, an individual trader bought 100000 USD/JPY at 113.09 then sold at 113.75:

P/L in pips is 113.75−113.09(66 profit) lot size is 100000 tick size is 0.01

P/L=P/L in pips×lot size×tick size÷current rate=66×100000×0.01÷113.75≈580 USD

4) P/L Pip Value of Cross Rates

The difference between this formula and the European term pip value is that in the calculation of the pip value there is an extra multiple with the base quote, which in Table 3-10 below is the current EUR/USD price, 1.3890. This makes the calculation a little more involved than the previous two. These extra calculations with base quote and division with current rate makes all the pip values between the cross rate pairs differ, and all the pip values will dynamically change relative to the current rate that itself changes constantly.

Table 3-10 Pip Value of Cross Rates: EUR/CHF Lot Size 100000

Type	Calculation	Quotation: 1.1500/620
Pip Value	lot size×tick size×base quote÷bid	100000×0.0001×1.3890÷1.1500=$12.07
P/L in Pips	sell-buy	1.1620−1.1500=0.0120(120profit)
P/L in $	p/l in pips × pip value	120×$12.07=$1448

An example helps to clarify the calculation. Peter buys 100000 units of EUR/JPY at 164.09 and he has EUR/JPY=164.10, and USD/JPY=121.35, as his selling prices. Peter profits in JPY pips=164.10−164.09=0.01yen=1 pip (recall that the Japanese yen exception: 1JPY pip=0.01yen).

total profit in JPY pips = 1×100000 = 100000 pips.

total profit in yen = 100000 pips÷100 = 1000 yen.

Because Peter only has the quote for USD/JPY = 121.35, to get profit in USD, Peter divides total profit in yen by the quote currency's conversion rate.

total profit in USD = 1000÷121.35 = 8.24 USD.

If Peter only has JPY/USD = 0.00824, which is equivalent to the above value, Peter uses the following formula to convert pips in yen to dollar:

total profit in USD = 1000×0.00824 = 8.24 USD, which is the same result obtained above.

An another example, for a 100000 EUR/GBP contract, an individual trader initially sold at 0.8498 and now closed at 0.8491, given current exchange rates as EUR/GBP = 0.8479/91, EUR/USD = 1.1228/32.

pip value: 100000×0.0001×1.1228÷0.8491

p/l in pips: 0.8498−0.8491⇒(7 profit)

P/L = 7×100000×0.0001×1.1228÷0.8491 = 92.56 USD

When calculate P/L bare into mind that FX market makers quote to their advantage. The individual trader, as a price taker, has to take the unfavorable prices to calculate profit/loss.

4.5 Value Date and Trade Date

1) Value Date

Value date is the date on which FX trades settle, i.e. the date that the payments of each currency are made. Value date is also known as settlement date or delivery date. There are 3 types of value date in spot trade. Suppose that today is Tue. and a trade arises today there are 3 types of value date as demonstrated below:

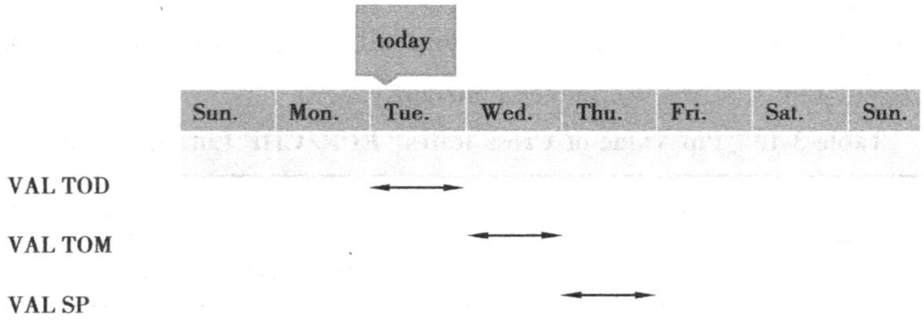

(1) Value Spot (VAL SP)

In the foreign exchange market, spot does not mean trade settled immediately after the deal contract is made. Considering the 24-hour's trading and global time difference, it is normally two banking days forward for the currency pair traded, which is depicted as T+2 days or is called value spot (VAL SP). For example, a standard spot trade agreed on 13th Mar. 2017 Monday (dealt for 13th Mar. 2017 Monday) is said to be for value on 15th Mar. 2017 Wednesday; unless either financial centre has a holiday on the 14th or 15th Mar. 2017, in which case it will be for value on the 16th. Weekends similarly extend the spot value date.

If a standard spot deal does not settle by the beginning of the second business day after the deal has been struck, interest will start to accrue against the party which has failed to deliver.

If not specified, it is FX market convention that FX spot trade is value spot. The ratio at which one currency is exchanged for another for settlement in two business days (value date) is the spot exchange rate.

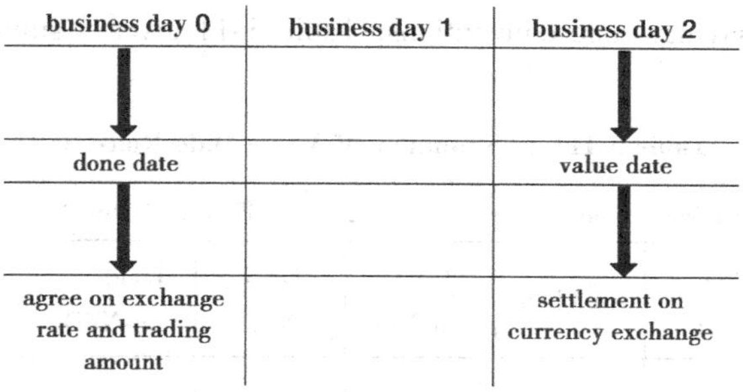

(2) Value Tomorrow (VAL TOM)

There are 7 currency pairs, however, are settled at T+1, they are USD/CAD, USD/MXN, USD/TRY, USD/PHP, USD/RUB, USD/KZT and USD/PKR. T+1 style settlement is called value tomorrow (VAL TOM). For example, a standard spot trade of USD/CAD agreed on 19th Jul. 2021 Monday (dealt for 19th Jul. 2021 Monday) is said to be for value on 20th Jul. 2021 Tuesday, i.e. in good business day. A good business day is a day that is not a holiday or weekend in either currency country.

(3) Value Today (VAL TOD)

Retail FX trade settlement between bank and individual clients usually takes the form of value today. With the development of intra-day settlement systems (such as real-time gross settlement systems—RTGS), deals may also be done to settle for cash (T+0).

2) Value Date Roll-Over

Most FX traders do not trade currency for delivery but for profits from speculation. They continually delay the settlement until trade turn profitable. If a FX spot contract is not delivered on time, this position is called "be held open" and will be rolled over to the next value day.

On an open position, interest is earned on the long currency and paid on the short currency during the rollover. For a long position if the interest rate associated with the base currency is higher than the quote currency, then the interest rate differential (positive rollover) is added to the trader's account. Vice Versa.

As interest is calculated everyday as long as the position is held, the number of days between rollovers can affect the amount of interest credited or debited. A weekend rollover (any T+2 trade that takes place after the settlement time on Wed. or Thu. for T+1 currency pair) involves 3 times as much interest as one-day rollover because there are 3 days between weekend rollovers. If the rollover period is extended due to holidays, then the additional holidays are counted as well.

All trading platforms make the above interest adjustment automatically. Most trading platforms inform the amount of interest rate differential for each currency pair that can be traded.

For all currency pairs except NZD/USD, FX market convention is that value dates roll forward at 5pm New York time. Value dates for NZD/USD roll forward at 7am Auckland time. This means that the local time of the value date roll-over varies throughout the year, depending on daylight savings time conventions. Table 3-11 gives a summary of value date roll-over as follows:

Table 3-11 A Summary of Value Date Roll-Over

with Effect from	Daylight Savings Time			Time of Value Date Roll-Over						
	London	New York	Auckland	GMT non-NZD	GMT NZD	London non-NZD	London NZD	NY NZD	Auckland non-NZD
2nd Sun. in Mar.	GMT	EDT	NZDT	21:00	18:00	21:00	18:00	14:00	10:00
last Sun. in Mar.	BST	EDT	NZDT	21:00	18:00	22:00	19:00	14:00	10:00
1st Sun. in Apr.	BST	EDT	NZST	21:00	19:00	22:00	20:00	15:00	09:00
last Sun. in Sep.	BST	EDT	NZDT	21:00	18:00	22:00	19:00	14:00	10:00
last Sun. in Oct.	GMT	EDT	NZDT	21:00	18:00	21:00	18:00	14:00	10:00
1st Sun. in Nov.	GMT	EST	NZDT	22:00	18:00	22:00	18:00	13:00	11:00

For most T+2 currency pairs, if T+1 is a USD holiday, then this does not normally affect the spot date. If a non-USD currency in the currency pair has a holiday on T+1, then it will make the spot date become T+3. If USD or either currency of a pair has a holiday on T+2, then the spot date will be T+3. For example, EUR/GBP can not have a spot date on 4th Jul. the Independence Day of the U.S. (although such a date could be quoted as an outright).

3) Trade Date

The trade date/time, also known as contract date, is a timestamp to record when a trade was executed. It is customary to store the trade date/time in GMT/UTC in a database, and for display purposes either to suffix it with "GMT" or "UTC", or otherwise to translate it to a user's local time zone. It is normal that the value date may sometimes not appear as expected in relation to the trade date. For example, to a customer in New York at 22:30 GMT, the spot date for EUR/USD appears as T+3; likewise to a customer in New Zealand at 20:30 GMT, the spot date for EUR/USD appears as T+1. Being a timestamp, the trade date does not change at the time of the value date roll-over.

Some systems include an additional trade date field to indicate the effective trade date for value date calculation purposes. This additional field should not incorporate a time and is not normally displayed to price takers.

4.6 Closing out a Position

An open position is one that is live and ongoing. As long as the position is open, its value will fluctuate in accordance with the exchange rate in the market. Any profits and losses will exist on paper only and will be reflected in trader's margin account.

To close out the position, one should conduct an equal and opposite trade in the same currency pair. For example, if one has bought ("gone long") one lot of EUR/USD (at the prevailing offer price) she can close out that position by subsequently selling one EUR/USD lot (at the prevailing bid price). Similarly, one can close out her position by purchasing if she has sold a currency pair.

§5 Fundamental Chart Patterns in FX Spot Trading

There are many set-ups one can use when trading currencies. FX traders may minimize some of the trial and error involved by using the chart patterns that have been proven by other traders as effective and have proven to be profitable set-ups, among which the following 3 are very basic to start with chart pattern trading approach.

5.1 Channel Pattern

The channel pattern is one of the most recognizable patterns in FX charts because it looks quite distinctive. As shown in Figure 3-11, it is two parallel trend lines that enclose price. These lines essentially govern the trend. Trades are usually entered that follow the trend when the price bounces off one of the trend lines. The profit target is usually within the domain of the opposite trend line. This strategy can be profitable if the assumptions are correct. Even when the price penetrates the trend lines, there is still the opportunity to earn since the trader can then trade on the breakouts.

Figure 3-11 Channel Pattern

5.2 Double Top

A double top is another very recognizable set-up. The double top happens when the price of the currency tests the resistance level on two different occasions and is not able to break the resistance. When this happens the price now breaks and assumes a bearish movement. When a trader sees this pattern on her chart she will commence her trade when the price breaks the neckline in Figure 3-12.

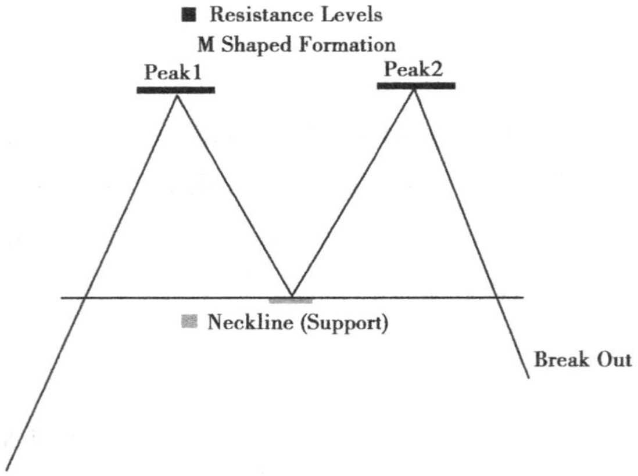

Figure 3-12 Double Top Formation

5.3 Asymmetric Triangle

The asymmetric triangle can be identified by checking the chart and looking for an asymmetric triangle where there is a trend line and one horizontal level that price will usually be able to penetrate. Trading with an asymmetric triangle pattern is similar to trading double tops: trade is entered after the currency price pulls back and goes to the broken horizontal level. This trade should be done with a strict stop loss.

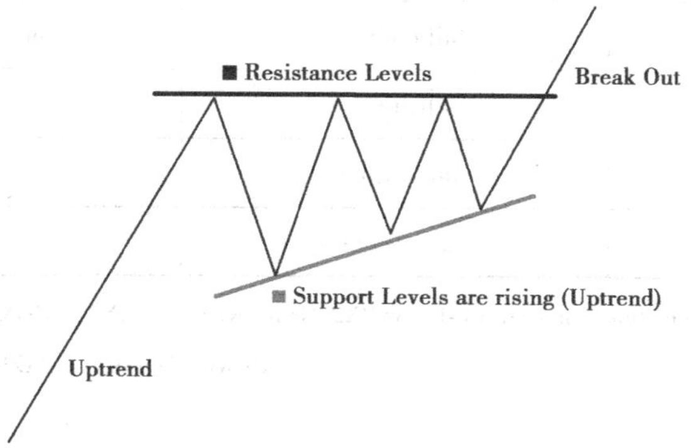

Figure 3-13 Ascending Triangle Formation

These three patterns are quite effective in providing FX traders with a useful and tested way of plotting out a strategy and giving signals on when to enter into a trade. There are many patterns for traders' reference, however, no one is proved to be 100% successful.

§6 Accurate Quotations

6.1 Short Scale and Long Scale

Currency amounts must be precise in foreign exchange conversation to avoid major blunders. Unfortunately, British and U.S. English are not always the same when quote FX. For example, the following table gives the major differences between British English and American English in number expression. Generally, American English adopts the short scale definition, whereby, three zeros (one thousand) are added each step; while British English uses the long scale definition, that is, six zeros (one million) are added each step. In the U.K, "1 billion" is 1 followed by 12 zeros while in the United States, it is 9 zeros. For the British, a "trillion" is a million billions, while in U.S., it is a thousand billions. To avoid confusion, foreign exchange traders use the word yard to describe a U.S. billion.

Table 3-12 Quotation Difference

Scientific Notation	US	UK
10^6	million	million
10^9	billion/yard	one thousand million
10^{12}	trillion	billion
10^{15}	quadrillion	billiard
10^{18}	quintillion	trillion

source: http://wenku.baidu.com/link? url=lM8yY-JEVVyBX2SGqMWKL3CWKyTX713L3GK9v7wnxDrKxFIDpS8wJ7Iof63IgbUPWon_ja9gQDchEDXZlgOJ-qMOk2sfuoox9dxGYrAV3x3

Typical interbank traded amounts in major currency pairs are usually quoted in millons. A 500000 GBP/USD contract would be said as "half a quid", 2000000000 JPY is said "2 yards of Yen" and "3 dollars" mean 3000000 USD.

6.2 Nick Names

Frequently traded currencies have nick names that have been widly used in FX market. U.S. dollar is called greenback because the paper notes issued during the American civil war in 1861 had a distinctive green coloring on the back. It is also called buck from times when deer skin (male deer is called buck) was used by American Indians for trading with dollars.

Euro currency's nickname fiber has the least known explanation, but many say that it comes from the fact that the paper used for Euro banknotes consists of pure cotton fiber which makes it more durable and gives it a special feel. Euro is often called single currency as it is used in 19 European countries.

British pound is officially called pound sterling. It sometimes gets abbreviated to either pound or sterling. Name sterling comes from times when the British pound had an equal value to one pound of sterling silver.

Loonie is a nickname for Canadian dollar as one dollar coin carries an image of a bird called "loon" that is a popular species in Canada.

New Zealand dollar has a nickname kiwi which represents the national symbol of New Zealand—a bird called kiwi. It is small, brown, furry and can't fly—just like a kiwi fruit.

GBP/USD currency pair is called the cable since there was a cable under the Atlantic ocean linking UK with U.S.A. It was used to synchronize British pound with U.S. dollar by a telegraph. The cable was laid in 1858 and made it possible to transmit currency prices from London's to New York's trading desks.

USD/RUB and EUR/RUB pairs are called Barnie and Betty respectively. These two nicknames are newcomers to the FX nickname family. Rubble is the currency in Russia.

EUR/GBP currency pair is sometimes called Chun which is an abbreviation of the Channel Tunnel that joins the channel between Britain and Europe.

§7 Offshore Chinese RMB Market: CNH①

China has been pursuing the internationalization of the Chinese yuan (CNY) since the financial crisis of 2008. The ultimate goal is to achieve full currency convertibility, thereby promoting use of the CNY as an international trade currency of choice.

The People's Bank of China (PBOC) and the Hong Kong Monetary Authority (HKMA) jointly announced on 19th Jul. 2010 that CNY may be deliverable in Hong Kong. This created a new offshore market in CNY, dubbed the "CNH" market. Since its introduction, this market has grown at a rapid pace, attracting widespread interest and activity.

This development is changing the character of the CNY markets and of the FX markets in general. CME Group currently offers futures based on the CNH vs. the US dollar (USD)②.

7.1 About CNY

The RMB or "people's currency" (designated as CNY or ¥ or RM ¥) is the official legal tender in Chinese mainland. This is the formal reference most frequently used to refer to the currency. Although there is no precise translation into English, it is generally analogous to a reference to the terms "money" or "legal tender."

The Chinese yuan refers to the standard unit of RMB and is analogous to the term "dollar" in English, i.e., the yuan represents the onshore or Chinese mainland spot currency market③. CNY

---

① http://www.cmegroup.com/education/files/offshore-chinese-renminbi-market.pdf.

② CME Group introduced futures based on the value of the US dollar vs. offshore Chinese yuan (CNH) in response to these developments. These contracts are quoted in terms of offshore CNY or CNH per USD. They call for the delivery of $ 100000 USD vs. an equivalent amount of CNH through Hong Kong domiciled banking facilities. Another CNH contract is available in an "Emicro" format which calls for the delivery of $ 10000 USD vs. an equivalent amount of CNH. Daily pays and collects are administered in CNH.

③ The "kuai" represents a slang reference for CNY and is analogous to the term "buck" in the US Similar references may be found in the United Kingdom where the British Pound may alternatively be referred to "sterling" (a formal reference), "pound" (in everydayusage) or "quid" (in slang).

is the ISO 4217 code for CNY① and is used to designated Chinese yuan or RMB in FX transactions.

For most of its early history after its introduction in 1948, the RMB had been pegged at 2.46 CNY per USD. The currency strengthened during the 1980s to a high of 1.50 CNY per USD by 1980s. Subsequently, as the PRC gradually transitioned from a centrally planned to a market driven economy, the currency was devalued to a low of 8.62 CNY per USD by 1994. Between 1997 and 2005, the currency remained steadily pegged at 8.27 CNY per USD.

As a result of the CNY's low peg and concerted industrialization, international trading activities intensified and PRC's current account surplus increased rapidly. These factors exerted upward pressure on CNY and the reference peg was amended as of July 2005, resulting in an immediate revaluation to 8.11 CNY per USD.

A peg was reintroduced in July 2008 in response to the financial crisis. But the PBOC announced in June 2010 that it would take further steps to reform its exchange rate regime, introducing enhanced flexibility. Since then, the CNY has generally strengthened vs. other world currencies.

The CNY remains subject to a "managed float" exchange rate regime which permits the currency to float within a specified range about the value of basket of world currencies. The basket is reported to largely be comprised of the US dollar (USD), EURO (EUR), Japanese yen (JPY), Korean won (KRW) with smaller proportions referencing the value of the Australian dollar (AUD), British pound (GBP), Canadian dollar (CAD), Russian ruble (RUB), Singapore dollar (SGD) and Thai baht (THB).

The range or band within which CNY is allowed to float about the official PBOC rate had been established at 0.3% on a daily basis. But the band was expanded to 0.5% as of May 2007. The band was further expanded to 1.0% in April 2012, a policy that has helped increase two-way interest in trading the currency. A 6.5 to 6.9 of USD/CNY trading band is anticipated by the end of 2021. This bolstered two-way trading in RMB.

Since 2014, the expansion has been further widened. From the chart below, a fluctuation of 11.32% was seen in year 2018.

① No official ISO code currently exists for CNH and it is simply referred to as "offshore CNY" or "offshore CNY" with the same ISO code, which can cause confusion distinguishing between onshore CNY and offshore CNY settlements and reporting.

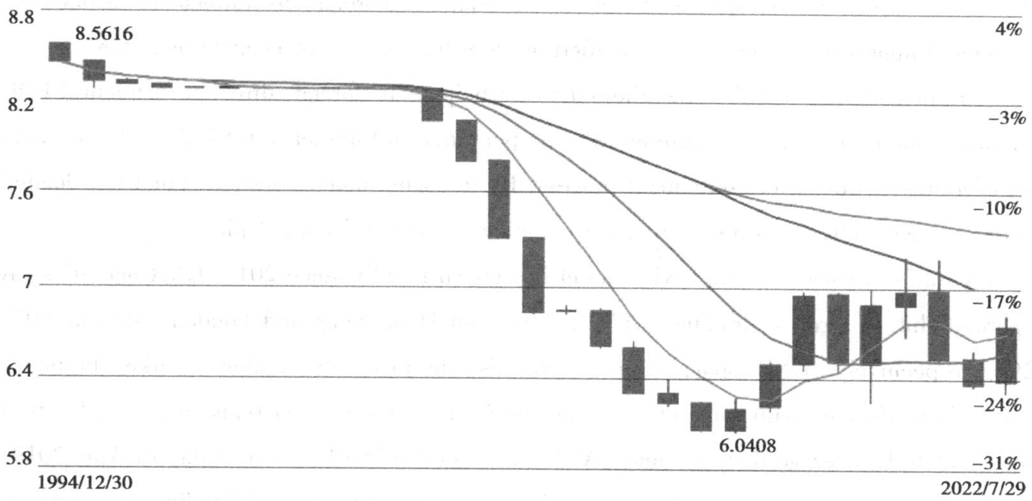

Figure 3-14 Annual USD/CNY

7.2 About CNH

Previously, RMB has been under-utilized as a medium for international trade relative to the significance of the Chinese economy. The Chinese economy has grown rapidly in recent years with 2020 GDP at 101.60 trillion yuan and second only to US GDP.

By the end of 2018, 28 countries and regines have applied RMB in international settlement. RMB has made significant gains by becoming the sixth most utilized international trade payment currency according to SWIFT's 2020 report.

Comparatively, RMB still has a long way to go to catch up with USD and EUR which account for 40.88% and 32.91% of transactions, compared to 1.79% for RMB.

This is a result of concerted steps having been taken to "internationalize" the RMB. This began with a December 2008 announcement from Premier Wen of a pilot program for cross border trade settlement of RMB with Hong Kong, Macau Special Administrative Region and Association of Southeast Asian Nations (ASEAN). The RMB became officially deliverable in Hong Kong SAR on 19th Jul. 2010 with a joint announcement between the People's Bank of China and Hong Kong Monetary Authority. Thus, the market for (Chinese Yuan in Hong Kong SAR) CNH was officially commenced.

Any offshore corporate entity or individual investor is allowed to buy, hold or sell CNH.

Corporate or individual investors not domiciled in Hong Kong SAR may participate in CNH markets by establishing CNH denominated nostro or non-resident accounts in Hong Kong SAR, frequently facilitated by a local bank with correspondent Hong Kong banking relationships.

Offshore FX market participants are, however, restricted from participating in the onshore

CNY market with some exceptions. Specifically, Qualified Foreign Institutional Investors (QFIIs) are granted quotas to participate in specified onshore trading and investment activities.

Certain corporate entities are allowed to participate in foreign direct investment (FDI) in mainland China. Offshore corporate entities are permitted to transact in CNY if the FX exchange is part of a cross-border trade settlement process. By the same token, onshore (or PRC domiciled) entities are generally constrained from participating in the CNH market place.

Figure 3-15 show that the CNH market has grown rapidly since 2017. CNH activities saw an important shift in terms of trading, with the shares of Hong Kong and London rising to 41% and 22%, respechively. CNH spot, swaps, forwards, futures, and options market liquidity has improved significantly with some OTC trading. BIS' Triennial Central Bank Survey of FX turnover shows that RMB average daily volume (ADV) surpassed $280 billion Per day in Apr. 2019. For the first time in over a decade, the relative importance of onshore CNY trading increased, while the share of CNH turnover declined, from 73% in 2016 to 64% in 2019.

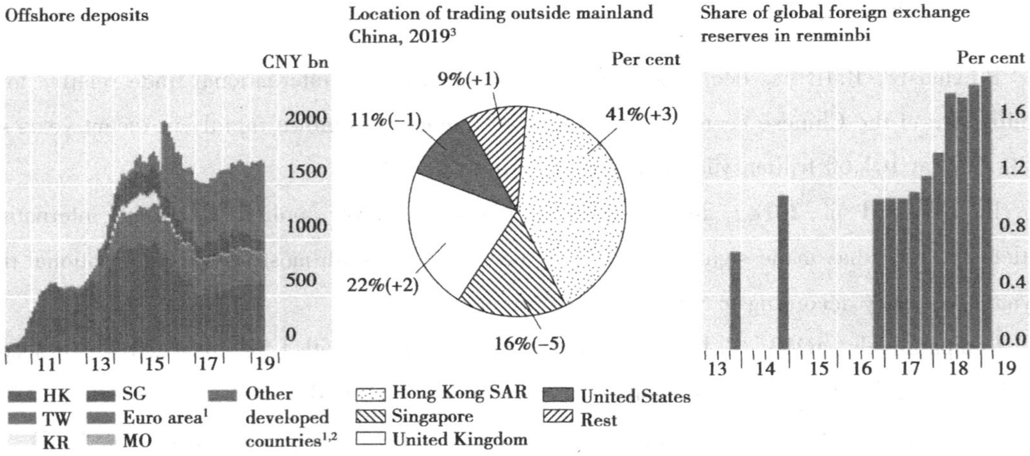

1 data are available from Q2 2012(as a part of Committee on the Global Financial System enhancements) and the coverage is partial

2 Australia, Canada, Denmark, Japan, Norway, Sweden, Switzerland, the United Kingdom and the United States

3 As a total of CNY trading excluding mainland China

Figure 3-15 Offshore RMB Deposits, Trading by Location and Share in Official Reserves

Source: People's Bank of China; CEIC; BIS locational banking statistics by residence and Triennial Central Bank Survey

Because the CNH market in Hong Kong SAR is limited to Hong Kong domiciled entities or those holding an ostro account in Hong Kong, the market is effectively regulated by the Hong Kong Monetary Authority (HKMA). However, the HKMA is not authorized to intervene in the market and, therefore, the market is open and operates akin to the markets for other deliverable currencies in Hong Kong.

While the People's Bank of China and the State Administration of Foreign Exchange (SAFE) regulate onshore CNY markets, they have no direct oversight in Hong Kong. Still, these bodies regulate RMB flows between onshore and offshore accounts and, therefore, may affect the supply and liquidity of CNH as well as the alignment between CNH and CNY rates.

7.3 Different Markets

While there is but a single Chinese RMB, the onshore and offshore environments for trading CNY and CNH are sufficiently insulated one from the other that two distinct markets have emerged for the two variations on the general theme.

This different exchange rates were observed in the CNY vs. CNH markets by design. Divergences may motivate cross-border flows of funds which will ensure convergence in the longer term. But in the shorter term, disconnects in relative value may be observed, noting that the supply of CNH remains relatively limited compared to CNY.

CNY weakened nearly 1.5% vs. USD since Feb. 2014 driven by the PBOC CNY fixing rate set weaker than expected. Some market participants explained the move on PBOC's intention to widen the trading band of CNY. Whatever the reason, the spike in volatility has led to short term divergence in the CNY/CNH spread.

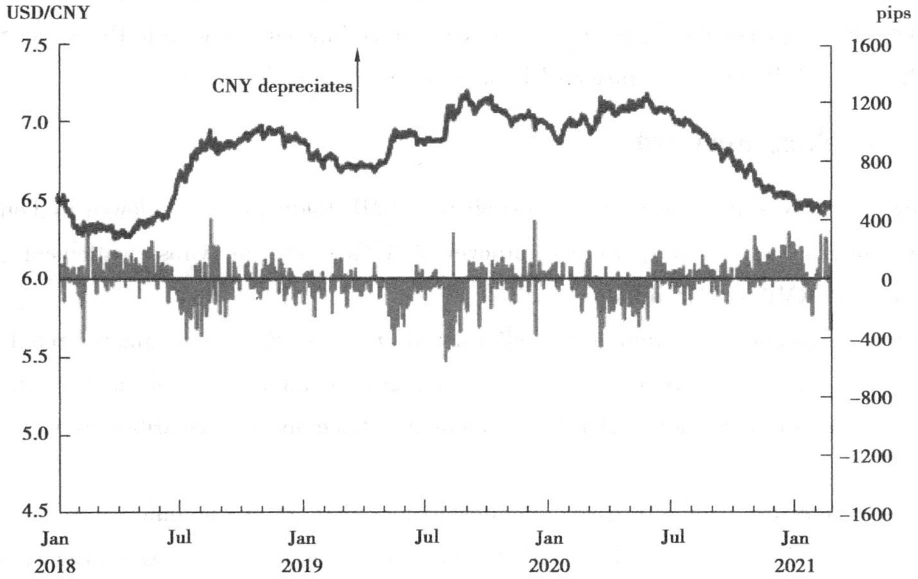

Figure 3-16 CNY and CNH Exchange Rates

Source: Bloomberg

The traditional offshore market for RMB in the form of USD settled non-deliverable forwards (NDFs) adds to the complexity further. These NDFs tend to trade independently of both onshore CNY and offshore CNH. Trading and hedging trends indicate that CNY NDFs are losing popularity as means of hedging or expressing onshore CNY views and rather, USD/CNH forwards and futures are picking additional liquidity as the favored derivative instruments.

7.4 Operational and Settlement Issues

The RMB settlement system in Hong Kong SAR is administered under the auspices of HKMA. The service uses the Hong Kong Real Time Gross Settlement (RTGS) infrastructure, which is further deployed for the settlement of Hong Kong dollars (HKD), USD and EUR along with the Central Clearing and Settlement System (CCASS). Real Time Gross Settlement (RTGS) is operated by HK Interbank Clearing Ltd.

The Bank of China (BOC) Hong Kong acts as the central clearing bank for the RMB Settlement System. Hong Kong banks wishing to use the service open accounts with BOC and payments can have the transactions cleared across those accounts.

The service covers check clearing, an automated system for remittance processing and CNY bankcard payments as well as interbank payments. Banks can square their RMB positions on a Payment versus Payment (PVP) basis. It further permits USD/CNY, HKD/CNY and EUR/CNY transactions to be concluded on a PVP basis.

Participating banks are allowed to convert foreign currency into CNY and vice-versa by buying or selling the foreign currency with BOC at the onshore exchange rate if the CNY is related to trade flows. BOC then squares their positions by buying or selling currency with PBOC in Shanghai vs. RMB. Thus, RMB may be transferred between onshore and offshore sources.

7.5 Looking Forward

Hong Kong now stands out as the largest offshore RMB trading center followed by London and singapore. For 2020 as a whole, average turnover of RMB Real Time Gross Settlement (RTGS) system stayed at RMB 1191.5 billion.

Hong Kong financial institutions now offer a wide range of RMB-denominated retail banking services including deposit-taking, currency exchange, remittance, debit and credit cards, checks, subscription and trading of RMB-denominated fixed income securities as well as RMB settlement.

RMB-denominated capital markets are developing and expanding quickly in Hong Kong. Trading in so called Dim Sum bonds, or CNH-denominated bonds issued in Hong Kong, rose from RMB 200 million in January 2011 to RMB 500-600bn in 2020 according to Figure 3-17. In April 2011, the first RMB-denominated IPO was listed on the Hong Kong Exchange by Hui Xian, part of Cheung Kong Group. The Dim Sum bond market is growing but remains insignificant compared to the trillion RMB onshore bond market.

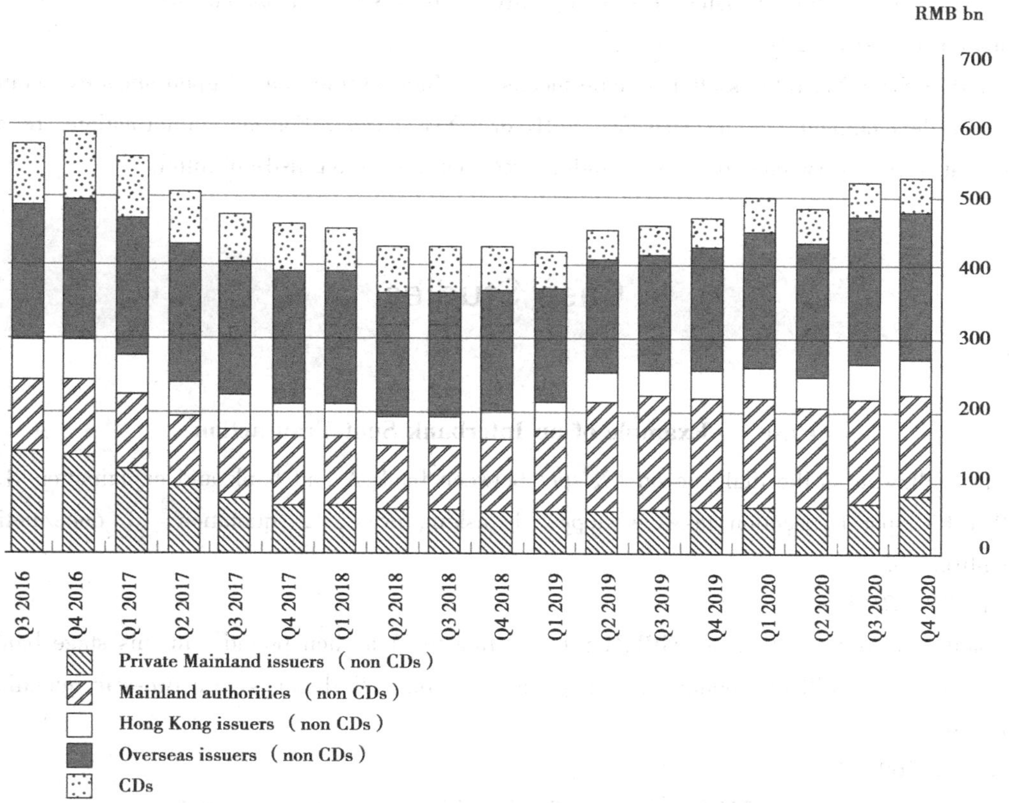

Figure 3-17 Outstanding Amount of CNH Debt in HK

Source: Newswires and HKMA staff estimates

In January 2012, UK Treasury and HKMA officials launched a joint private sector forum that aims to improve cooperation between the UK and Hong Kong SAR to support the development of offshore RMB trading.

On 22nd Jun. 2013, Governor Zhou Xiaochuan and former Governor Mervyn King signed an agreement to establish a 3-year GBP/CNY currency swap line with a maximum value of RMB 200bn ($33bn) to promote bilateral trade between the UK and China.

7.6 Conclusion

The rapid emergence of offshore trading in Chinese yuan (the "CNH" market) domiciled in Hong Kong SAR represents a significant development towards the internationalization of the CNY as the PRC continues to assert itself on the world economic stage. These developments merit close consideration in light of the economic significance of the PRC now and continuing into the futures.

As the underlying cash market grows, there will be a proliferation of derivative hedging products for clients to manage their CNY risk. In particular, CNH options have grown in liquidity and popularity as a risk management tool. CNH option liquidity is estimated around $3-5bn by local market traders though patchiness in liquidity exists. CME then planed launching USD/CNH options on futures for 2014.

CME USD/CNH futures offer a facile means by which to trade based upon one's expectations of further developments in the off-shore RMB or CNH market. For more information, refer to website at http://www.cmegroup.com/trading/fx/emergingmarket/usd-cnh.html.

Case Studies

Case 1 Example of an Interbank Spot Transaction

The following is the dialogue on FX spot between bank A and bank and explaination B. To fulfill a FX spot transaction takes 4 steps: ① asking price, ② quotation, ③ done/noting, ④ confirmation

A: SP GBP 5 mio.

Bank A asks bank B about GBP/USD spot rate for 5 million pounds. In this stage bank A does not state if it will buy pounds or sell pounds, so bank B should give a two-way quotations: bid-ask price.

B: 1.2369/82.

Bank B offers bid 1.2369 and ask 1.2382, which means that it will buy one pound with 1.2369 dollar, or it will sell pounds to bank A as 1.2382 dollar per pound. As the contract is 5 million pounds, the total dollar they are talking about is either 1.2382×5 million = 6.191 million dollars or 1.2369×5 million = 6.1845 million dollars.

A: My risk.

Bank A is not satisfied with the price, it prefers waiting for new rate or asking other dealer's offer. Bank A understands that spot rate may not hit its favorite level during this time, so it replies that it will shoulder any possible loss arises from this period of waiting time.

A: Now pls.

Bank A then requires bank B offer the newest price.

B: 1.2375 choice.

This time, bank B gives only one price. It means that bank B could either sell or buy pounds with this price, leaving bank A to decide the trade direction.

A: Sell pls. My USD to A NY.

Bank A chooses to sell pounds to bank B and it requires bank B to put dollars into its New York branch.

B: OK. Done, at 1.2375 we buy GBP 5 mio ag USD. Val 20 May. GBP to my London. Tks for deal. BIBI

Bank B closes the deal by repeating the contract. The last 2 sentences actually compose a formal FX spot contract between bank A and bank B:

Contract size: 5 million pounds

Price: 1.2375 dollars

Seller: bank A with its branch in New York

Buyer: bank B with its branch in London

Contract signed on May.18 and will be executed on May. 20.

Case 2 Chinese yuan: On-Shore Market and Off-Shore Market

Since 2011 China has been attempting to internationalize its currency by allowing more cross-border trade to be settled in RMB. Via RMB Trade Settlement Scheme, trade partners are able to pay and to be paid in RMB off-shore. As Chinese yuan is not freely traded yet, there are two markets that are dealing with RMB trading: CNY refers to the onshore RMB and CNH refers to the off-shore RMB①.

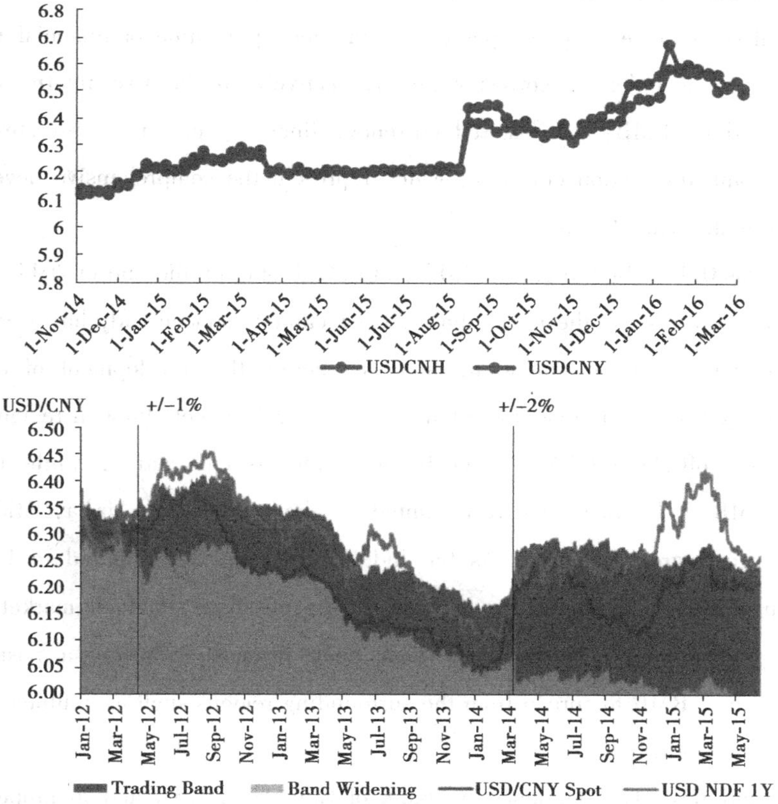

Figure 3-18 RMB Fluctuations within the Band Both On-Shore (CNY) and Off-Shore (CNH)

Source: Bloomberg

① Seven major RMB offshore markets are Australia, Brazil, Hong Kong, Korea, Malaysia, Singapore, and United Kingdom.

The development of off-shore financial market is a double-edged sword, the smooth development can enhance the process of RMB internationalization, promote the reform and perfect in bank financial market, guide the marketization of interest rate and exchange rate regime reform.

Without adequate supervision, however, systemic risk will be induced in the onshore market through the linkage relationship between the offshore and onshore market, destroying the stability of domestic financial system. China thus need to strengthen the international supervision and coordination between off-shore and onshore markets.

On 11th Mar. 2014, in Beijing, Bank of China issued worldwide the initial "Off-shore RMB Index" (BOC ORI). It is another index launched by Bank of China to comprehensively represent the international level of RMB by giving play to its study capacity and professional advantage, after launching the "Cross-border RMB Index" (CRI) last year.

BOC ORI mainly tracks the development level of CNY in the off-shore financial market, including capital stock scale, capital operation status and application of financial instruments. It sets five categories of indexes, corresponding respectively to the five international monetary functions exercised by RMB: value-stored currency, financing currency, investment currency, reserve currency and transaction currency, which represent the comprehensive development level of RMB after weighted calculation.

BOC ORI was 0.91% by the end of 2013 and 0.32% only by the end of 2011, with a growth of 1.84 times in two years. As the index shows, CNY capital stock already has a certain scale on the off-shore market, as is an important factor promoting the development of off-shore RMB market. Hong Kong SAR is the most important off-shore RMB center. In such regions as Southeast Asia and Europe, off-shore CNY market becomes increasingly active, while the stock and application of RMB is by now relatively limited in the markets of Africa, Middle East and America, but with a great potential. As the index indicates, as compared to USD and other international currencies, the total share of RMB in the off-shore financial market is not yet so high, but its promotion is at a relatively high rate, primarily showing a positive trend for internationalization of RMB to spread from the surrounding regions such as Southeast Asia to other regions all over the world.

CNY ORI and RMB CRI launched by Bank of China in 2013 acted in proper coordination with each other. The two indexes represent different indicators such as content, nature and emphasis, but they are mutually associated, supplemented and confirmed, forming, together, an integral system for tracking and studying the internationalization level of CNY.

Case 3 Exchange Rate in International Trade

Chinese exporters may need to convert the offers from RMB price to foreign price or from foreign price to RMB, under direct quotation, the rule is:

Bid rate is applied to convert offer from RMB to foreign price;

Ask rate is applied to convert offer from RMB to foreign price.

For example, a Chinese exporter is selling equipment as 1 million yuan per set, and she is required to offer dollar price. Given spot exchange rate as USD/CNY = 6.9189/95,

her dollar price = 1000000 ÷ 6.9189 = $ 144531.65 per set

Another Chinese exporter is selling garments as € 50 per suit, and she is required to offer RMB price. Given spot exchange rate as EUR/CNY = 7.3605/00,

her RMB price = 50 × 7.3700 = ¥ 368.5 per suit

Case 4 President Trump's Twitter Feed: Currency Exchange Rate Volatility

The valuation of a country's currency is dependent upon many factors that relate to its adopted monetary policy, domestic economic health and growth prospects. Accordingly, any statement made by the President of the United States regarding a change in the diplomatic and economic relationship between the US and another country may have a widespread impact upon global currency values. In the event that a Twitter release is the conduit by which the statement is made, a rapid and substantial reaction may be experienced by the FX market.

Perhaps the currency valuation most affected by Trump's twitter activity has been that of the Mexican peso (MXN). Mexico's economic relationship and business dealings with the United States was a notable theme in the 2016 US presidential election. Trump's public views towards Mexico during the election and since then have signaled a change in US policy towards the areas of immigration and commerce.

On 3rd Jan. 2017, Trump addressed the auto industry's involvement in Mexico via his Twitter feed: "General Motors is sending Mexican made model of Chevy Cruze to US car dealers-tax free across border. Make in USA or pay big border tax!"

The fallout from the statement was multifaceted:

- GM shares initially traded up 1.69% after the announcement.
- Competitor Ford announced plans to cancel a proposed production facility, which was slated to inject US $ 1.6 billion and 2800 jobs to Mexico.

- The USD/MXN traded down 2% in the immediate aftermath of the tweet to a record-low of 21.619 pesos to the dollar in Figure 3-19.

Figure 3-19 Monthly USD/MXN

- During extended trading, the MXN dropped 3.5% against the USD, triggering intervention by Mexico's Central Bank (Banxico).

Ultimately, Trump's tweet signaled a potential change in the business practices that are to be allowed under his administration. As a result, the domestic currency of an economic beneficiary experienced a dramatic reaction in terms of volatility and valuation. Albeit indirectly, Mexico's economic prospects came into question by FX traders and investors, with the end result being a depreciation of the domestic currency.

Exercises

Ⅰ. *For the follow questions, consider each of the choices separately and choose all that apply.*

1. A FX pip is a unit utilized to denote value changes for currency pairs. One pip is 0.0001 in case of (　　).

A. EUR　　B. GBP　　C. JPY　　D. CNY

2. Market makers consider ( ) factors before offering official bid-ask prices.
   A. inventory holding costs
   B. currency pair's liquidity or trading volume
   C. exchange rate volatility (market uncertainty)
   D. number of dealers (market competition)
3. The arbitrage opportunities rarely exist or are rarely exploitable because that ( ).
   A. market will be bias once the price deviates from the equilibrium
   B. arbitrage actions kill arbitrage opportunities
   C. investors are not participating in inefficient market
   D. the difference in buying and selling rates is ignored
4. With the following information, one can exploit risk free profits with no initial investment if ( ).

bank	currency pair	quotes
A	X/Y	bid_A/ask_A
B	Z/Y	bid_B/ask_B
C	X/Z	bid_C/ask_C

   A. $ask_B \times ask_C < bid_A$
   B. $ask_B \times ask_C > bid_A$
   C. $bid_B \times bid_C > ask_A$
   D. $bid_B \times bid_C < ask_A$
5. A 1 pip difference means that ( ).
   A. a change from 114.05 to 114.06 for the USD/JPY
   B. a change from 1.2351 to 1.2350 for the EUR/USD
   C. a change from 1.41342 to 1.41343 for the GBP/USD
   D. a change from 6.311 to 6.310 for the USD/CNY

Ⅱ. ***Numerical works.***

1. *Cross exchange rates with no transaction costs: suppose that* $S_{EUR/USD} = 1.5$ *and* $S_{GBP/USD} = 2$, *work out* $S_{EUR/GBP}$.

2. *Fill in how far to the right of the decimal point for the following currency pairs.*
   EUR/USD:
   USD/JPY:
   USD/CNY:

3. *Given spot exchange rates as EUR/USD = 1.1325, EUR/GBP = 0.7805, GBP/USD = 1.4528, work out possible way for triangular arbitrage and explain potential risk.*

4. *Is there any triangular arbitrage? (round to 4 decimal places)*
   Barclays: GBP/USD = 1.8400/27
   Deutsche: GBP/EUR = 1.5085/109
   Citibank: EUR/USD = 1.2211/33

5. *Given a 10∶1 leverage ratio, what is the corresponding margin? If the margin is 0.02, what is the corresponding leverage?*

6. *Calculate margin requirements for a trade and the remaining account equity. You have $3000 in your account. You want to buy 100000 EUR with a current price of 1.0621 USD, and your broker requires a 2% margin. What is the required margin? How many more Euros could you buy after commit the margin?*

7. *How much should one trader to pay to buy 10 lots USD with an account that its leverage is 50∶1 ?*

8. *Suppose that one trader has a $10000 account and she has some open positions with the total margin of $900 and her positions are $400 in profit. What is her equity and how much left for her free margin?*
   equity = $10000 + $400 = $10400
   free margin = $10400 − $900 = $9500

9. *Solve for cross rates with two sided quotes.*
   USD/CHF = 1.6545/50 and NZD/USD = 0.6195/0.6200, NZD/CHF = ?

10. *A German student plans a trip to St. Petersburg, Russia. She leaves Berlin with € 1000 in her money pouch, wanting to exchange all of these for Russian rubles. She obtain the following quotes:* $S_{EUR/USD} = 1.0792/98$, *and* $S_{USD/RUB} = 54.45/56$. *How much rubles will she obtain from her Euros?*

11. *If* $S_{USD/JPY} = 109.86/93$ *and* $S_{USD/CAD} = 1.3556/62$, *solve for* $S_{CAD/JPY}$.

12. *If* $S_{GBP/USD} = 1.2778/82$ *and* $S_{USD/MXN} = 18.8068/73$, *solve for* $S_{GBP/MNX}$.

13. *If* $S_{OMR/USD} = 2.5988/07$ *and* $S_{BHD/USD} = 2.6568/92$, *solve for* $S_{BHD/OMR}$.

14. *On 31st Dec. 2015,* $S_{USD/JPY} = 120.21$, *while one year later on 30th Dec. 2016,* $S_{USD/JPY} = 116.95$. *Calculate the magnitude of percentage appreciation or depreciation for the base currency USD.*

15. *Given rates found on the following currency pairs EUR/USD = 1.0798, EUR/JPY = 119.53, USD/JPY = 110.07, work out possible way for triangular arbitrage if there is any.*

16. *How is the central parity of RMB against USD determined?*

17. *Explain the dialogue of FX spot transaction between bank A and bank B.*

    A: GBP 5 Mio.
    B: 1.4131/1.4137.
    A: My risk.
    B: 1.4134 Choice.
    A: Sell PLS. My USD To ANY.
    B: OK, done. At 1.4134 We Buy GBP 5 Mio AG USD Val March-26 GBP To My London, TKS for deal, BIBI.

18. *For currency pair EUR/USD, bank A offers prices as EUR/USD = 1.244 5/51 and bank B offers prices as EUR/USD = 1.245 4/60. There is a two-currency arbitrage. Give two ways to exploit the arbitrage.*

19. *What does the quote USD/CHF = 0.9618/23 indicate?*

Chapter 4
Foreign Exchange Forwards

A Chinese stationary manufacturer has a large order to be shipped to America and will receive USD in half a year. There is a depreciation trend of USD against CNY. This manufacturer may consider to apply FX forward to hedge against the exchange rate risk. Hedging engages in a currency forward which is to sell 10 million USD in exchange for CNY at a forward rate of $0.1586 per Chinese yuan. Therefore, the Chinese stationary manufacturer is obligated to deliver 10 million USD at the specified rate on the specified date, 6 months from the current date, regardless of fluctuating currency spot rates.

FX forward contracts are transactions that agree to exchange a specified amount of different currencies at some future date, with the exchange rate being set at the time the contract is entered into. Forward exchange rate is the rate agreed today for delivery of the currency at a future time. A FX forward contract is a binding contract in the foreign exchange market that locks in the exchange rate for the purchase or sale of a currency on a future date. It is essentially a hedging tool that does not involve any upfront payment. It can be tailored to a particular amount and delivery period. Forward settlement can either be on a cash or a delivery basis, provided that the dealing is mutually acceptable and has been specified beforehand in the contract. FX forward, also known as an "outright forward" is over-the-counter (OTC) instruments. This chapter explains:

- Definition and types of FX forward;
- Interest parity application in forward point determination;
- FX forward in China;
- NDF and its applications.

§ 1 Conventions

1.1 Derivatives and an Overview of FX Forward

A financial instrument that is derived from some other assets, indices, events, values or conditions is called a derivative. FX derivatives, most commonly used by end-users, are broadly categorized into forward, swap, futures, and option. The gross market value of OTC derivatives after netting is 1 trillion USD[①]. The UK accounts for almost half of daily global OTC derivatives turnover. North America is 24%, continental Europe is 18% and Asia-Pacific is 8%. Rather than trade or exchange the underlying asset itself, derivative traders enter into an agreement to exchange cash or assets over time based on the underlying asset such as foreign exchange.

FX derivatives are widely used in foreign exchange risk management. Multinational corporations and financial institutions often use FX forward to hedge future payables or receivables denominated in a foreign currency against foreign exchange risk.

Forward contract or forward, also known as a forward outright contract, is the simplest type of derivatives, and is usually exchanged in the interbank market. As one fundamental derivative product, forward contract can be used as an example to provide a general understanding of more complex derivative instruments such as swap, futures, and option. Forward contracts are very popular because they are barely regulated.

Flexible they are, forward contracts have disadvantages: lack of transparency, no clearinghouse to prevent counter party risk, etc.

Among forwards, FX forward is about currency trade that contracted today but with delivery and settlement in the future. Banks typically quote forward rates for major currencies in maturities of 1, 3, 6, 9 or 12 months. Very few banks provide quotations for greater maturities available up to 5 or 10 years. In FX forward, an investor who agrees to buy the base currency is said to enter into a long forward contract or to take a long forward position. If an investor agrees to sell the base currency, is said to enter into a short forward contract or to take a short forward position. For example, when some trader agrees to sell euros for dollars on a future date at a rate fixed on today, she has "sold euros forward" and bought "dollars forward".

Foreign exchange forward contracts are considered a form of derivative since their value depends on the value of the underlying currencies. It does not require payment at the time when a FX forward contract is exchanged. The main reasons for engaging in FX forward contracts are speculation for profits and hedging to limit risk. Although FX forward hedging lowers foreign exchange risk, it also eliminates the potential profits.

1.2 Characteristics of FX Forward

1) Private Legal Contract

FX forward contracts are private legal contracts between two parties. Both parties are committed to trade the specified currencies at the specified exchange rate on the specified date. If the exchange rate went against the trader's interest, this disadvantage can be reduced by creating a second forward contract that is in opposite side to offsets the first. Each FX forward contract brings commission fees to the forward broker. To ensure transparency, many regulators require OTC derivatives trade reporting.

---

① Source: McKinsey; International Swaps and Derivatives Association (ISDA)

2) Customized

FX forward contracts are customized in terms of contract size, maturities, settlement details. This flexibility is obtained with the sacrifice of liquidity. FX forward contracts are not so easy to be exchanged cross the market. Most FX forward contracts thus conclude with the actual currency delivery.

3) An Obligation

A FX forward usually is used to hedge the foreign exchange exposure of a loan or an equity stake. Long position is used to hedge against the appreciation of the payable and short position for the depreciation of the receivable. FX forward represents a binding obligation. Traders must fulfill the obligation even if the "locked in" rate turned out to be adverse. It might not be a good choice if the trader's goal is to maximize profits.

FX forwards typically do not require an upfront payment when used by large corporations and banks. To compensate for the risk of non-delivery or non-settlement, financial institutions that deal in FX forwards may require a deposit from retail investors or smaller firms.

4) Zero-Sum Game

There are two parties in a FX forward: buyer and seller. The loss of one party will be the gain of the other.

More specifically, the party holding a long forward contract with delivery date T will benefit if the spot exchange rate S_T rises above the contract forward rate F. If S_T falls below the forward rate F, then the holder of a long forward contract will suffer a loss. The payoffs could be positive, negative or zero. The payoff for a long forward position is $S_T - F$. The payoff for a short forward position is $F - S_T$. If add up both payoffs of long position and short position, the sum would be zero.

Each participant's gain or loss in a FX forward contract is thus exactly balanced by the losses or gains of the other participants.

1.3 Forward Quotations

There are mainly 3 ways to quote FX forwards.

1) Outright Forward Rate

An outright forward rate is usually quoted as $F_N(q/b)$, which refers to the price of one unit of base currency b in terms of currency q for delivery in N months. Both q and b here are currency symbols. Forward maturities of 1 week, 2 weeks, and 1—12 months are common, although other maturities are available. Take 3-month EUR/USD forward for instance, the outright rate symbol is expressed as $F_3(\$/€)$. Outright forward contracts are not traded in inter-bank market but are very popular with corporate customers.

In newspapers, forward rate quotations usually appear directly under the spot rate quotations for 4 major frequently-traded currencies (GBP, CAD, JPY, CHF) for 1-, 3-, and 6-month maturities. Table 4-1 shows published in Wall Street Journal spot and forward closed middle rates of last trading day.

Table 4-1 Outright Forward Rate

Currencies

U.S.-dollar foreign-exchange rates in late New York trading. .6491 = 1/1.5402

------Wednesday------ ------Wednesday------

Country/currency	in US $	per US $	Country/currency	in US $	per US $
Canadian dollar	.9984	1.0016	Euro area euro	1.3092	.7638
1-mos forward	.9986	1.0014	1-mos forward	1.3093	.7638
3-most forward	.9988	1.0012	3-most forward	1 3098	.7635
6-mos forward	.9979	1.0021	6-mos forward	1.3107	.7630
Japanese yen	.010094	99.07	British pound	1.5405	.6491
1-mos forward	.010095	99.06	1-mos forward	1.5402	.6493
3-most forward	.010099	99.02	3-most forward	1.5396	.6495
6-mos forward	.010106	98.95	6-mos forward	1.5389	.6498

source: Wall Street Journal

From Table 4-1 one can find that market participants expect a strong EUR on that trading day because 1-month EUR is closed at $F_1(\$/€)= 1.3093$, 3-month EUR is closed higher in $F_3(\$/€)= 1.3098$, and 6-month EUR is closed even more expensive, $F_6(\$/€)= 1.3107$.

A 3-month CAD closed at 0.9988 USD, which is more expensive than its spot rate, 0.9984. The market participants expect that CAD will appreciate against USD in 3 months. But it drops down to 0.9979 USD in 6 month.

If the outright rate is higher than the spot rate, the base currency is said at premium.

If the outright rate is lower than the spot rate, the base currency is said at discount.

When forward rate equals to the spot rate, it is "at par".

Outright forward contracts are typically between a bank and its commercial or retail customers. International traders who have payments due in the future can enter into outright forward contracts with banks to lock in the purchase or sale price of the payment currency.

2) Forward Quotations on a Points Basis

The forward rates can be quoted in terms of points. Forward points are widely used in interbank market, day-to-day business. Forward points are equivalent to pips in the spot market. A point is the last digit of a quotation, with convention dictating the number of digits to the right of the decimal point. Forward points are usually quoted to an accuracy of 2 decimal places of one point. FX forward points are an adjustment to the spot rate to reflect the interest rate differential.

Because forward points represent a difference in rate as opposed to being a rate, there is no big figure. For example, to represent a difference in GBP/USD between 1.2428 and 1.2439, the forward points would be 11, because one pip or point is worth 0.0001 in GBP/USD. To represent a difference in EUR/USD between 1.0323 and 1.03275, the forward points would be 4.50.

Corresponding to "bid and ask", the two sides of a forward price are sometimes called "left-hand-side" (LHS) and "right-hand-side" (RHS).

Forward points may be positive or negative. Take USD/JPY forward for instance, it is offered in the following Table 4-2.

Table 4-2 FX Forward Quotation

Name	Bid	Ask	High	Low	Chg	Time
USDJPY ON FWD	-0.3300	-0.2300	-0.2590	-0.2890	-0.0400	6:41:00
USDJPY TN FWD	-0.2700	-0.2400	-0.2200	-0.2900	0.0450	8:04:00
USDJPY SN FWD	-0.3000	-0.2600	-0.2830	-0.3100	0.0220	8:03:00
USDJPY SW FWD	-4.1900	-3.7700	-3.8900	-5.0700	0.9200	8:02:00
USDJPY 2W FWD	-7.0100	-6.5700	-6.8600	-8.0200	1.3200	8:04:00
USDJPY 3W FWD	-9.8800	-9.5500	-9.7200	-10.9900	1.2800	8:04:00
USDJPY 1M FWD	-13.1000	-12.8400	-12.6900	-14.5600	1.7000	8:04:00
USDJPY 2M FWD	-26.7000	-26.0400	-26.0200	-28.9100	1.3100	8:04:00
⇨ USDJPY 3M FWD	-40.3100	-38.8800	-39.2200	-41.1000	1.1400	8:04:00
USDJPY 4M FWD	-57.0100	-56.2500	-56.2700	-58.8700	2.5000	8:04:00
USDJPY 5M FWD	-70.5500	-70.1400	-70.0000	-72.4000	2.0500	8:04:00
USDJPY 6M FWD	-86.0300	-84.3700	-84.4200	-87.5000	1.0700	8:04:00
USDJPY 7M FWD	-104.8200	-104.4900	-104.0000	-106.8600	2.2800	8:04:00
USDJPY 8M FWD	-121.4000	-119.8000	-118.5300	-122.6000	1.6000	8:04:00
USDJPY 9M FWD	-137.8000	-136.0000	-136.4000	-139.5700	1.4000	8:04:00
USDJPY 10M FWD	-162.7500	-160.2500	-161.0400	-164.4600	2.7000	8:04:00
USDJPY 11M FWD	-179.1400	-177.4700	-177.3800	-180.6000	3.2600	8:04:00
USDJPY 1Y FWD	-198.0000	-193.7500	-195.4500	-199.0000	2.0000	8:04:00
USDJPY 15M FWD	-260.2500	-249.7500	-255.7500	-263.7400	-1.1800	8:01:00
USDJPY 21M FWD	-394.8700	-379.7700	-385.0000	-395.5000	-3.3700	8:04:00
USDJPY 2Y FWD	-462.5000	-453.5000	-457.5000	-466.0000	3.5000	8:04:00
USDJPY 3Y FWD	-763.0000	-751.0000	-761.0000	-771.0000	8.0000	8:04:00
USDJPY 4Y FWD	-1082.3900	-1044.8900	-1075.0699	-1066.1600	2.8100	7:59:00
USDJPY 5Y FWD	-1392.0000	-1352.0000	-1389.3000	-1373.7000	22.1000	8:03:00
USDJPY 6Y FWD	-1926.0000	-1876.0000	0.0000	0.0000	0.0000	27/03
USDJPY 7Y FWD	-1996.0000	-1925.0000	-1996.0000	-1939.0000	2.0000	6:31:00
USDJPY 8Y FWD	-2277.0000	-2196.0000	-2277.0000	-2211.0000	3.0000	6:31:00
USDJPY 9Y FWD	-2540.0000	-2450.0000	-2540.0000	-2467.0000	4.0000	6:31:00
USDJPY 10Y FWD	-2790.0000	-2689.0000	-2790.0000	-2707.0000	2.0000	6:31:00
USDJPY 12Y FWD	-3611.0000	-3486.0000	0.0000	0.0000	0.0000	27/03
USDJPY 15Y FWD	-4196.0000	-4056.0000	0.0000	0.0000	0.0000	27/03
USDJPY 20Y FWD	-4942.0000	-4792.0000	0.0000	0.0000	0.0000	27/03
USDJPY 30Y FWD	-5683.8101	-5559.4502	0.0000	0.0000	0.0000	01/02

source: Financial Times

"3-month dollar/yen 40.31 at 38.88." said by the trader means that the 3-month points quotations for the JPY in Table 4-2 are −40.31 bid and −38.88 ask. The first number, −40.31 refers to points away from the spot bid; and the second number, −38.88, refers to points away from the spot ask. Given the spot quotes of 110.64 bid and 110.66 ask, $S_{USD/JPY}=110.64/66$, the outright 3-month forward rates are calculated as follows:

	bid	ask
outright spot	110.64	110.66
Plus 3-months points	−40.31÷100	−38.88÷100
Outright forward	110.24	110.27

If forward rate exceeds the spot rate, base currency appreciates against quote currency, the base currency is said "at a premium". The forward points should be added to the spot rate.

If forward rate is lower than the spot rate, base currency depreciates against quote currency, the base currency is said "at a discount". The forward points should be subtracted from the spot rate.

Given $S_{CHF/USD}=0.9630/40$, and 6-month forward points quote is 32/27, the forward points are in descending order. If the forward pips decline from left to right, the currency is at a discount and the forward pips are deducted from the spot rate, then the 6-month forward rate is $F_6(\$/Fr)=$ 0.9598/13.

Suppose that $S_{EUR/USD}=1.5554/59$, a 3-month forward points quote is 14/21, the forward points are in ascending order. If the forward pips rise from left to right, the currency is at a premium and the forward points are added to the spot, then the 3-month forward rate is $F_3(\$/€)=$ 1.5568/80.

Forward points are based on spot rate and are mainly influenced by interest rates, thus must be updated for every move in the spot rate. It is easier for customers to compare the quotes of market makers and make deal with the best offer. In practice, the FX forward trading book is separated from the spot trading book. The forward desk actually belongs to the money market department. Forward deals are most frequently used as a part of FX swap transactions in the interbank market, and swaps are dominated by the interest differential.

3) Forward Quotations in Percentage Terms

Premium or discount of a forward FX rate can be expressed as an annualized percentage deviation from spot FX rate.

① Under European terms, which USD is the base currency, the formula for the premium or discount is given as:

$$F_n(q/\$)=\frac{S-F}{F}\times\frac{d}{n}\times 100\% \tag{4.1}$$

where d is days in year and n is number of forward valid days,

Given $S_{(USD/JPY)}=112.38$ and a 3-month forward is offered as 112.49, then

$$F_{3(¥/\$)} \text{ or } F^{¥}=\frac{112.8-112.49}{112.49}\times\frac{360}{90}\times 100\%=-0.39\%$$

The sign is negative, indicating that the 3-month forward yen is selling at a 0.39% per annual discount over the dollar.

Given $S_{(USD/CHF)}=1.0069$ and a 1-month forward is offered as 1.0053, then

$$F_{1(Fr/\$)} \text{ or } F^{Fr}=\frac{1.0069-1.0053}{1.0053}\times\frac{360}{30}\times 100\%=1.91\%$$

The sign is positive, indicating that the 1-month forward Swiss Franc is selling at a 1.91% per annual premium over the dollar.

② Under American terms, where USD is quote currency, the formula for the premium or discount is given as:

$$F_n(\$/b)=\frac{F-S}{S}\times\frac{d}{n}\times 100\% \tag{4.2}$$

where d is days in year and n is number of forward valid days.

Given $S_{(GBP/USD)}=1.2412$ and a 6-month forward is offered as 1.2157, then

$$F_{6(\$/£)} \text{ or } F^{£}=\frac{1.2157-1.2412}{1.2412}\times\frac{360}{180}\times 100\%=-4.11\%$$

The sign is negative, indicating that the 6-month forward sterling is selling at a 4.11% per annual discount over the dollar.

Given $S_{(EUR/USD)}=1.0818$ and a 3-month forward is offered as 1.0901, then

$$F_{3(€/\$)} \text{ or } F^{€}=\frac{1.0901-1.0818}{1.0818}\times\frac{360}{90}\times 100\%=3.07\%$$

The sign is positive, indicating that the 1-month forward Euro is selling at a 3.07% per annual premium over the dollar.

1.4 Deriving Forward Cross Rate

As USD is the viechle currency, in the interbank forward market other currencies are usually quoted against USD (except for EUR/GBP). Cross currency pairs, although not as actively traded as pairs with USD, are occasionally in need.

Like spot rate, forward cross rate is a bilateral exchange rate calculated from two other exchange rates involved USD. 3 examples are illustrated to show the deriving process.

1) Both Currency Pairs Have USD as Base Currency (European Terms)

To calculate an outright rate of DKK/SEK, the resulting DKK/SEK forward points should be added to the DKK/SEK spot rate to produce a DKK/SEK outright rate. It is similar with examples of the spot cross rate discussed in chapter 3.

First, work out outright expression of each currency pair, then apply the rule of spot cross rate.

Suppose that $S_{USD/DKK}=7.0437/45$, 3-month point is 12/20; $S_{USD/SEK}=9.0243/56$, 3-month point is 22/15. To work out 3-month DKK/SEK, one should first get 3-month USD/DKK and 3-month USD/SEK.

Because that forward point of USD/DKK is in ascending order, its 3-month forward is obtained by adding the points to spot rate:

3-month forward rate of USD/DKK

$bid_{DKK}=7.0437+0.0012=7.0449$

$ask_{DKK}=7.0445+0.0020=7.0465$

Because that forward point of USD/SEK is in descending order, its 3-month forward is obtained by deducting the points from spot rate:

$bid_{SEK}=9.0243-0.0022=9.0221$

$ask_{SEK}=9.0256-0.0015=9.0241$

Then apply spot cross rate methods to work out forward cross rate. Recall that to derive spot cross rate, given $USD/X=bid_x/ask_x$ and $USD/Y=bid_y/ask_y$, bid price of $X/Y=bid_Y \div ask_X$ and ask price of $X/Y=ask_Y \div bid_X$.

let X be DKK, y be SEK,

bid price of 3-monthDKK/SEK $=bid_{SEK}\div ask_{DKK}=9.0221\div 7.0465=1.2804$

ask price of 3-month DKK/SEK $=ask_{SEK}\div bid_{DKK}=9.0241\div 7.0449=1.2809$

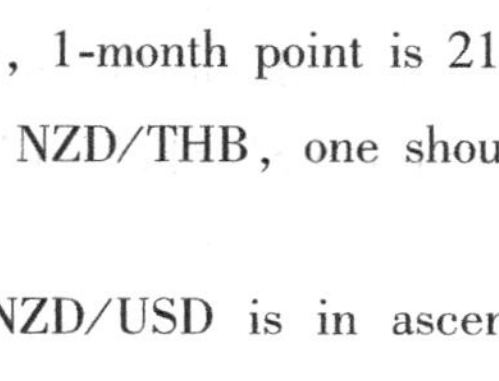

2) One of the Pairs Has USD as Quote Currency

Suppose that $S_{USD/THB}=34.45/54$, 1-month point is 21/15; $S_{NZD/USD}=0.7003/09$, 1-month point is 08/11. To work out 1-month NZD/THB, one should first get 1-month USD/THB and 3-month NZD/USD.

Because that forward point of NZD/USD is in ascending order, its 1-month forward is obtained by adding the points to spot rate:

$bid_{NZD}=0.7003+0.0008=0.7011$

$ask_{NZD}=0.7009+0.0011=0.7020$

Because that forward point of USD/THB is in descending order, its 1-month forward is obtained by deducting the points from spot rate:

1-month forward rate of USD/THB

$bid_{THB} = 34.45 - 0.21 = 34.24$

$ask_{THB} = 34.54 - 0.15 = 34.39$

Then apply spot cross rate methods to work out forward cross rate. Recall that to derive spot cross rate, given $X/USD = bid_X/ask_X$ and $USD/Y = bid_Y/ask_Y$, bid price of $X/Y = bid_X \times bid_Y$ and ask price of $X/Y = ask_X \times ask_Y$.

Let NZD be X and THB be Y,

big price of 1-month $NZD/THB = bid_{NZD} \times bid_{THB} = 0.7011 \times 34.24 = 24.01$

ask price of 1-month $NZD/THB = ask_{NZD} \times ask_{THB} = 0.7020 \times 34.39 = 24.14$

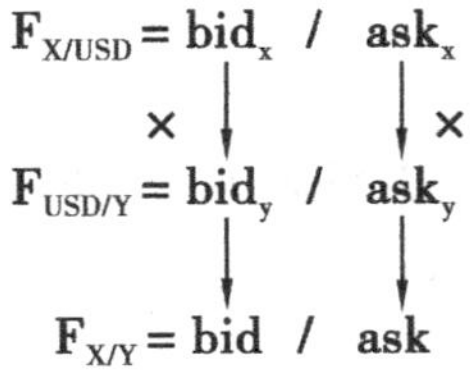

3) Both Currency Pairs Have USD as Quote Currency (American Terms)

Suppose that $S_{EUR/USD} = 1.0810/12$, 3-month point is 46/47; $S_{AUD/USD} = 0.7638/40$, 3-month point is 13/12. To work out 3-month EUR/AUD, one need first get 3-month EUR/USD and 3-month AUD/USD.

Because that forward point of EUR/USD is in ascending order, its 3-month forward is obtained by adding the points to spot rate:

$bid_{EUR} = 1.0810 + 0.0046 = 1.0856$

$ask_{EUR} = 1.0812 + 0.0047 = 1.0859$

Because that forward point of AUD/USD is in descending order, its 3-month forward is obtained by deducting the points from spot rate:

3-month forward rate of AUD/USD

$bid_{AUD} = 0.7638 - 0.0013 = 0.7625$

$ask_{AUD} = 0.7640 - 0.0012 = 0.7628$

Then apply spot cross rate methods to work out forward cross rate. Recall that to derive spot cross rate, given $X/USD = bid_X/ask_X$ and $Y/USD = bid_Y/ask_Y$, bid price of $X/Y = bid_X \div ask_Y$ and ask price of $X/Y = ask_X \div bid_Y$.

Let EUR be X and AUD be Y,

big price of 3-month $EUR/AUD = bid_{EUR} \div ask_{AUD} = 1.0856 \div 0.7628 = 1.4232$

ask price of 3-month $EUR/AUD = ask_{EUR} \div bid_{AUD} = 1.0859 \div 0.7625 = 1.4241$

$$F_{X/USD} = bid_x \ / \ ask_x$$
$$\div \qquad\qquad \div$$
$$F_{Y/USD} = bid_y \ / \ ask_y$$
$$F_{X/Y} = bid \ / \ ask$$

1.5 Forward Points and Premium/Discount Calculation

As forward rates are calculated from interest rate differentials, with any forward transaction the quotations are based on the relationship between the prevailing interest rates of the two currencies concerned.

1) Interest Rates Compounded on a Discrete Basis

The FX forward market is in fact an interest rate market. Forward rate is not only affected by the value of one currency against another, but also by the interest rate of one currency in comparison to another over a period. Forward traders are therefore interest rate traders, and as such, some banks include FX forward traders under their interest rate division rather than their FX division. The future value of a currency is the sum of the present value of the currency and the interest that it earns over time. Using simple annualized interest, the future value of currency can be represented as $FV = P(1+R)^n$, where FV is future value of currency, P is principal, R is interest rate per year, and n is number of years. If the forward exchange rate equalizes the future values of the base and quote currency, then the following equation holds:

forward exchange rate×FV of base currency = spot exchange rate×FV of quote currency

Dividing both sides by the FV of the base currency yields

forward exchange rate = spot exchange rate×(FV of quote currency÷FV of base currency)

$$F_n(q/b) = S(1 + R)^n \div (1 + R^*)^n \tag{4.3}$$

Where S is spot rate, R is interest rate of quote currency, R^* is interest rate of base currency.

If $R < R^*$, then forward exchange rate < spot exchange rate, the base currency is said at discount;

If $R > R^*$, then forward exchange rate > spot exchange rate, the base currency is said at premium;

If $R = R^*$, then forward exchange rate = spot exchange rate, it is at par.

The above equation is essentially the interest rate parity, but requires further improvement on 3 aspects before put into use:

① the bid and ask difference;

② the different interest rate year conventions (360-day basis and 365-day basis);

③ interest rate change during interest-compounding periods.

In practice, forward rate is usually simplified as $F_n(q/b)=S+S(R-R^*)$, which ignored the interest cost of the base currency during the forward period. If not specified, this book deals with the accurate way of forward rate calculation, i.e. $F_n(q/b)=S(1+R)^n \div (1+R^*)^n$.

2) Interest Rates Compounded on a Continuous Basis

Given continuous risk free interests, r and r^*, the above equation could be expressed as

$$F_n(q/b) = S\, e^{(r-r^*)(T-t)} \tag{4.4}$$

Where e is a mathematical constant that is the base of the natural logarithm (the unique number whose natural logarithm is equal to one). $T-t$ is the time left before forward to be expired.

As stated above, forwards deal at either premiums or discounts. Premium forward points must be added to the spot rate, making the forward rate higher than the spot rate. Discount forward points must be subtracted, making the forward rate lower. If one trader a long position of the forward, then premium points work against her; if she wants to short the forward, premium points work in her favor. The conditions are reversed for discount points. For example, suppose one trader is interested in buying USD forward versus CAD with $S_{USD/CAD}=1.3328/31$ and the 6-month forward point is quoted 21/76. The premium forward points make the forward rate less attractive. Similarly, discount forward points work against forward sellers. The difference here represents the interest rate differential that intrinsically is paid or received. This differential is known as the cost of carry, which is the cash flow involved in maintaining a long or short position. On an open position, interest is earned on the long currency and paid on the short currency every time the position is rolled over.

3) Computing Premium/Discount

Premium or discount points are in fact forward points. The equation is given as

$$\text{premium/discount} = S\left(\frac{1+R}{1+R^*} - 1\right)$$

For example, given the following market conditions, work out the 6-month forward points.

Annual interest rate of USD is 1.2%, annual interest rate of CHF is 1.8%, $S_{USD/CHF}=1.0007$

Base currency in this case is USD, quote currency is CHF.

$$1.0007 \times \left(\frac{1+0.018\times 6 \div 12}{1+0.012\times 6\div 12} - 1\right) = 0.002984$$

As currency prices for the USD are expressed to four decimal points, its forward points thus need multiply by 10000. 6-month USD/CHF forward points are 29.84. It is positive, meaning USD is at premium.

§ 2 Forward Contracts

2.1 Types

FX forward contracts are widely used for hedging to limit risk and speculation for profits. To serve different demand, FX forward contracts evolve into different types, in addition to the "mainstream" FX forward contracts.

1) Outright Forward and NDF

Outright FX forward contracts are most commonly traded. The parties to an outright FX forward agree to buy or sell a currency at a specified exchange rate, at a specified quantity and on a specified future date. On the specified future date, the two parties exchange the currency amounts to settle their claims under the contract. Unless otherwise noted, the FX forward agreement entails physical delivery of the specific currencies.

But monetary authorities of some countries' impose restrictions on their currency's convertibility in order to regulate the currency's inflow and outflow. Ordinary outright FX forward contracts are not available as currency transactions might not be allowed under the jurisdiction. To meet the hedge or speculation demand on FX forward, markets for non-deliverable forwards (NDF), which do not require the exchange of the non-convertible currency, have developed.

NDF is a cash-settled forward contract, which involves no actual delivery. It settles against a fixing rate at maturity, with the net amount in USD, or another fully convertible currency, either paid or received. At expiry of NDF, the underlying forward is liquidated relative to the spot rate.

More details of NDF will be elaborated later in this chapter.

2) Fixed Term and Optional Term

FX forward can be further differentiated into fixed term and optional forward contracts.

A fixed term contract involves a specified date on which the currency transfer can take place. If delivery date is to be rearranged after the fixed term contract has been signed, an adjustment of the exchange rate should also be agreed.

An optional term contract offers more room for the time the money be transferred. Instead of one specific date, it is a period of time the customer of optional FX forward states about the payment time. This period of time is usually no longer than a month.

2.2 Dates

Spot value dates are employed to calculate forward value dates and the trading date. Except for USD/CAD, most FX spots are settling in two business days. As spot value date is 2 business days after the trading date, forward value dates will usually settle more than 2 business days from the trading date. For a 1-month forward deal signed on Wed. 1st Apr. 2020, spot value is Fri. 3rd Apr. 2020. As one month later is Sun. 3rd May. 2020, forward value should be deferred to the next day, 4th May. 2020.

The following figure states that the value date of a *N*-month forward transaction is *N* calendar months from the spot value date for the currency.

Figure 4-1

Suppose that today is Mon. 13th Mar. 2017, a customer buys F_3($/€) at 1.2563, then forward execution date is Mon. 13th Mar. 2017 and forward delivery date is Thu. 15th Jun. 2017 (forward value date).

If the theoretical value date of an outright is on weekend or holiday, the value date is deferred to the next working day. If the spot value date of an outright is on the last working day of a month, it is called the end deal, the value date is the last working day. For example, the trading day of a one-month outright deal is on Mon. 29th Mar. 2021, value date of the spot deal would be on Wed. 31st Mar. 2021, the value date of the outright deal is on Fri. 30th Apr. 2021, the last bank day in April.

Because interbank forward points are always quoted against USD, it is impossible to calculate accurate forward points for any cross currency for settlement on a USD holiday, e.g. 4th Jul.. Although 4th Jul. or any other USD holiday could never be a standard tenor date (including spot) for this reason, it is possible to settle a non-USD currency pair (e.g. EUR/GBP) on 4th Jul. as a broken date (an illiguid period), but the spread would be very wide.

The forward value date or delivery date is simply the agreed upon date for mutual delivery of the currencies specified in a forward contract. This date can be days, months or even years after the transaction date. If the trade is a weekly trade, settlement is on the same day of the week as the forward trade, unless it is a holiday, then settlement is the next business day.

If it is a monthly trade, then the forward settlement is on the same day of the month as the initial trade date, unless it is a holiday. If the next business is still within the settlement month, then the settlement date is rolled forward to that date. If the next good business day is in the next month, then the settlement date is rolled backward, to the last good business day of the settlement month.

As a result of this flexibility in value dates, a forward contract can easily be tailored to meet a hedger's specific currency delivery needs based on their expected currency cash flows.

Furthermore, how the exchange rate moves between the forward transaction date and its value has little impact, other than from a credit risk standpoint. This is because the counterparties have already agreed upon a rate of exchange for the currencies involved that will be used when the value date for settlement of the currencies finally arrives.

2.3 Transfer of FX Forward

Forward contracts are typically exchanged in the OTC forward market between counterparties. Over the telephone or telegraph, traders work out the FX forward contract's terms. A transfer of FX forward involves 3 processes: execution, clearing and settlement.

Since the value of forward contracts is based on the spot rate and interest rates difference, executing a forward transaction usually involves first doing a spot trade in the desired currency amount. Secondly, to obtain the forward rate, the counterparties will add or subtract from the spot rate the FX swap points. The FX swap points are interest rates difference for the desired forward value date that pertain to the particular currency pair involved.

Once the FX forward contract is signed, traders launch the transaction. All the processes that lead up to settlement is referred to as clearing, such as recording the transaction. There are 2 types of clearing: Central Counter Party and Bilateral Clearing.

Settlement is the actual exchange of money between the parties of a FX forward on the settlement date. FX forward traders could also choose an opposite FX forward to net the final payment. Given FX forward contracts are quite term-tailored, it is not easy to net.

2.4 Payoff of Forward at Delivery

There is no payment on the day when two traders sign the forward contract, which sets the forward exchange rate as $F_{(0,T)}$. At delivery, the one who has a long position receives the amount of $S_T - F_{(0,T)}$ by buying the underlying base currency for the exchange of $F_{(0,T)}$ and selling it for the market price S_T. The payoff for the short forward position is $F_{(0,T)} - S_T$, by buying it for the market price S_T and selling the underlying base currency for the exchange of $F_{(0,T)}$. If add their payoffs up, one will find that a forward contract is a zero-sum game. If, instead of time 0, the FX forward contract is initiated at time t<T, then use $F_{(t,T)}$ for the forward price, the payoff at the delivery being $S_T-F_{(t,T)}$ for a long forward position and $F_{(t,T)}-S_T$ for a short position, it is still a zero-sum game. One of the two parties to a FX forward contract will be losing money, which is exactly what the other one earns. When delivered the payoffs for long and short forward positions are the difference of spot prevailing on dilivery date and forward rate as listed in Figure 4-2 below.

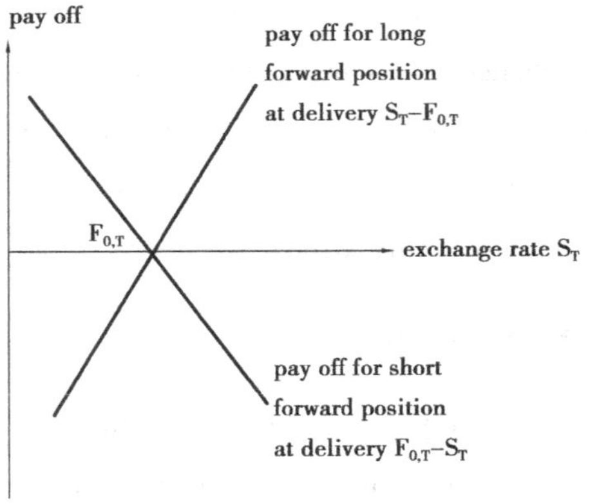

Figure 4-2 Payoffs of Long and Short FX Forward Positions are Mirror Images

2.5 Risks Associated with FX Forward Contracts

Although a forward contract may lower currency risk, it does not eliminate all risks. Two main types of exposures arise upon entering a FX forward contract. One risk is from forecast error and the other risk arises from financial accounting practice.

When exposures transform from anticipated to commitment, there will be some residual risk resulting from forecast error. If the actual exposure is greater/less than expected, the trader will be under-hedged/over-hedged. The long position, which was applied to hedge against appreciation of base currency, ends up with depreciation of base currency. Even if the forecast and actual figures are identical, traders may still be subject to risk in the form of a timing mismatch. This would arise when flows do not occur as expected. For example, delays in receipt/disbursement schedules can result in being under/over forecast. Whether there is a mismatch in magnitude or timing, a firm may need to enter the spot market to meet its obligations. In this case the direction of the quote currency, mostly USD, decides whether or not the trader has suffered a loss.

In addition, financial accounting requires that the change in value of that forward must be reported at the mark-to-market value on a quarterly basis. During holding of the forward, any drop in forward contract value can lead to unfavorable swings in reported earnings. So even if the forecast error is zero, the value of that forward contract may change through time, and those gains/losses must pass through the income statement at quarter's end. The danger lies in the fact the value of the underlying exposure may not be realized until sometime after that.

§3 FX Forward Point Determination: IRP

When there is no arbitrage opportunity and markets are in equilibrium, all international parity conditions hold, so does Interest Rate Parity (IRP). When international financial markets are in equilibrium there is no arbitrage opportunity. Given free movement of capital, international financial markets should be efficient. Arbitrage eliminates any discrepancies. In a nutshell, IRP is the market's tendency to correct itself against arbitrage. Arbitrage is the purchase and sale of an asset in two separate financial markets in order to profit from a price difference between the two. IRP describes the relationship between forward exchange rates, spot exchange rates, and interest rates between two countries. A forward contract is in fact a spot exchange rate transaction that incorporates the interest rate structure of each country. By IRP, FX forward point can be derived.

3.1 Two Ways to Derive IRP

1) The First Way: A Speculator's Choice

If FX forward is applied to hedge, exchange rate risk is said to be "covered", IRP is then known as covered interest rate parity. To demonstrate how the theory of IRP processes an imaginary two-country-world is applied. Suppose that a speculator has one unit of domestic currency, and that market conditions are given as follows:

The spot exchange rate is S;

The one-period forward exchange rate is F;

The one-period interest rate in quote currency is R;

The one-period interest rate in base currency is R^*.

Q stands for quote currency;

B stands for base currency;

This speculator has two alternative ways of investing as illustrated in Figure 4-3 (only default-free investments are considered).

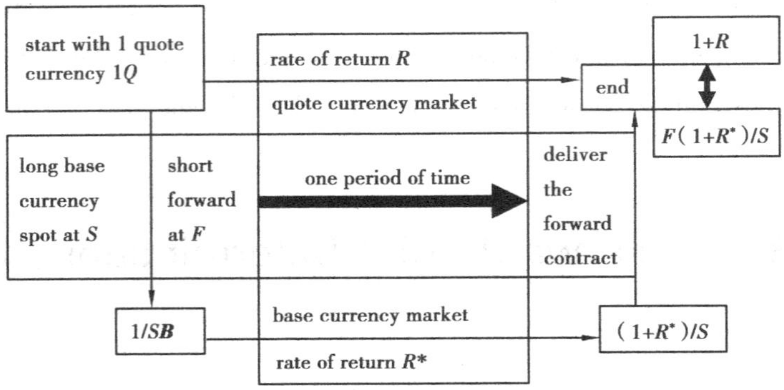

Figure 4-3 Exchange Rate Movement

According to the above figure, alone the top line, if at time 0, the speculator chooses to invest in a quote money market instrument, the speculator would earn R. At the end of the period, time 1, this speculator would have $1+R$ in her account. Or, this speculator can:

at time 0, exchange this one unit of quote currency at the spot rate of exchange for $1/S$ units of base currency;

at time 0, hedge the exchange risk by selling the maturity value, $(1+R^*)/S$, of the investment forward at F;

at time 0, invest the base currency in a money market instrument, and at time 1, gain $(1+R^*)/S$;

at time 1, convert the resulting proceeds back to quote currency, receiving $F(1+R^*)/S$.

With forward contract, this speculator has not only re-denominated the foreign investment in quote currency but also has effectively hedged the exchange risk. She will then compare $1+R$ with $F(1+R^*)/S$ and choose whichever offers the higher return. If the economy is in equilibrium, the returns of these two financial instruments are equal: $1+R=F(1+R^*)/S$. If rearranged, the formal statement of IRP can be expressed as:

$$F = S\frac{1+R}{1+R^*} \tag{4.5}$$

Equation 4.5 indicates that the forward exchange rate will deviate from the spot rate as long as the interest rates of the two countries are not the same. The approximation form of IRP could be derived as $F=S\frac{1+R}{1+R^*} \Rightarrow R=R^*\frac{F-S}{S}+R^*+\frac{F-S}{S}$, since $R^*\frac{F-S}{S}$ is a small number, the IRP relationship could be approximated as

$$R - R^* = \frac{F-S}{S} \tag{4.6}$$

This approximation form is frequently used to make quick judgment in searching for arbitrage opportunities. To calculate the specific arbitrage quantity, however, one should use the exact version of IRP, not the approximate version.

The process to achieve IRP confirms that IRP is a manifestation of the law of one price applied to international money market instruments.

2) The Second Way: Cash Flow Analysis

Alternatively, IRP can be derived by analyzing the cash flow of the following portfolio:

Borrow S units of quote currency with which long 1 unit of base currency at the spot exchange rate;

Lend out 1 base currency at the interest rate R^* for one period of time;

Sell the maturity value of the investment forward, and repay the loan.

The cash flow occurred from this portfolio is summarized in Table 4-3, where CF_0 denotes the cash flow at the start, time 0; CF_1 is the cash flow in the end, time 1, and S_1 is the spot exchange rate prevailing in time 1.

Table 4-3 The Cash Flow Analysis of a Portfolio

Transactions		CF_0	CF_1
1	Borrow quote currency	S	$-S(1+R)$
2	Lend in country that issues base currency	$-S$	$S_1(1+R^*)$
3	Short the base currency receivable forward	0	$F(1+R^*)-S_1(1+R^*)$
Net Cash Flow		0	$F(1+R^*)-S(1+R)$

As equilibrium requires no risk-free profit, the net cash flow on the maturity date should be zero:

$$F(1+R^*) - S(1+R) = 0 \tag{4.7}$$

If rearranged, equation 4.7 is in fact the same as equation 4.5.

IRP statements equation 4.5, 4.6 and 4.7 provide a linkage between interest rates in two different countries. More specifically, if the base currency is at a forward premium, $F>S$, then the base currency interest rate R^* is supposed to be lower than the quote one R. The exchange rate gain of any investment in base currency country is offset by low base interest. On the other hand, if the base currency is at a forward discount, $F<S$, then the base currency interest rate would be higher than the quote one $R^*>R$. The exchange rate loss of any investment in base currency country could be compensated by base currency interest. When IRP holds, one will be indifferent between investing in any country with forward hedging.

For example, one U.S. investor has \$1 to invest for one year. She has two portfolios: ① Invest in the U.S. treasury securities at R for one year; or ② Invest in foreign UK treasury securities at R^*, and hedge foreign exchange risk by selling maturity value of pounds forward one year. (round to 2 decimal).

Portfolio one, in the U.S., her payoff (maturity value) in one year will be: \$1(1+ R). In equilibrium this should be the same as her payoff in UK.

Portfolio two, she could:

Sell \$1 for pounds to get £ 1/S;

Invest pounds at UK with payoff=£$(1+R^*)/S$;

Sell pounds forward at F_{12}(\$/£) for the maturity value of the UK investment, to get a guaranteed amount of dollars.

For portfolio two, she has completely hedged (covered) foreign exchange risk with the forward contract. For either portfolio, she starts and ends with the U.S. dollars. If IRP holds, both porfolio provide the same payoff. $1+R=F(1+R^*)/S$, if rearranged $F=S\dfrac{1+R}{1+R^*}$.

3.2 Interest Rate Parity Line

Figure 4-4 below illustrates the conditions for equilibrium between interest rates and exchange rates. The vertical axis indicates the forward premium/discount in percentage. The horizontal axis indicates the interest rate differential, also in percentage. If IRP is maintained, the difference in the national interest rates for securities of similar risk and maturity should be equal to the forward rate discount or premium for the foreign currency, except for transaction costs. That is, differences in nominal interest rates, normally the midpoint of the saving/borrowing spread, between currencies determine the premiums or discounts on currencies in the forward foreign exchange market. All the combinations of interest rate difference and forward discount/premium that meet the IRP make a 45-degree line drawn from the origin.

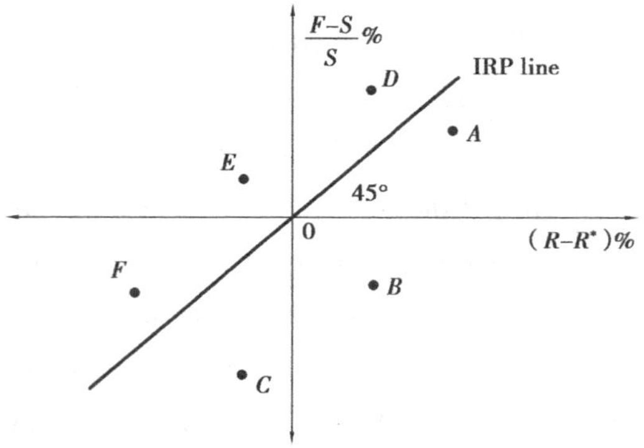

Figure 4-4 Interest Parity Line

IRP line gives another way to understand IRP: $R-R^*=(F-S)/S$ shows that interest rates (bond prices) are directly linked with S and F exchange rates.

The above equality can be represented graphically in IRP line in Figure 4-3 (note: units for both axes are %). Points deviate from the IRP line allow arbitragers to earn a riskless profit. Any point above the IRP line $R-R^* < \frac{F-S}{S}$ represents profits by either ① investing in base currency instead of quote currency, or by ② borrowing in quote currency and lending in base currency (arbitrage).

Any point below the line $R-R^* > \frac{F-S}{S}$ represents profit opportunities by either ① investing in quote currency or ② borrowing in base currency and lending in quote currency (arbitrage).

Every point in the IRP line represents exchange rate gain/loss is exactly offset by interest loss/gain and there should be no expected excess return from arbitraging across currencies.

3.3 Covered Interest Arbitrage (CIA)

IRP is the evidence that the forward, spot and credit market prices are mutually consistent. The prevailing forward rate will guarantee that the initial net present value of the forward contract is zero, thereby ensuring the inter-market consistency. In reality, spot and forward exchange markets are not always in the state of equilibrium following the IRP. When IRP does not hold, it gives rise to covered interest arbitrage (CIA). For instance, whichever point that is deviated from the IRP line demonstrated in Figure 4-4, the arbitrager will recognize this imbalance, and will take advantage of this disequilibrium by investing in whichever currency offers the higher return on a covered basis.

1) CIA Strategy when Market Situation is Located Below the IRP Line

For any point below the IRP line, such as point A, B, and C in Figure 4-4, $R-R^* > \frac{F-S}{S}$. Quote currency offers higher return that is more than enough to cover the loss caused by depreciation of the quote currency. In order to gain risk-free profit, an arbitrager can employ strategy Ⅰ shown in Figure 4-5 below (B for base currency, Q for quote currency):

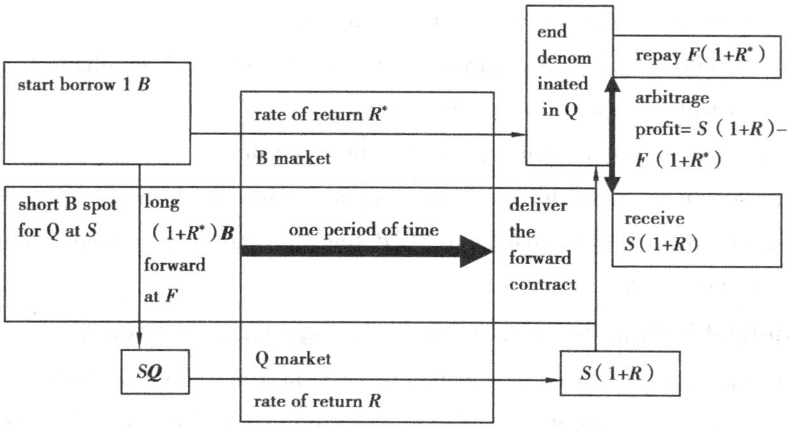

Figure 4-5 Strategy Ⅰ

① Borrow base currency loan for one period of time.

② Sell base currency for quote currency in spot market, and purchase forward of base currency with the same maturity value and time as the base currency loan.

③ Invest in quote currency country, get revenue when due.

④ Sell forward in exchange for base currency and repay the loan.

When market situation is located below IRP line, the above arbitrage brings risk free positive profit as $S(1+R)-F(1+R^*)$.

2) CIA Strategy when Market Situation is Located above the IRP Line

For any point above the IRP line, such as point D, E and F in Figure 4-4, $R-R^* < \frac{F-S}{S}$. Base currency appreciation outweighs its interest cost. In order to gain risk-free profit, an arbitrager can implement strategy Ⅱ shown in Figure 4-6 below (B for base currency, Q for quote currency):

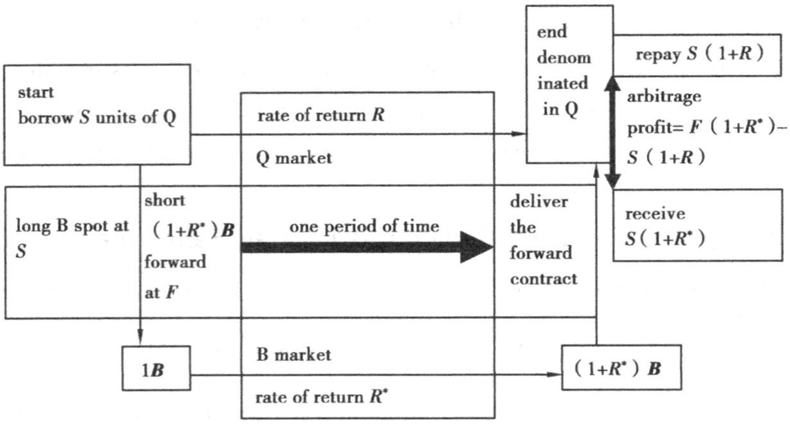

Figure 4-6 Strategy Ⅱ

① Borrow quote currency loan for one period of time.

② Sell quote currency for base currency in spot market, and simultaneously take a short position in forward with the same time as the loan.

③ Invest in base currency country, get revenue when due.

④ Sell forward in exchange for quote currency and repay the loan.

When market situation is located above IRP line, the arbitrage produces risk free positive profit as $F(1+R^*)-S(1+R)$.

3) Numerical Examples on CIA and Arbitrage Rule of Thumb

To explain the CIA process more specifically, it is best to apply the above strategies to some numerical examples. To simplify the calculation, all the numerical cases so far ignore the bid and ask difference and take midpoint instead.

Suppose, for one year, at point A in Figure 4-4 $R=4\%$, $R^*=1\%$, $F=2.02$, $S=2$. The interest rates difference is $R-R^*=4\%-1\%=3\%$. There is one-year forward premium $\frac{F-S}{S}=(2.02-2)\div 2=0.01$, or the base currency is trading at 1% premium versus the quote currency for delivery in one year. Point A is located below the IRP line. The interest rates difference in point A is greater than the forward premium: $R-R^*>\frac{F-S}{S}$. The quote currency interest return is high, even taken account in the depreciation of quote currency, there still exists extra return. Arbitrage arises from this violation of IRP. Because the interest rates gain 3% is greater than the forward cost 1%, an arbitrager would implement Strategy Ⅰ to perform the follow CIA transaction:

① Borrow one unit of base currency. Repayment in one year will be $1+R^*=1+1\%=1.01$ units of base currency.

② Sell this one unit of base currency in spot market for $S=2$ units of quote currency and purchase 1.01 units one-year forward of base currency, in exchange for $1.01F=1.01\times 2.02=2.0402$ units of quote currency.

③ Invest 2 units of quote currency. In one year, the maturity value will be $S(1+R)=2\times(1+4\%)=2.08$ denominated in quote currency.

④ To repay the loan, need 2.0402 units of quote currency to deliver the forward for 1.01 units of base currency.

The arbitrage profit will thus be $2.08-2.0402=0.0398$ units of quote currency.

The cash flow occurred from this arbitrage is summarized in Table 4-4, where CF_0 denotes the cash flow to start with, CF_1 is the cash flow in the end and S_1 is the spot exchange rate prevailing in the future.

Table 4-4　The Cash Flow Analysis of Arbitrage Strategy Ⅰ

Transactions		CF_0	CF_1
1	Borrow 1 unit of B	S	$-S_1(1+R^*)$
2	Lend in Q country	$-S$	$S(1+R)=2.08$
3	Long B receivable forward	0	$S_1(1+R^*)-F(1+R^*)$
Net Cash Flow		0	$S(1+R)-F(1+R^*)=0.0398$

It is left to the reader to figure out the arbitrage strategy and transaction for the other two points below the IRP line:

Point B: $R=1.1\%$, $R^*=1\%$, $F=2$, $S=2.5$;

Point C: $R=1\%$, $R^*=1.1\%$, $F=2$, $S=2.5$.

Point above the IRP line compose another case for CIA. Take point F in Figure 4-4 for instance, the market condition for point F is summarized as $R=1\%$, $R^*=5\%$, $F=1.99$, $S=2$. The base currency offers higher interest with the interest rates difference of $R-R^*=1\%-5\%=-4\%$, and is trading at 0.5% discount, since $\frac{F-S}{S}=(1.99-2)\div 2=-0.005$. Even with the depreciation, the base currency provides extra return. In order to realise the arbitrage opportunity, an arbitrager can implement Strategy Ⅱ to perform the following CIA transaction:

① Borrow $S=2$ units of quote currency. Repayment in one year will be $S(1+R)=2\times(1+1\%)=2.02$ units of quote currency.

② Sell this 2 units of quote currency in spot market for one base currency (spot exchange rate is 2) and simultaneously long $1.05F=1.05\times2=2.1$ units of one-year forward quote currency, which will cost $1+R^*=1+5\%=1.05$ units of base currency when it is due.

③ Invest this unit of base currency. In one year, the maturity value will be $1+R^*=1+5\%=1.05$ denominated in base currency.

④ To repay the loan, delivery the forward for 2.1 units of quote currency.

The arbitrage profit will thus be $2.1-2.02=0.08$ units of quote currency.

The cash flow occurred from this arbitrage is summarized in Table 4-5.

Table 4-5 The Cash Flow Analysis of Arbitrage Strategy Ⅱ

Transactions		CF_0	CF_1
1	Borrow S units of Q	S	$-S(1+R)=-2.02$
2	Lend in B country	$-S$	$S_1(1+R^*)$
3	Short B receivable forward	0	$F(1+R^*)-S_1(1+R^*)$
Net Cash Flow		0	$F(1+R^*)-S(1+R)=0.0695$

It is left to the reader to figure out the arbitrage strategy and transaction for

Point D: $R=2\%$, $R^*=1\%$, $F=3$, $S=2$;

Point E: $R=1\%$, $R^*=2\%$, $F=3$, $S=2$.

Following case gives a more detailed example of a covered interest arbitrage strategy on EUR/USD applied in practice. Spot rate is 1.35, EUR interest rate $R^*=4\%$, USD interest rate $R=1\%$.

To initiate a covered interest arbitrage strategy, the currency trader would first need to determine what the forward rate between USD and EUR should be in an efficient interest rate environment. To make this determination, the trader would divide the EUR spot rate by one plus the European annual risk-free rate, and then multiply that result by one plus the annual US risk-free rate.

$$F = S \div (1 + R^*) \times (1 + R) = [1.35 \div (1 + 0.04)] \times (1 + 0.01) = 1.311$$

In this case, the one-year forward contract between USD and EUR should be selling for 1.311. Since the one-year forward contract in the open market is selling at 1.50, the currency trader would know that the forward contract in the open market is overpriced. Accordingly, an astute currency trader would know that anything that is overpriced should be sold to make a profit, and therefore the currency trader would sell the forward contract and long EUR in the spot market to earn a risk-free rate of return on the investment.

The covered interest arbitrage strategy can be achieved in four simple steps:

① The currency trader would need to take $1.298 dollars and use it to buy € 0.962 euros.

To determine the amount of U.S. dollars and euros needed to implement the covered interest arbitrage strategy, the currency trader would divide the EUR spot rate of $ 1.35 by one plus the European annual risk-free rate of 4%: 1.35÷(1+0.04)= 1.298.

In this case, 1.298 U.S. dollars would be needed to facilitate the transaction. Next, the currency trader would determine how many euros are needed to facilitate this transaction, which is simply determined by dividing one by one plus the European annual risk-free rate of 4%: 1÷(1+0.04)= 0.962, the amount that is needed is 0.962 euros.

② The trader would need to sell a forward contract to deliver 1.0 euro at the end of the year for 1.50 U.S. dollars. (the forward rate)

③ The trader would need to hold the euro position for the year, earning interest at the European risk-free rate of 4%. This euro position would increase in value from 0.962 euro to 1.00 euro: 0.962×(1+ 0.04)= 1.000.

④ On the forward contract expiration date, the trader would deliver the 1.00 euro and receive 1.50 U.S. dollars. This transaction would equate to a risk-free rate of return of 15.6%, which can be determined by dividing 1.50 U.S. dollars by 1.298 U.S. dollars and then subtracting one from the answer to determine the rate of return in the proper units: 1.50÷1.298−1=0.156.

The mechanics of this covered interest arbitrage strategy are very important for investors to understand, because they illustrate why interest rate parity must hold true at all times to keep investors from making unlimited risk-free profits.

4) Economic Adjustment to CIA

Suppose that the market condition is summarized as follows, is there any CIA opportunity? If there is, show the CIA process. What will happen over time?

The annual interest rate is R=5% in the U.S.;

The annual interest rate is R^* =8% in the UK;

The spot exchange rate is $S_{GBP/USD}$ = 1.50;

The forward exchange rate with one-year maturity is $F_{12}(\$/£)$= 1.48.

Since $R-R^* < \frac{F-S}{S}$, IRP does not hold and CIA can be exploited. Nominal interest rates are 3% higher in UK than U.S.. GBP should depreciate by approximately 3% if IRP holds. But rate of depreciation of the foreign currency is $(F-S)/S \times 100 \Rightarrow (1.48-1.50) \div 1.50 \times 100 = -1.333\%$. GBP is expected to depreciate by only 1.33% instead of 3%. The market is not in equilibrium. UK market brings higher return. It is profitable to invest in UK.

CIA involves that

Borrow dollars at $R=5\%$, long GBP spot at $S_{GBP/USD}=1.50$;

Invest (lend) in UK and earn $R^*=8\%$;

And sell pounds forward at $F_{12}(\$/£)=1.48$, to cover exchange rate risk.

Investing in UK includes 2 simultaneous investments: ① the UK security and ② the British pound.

$1+R=1.05$ in U.S. vs. $(1+R^*)F/S=1.08\times1.48\div1.50=1.0656$ in UK

$1.05<1.0656 \Rightarrow 1+R<(1+R^*)F/S$

Returns in UK (6.56%) are higher than in US (5%) by more than 1.5%. one can

Borrow \$1 m in U.S. at 5%, promise to pay \$1.05 m back in one year.

Buy pounds at $S_{GBP/USD}=1.50$ for 1 m÷1.5=£ 666667.

Invest £ 666667 in UK at 8% to get guaranteed payoff in one year, that is £ 666667×1.08=£ 720000.

Enter into a 1-year forward contract to sell £ 720000s at $F_{12}(\$/£)=1.48$, for \$1065600 is guaranteed in one year.

Pay back \$1050000 on the loan in U.S., and make \$15600 profit.

If IRP did not hold, arbitrage would be possible. But continuing arbitrages would restore parity.

Interest rate R will rise due to borrowing pressure.

Interest rate R^* will fall as money rush into UK seeking for investment return.

GBP will appreciate in spot market due to buying pressure (S will rise) and will depreciate in the forward market, due to selling pressure (F will fall).

The difference between the two interest rates (3%) will be narrowed down and the difference between the S and F will grow wider (the forward discount for GBP will increase from 1.33%), until IRP is restored, possibly at a forward discount of 2% for GBP, until the interest rate spread is EXACTLY equal to the forward discount in GBP. Suppose interest rates end up at 5.5% in U.S. and 7.5% in UK, and GBP sells at a forward discount of 2%. IRP is restored, partly by a decrease in the interest rate differential and partly by an increase in the forward premium.

From the above cases one can see that arbitrage opportunities can only last for a short while. Because foreign exchange market traders that detect any deviations from IRP will immediately carry out CIA transactions, IRP can soon be restored.

Given market is located at point D in Figure 4-7 below, $R-R^{*}<\frac{F-S}{S}$, then

① Every trader borrows quote currency, quote interest rate will be driven up, $R\uparrow$.

② Selling quote currency for base currency in spot market will cause base currency appreciate in the spot market, $S\uparrow$.

③ Short base currency forward, and the base currency will depreciate in the forward market, $F\downarrow$.

④ Investing base currency will pull down base interest rate, $R^{*}\downarrow$.

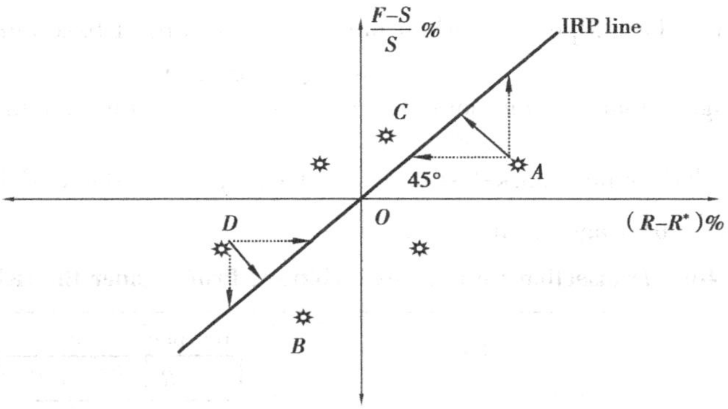

Figure 4-7 Adjustments to Restore IRP

These adjustments raise interest difference $(R\uparrow -R^{*}\downarrow)\uparrow$ and at the same time lower the forward discount $\frac{F-S}{S}\downarrow$ squishing out the arbitrage profit till both sides are equalized and IRP restored.

Figure 4-7 depicts the above adjustment process. As point D is substantially off the IRP line, once market participants sense this arbitrage opportunity, they implement CIA. Those arbitrages increase the interest rate difference (as indicated by the horizontal dotted arrow), and at the same time, lower the forward discount (as depicted by the vertical dotted arrow). Because these adjustments happen simultaneously, the foreign exchange market and money market share the adjustment, the actual path of adjustment to IRP is the hard arrow.

When the initial market condition is located at point A, arbitrage behavior will make IRP be restored through the hard arrow partly by an increase in the forward premium, and partly by a decrease in the interest rate differential.

5) Reasons for Non-Profitable IRP Deviation

(1) Transaction Costs

Empirical researches show that even IRP does not hold precisely, arbitrage opportunity is scarce. At least two reasons explain this situation: transaction costs and capital controls.

In reality, the interest rate at which one arbitrager borrows tends to be higher than the rate which she lends. It is called saving/borrowing spread. Let subscripts a and b denote the ask and bid prices of exchange rates and interest rates, then for any individual arbitrager $R_a>R>R_b$, $R_a^*>R^*>R_b^*$, $S_a>S>S_b$, $F_a>F>F_b$.

Suppose the market condition is located below the IRP line, the interest rate with which one individual arbitrager borrows R_a^* is higher than the midpoint R^*, $R_a^*>R^*$. The interest rate she lends R_b is lower than the midpoint R, $R_b<R$. $|R-R^*|>|R_b-R_a^*|$. The actual market condition point this arbitrager could obtain should move horizontally towards IRP line (or original point 0). When selling base currency for quote currency in spot market, this arbitrager takes bid price, S_b, which is lower than the midpoint S; when purchasing forward of base currency, she takes ask price F_a, which is higher than the midpoint F. $\frac{F-S}{S}<\frac{F_a-F_b}{S_b}$ the actually point, thus, moves up vertically towards IRP. When market situation is located below the IRP line, take account in the bid ask spread, the arbitrage room shrinks down.

Table 4-6　Transaction Costs Erase Arbitrage Profit Under the IRP Line

borrow B	cost higher $R_a^*>R^*$	revenue　cost $S(1+R)-F(1+R^*)>0$
short B	get less $S_b<S$	decrease　increase
Invest in Q	gain less $R_b<R$	$S_b(1+R_b)-F_a(1+R_a^*)$
long B forward	spend more $F_a>F$	decreased revenue　increased cost

Same applies when market situation located above the IRP line:

Table 4-7　Transaction Costs Erase Arbitrage Profit Above the IRP Line

borrow Q	cost higher $R_a>R$	revenue　cost $F(1+R^*)-S(1+R)>0$
long B	spend more $S_a>S$	decrease　increase
Invest in B	gain less $R_b^*<R^*$	$F_b(1+R_b^*)-S_a(1+R_a)$
short B forward	get less $F_b<F$	decreased revenue　increased cost

Taking account in these transaction costs, the arbitrage profit is rare. Only points that deviate far away from the band, as shown in Figure 4-8, can possibly provide some arbitrage opportunity.

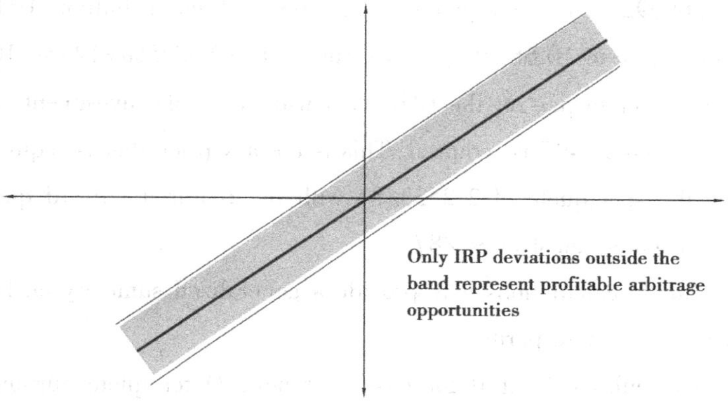

Figure 4-8 IRP with Transaction Costs

(2) Capital Controls

Capital controls also can cause the deviations from IRP with no arbitrage opportunity. In order to improve the balance-of-payment situations and to keep the exchange rate at a desirable level, governments usually impose capital controls by means of jawboning, imposing taxes, or outright bans on cross-border capital movements. Arbitrage process thus is impaired despite deviation from IRP.

3.4 Bid and Ask Forward Points Based upon IRP

1) Computing Outright Rate with Bid and Ask Rates

If markets are efficient, interest rate parity must hold after taking bid and ask spreads into account. This is the principle by which banks offer bid and ask forward price.

Suppose that a trader face the following market conditions: $S_{USD/CHF} = 2.2533/84$, one-month dollar interest rates is $R_1^{USD} = 10.6875\% \sim 10.8125\%$, one-month Swiss Franc interest rates is $R_1^{CHF} = 5.875\% \sim 6\%$. At the end of the month, this investor who borrowed 1 million USD for one month owes $1\text{mil} \times (1 + 10.8125\% \div 12) = \$1009010.417$. The investor can take the 1 million USD of borrowing and buy CHF in the spot market. Buying CHF is the same as selling USD, so the proceeds of the sale of the USD are $1\text{mil} \times 2.2533 = \text{Fr}2253300$. Lending the CHF proceeds at 5.875% yields $2253300 \times (1 + 5.875\% \div 12) = \text{Fr}2264331.781$ by the end of the month. To break even, this investor needs to buy USD at a rate that provides an amount sufficient to pay off the loan. Hence the sale price needs to be $2264331.781 \div 1009010.417 = 2.2441$. This is the outright bid forward price that the market maker is willing to offer in a fully competitive market without transaction costs other than the spread.

Alternatively, continuing to use the same market interest and exchange rates, the investor can borrow 2258400 CHF at the interest rate of 6%, results in a loan balance of 2258400 ×

(1+6%÷12)= Fr2269692. The loan proceeds can be sold for 1 million USD, which, when invested at the interest rate of 10.6875%, yields 1mil×(1+10.6875%÷12)=$1008906.25 by the end of the month. In order to pay off the CHF loan with the USD investment, an exchange rate of 2269692÷1008906.25=2.2497 is required. This is the ask price that is required for an outright forward. Comparing the spot quote of 2.2533/84 with the required forward quote of 2.2441/97 shows that the forward points must be 92/87.

The following sample calculations may provide a generalized summary on how to set forward bid and ask to meet interest rate parity.

To simplify the calculation, set B for base currency, Q for quote currency; given annual interest rates of quote currency as R_a and R_b; annual interest rates of base currency as R_a^* and R_b^*; bid and ask spot rate as S_a and S_b; set one time period as one year, the bid and ask price of forward would be derived from the perspective of a market maker as follows.

(1) Bid of Forward

Suppose that at the beginning of the year, one customer goes to bank to short forward, i.e. she is asking the bank to offer bid of forward. Once receives the order from the customer, this bank, as the price maker, should consider the following to work out how much forward rate to offer.

Bid price of a forward indicates that the bank signs itself into a forward contract promising to buy base currency in the future. In order to square this long position, this bank should short spot. It, unfortunately, does not have base currency on hand. This bank has to borrow, as a price taker, from money market. Once borrows 1 base currency, this bank put itself in debt of $1+R_a^*$, which needs to be paid up in one year.

Before the loan is due, this bank can compensate its debt by exchanging into quote currency and depositing for interest R_b as a price taker. To trade base currency for quote currency in spot, this bank, as a price taker in FX market, can only sell for S_b. By the time the loan is due, this bank has $S_b(1+R_b)$ on hand.

This bank can exercise FX forward by paying F_b to buy base currency from customer, and fulfill its debt obligation. According to the no-arbitrage principle, what this bank earns exactly covers its debt obligation:

$$S_b(1+R_b)/F_b = 1+R_a{}^* \Rightarrow$$

$$F_b = S_b\frac{1+R_b}{1+R_a^*} \tag{4.8}$$

Figure 4-9 depicts the bank's processes of deriving bid of forward. Among all bank's activities, it acts as a price taker except for offering bid of forward, which is highlighted by an italic font.

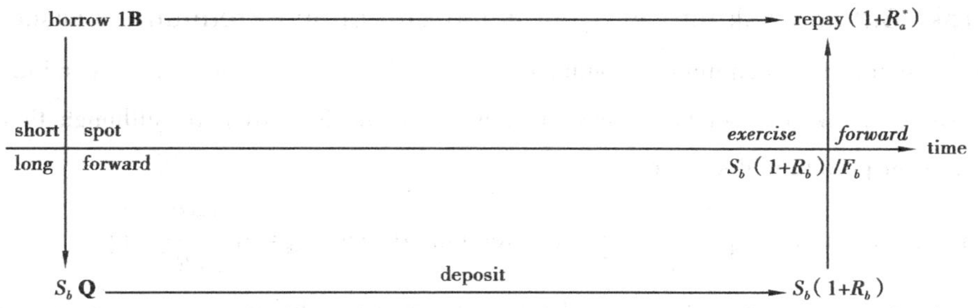

Figure 4-9 Deriving Bid of forward F_b

(2) Ask of Forward

When customer needs to buy base currency in future, she can sign a forward contract with a bank. This time, bank should offer ask of forward to the customer. Bank works out the ask rate of forward according to the no-arbitrage principle.

With the order from customer, bank goes to money market and FX market to prepare forward. Bank borrows quote currency to long base currency in spot, and deposits base currency till forward is due. Bank acts as a price taker for all the above preparations in money market and FX market. The borrowing cost for this bank is R_a, the spot rate bank can have in FX market is S_a, and the interest rate this bank earns is R_b^*. By the time to execute forward, this bank has $(1+R_b^*)$ to cover $S_a(1+R_a)$. The forward rate this bank offers to customer should be just enough to make its revenue and cost even.

$$F_a(1 + R_b^*) = S_a(1 + R_a) \Rightarrow$$

$$F_a = S_a \frac{1 + R_a}{1 + R_b^*} \tag{4.9}$$

Figure 4-10 shows how the bank works out ask of forward. Bank in this case is like a businessman who needs to go to money market and FX market to buy raw material for assembling the final product, forward, to sell. Among all activities, bank acts as a price taker except for offering ask of forward, which is highlighted by an italic font.

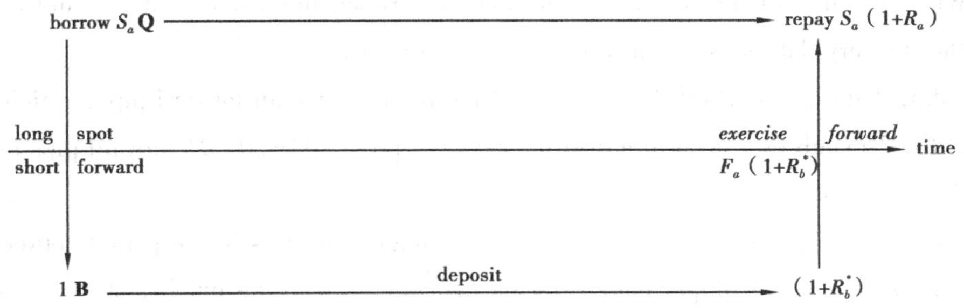

Figure 4-10 Deriving Ask of forward F_a

2) Take Bid and Ask into Account when Computing Premium or Discount

When compute the premium/discount, the calculation may be done with the midpoint of the spot rate. Bid and ask for spot has almost no impact on the forward point although there are bid and ask price in premium/discount.

$$\text{premium/discount}_{\text{bid}} = S\left(\frac{1+R_b}{1+R_a^*}-1\right) \text{ and premium/discount}_{\text{ask}} = S\left(\frac{1+R_a}{1+R_b^*}-1\right)$$

Interest rates are essential for forward rate determination. In practice, however, banks need consider many other factors besides interest rates to offer forward rate. If one bank would reduce some currency position, it may offer lower forward rate to get rid of it. If one bank senses some positive trend in favor of one country, it will bid higher forward rate for that currency. If one bank has some expansionary strategy in FX market, it may adjust its forward offer... All those factors have complex impacts on forward rate. (4.8) and (4.9), provide just benchmarks for forward rates offers. Traders may find different banks offer different forward rates on the same currency pair. They thus can shop around FX market for their favorite offer.

3) Forward Point Calculation for Broken Dates

FX forwards are mostly quoted in standard time. Occasionally, people require forward for a certain period that is other than the standard time that is called broken dates. FX forward rate for broken dates can be calculated by linear interpolation of the two nearest forward rates. That is to interpolate between the two standard date quotations on either side of the desired maturity.

For example, to work out the forward pips for the dollar against the Japanese yen for one and half months, 45 days, assume the following rates:

$S_{USD/JPY} = 106.85/95$

1-month forward pips 20/10

2-month forward pips 41/37

The bid and ask of a broken-dated forward can be calculated through 4 steps:

① Work out the number of days in the period between the 1-and 2-month forward quotes, because the delivery date falls within this period. (45 days)

② Subtract the bid 1-month forward pips from the bid 2-month forward pips, which will then show what the 2-month pips are worth over the 1-month pips. (41−20=21 forward pips for bid and 37-10=27 forward pips for ask)

③ Divide the difference in forward pips, by the number of days in the period between the two standard quotes, 30, and multiply the answer by the difference in the number of days between the required date and the last day of the 1-month quote. (21÷30×15=10.5 and 27÷30×15=13.5)

④ The sum of the above result and the 1-month forward pips is the bid and ask of one and half months forward. (30.5/23.5)

For another example, given market conditions as $S_{EUR/USD}$ = 1.0681/83, 6-month forward points are 97.75/98.71, 9-month forward points are 151.75/155.36. One trader plans to sell EUR 8-month forward. What is the forward rate?

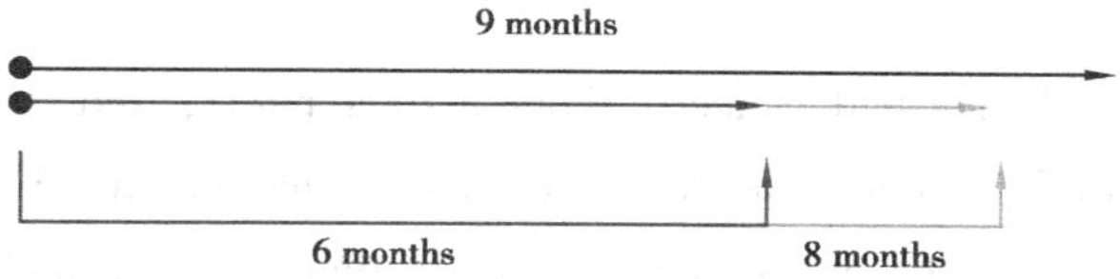

8-month forward is between the 6-month and 9-month forwards. As this trader plans to sell EUR, the bid applies.

This difference between the 6-month and 9-month forwards is 151.75−97.75 = 54 pips. If the EUR/USD forward curve runs linear, this trader can assume that between the 6-month and 9-month forwards the premium per month has to be 54÷3 = 18 pips. So this trader would have an estimated 8-month forward rate of 1.068 1+0.001 8×2 = 1.0717.

3.5 Departures from IRP in Real Life

During the financial crisis period of 2007−2008, forward points were bias far away from what IRP would have suggested. As shown in Figure 4-11, where 3-month dollar LIBOR is compared to the implied dollar interest rate extracted from the forward market for EUR/USD, LIBOR rates were less than forward-implied rates. In the middle of Sep. 2008 when the investment banking firm of Lehman Brothers failed—forward implied LIBOR rates extending hundreds of basis points over LIBOR rates.

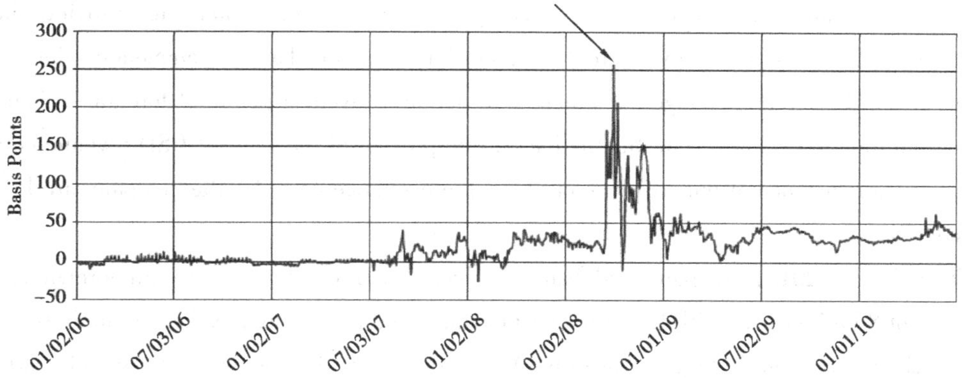

Figure 4-11 Departures from IRP

source: Bloomberg Finance L.P.

During the crisis, demand for dollar funding increased. Financial institutions borrowed in local currency, longed USD in spot, and shorted USD forward for local currency. There was a significant violation of IRP in financial crisis. The deviation from IRP may not have been a true arbitrage opportunity, but rather an illusion of potential profit, in that there was no actual way to execute the suggested trade. Arbitrage LIBOR against the forward market was not available as trading lines became scarce when counterparties scaled down or even closed trading relationships due to credit risks.

Besides credit risk, banks had concern about market panic, and had quoted LIBOR rates below actual market levels. Under the financial crisis, market would doubt banks' capital adequacy if quoting high rate. Given asymmetric information, quoting higher but correct interest rate would even have created suspicion that this bank was either in trouble or was simply desperate for funds①. So, during financial crisis of 2008, even there were measured deviations from IRP, it is not clear that those anomalies constituted actual profit opportunities.

§4 FX Forward in China

4.1 FX Forward Application in International Trade

As the top country in international trade, China has demand on FX forward for hedging. In October 2015, a large equipment export company came to a bank in China to make consultation on a business of forward value maintenance. The company was expected to reach a forward import contract of 8 million USD with an American exporter in Nov. 2016. Considering that the collected currency was non-local currency, the company wanted this bank to provide hedging instruments. Taking the company's actual situation into account, bank recommended the company with the forward foreign exchange settlement transaction to avoid a potential foreign exchange loss arising from foreign exchange rate fluctuations in the process of the forward USD revenue collection during the signature of the import contract. Thus the exchange costs for the company are locked in advance.

On 3rd Nov. 2015, company and bank conducted a transaction of forward foreign exchange settlement of 8 million USD with the term of 10 months, and at a foreign exchange rate of 6.5328. On 5th Sep. 2016, upon the USD payment to its American trader, the company immediately carried out the delivery procedures for transaction mentioned above. USD spot rate was 6.6794 on that day. Therefore, compared with such a spot transaction of foreign exchange settlement, this company hedged a potential loss of 8 million × (6.6794 − 6.5328) = ¥ 1172800 via the forward foreign exchange settlement transactions.

---

① Finch, Gavin, Elliott Gotkine. LIBOR Banks Misstated Rates, Bond at Barclays Says, Bloomberg News, 2008, May 29.

Usually, international traders long/short forward to hedge against payable/receivable in case of the appreciation of payable/the depreciation of receivable. In 2021, the scale of enterprises using foreign exchange derivatives such as forwards to manage exchange rate risks increased by 59% year on year.

4.2 FX Forward Trade Provided by Banks

FX forward in China is mainly about settlement and sale of foreign exchange between companies and banks. According to Regulations Governing the Purchase and Sale of Foreign Exchange, FX forward should be based on real international trade. FX forward in China means a customer enters into agreements with a bank to determine the currency, sum, term and exchange rate of foreign exchange to be sold or purchased and transacts the RMB-FX trading as per the currency, sum and exchange rate specified therein.

FX forward provides fixed cost and hedging. By getting into such forward, international trade companies may fix the costs in terms of foreign exchange to gain, which will serve to ensure currency value and facilitate the financial personnel of a company to accurately predict the cost and benefit.

Banks in China usually offer two types of forward: fixed date transaction and option forward transaction. Fixed date transaction means that the settlement date is a fixed date in the future. However, if a company will receive or pay any foreign currency at an unfixed date in the future, it may choose option forward transaction, which enables the company to flexibly choose a transaction date and to make good use of the fluctuation of exchange rate immediately.

Forward in China is very frequent under current account usage. Forward RMB-FX trading is applicable for foreign exchange receipts and disbursements, which may transact RMB-FX trading according to Regulations on Management of Settlement, Sale, and Payment of Foreign Exchanges. All the valid certificates required for RMB-FX trading shall be provided by the customer during the completion of forward RMB-FX trading upon maturity.

Forward RMB-FX trading under capital account in China is limited to the following 6 circumstances:

① Foreign exchange loan of a local Chinese bank;

② Compensation of foreign loan registered with the State Administration of Foreign Exchange (SAFE);

③ Foreign exchange receipts and disbursements in direct investment registered with the SAFE;

④ Foreign exchange capital earning of foreign-invested enterprise registered with the SAFE;

⑤ Foreign exchange earning of domestic institutions that go public out of China, registered with the SAFE;

⑥ Other foreign exchange receipts and disbursements that are approved by the SAFE.

4.3 Price of Forward RMB-FX Trading

The forward rate calculation in China follows the same principles before shared: spot exchange rate±premium/discount points; the trade price in one bank, however, shall be in conformance with the trade prices of all the local banks.

For example, given the spot rate of USD/CNY as 6.8218 and the USD premium is 45 points in 6 months. If a customer is obligated to pay USD 30000000 in 6 months later, the customer may enter into agreement with the bank for purchase of USD of 6 months later to prevent dollar appreciation. Then the bank will sell USD at the agreed exchange rate of 6.8263 (6.8218+0.0045), the transaction date of which will be 6 months later. If the USD/CNY exchange rate rises to 6.8275 in 6 months, the customer may obtain an underpayment of 30000000×(6.8275−6.8263)= ¥ 36000.

4.4 Development of FX Forward Market in China

China's steps to open its capital account are transforming the country's onshore foreign exchange forward market by allowing interest rates to replace expectations of currency trends as the main driver of the forward curve. China's forward curve increasingly behaves the same way as those in open economies where capital can flow freely across borders. That means that the interest rate differential is becoming the key driver of movements in the USD/CNY forward curve.

For example, in late Aug. 2011, one-year USD/CNY forwards were at a premium of 585 points, meaning that CNY forward was more expensive than CNY spot. But that situation has radically reversed showing the deep CNY discount at 1360 points. The divergence in CNY and USD interest rates in the following year closely matched the rise of the CNY forward discount, which implies higher interest rates in CNY than in USD. A key reason that interest rate differentials exerted a stronger influence on forward rates is China's incremental steps towards capital account opening in 2012. In Mar. 2012, Chinese authorities raised the long-term foreign debt quota allocated to foreign banks. In Apr. 2012, the quota for qualified foreign institutional investors (QFII) were scheme doubled. (the main channel for foreign investment in Chinese securities is QFII) Restrictions on converting dollars to RMB prevented investors from executing carry trades designed to profit from then higher RMB interest rates in China than in other markets. The ability to conduct such arbitrage is the reason that interest rate differentials determine forward currency prices in economies where capital can flow freely across borders. When China's capital account is fully open, the forward curve will fully reflect the differential. An expansion of the forwards market is an important step in helping China fulfill its vows to free up the RMB to market forces. Before 2010, a Chinese bank was required to have an annual foreign exchange turnover of at least $20 billion to apply for a license of selling currency forwards. Smaller Chinese banks that were previously barred from selling currency forwards can now partner their bigger, approved counterparts to offer forward contracts to clients.

Figure 4-12 gives a summary of FX forward traded in China since 2015. As forward contracts are usually based on real international trade, forward market may have more potential to reveal.

Figure 4-12 FX forward Monthly Turnover (**100million CNY**)

Source: collected and rearranged from SAFE

FX forwards are traded mainly in interbank market in China. Till Dec. 2021, there are 115 banks and financial institutions in China provide forward settlement and sale of foreign exchange to companies, according to SAFE.

The offshore RMB market officially launched in Hong Kong SAR in July 2010 and the offshore deliverable forward market was established two months later.

Shanghai Clearing House launched its central clearing service for RMB/FX forwards and swaps on 3rd Nov. 2014. This is a further step in China's endeavor to regulate OTC derivatives market and marks a significant development following the mandatory central clearing of RMB interest rate swaps on 1st Jul. 2014.

Shanghai Clearing has published a set of clearing rules and guidelines governing the new FX Clearing Service, including the Clearing Rules, the Risk Management Rules, and the Guidelines for Central Counterparty Clearing of RMB-FX Request-for-Quote Transactions.

In Apr. 2016, China's central bank revealed its short foreign-currency positions in forwards and futures for the first time, a decision that will help show the extent of the monetary authority's support of the CNY. Hedging demand from companies has increased since 2015 as the yuan became more flexible against the dollar. Banks in China keep providing such products as FX forward based on real needs when the forwards contracts mature.

§5 Non-deliverable Forwards

5.1 Definitions

The Non Deliverable Forward is a contract for difference of one currency against a value of USD, or other given currency. Transactions are made for future value dates for one currency against, normally USD at agreed rates. On maturity the currency flow is netted off against the agreed benchmark for fixing. The resultant difference in USD cash flows is either paid to the counterparty, or received from the counterparty. The counterparties to an NDF thus do not exchange the notional amount, they simply pay each other a cash sum based on the difference between the NDF rate and a reference FX spot rate① at the contract's maturity.

The NDF market began to grow in the early 1990s, focused mostly on emerging market currencies in Latin America. NDFs help investors in emerging markets manage their exposures to non-convertible currencies, or to currencies whose forward markets are restricted. Because NDF trading was primarily used as a means to hedge exchange rate risk for non-convertible currencies, market growth has been greatest for currencies of countries with increasingly active investors (portfolio and/or foreign direct investment) and countries with uncertain exchange rate regimes. NDF markets in currencies that were becoming increasingly convertible have disappeared. Throughout the 1990s, increasing investments in emerging markets in Asia and Eastern Europe further expanded the NDF market. By 1997 the International Swaps and Derivatives Association added provisions for NDF transactions to its definitions.

The buyer of an NDF is, like in a conventional FX forward transaction, is the buyer of the base currency (only notional amount). Take USD/CNY for instance, any trader buys this NDF, she has a long USD position and she must have expected USD is going to appreciate against CNY. Should the NDF come to maturity and the USD/CNY rate rises above the NDF rate, according to the spot CNY reference published by the China Foreign Exchange Trade System, the buyer receives a compensation payment from the seller. Foreign companies with asset exposures in the non-convertible currency or investors speculating on a depreciation of the non-convertible currency are natural buyers of NDFs on the hard currency, usually USD.

---

① This reference FX spot rate is an official fixing which is determined by a certain bank panel at a certain time. Market-based exchange rate reference of RMB has been published according to market requirements on each trading day since 24th Aug. 2015.

On the other hand, the seller of an NDF can receive a compensation payment from the buyer if the hard currency depreciated against the non-convertible currency.

5.2 NDF Risk

1) Market Risk

NDF is cash-settled currency forward, the instrument provides an offshore mechanism to hedge currencies against USD. Customers who use this instrument can lock in future exchange rates and hedge from FX market risk. Still, a party to an NDF is exposed to the risk that spot rate moves to an adverse direction. Major financial institutions are primarily involved in the NDF markets through their market-maker activities. They frequently offset the risk assumed through the broker market, with other banks and onshore market participants and exchanges. These market-making firms are exposed to market risk—the risk that offsetting contracts might settle at different rates in the event of a disruption. The market risk is the risk of a loss due to market price changes, here the exchange rate. The market risk of an NDF is the same as that of a traditional FX forward.

2) Credit Risk

The credit risk or counterparty risk is the risk of a loss due to a default of the counterparty. With NDFs there is the risk that the counterpart does not pay the compensation payment. This kind of credit risk is called replacement risk. It is the same for NDFs as for traditional FX forward.

Another kind of credit risk is the settlement risk, which only occurs with exchange transactions. If one party has already fulfilled its part of the contract, the other party fails to fulfill the remaining part, settlement risk arises. As there is only a cash settlement for NDFs and no exchange of principal, NDF may involve settlement risk.

3) Convension Risk

In times of crisis, the fixing rate in NDF can differ from the market rate considerably, turning a possible gain into loss. NDFs, when used as a hedging instrument, have additional risks which need to be considered. The main risk concerns the spot rate at which the contract settles. This spot rate is often a rate posted by onshore authorities or offshore organizations and there is no guarantee that NDF parties will actually be able to convert their onshore currency at that rate. In particular, in times of market crisis or when a change in exchange rate regime is increasingly likely, the likelihood that the NDF fixing rate is an indication of where the spot market is trading may be significantly diminished. This may affect the usefulness of NDFs as a hedging product because protection from the contracts would be most desired during episodes of market distress.

The process for determining the spot rate varies by currency and jurisdiction. For some currencies, the market exchange rate is determined using a similar process to that which determines LIBOR. For example, the reference rates for the Indonesian rupiah, Malaysian ringgit, Singapore dollar, and Thai baht are overseen by the Association of Banks in Singapore (ABS). For these currencies the ABS collects quotes from a panel of participating banks, excludes a proportion of the highest and lowest bids, and averaging the remaining values to determine the spot rate.

Probes into the LIBOR rigging scandal have raised concerns that spot rates on NDF contracts might also have been manipulated for some currencies, including the Malaysian ringgit and the Indonesian rupiah. The concerns are that traders could have attempted to move spot rates in order to profit when settling NDFs carried on their books. In the summer of 2012 the Monetary Authority of Singapore ("MAS") instructed banks to review their processes to set foreign-exchange rates used to settle certain currency forward contracts. As of November 2012, both UBS and RBS had suspended Singapore-based FX traders following internal probes into the manipulation of NDF rates and pending an investigation into the manipulation of the NDF spot rates by the MAS. Citigroup is also being investigated. In January 2013, a Reuters news article cited an unnamed source with knowledge of the inquiries and reports and stated that the probes found evidence showing that traders from several banks colluded to fix NDF rates in order to benefit their trading books.

5.3 NDF Trading Convention and Settlement

Suppose that an American company, A, will receive IDR 10^{10} (Indonesian Rupiah) three months from today as a result of an investment in Indonesia. Upon receipt, Company A is planning to convert the payment into USD at the then available spot rate; Indonesian authorities permit this spot market transaction. In contrast, NDF contracts are available for IDR, so in order to hedge the exchange rate risk between IDR and USD, Company A enters into an NDF with a bank in Singapore. The NDF contract specifies a notional of IDR 10^{10} a maturity of three months, and the agreed upon forward rate of 9870 which equals the current spot rate ($S_{USD/IDR} = 9870$). The spot rate for IDR is set by the ABS, which calculates the rate based on data submitted by banks (using a process similar to the one used to calculate LIBOR and other global reference benchmarks). Three months later, at maturity, this spot rate is 10201. The close-out payment of the NDF is calculated:

$$(10^{10} \div 9870) - (10^{10} \div 10201) = 1013171 - 980296 = \$32875$$

In terms of RMB, while the level of CNY is determined by market factors such as interest rate differentials, CNY NDFs are settled against the midpoint announced daily by the People's Bank of China.

Suppose $S_{USD/CNY} = 6.3010$, a trader expects CNY will appreciate more and buy CNY NDF (long CNY, short USD) of 1 month for USD 1000000.

If CNY appreciated to 6.2800 on valuation date, as shown in Figure 4-13 the settlement currency amount = $1000000×(6.2800÷6.3100−1) = $4777.07. The trader obtains $4777.07 from bank on settlement day.

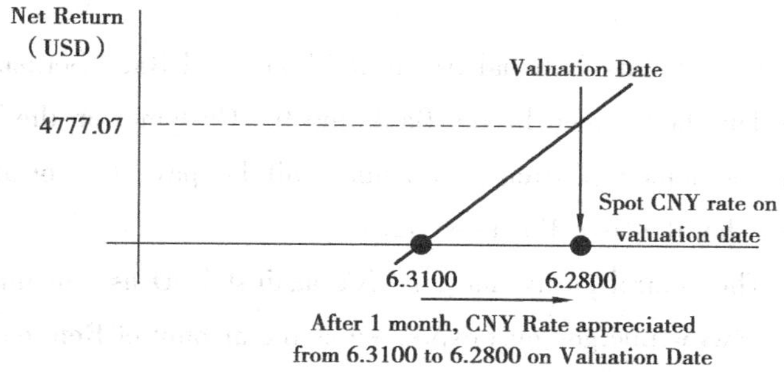

Figure 4-13 Profit-Loss

If CNY depreciated to 6.3300 on valuation date as in Figure 4-14, the settlement currency amount = $1000000×(6.3300÷6.3100−1) = $3159.56. The trader pays $3159.56 to bank on settlement day.

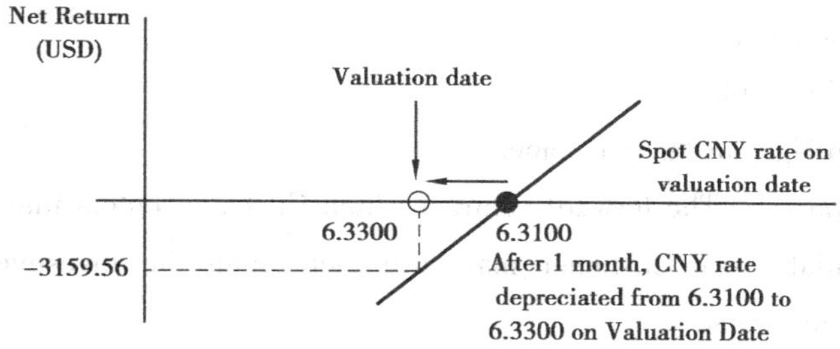

Figure 4-14 Profit-Loss

The rude is that settlement amount = contract size×(midpoint announced by PBOC−NDF)÷midpoint announced by PBOC

5.4 CNY NDF

Many banks in China offers CNY NDF. The following is CNY NDF provided by China Construction Bank

Minimum Transaction Amount: USD 30000

Transaction Tenors: 1, 2, 3, 6, 12 months

Forward Rate: The exchange rate (expressed as the amount of Reference Currency per one unit of Settlement Currency) agreed between the Bank and the Customer on the Trade Date

Notional Amount: The reference amount in the Settlement Currency agreed by the Bank and the Customer on the Trade Date, or if denominated in the Reference Currency, it means the stipulated quantity of Reference Currency divided by the Forward Rate

Reference Currency: Chinese Yuan (CNY)

Settlement Currency: United States Dollars (USD)

Settlement Currency Amount: An amount expressed in the Settlement Currency calculated as follows.

Settlement Currency Amount = Notional Amount×(1-Forward Rate÷Settlement Rate)

Settlement Date: The date agreed by the Bank and the Customer on the Trade Date as being the date on which the Settlement Currency Amount shall be payable (or if that day is not a Business Day, the next day that is a Business Day)

Settlement Rate: The central parity rate for CNY against USD as announced by the People's Bank of China at http://www.pbc.gov.cn (expressed as the amount of Reference Currency per one unit of Settlement Currency) on the Valuation Date

Spot Date: In relation to a CNY NDF Transaction, the second Business day after the Trade Date of such CNY NDF Transaction

Trade Date: The date on which the Bank and Customer enter into a CNY NDF Transaction

Valuation Date: The second Business Day prior to the Settlement Date

No principal protection

No callable by the Bank

Early liquidation right by the Customer

Embedded derivatives: The forward contract which Customer enters into is a derivatives

Maximum potential loss: Customer may lose more than the investment amount and the potential loss can be unlimited

By entering into a CNY NDF Transaction, the "Notional Amount", "USD/CNY Forward Rate" and "Settlement Date" are pre-determined and agreed between the customer and the bank.

On the Settlement Date, the transaction is settled by either party making a net payment to the other party, of an amount in USD which is proportional to the difference between the agreed Forward Rate and the Settlement Rate. The whole process does not involve the actual delivery of CNY.

2) Arbitrage Between CNY Forward and NDF

On 14th Oct. 2009 in Hong Kong market, NDF gives the following rates:

Table 4-8 NDF Offers

Period (in months)	Bid	Ask	Spread
1	6.8160	6.8270	0.0110
2	6.8020	6.8190	0.0170
3	6.7890	6.8060	0.0170

Continued

Period (in months)	Bid	Ask	Spread
4	6.7760	6.8010	0.0250
5	6.7548	6.7758	0.0210
6	6.7360	6.7590	0.0230
7	6.7186	6.7436	0.0250
8	6.7013	6.7283	0.0270
9	6.6850	6.7140	0.0290
10	6.6662	6.6972	0.0310
11	6.6474	6.6804	0.0330
12	6.6280	6.6630	0.0350

While in FX market mainland China, one can have CNY forward rates shown below:

Table 4-9 CNY Forward

Period (in months)	Bid	Ask	Spread
1	6.8019	6.8575	0.0556
2	6.8036	6.8598	0.0562
3	6.8037	6.8593	0.0556
4	6.7989	6.8552	0.0563
5	6.7958	6.8521	0.0563
6	6.7879	6.8436	0.0557
7	6.7814	6.8391	0.0577
8	6.7762	6.8339	0.0577
9	6.7686	6.8271	0.0585
10	6.7540	6.8224	0.0684
11	6.7598	6.8176	0.0578
12	6.7540	6.8125	0.0585

There is a gap between ask price in Hong Kong and bid price in Chinese mainland. Start from 5-month forward, bid price in Chinese mainland is higher than ask price in Hong Kong.

period	buy (ask in HK)	sell (bid in mainland China)	p/0
1	6.827	6.8019	-0.0251
2	6.819	6.8036	-0.0154
3	6.806	6.8037	-0.0023
4	6.801	6.7989	-0.0021
5	6.7758	6.7958	0.02
6	6.759	6.7879	0.0289
7	6.7436	6.7814	0.0378
8	6.7283	6.7762	0.0479
9	6.714	6.7686	0.0546
10	6.6972	6.754	0.0568
11	6.6804	6.7598	0.0794
12	6.663	6.754	0.091

12-month forward shows the greatest profit, if one buys from Hong Kong and sells to Chinese mainland. It turned out that by the forward value date 16th Oct. 2010, spot rate is $S_{USD/CNY}=6.6450$.

This trader has gained profit in Chinese mainland: 6.7540−6.6450=￥0.109.

She has suffered a loss in Hong Kong: 6.6450−6.6630=−￥0.018.

In total, she has a net profit as 0.109−0.018=￥0.091.

3) Some Research on Relationship Between CNY NDF and DF

Since the foundation of FX forward in China in 2005, the pricing mechanism of CNY forward exchange rate has been greatly improved. Although CNY forward transactions are still traded among large commercial banks, the forward rate is mostly determined by covered interest parity. Chinese foreign exchange dealers actually have been applying interest rate parity as the principle of calculating CNY DF since the business of forward settlement and sales was put into service by People's Bank of China in Apr. 1997. Literature shows that RMB onshore and offshore forward exchange markets are closely related as the degree of marketization of CNY DF market gradually increased. Still, DF and NDF have significant quotation difference between each other due to the institutional constraints in Chinese mainland①. Some research has found that NDF is a better estimator of future spot exchange rate as it meets the expectation for CNY future exchange rate and

① Ren and Ning (2004)

could quickly absorb market information[①]. Some papers even conclude that NDF was the key factor of CNY DF determination in the long-run[②]. However, after the foreign exchange reform, domestic CNY gained more influence power[③]. It is generally believed that as CNY DF is fixed mostly by covered interest parity while NDF is determined by market expectation, there is a gap between two forward rates.

§ 6 Optional Forwards

6.1 Definition

Optional forward transactions are only traded by retail customers. There is no optional forward in the interbank market. When bank offers optional forward, the optional forward transaction of foreign exchange refers to the foreign exchange forward deal that enables customers to settle with prescribed foreign exchange rate on any working day within a certain contracted period in the future. Customers can choose the settlement date by themselves.

Some banks such as Bank of China and Agricultural Bank of China provide optional forward transaction. One may find details of such service online: http://www.boc.cn/th/en/cbservice/cb3/201109/t20110909_1589840.html

http://www.abchina.com/en/corporate-banking/trading/foreign-exchange-trading/

Customers entrust bank to settle with the contracted foreign exchange rate within a certain designated period. When the settlement date is uncertain, bank can fix the foreign exchange rate of a certain period in the future at a level on the settlement date to fully lock up the exchange rate risk, and to reduce the probability of credit risk.

Contrary to traditional FX forward contracts, the settlement of an optional forward transaction is not on a specified day but within a specified period of time. The terms "optional" therefore relates to the date of settlement. Customers use optional forward for hedging when the exact date of payment is not known. As a cost for time flexibility, customers have to accept an unfavorable rate compared to the rate of a traditional forward contract. Professional FX traders thus prefer traditional forward deals and compensate any differences in the date of settlement with FX swaps that will be discussed in next chapter.

---

① Zhang and Wang (2005)

② Ye et al. (2006)

③ Huang and Wu (2006)

6.2 Pricing Optional Forward

Because that bank is offering time flexibility during optional forward transaction, bank requires higher price to compensate; customers therefore can only have the most unfavorable price under optional forward. More specifically, banks, as market makers, would follow the following rule to offer optional forward price:

(1) When there is a forward premium, choose the earliest possible settlement premium to calculate bid the rate; the latest possible settlement premium to calculate the ask rate.

For example, given

$S_{EUR/USD} = 1.0681/83$

6-month forward points are 97/98

9-month forward points are 151.75/155.36

What are the rates for an optional forward from 6 to 9 months?

Possible combination is

	Bid	Ask
Spot	1.0681	1.0683
6-month	97 ⇒***1.0778***	98 ⇒1.0781
9-month	151.75 ⇒1.0832	155.36 ⇒***1.0838***

Bank offers two worst rates to optional forward trader, from 6 to 9 months: 1.0778−1.0838.

(2) When there is forward discount, choose the latest possible settlement discount to calculate bid rate; the earliest possible settlement discount to calculate ask rate.

For example, given

$S_{USD/JPY} = 111.60/63$

3-month forward points are 41/40

6-month forward points are 90/88

What are the rates for an optional forward from 3 to 6 months?

Possible combination is

	Bid	Ask
Spot	111.60	111.63
3-month	41 ⇒111.19	40 ⇒***111.23***
6-month	90 ⇒***110.70***	88 ⇒110.75

Bank offers two worst rates to optional forward trader, from 3 to 6 months: 110.70−111.23.

6.3 Optional Forward Risk (from the perspetive of banks)

The optional forward pricing is based on the most unfavorable settlement date. The hedging of this position is also done for this most unfavorable settlement date. The bank assumes that at any other settlement date the result will be better. This assumption is flawed, because discount and premium may sometime turn into each other. When the exchange rate goes to opposite direction, bank is going to suffer from loss.

For example, given

$S_{GBP/USD} = 1.2467/70$

11-month forward points are 116/119

12-month forward points are 130/132

A customer sells an optional forward from 11 to 12 months.

Possible combination is

	Bid	Ask
Spot	1.2467	1.2470
11-month	116 ⇒***1.2583***	119 ⇒1.2589
12-month	130 ⇒1.2597	132 ⇒***1.2602***

Bank offers the bid price for the earliest settlement, i.e. 1.2583. Then bank hedge for 11 months assuming that the result will improve when customer settles on a later date as then bank could roll-over the hedging position with premium. But, if after 11 months the GBP depreciated, then GBP/USD is quoted with discount. If the customer settles the deal on a later date, the bank has to roll-over its position with discounts, which impairs its result.

Case Studies

Case 1 China to Curb Speculation in Forward FX Transactions

Updated: Sep. 9, 2015 9:36 AM

BEIJING (Xinhua)—China's new measure requiring commercial banks to pay risk deposit for forward foreign exchange sales aims to raise the cost of FX speculation and avoid excessive fluctuation, the central bank said on Sep. 8.

The People's Bank of China (PBOC) announced last week that commercial banks will have to pay a 20 percent deposit for their forward FX sales to companies as of Oct 15.

In forward exchange sales, commercial banks agree to sell a foreign currency to a company at a specific time in the future to help the company ward off risks from exchange rate fluctuations.

The new move is conducive to curbing excessive fluctuation on the FX market, preventing financial risks and promoting prudent operation of banks, the PBOC said in an online statement.

This measure was rolled out as forward exchange sales from commercial banks surged to three times as high as the monthly average of the first seven months in August. "It shows there were speculative transactions," the PBOC said.

On Aug. 11, the central bank decided to let the market have a greater say in forming the yuan's central parity rate against the US dollar, leading to a depreciation of more than 4 percent last month.

The measure is not capital control as it does not restrict transaction volume, nor does it require approval for each single transaction, the PBOC said.

The deposit allows banks to make preparations for their possible losses in the future, curbing speculative transactions and raising the overall cost, the central bank said.

Offshore one-year non-deliverable forwards contracts (NDFs), considered the best available proxy for forward-looking market expectations of the yuan's value. One-year NDFs are settled against the midpoint, not thespot rate.

There are three consequences of this move, one of which is already filtering into the broader market. The onshore market, relative to the offshore market, as an increasingly unbiased predictor of market value for the RMB takes a hit because of the higher hedging costs which translates into lesser demand for dollars.

Two, a potential for a US liquidity dollar shortage looms because not all banks have unlimited access to dollars, not to mention tenor mismatches. And thirdly, there will be a growing dissonance between the offshore and the onshore value of the Chinese currency, as long as these controls remain, adding to greater volatility on corporate balance sheets and to the frustration of proponents of a "unified value" of the RMB.

Of course, this will lead to a reduction in "hot money" capital outflows disguised as cross-border arbitrage activities as more US dollar buying will be pushed to the offshore market where the RMB is worth even lesser than onshore. But perhaps, what authorities will be rooting for, is that corporate confidence in the RMB will not waver.

Huszar, Z. R., Zhang, W., & Tan, R. S. K. (2016) explore the presence and the relative strength of market efficiency in the onshore and offshore RMB forward marketsby examining the covered interest rate parity. They have concluded that the offshore market is more efficient than the onshore market in conveying private information about investors' expectation. They suggest that by opening the offshore market to domestic participants and the onshore market to more foreigners, the forward rates may become more informative with a greater investor mix.

Case 2 Example of an Interbank Forward Transaction

The Following Dialogue is FX Forward Between Bank A and Bank B.

A: GBP 0.5 mio.

Bank A asks bank B about GBP/USD spot rate for half million pounds. In this stage bank A does not state if it will buy pounds or sell pounds, so bank B should give a two-way quotations: bid-ask price.

B: GBP 1.8920/25.

Bank B offers bid 1.8920 and ask 1.8925, which means that it will buy pounds with 1.8920 dollar, or it will sell pounds to bank A as 1.8925 dollar per pound. As the contract is half million pounds, the total dollar they are talking about is either 1.8920×0.5 million = \$ 946000 or 1.8925×0.5 million = \$946 250.

A: Mine, pls adjust to 1 month.

"mine" means that bank A is interested in buying GBP. It, however, plans to long GBP forward. With bank B's spot price, bank A is able to have an idea what the forward price may turn out to be, considering interest rates in Britain and in the U.S.

B: OK. Done spot/1 month 93/89 at 1.883 6. We sell GBP 0.5 mio. Val June 22. USD to my NY.

Bank B closes the deal by repeating the contract, which contains all the information of one formal FX forward contract between bank A and bank B:

contract size: 0.5 million pounds

forward rate is based on spot rate: 1.8925−0.0089 = 1.8836 dollars

seller: bank B with its branch in New York

buyer: bank A with its branch in London

value date is on 22nd Jun.

A: OK. All agreed. My GBP to my London. Tks, BI.

Bank A confirms the contract and informs its remittance details.

B: OK. BI and Tks.

Case 3 Example of an interbank forward transaction

The following dialogue is FX forward between bank A and bank B.

A: Cable Outright GBP 5 Mio Val 3 Month.

Bank A is asking 3 month sterling forward price.

B: SW 35/29 SP 88/94.

Bank B offers both forward points and spot prices. Notice that for spot rate, bank B ignores the big number. The forward points are in descending order, then should be deducted from spot rates.

A: Buy.

Bank A would like to enter a long forward contract with bank B.

B: 5 Mio Agree, To CFM at 1.4065 I Sell 5 Mio GBP Val 4 Jul 2018 My USD to B Bank NY Thanks and Bye.

Bank B closes the deal by repeating the contract, which contains all the information of one formal FX forward contract between bank A and bank B:

contract size: 5 million pounds

forward rate is based on spot rate: 1.4094−0.0029=1.4065 dollars

seller: bank B with its branch in New York

buyer: bank A with its branch in London

value date is on Jul. 4, 2018.

A: Ok Agreed My GBP to A Bank LDN. Thanks and Bye.

Bank A confirms the contract and informs its remittance details.

Exercises

Ⅰ. *Mutiple choice Question, choose All that apply.*

1. FX forward contract is (　　).

   A. a private legal contract　　B. customized

   C. a zero-sum game　　D. for hedging

2. Financial derivatives are powerful tools that can be used by management for purposes of (　　).

   A. speculation　　B. hedging

   C. human resource management　　D. profit maximization

3. To get outright forward quotes, one (　　).

   A. should add the forward point to the spot rate if forward points are in descending order

   B. should add the forward point to the spot rate if forward points are in ascending order

   C. should deduct the forward point from the spot rate if forward points are in descending order

   D. should deduct the forward point from the spot rate if forward points are in ascending order

4. Given S_a, S_b, R_a, R_b, R_a^*, R_b^*, the forward rates that follow the interest rate parity are ( ).

A. $F_b = S_b(1+R_b)/(1+R_a^*)$

B. $F_b = S_b(1+R_a^*)/(1+R_b)$

C. $F_a = S_a(1+R_b^*)/(1+R_a)$

D. $F_a = S_a(1+R_a)/(1+R_b^*)$

5. For any point above the IRP line, an arbitrager can ( ).

A. invest in quote currency country

B. invest in base currency country

C. borrow quote currency loan, long spot and short receivable forward

D. borrow base currency loan, short spot and long receivable forward

Ⅱ. *Numerical Work.*

1. *In the London FX market, $S_{USD/JPY} = 130.47/57$, the points of 1-month USD is 40/50; $S_{USD/EUR} = 1.8252/62$, the points of 1-month USD is 30/20. work out F_1(¥/\$), F_1(€/\$) and F_1(¥/€).*

2. *Company A expects to receive € 100 million 6 months from now and enters into a cash settlement currency forward to exchange these euros for U.S. dollars at \$1.0613/€. If market exchange rate is \$ 1.0615/€ at settlement, what is the amount of the payment to be received or paid by company A?*

3. *$R = 5\%$, $R^* = 8\%$, $F_{GBP/USD} = 1.458333$ and $S_{GBP/USD} = 1.50$. If round to two decimals, is there any arbitrage opportunity?*

4. *Read the following news on Mar. 27, 2015, explain the relationship among onshore RMB rate, offshore RMB rate and NDF.*

5. *Convert forward quotations expressed on a points basis into an outright forward quotation: Given $S_{USD/CHF} = 1.6557/68$ and the forward points as 25/15, solve for the outright forward.*

6. *Convert forward quotations expressed in percentage terms into an outright forward quotation: Swiss franc is selling forward at a 3.96% per annum premium over the dollar at the 3-month forward rate, $S_{USD/CHF} = 1.4800$, what is the 3-month outright forward quotation, F_3(Fr/\$) = ?*

7. $S_{EUR/USD}$ = *1.0681/83, 6-month forward points are 97/99, 9-month forward points are 151/156. One trader plans to buy EUR 8-month forward. What is the forward rate?*

8. *Given* $S_{USD/CHF}$ = *1.5000/10, annual interest rate of dollars is 5.875% and 6% while annual interest rate of Swiss Franc is 2% and 2.125%, considering bid and ask, what are the 6-month forward points and outright rates?*
According to the FX convention, base currency is USD and quote currency is CHF.

9. $S_{EUR/USD}$ = *1.0645/53, 3-month forward points are 62/63, 6-month forward points are 97/99. What are the rates for an optional forward from 3 to 6 months?*

10. $S_{GBP/USD}$ = *1.2778/84, 1-month forward points are 43/42, 3-month forward points are 69/67. What are the rates for an optional forward from 1 to 3 months?*

11. $S_{USD/CAD}$ = *1.3500/06, annual interest rates of Canadian dollar are 5.98% and 6.02%, annual interest rates of US dollar are 3.92% and 3.98%. If one Canadian company needs USD in 90 days, what forward price it could have should the IRP holds? If one US company needs CAD in 90 days, what forward price it could have should the IRP holds?*

Chapter 5
Foreign Exchange Swaps

Company A, which has good reputation in the U.S., plans to set a branch in Japan. It needs to borrow JPY to finance its business expansion. Unfortunately, local banks in japan have few information about company A and pre-loan investigation costs more than the interest bank can earn from this loan. Meanwhile company B, well established in Japan, happens to need USD. A and B may borrow local currency, and exchange loans to meet their financing targets. Of course, they need to come to an agreement on loan duration and make sure that USD amount is equivalent to JPY both at the beginning of the loan and by the end of the loan. A and B can apply a spot and forward exchange solution for international borrowing and lending problems. This spot plus a reversed forward solution is called FX swap. Given an increase trend of globalization, international banking amount is growing dramatically. Asymmetrical information is one of the main obstacles stand in the way of international expansion. FX swap, as a handy financial derivative, has proved to be quite efficient to solve asymmetrical information problem and to cultivate globalization.

FX swap is a simultaneous purchase and sale of identical amounts of one currency for another with two different value dates (normally spot to forward). An FX swap allows sums of a certain currency to be used to fund charges designated in another currency without acquiring foreign exchange risk. It permits companies that have funds in different currencies to manage them efficiently.

This chapter introduces FX swap knowledge about

- definition and conventions;
- main types;
- calculations;
- basic application.

§ 1 Quotation

1.1 Overview

1) Definition

A FX swap or time arbitrage, is a contract to long/short an amount of the base currency at an agreed rate, and simultaneously short/long the same amount of the base currency for a later value date to the same counterpart, also at an agreed rate. Let Q for quote currency and B for base currency, the mechanism of FX swap is illustrated in the following figure. Figure 5-1 shows that FX swap can be treated as a combination of a spot and a reverse forward:

Figure 5-1 FX Swap Mechanism

An FX swap is so-named because it swaps one currency for another over a given period, mostly within one year. The market risk is the interest rate differential over that period. FX swaps can be viewed as form of collateralized borrowing and lending, with the repayment obligation to the counterparty being the collateral, and the repayment being fixed at the FX forward rate at the commencement of the contract.

According to Bank of International Settlement, FX swap agreement is a contract in which one party borrows one currency from, and simultaneously lends another to, the second party. Each party uses the repayment obligation to its counterparty as collateral and the amount of repayment is fixed at the FX forward rate as of the start of the contract. Thus, FX swaps can be viewed as FX risk-free collateralized borrowing/lending.

FX swaps have been employed to raise foreign currencies, both for financial institutions and their customers, including exporters and importers, as well as institutional investors who wish to hedge their positions. They are also frequently used for speculative trading, typically by combining two offsetting positions with different original maturities. As FX swaps are generally considered a high-end financial instrument, used by large companies, high-net-worth investors, and institutional traders to control risk and gain a financial edge, they are not generally available as a tradable instrument at retail brokerages. As swap points determine the rollover costs associated with keeping positions open overnight, individual traders should look at the swap points offered by various brokerages, and consider this alongside other factors such as spread sizes and execution types when choosing who to trade with.

2) Evolution

FX swaps between corporations are said to be dated back to the late Middle Ages, when trades began to resurface in the Italian cities and the Hansastädte. In medieval Italy, when it was immoral to charge interest on a loan①, Lombards made compensation on interest by exchange rate difference.

One of the first swap deals nowadays was the IBM-World Bank swap of 1981. The World Bank wanted to borrow funds in German Deutsche marks and Swiss francs to finance its operations, but had borrowed its limit in these two countries and was blocked by authorities. At the same time, IBM had already borrowed large sums of Swiss francs and Deutsche marks, and sought to borrow dollars in the United States, but was hesitating because dollar interest rates were very high for companies there. The solution, invented by bankers at Solomon Brothers, was to have the World Bank and IBM swap their debts. IBM deposited its borrowed Deutsche marks and Swiss francs with the World Bank, and the World Bank borrowed U. S. dollars and then deposited them with IBM. This example shows what swaps could accomplish for global corporations: the deal circumvented national capital controls and shielded IBM from changes in the value of Swiss francs and Deutsche marks, while allowing the World Bank to borrow Swiss francs and Deutsche marks. This specific derivative contract transcended national regulatory barriers and created a cohesive global market mechanism.

FX swap has evolved greatly. The following chart shows that trading in FX markets averaged $5.1 trillion per day in April 2016 and this was down from $5.4 trillion in April 2013; then rallied back to $6.7 trillion in 2019 and continued growing to $7.5 trillion in 2022. The rise in trading was led by FX swaps. Spot trading fell to $1.7 trillion per day in April 2016 from $2.0 trillion in April 2013; and in year 2019 reached to almost $2 trillion. Trading in outright forwards rose by 43% to $999 billion per day. From 2019 the share of spot trades fell to 28% and that of outright forwards remained at 15% while the turnover of FX swaps accounted for 51%, up from 49% in year 2019. The trading of FX swaps, which is concentrated in maturites of less than a week, accounted for most of the overall increase in FX trading.

---

① As in the Middle Age, church was powerful. The Bible (Deuteronomy 23:19) requires: "Thou shalt not lend upon usury to thy brother; usury of money, usury of victuals, usury of any thing that is lent upon usury."

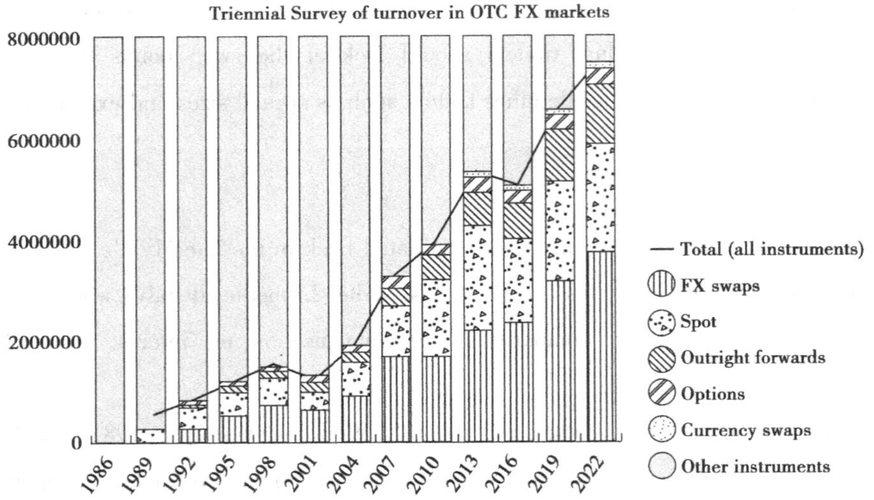

source: BIS

3) Functions

The main purpose of FX swap is to net cash flow gap caused by different maturity. It comprises of different values for currencies that have gone through the same transaction at that point of time. Although FX swaps originally were used to get around exchange controls and to give each party access to enough foreign currency to make purchases in foreign markets, market participants gradually arrange FX swaps as a way to enter new capital markets or to provide predictable revenue streams in another currency, typically as a hedge against currency risk exposure.

(1) adjust cash flow dates or cash position

A FX swap will often be used when a trader or hedger needs to roll an existing open FX position forward to a future date to avoid or delay the delivery required on the contract. Nevertheless, a FX swap can also be employed to bring the delivery date closer. The "rollovers" in chapter 3 is more technically known as tomorrow/next swaps, is applied to extend the value date of what was formerly a spot position entered into one day earlier to the current spot value date. Some retail FX brokers (top list of trusted brokers) will even perform these rollovers automatically for their clients on positions open after 5pm EST.

For cash position purpose, FX swaps are valuable to those who have liquidity in one currency but need liquidity in another currency. Typically, a client will buy spot and sell forward to generate liquidity in the currency purchased at spot. If a client exchanges USD for EUR at spot and simultaneously exchanges EUR forward for USD, the client has created liquidity in EUR until the forward date. A FX swap thus is an alternative to straight borrowing in a foreign currency.

(2) hedge or speculation

The decision to utilize a FX swap may be driven by the benefits of certainty in pricing. A corporation might wish to use a FX swap for hedging purposes if an anticipated currency cash flow, which had already been protected with a forward outright contract, was actually going to be delayed. In this case, the corporation could simply roll their existing forward outright contract hedge out by agreeing to a FX swap in which the existing near date contract is closed out and a new one for the desired date in future is opened.

As a means of converting debt issued overseas to home currency, FX swaps are widely used by financial and non-financial institutions. The product allows firms to diversify their investor base and benefit from potentially favorable funding costs elsewhere without exposing them to mismatches in interest rates and currency.

(3) business expansion: financing convenience

For the purpose of expanding themselves into the exchange market, most companies will try to fence their FX exposure. However, this is not always feasible. For instance, an Europe based company plans to raise CNY to set up a production plant in China, and to pay off the expense in one of its local regions. The majority of the plant yield is sold throughout Europe and only a small portion of its receipts will be denominated in CNY. To meet up to the repayment requirements the company can swap EUR generated from the plant's output into CNY.

FX swap thus can help bring two bodies, each who has an advantage in a specific market together. It enables both parties to get a comparative advantage of the local market.

A swap has two "legs," spot and forward, thus there are two value dates and two sets of cash flows. The two legs of a swap are based on the same spot rate, but differ by the forward points. In the first leg of a FX swap transaction, a particular quantity of a currency is bought or sold versus another currency at an agreed upon rate on an initial date. This is often called the near date since it is usually the first date to arrive relative to the current date.

In the second leg, the same quantity of currency is then simultaneously sold or bought versus the other currency at a second agreed upon rate on another value date, often called the far date.

FX swap deal effectively results in no (or very little) net exposure to the prevailing spot rate, since the first leg opens up spot market risk, while can be immediately closed down by the second leg.

4) Main Participants in FX Swap Trading

The FX swap market is a liquidity/treasury management tool. The most significant users by order of importance, are:

① Asset managers who want to invest in non-domestic markets without taking the FX spot risk, include classical funds managing all kind of assets pension funds, and life insurers. They usually trade swaps with classical maturity of 1 month to 3 months in EUR/USD or GBP/USD and can go up to 6 months in USD/JPY. They are lenders of the domestic currency against the foreign currency they need to fund.

② Bank treasurers who have the obligation to arbitrage between the pricing of their own funding/Certificate of Deposit per currency and the FX swaps markets, according to their needs in order to lower their overall cost of liquidity across currencies. The maximum maturity of the FX swaps they trade is one year.

③ Central banks who manage their reserves liquidity profiles, or act on behalf of other central banks. Central banks deal FX swaps with classical maturity of 1 to 3 months and they go up to 1 year.

④ Corporate treasurers that care about their respective treasury ladder per currency and the overall trade balance of each country. They are mainly from international trade companies, and both act like banks for their short term funding, and to manage natural cash-flows in the different currencies, i.e. their treasury position in the different currencies. The bulk of their flow is below 1 month, but they can go to 1 year and even beyond 5 years.

5) FX Swap, Currency Swap and Outright Forward

The trades that the interbank FX forward market uses are FX swaps, not to be confused with currency swaps. Currency swaps are contracts which commit R_1 counterparties to exchange streams of interest payments in different currencies for an agreed period of time and/or to exchange principal amounts in different currencies at a pre-agreed exchange rate at maturity. In a FX swap the interest rate differential between two currencies is taken into account in the forward points for the forward delivery date, while for a currency swap the interest rate differential is paid during the life of the swap at each payment date.

Figure 5-2 illustrates the cash flows in a typical FX swap (EUR/USD swap). At the beginning of the contract, party A borrows X · S USD from, and lends X EUR to party B, with S being the FX spot rate i.e. 1 EUR=S USD. At the expiry of the contract, A returns X · F USD to B, with F being the FX forward rate at the beginning of the contract, and B returns X EUR to A.

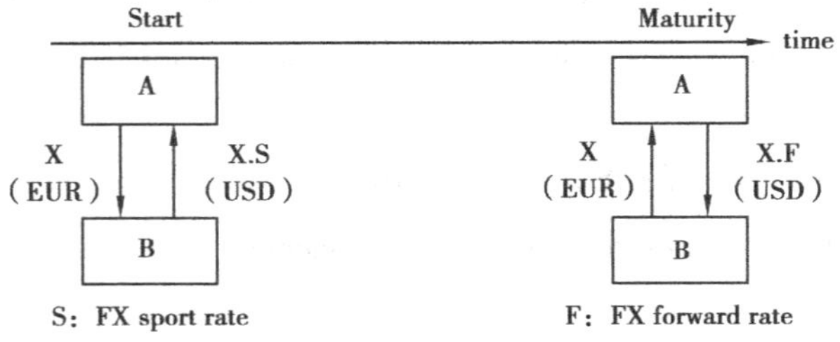

Figure 5-2 Cash Flow in an FX Swap

source: BIS

Figure 5-3 gives an example of currency swap where the interest is paid during the life of the swap quarterly.

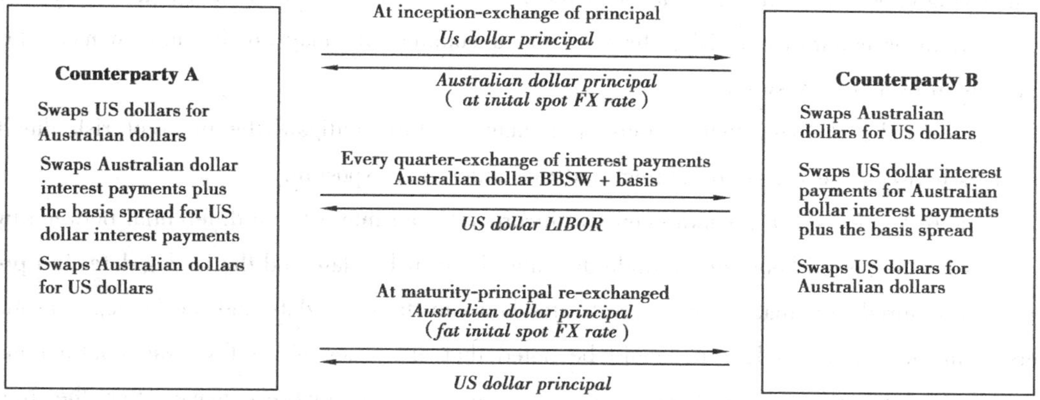

Figure 5-3 Cash Flows in a Stylized Currency Swap

source: RBA

FX swaps combined with some interest rate swaps are currency swaps. One company would seek to swap their cash flow for a fixed rate debt in USD denomination for a floating-rate debt that is denominated in EUR. These types of currency swaps are particularly common in Europe where organizations shop for the least expensive debt regardless of its type of denomination and then seek to swap it for the debt in their desired currency.

An outright forward is exposed to a FX risk for the full nominal amount, while in a FX swap contract the FX risk of the spot transaction is offset by the forward transaction. FX swaps thus are exposed to an interest rate risk rather to an FX risk.

Although forward points equal to swap points, outright forward price does not equal to forward price under a swap as demonstrated in Table 5-1.

Table 5-1 Difference Between an Outright Forward and a FX Swap

Quote Party in Outright	Quote Party in Swap
long: S_{bid}+/−F_{bid} point	short spot and long forward: S_{ask} and S_{ask}+/− F_{bid} point
or	or
short: S_{ask}+/− F_{ask} point	long spot and short forward: S_{bid} and S_{bid}+/− F_{ask} point

6) Risks Associated with a FX Swap Contract

Traders involved in a FX swap may confront 4 main risks:

① Market risk: the risk that exchange rate movements may adversely affect the owner of the contract. (Normally a FX swap contract will hedge against unexpected movements, however should an underlying exposure such as, an account receivable be cancelled, unwanted risk may arise).

② Credit or counterparty risk: the risk that a counterparty may not be able to meet their obligations to execute FX swap.

③ Basis risk: the risk that a transaction may not fully mitigate the inherent risk due to differences between the FX swap contract and the underlying exposure.

④ Interest rate risk: a FX swap contract incorporates an interest rate differential between two currencies for the period between the trade date and the near leg date and the far leg date. If a pre-delivery is required, fluctuations in interest rates between the trade date and the far leg date may adversely impact on the hedge. It should be noted that either leg of an FX swap contract may become in-the-money or out-of-the-money depending on how markets move after the trade date. This does not change the obligation to exchange currency on the near leg date and the far leg date at the fixed rate agreed to on the trade date. There is no cooling off period applicable to FX swap contracts.

7) Making an Early Exit

Sometimes, one of the FX swap parties may need to get out of the deal before the pre-agreed termination date. There are four ways in which an early exit from a swap deal can be achieved:

① Buying out the counterparty: as a FX swap contract has a market value, it is possible to terminate the contract by paying the market value to the counterparty. This way requires that both counterparties reach to an agreement or have such option specified in the swap contract before hand. It is not a universal feature of a swap contract.

② Selling on the swap contract: a FX swap has a calculable market value, which means that theoretically it could be sold to a third party. Still, this selling need the consent of the counterparty.

③ Using an offsetting swap: by entering into a new swap that is the opposite of the old FX swap, the effect of the first swap can more or less be canceled out.

④ Using a swaption: a swaption is an option on a swap. A potentially offsetting swap is allowed to set up at the time the original swap is entered into, and has the option of triggering it at a later date. This reduces the risks of entering into an offsetting swap at a later date when market conditions have moved against trader's original position.

1.2 Types

1) Classified According to Counterparties

(1) Pure Swap

FX swap includes two transactions: a FX spot and a reverse FX forward. FX swap maturities are negotiable for up to 10 years, making them a very flexible foreign exchange instrument.

(2) Engineered Swap

Engineered swap, also referred to manufactured swap, is the swap in which one buys from one trader and sells to another trader. There are more than 2 parties involved in an engineered swap.

2) Classified According to Legs

Like FX forward contracts, the far legs of FX swaps are regularly for periods of 1, 2, 3, 6 and 12 months from the spot value date. A swap has two legs in one trade in that there are two value dates and two sets of cash flows. The date can also be customized to meet a client's needs. Given the leg of a swap with the first value date is known as the near leg, whereas the leg of a swap with the second value date is known as the far leg, swap could be classified according to the dates the two legs are located.

(1) Spot Against Spot

This kind of swap settles before regular spot settlement date. It is popular in interbank market because it deals with short term currency transaction. The most traded spot against spot are:

① O/N: over night, the near leg is the very day of swap agreement is reached and the far leg is the next day. Let Q stand for quote currency, B for base currency.

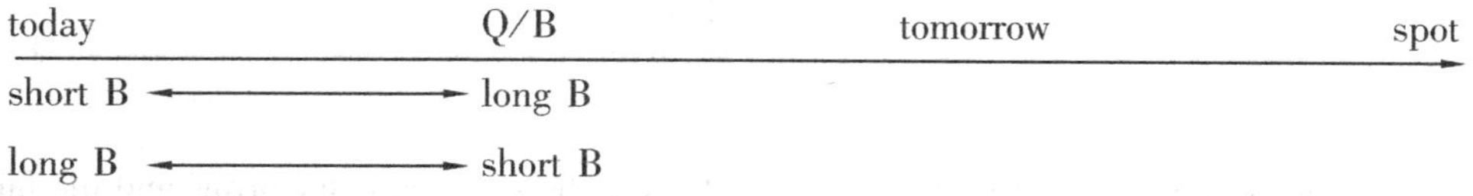

Individual traders often confront swap when leaving a position un-closed overnight.

As shown in the following figure, a trader did not close up her position of shorting one lot EUR yesterday, causing a \$16 over-night interest. If she closed her position today, a O/N swap (also known as rollover) come into being.

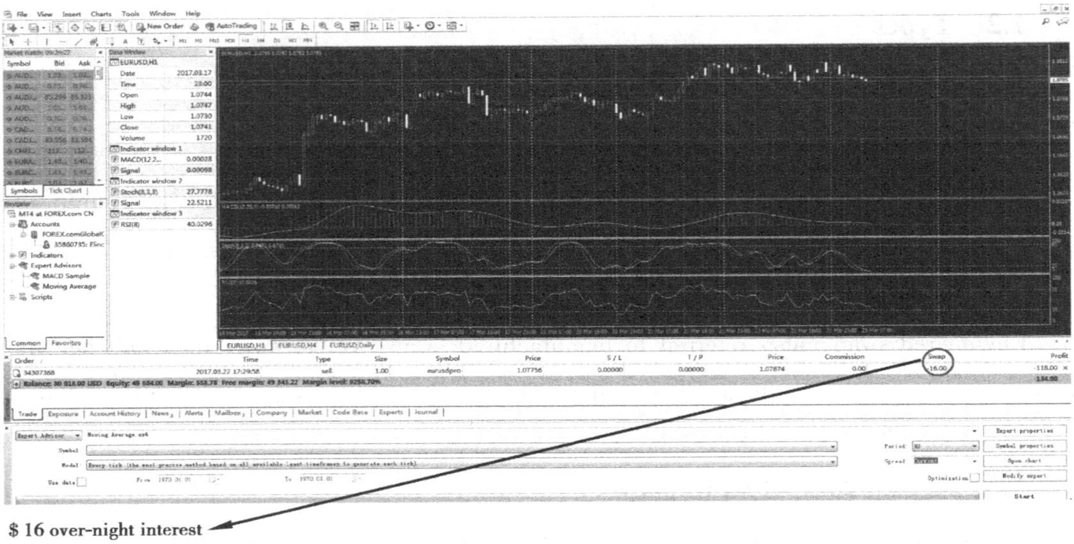

Figure 5-4 Swap is Essentially Interest Added or Deducted for Holding an Open Position

A FX rollover/swap is the interest added or deducted for holding a position open overnight (long/short). The rollover/swaps are calculated and applied on every trading night. On Wednesday night rollover/swaps are charged at triple rate as illustrated in Table 5-2.

Table 5-2 A Summary of Interest Payable for an Individual Trader's Open Position

Contract Signed Date	Settlement Date	Days Interest Payable/Receivable
Mon. ~ Tue.	Wed. ~ Thu.	1
Tue. ~ Wed.	Thu. ~ Fri.	1
Wed. ~ Thu.	Fri. ~ next Mon.	3
Thu. ~ Fri.	next Mon. ~ next Tue.	1
Fri. ~ next Mon.	next Tue. ~ next Wed.	1

② T/N: tomorrow next, swap deal is signed today, the near leg is tomorrow and the far leg is the day after tomorrow, which is the next working day after the near leg, usually it is on spot settlement date.

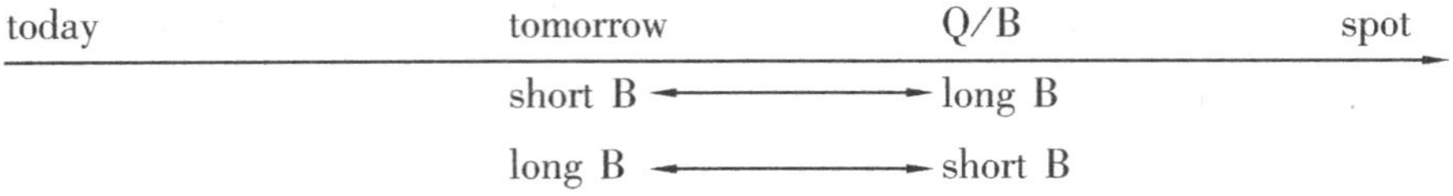

(2) Spot Against Forward

This kind of swap has the near leg as spot and far leg as forward. The most common spot against forward are:

①S/N: spot-next, the near leg is on spot settlement date, and the far leg is on the day after.

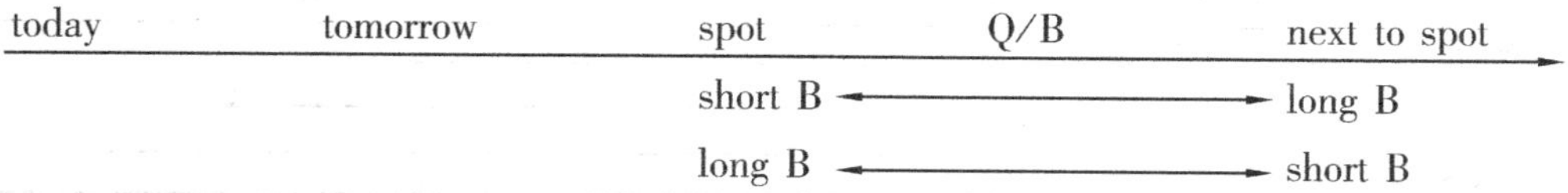

② S/W: spot-week, the near leg is on spot settlement day and the far leg is one week following the spot settlement date.

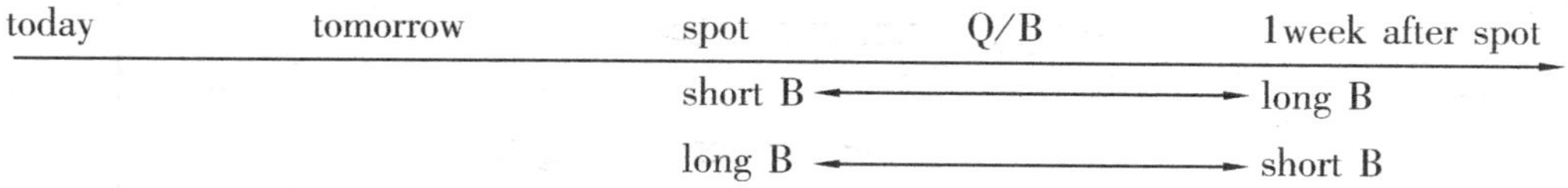

③ S/nM: spot-n months, the delivery of the currency n months following the spot settlement date. For example, one could buy EUR spot and sell the same amount as a 3-month forward. This type is the mostly traded swap in FX market.

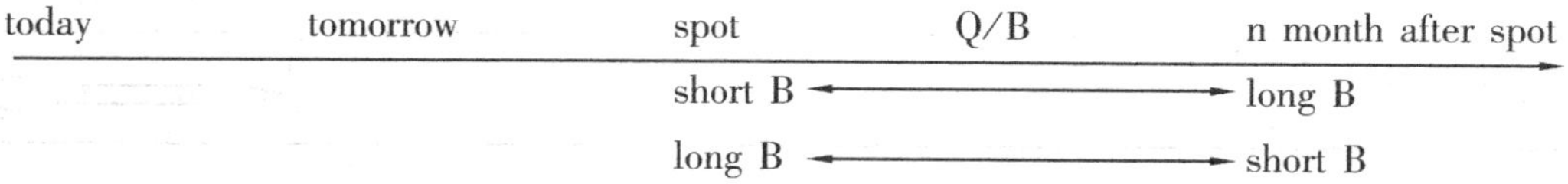

O/N, T/N, S/N and S/W are also classified as short dated swaps and S/nM is middle date while the following forward against forward is long date. Find Figure 5-5 to have an overview of short dated swaps.

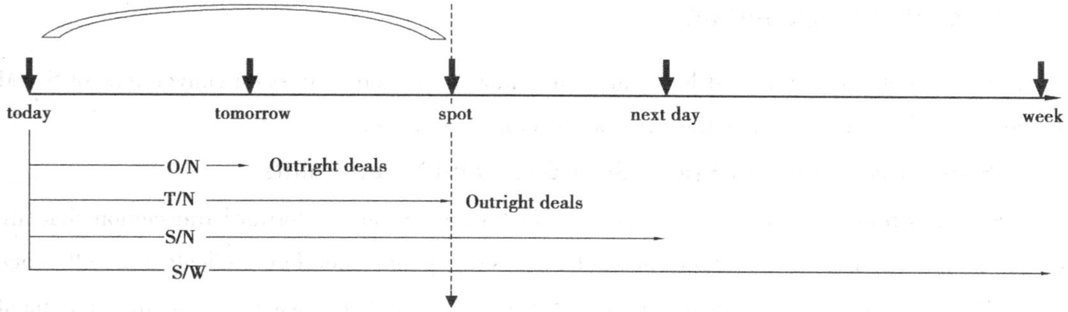

Figure 5-5 Trade Date and Settlement Date of Short Dated Swaps

(3) Forward Against Forward

Both the near and far legs are after the spot date is a forward against forward swap also called a forward swap. It is a swap between two forward dates and is equivalent to the combination of two separate swaps each based on the same spot.

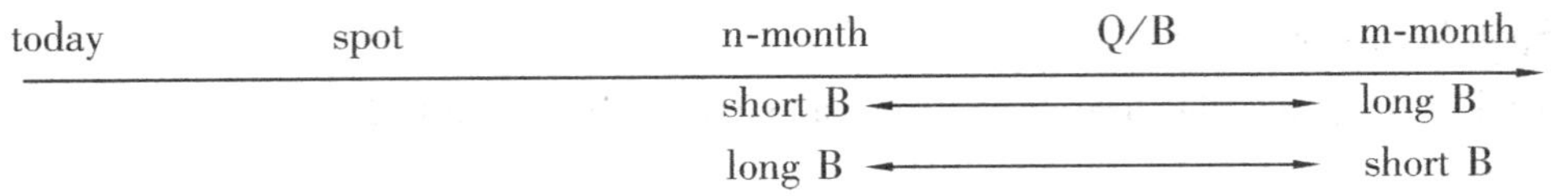

All together, FX swaps may take the following forms shown in Figure 5-6:

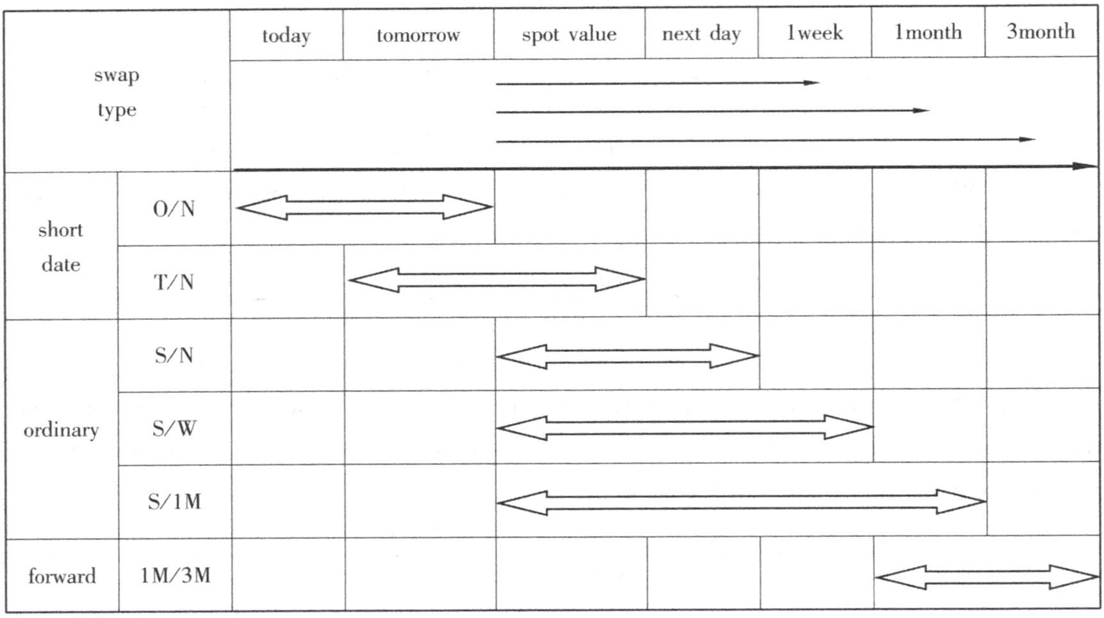

Figure 5-6　FX Swap Types

It is also possible to trade mismatched, uneven or non-round swaps whereby the amounts vary on each leg of the swap. These types of swaps may carry spot risk.

1.3 Ordinary Quotation

As S/*n*M is the mostly traded FX swap, the following section focuses on conventions of S/*n*M quotation. Short dated swap quotation will be explained in section 5.

1) Spot Price, Forward Price, Spot Basis and Swap Points

A FX swap trade consists of two legs: a spot transaction and a forward transaction that are executed simultaneously for the same amount, the swap points therefore indicate the difference between the spot and forward rates. Physical transfer of principal takes place on the settlement dates. The term "FX swap" can refer to the amount of pips or "swap points" that traders add or subtract from the initial value date's exchange rate, often the spot rate, to obtain the forward exchange rate when pricing a foreign exchange swap transaction.

Table 5-3 and Table 5-4 below are two examples of Reuters pages that help understanding.

Table 5-3 FX Swap Points

EURON=	-0.385	-0.335	CADON=	2.96	3.01
EURTN=	-1.25	-1.21	CADTN=	2.70	2.80
EURSN=	-0.41	-0.38	CADSN=	0.73	0.78
EURSW=	-3.29	-3.24	CADSW=	5.25	5.55
EUR2W=	-5.8	-5.7	CAD1M=	23.30	23.70
EUR1M=	-12.67	-12.42	CAD2M=	48.70	49.50
EUR2M=	-23.66	-22.66	CAD3M=	74.00	75.00
EUR3M=	-33.05	-32.55	CAD6M=	154.50	157.00
EUR4M=	-43.01	-42.61	CAD9M=	239.00	243.00
EUR5M=	-53.04	-52.54	CAD1Y=	317.00	322.00 ⇦
EUR6M=	-62.05	-61.65	CAD2Y=	580	605
EUR7M=	-71.2	-70.2	CAD3Y=	790	830
EUR8M=	-80.6	-79.6	CAD4Y=	900	950
EUR9M=	-89.20	-88.00	CAD5Y=	1 056	1 093
EUR10M=	-97.62	-96.37			
EUR11M=	-105.63	-104.38			
⇨ EUR1Y=	-112.60	-111.40			
EUR2Y=	-177.5	-172.5			
EUR3Y=	-215	-195			
EUR4Y=	-219	-189			
EUR5Y=	-214	-174			
EUR10Y=	-191	-91			

source: Reuters

In a swap, there are two counterparties: quoting party and calling party. Quoting party offers the swap points that are actually the forward points under a swap contract. The last digit of the points is in the same place as the last digit of the spot price. Calling party is usually the one who starts a trade by asking for quots. In a regular FX swap the base currency's volume both for the spot and the forward transaction is the same.

Unlike a FX spot, a FX swap trade is either a "buy and sell" or a "sell and buy". It is the action on the far date that is significant to the pricing in that quoting party buys on the left hand side and sells on the right hand side, similarly to spot. That is, quoting party buys at the bid rate of swap and sells at the ask rate of swap. In FX swap convention, the term "sell" or "buy" refers to the far(forward) leg as demonstrated in Table 5-4.

Table 5-4 Bid and Ask of a FX Swap

swap	bid	ask
quoting party	Sell+**Buy**	Buy+**Sell**
calling party	Buy+Sell	Sell+Buy

Because an ordinary FX swap is a combination of a spot and a forward, the bid price of swap offered by quoting party is usually the difference between the spot ask and the outright forward bid; the ask price of swap offered by quoting party is the difference between the spot bid and the outright forward ask. The corresponding swap for quoting party is therefore either "short spot and long forward" (bid price of swap) or "long spot and short forward" (ask price of swap).

Quoting party's actions under a FX swap is summarized as follows:

$SWAP_{bid}$:	$SWAP_{ask}$:
short spot: S_{ask} long forward: S_{ask} +/− F_{bid} point	long spot: S_{bid} short forward: S_{bid} +/− F_{ask} point

Take EUR/USD for instance, if $S_{EUR/USD}$ = 1.0676/77 and 1-year swap points are 112.60/111.40, then for a quoting party to "buy" a swap (Sell/Buy) includes:

- Short spot with 1.0677, quoting party shorts EUR in spot market for 1.0677 USD, and at the same time.
- Long forward with 1.0677−0.01126 = 1.05644, quoting party longs 1-year EUR forward with 1.05644 USD.

On the other hand, a quoting party to "sell" (Buy/Sell) swap includes:

- Long spot with 1.0676, quoting party longs EUR in spot market with 1.0676 USD, and at the same time.
- Short forward with 1.0676−0.01114 = 1.05646, quoting party shorts 1-year EUR forward with 1.05646 USD.

Swap	Bid	Ask
Spot	**1.0676**	**1.0677**
∵ in descending order, ∴ −swap point	*112.60*	*111.40*
1-y forward in swap	**1.05644**	**1.05646**
outright 1-y forward	1.05634	1.05656

Suppose that $S_{USD/CAD}=1.3389/91$ and 1-year swap points are 317/322, then a "buy" swap of quoting party (Sell/Buy) includes:

- Short spot with 1.3391, quoting party shorts USD in spot market for 1.3391 CAD, and at the same time.
- Long forward with 1.3391+0.0317=1.3708, quoting party longs 1-year USD forward with 1.3708 CAD.

On the other hand, a "sell" swap (Buy/Sell) includes:

- Long spot with 1.3389, quoting party longs USD in spot market with 1.3389 CAD, and at the same time.
- Short forward with 1.3389+0.0322=1.3711, quoting party shorts 1-year USD forward with 1.3711 CAD.

Swap	Bid	Ask
Spot	**1.3389**	**1.3391**
∵ in ascending order, ∴ +swap point	*317*	*322*
1-y forward in swap	**1.3708**	**1.3711**
outright 1-y forward	1.3706	1.3713

The spot price in a swap calculation is called spot basis. In practice spot basis in a S/*n*M swap could be the bid or ask or mid-point of spot, as long as it is agreed by both swap dealers. It is not important which spot price to be the spot basis, because what really matters in a swap is the swap point. Usually both counterparties choose the spot mid rate as spot basis. If the mid rate is an uneven figure, it is, by convention, rounded to the nearest round lot, which lies within the spot quote. For example, if $S_{EUR/USD}=1.0647/52$, then spot basis is set at 1.0650. That is $(1.0647+1.0652)\div 2=1.06495$ rounded to the nearest round lot. Given 6-month swap points as 62.05/61.65, the 6-month forward swap is quoted as

Swap	Bid	Ask
Spot	**1.0647**	**1.0652**
mid point	**1.0650**	
∵ *in descending order*, ∴ *-swap point*	*62.05*	*61.65*
6-month forward in swap	**1.058795**	**1.058835**
outright 6-month forward	1.058495	1.059035

2) Swap is a Better Offer

Swap is a better offer than spot+forward set because it requires narrower spread.

Outright forward price is not equivalent to forward under swap, even they share the same pair of points. Because that outright forward is exposed to exchange risk, it has wider spread than FX swap. To prove, given the following data

	Bid	Ask
Spot	b	a
Points	x	y

(1) if $x<y$

To make sure the swap spread is positive, x and y are quoted to let $(b+y)-(a+x)>0$

If $x<y<b<a$ and $(b+y)-(a+x)>0$	Bid	Ask	Spread
outright forward price	$b+x$	$a+y$	$a-b+y-x$
forward under swap	$a+x$	$b+y$	$b-a+y-x$
take mid-point or S_b or S_a as spot basis	$\frac{a+b}{2}+x$ or S_b+x or S_a+x	$\frac{a+b}{2}+y$ or S_b+y or S_a+y	$y-x$

outright forward spread-swap spread $=(a-b+y-x)-(y-x)=a-b>0$;

or outright forward spread-swap spread $=(a-b+y-x)-(b-a+y-x)=2(a-b)>0$.

In both cases, outright forward spread>swap spread

(2) If $x>y$

To make sure the spread is positive, x and y are quoted to let $(a-x)-(b-y)>0$

If $y<x<b<a$ and $(a-x)-(b-y)>0$	Bid	Ask	Spread
outright forward price	$b-x$	$a-y$	$a-b+x-y$
forward under swap	$a-x$	$b-y$	$b-a+x-y$
take mid-point or S_b or S_a as spot basis	$\frac{a+b}{2}-x$ or S_b-x or S_a-x	$\frac{a+b}{2}-y$ or S_b-y or S_a-y	$x-y$

outright forward spread−swap spread $=(a-b+x-y)-(x-y)=a-b>0$;

or outright forward spread−swap spread $=(a-b+x-y)-(b-a+x-y)=2(a-b)>0$.

In both cases, outright forward spread>swap spread

Although forward points equal to swap points, outright forward price does not equal to forward price under a swap. Outright forward spread is wider than swap spread because that outright forward is exposed to exchange risk, which is called exchange rate risk premium.

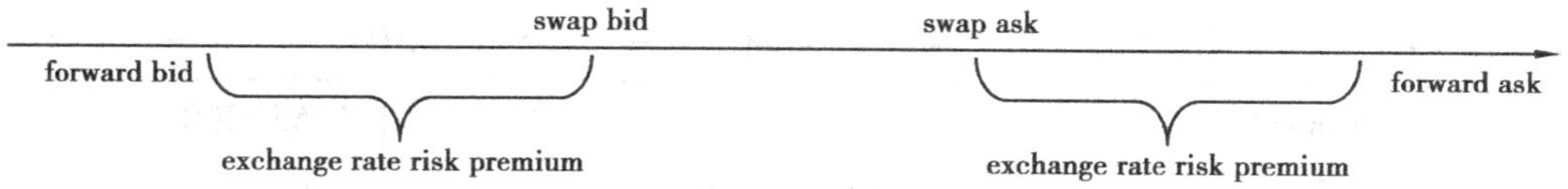

According to the above analysis, one can conclude that:

① A FX swap is a pair of offsetting FX transactions for different value dates, mature at the same time and on the same deal ticket with the same counterpart.

② swap trader is actually borrowing one currency for one period of time and lending the other currency over the same time length.

③ the FX swap is a pair of money market deals effected by means of FX transactions.

④ at the bid rate of swap the quoting party buys the swap (short spot and long forward) while the calling party sells the swap (long spot and short forward); at the ask rate of swap the quoting party sells the swap (long spot and short forward) while the calling party buys the swap (short spot and long forward).

Today		Near Leg: Spot	Far Leg: Forward
sign	quoting buy swap (S/B)	short	long
a	price	$S_{mid-point}$	$S_{mid-point}$ +/− F_{bid} point
swap	calling sell swap (B/S)	long	short

Today		Near Leg: Spot	Far Leg: Forward
sign	quoting sell swap (B/S)	long	short
a	price	$S_{mid-point}$	$S_{mid-point}$ +/− F_{ask} point
swap	calling buy swap (S/B)	short	long

1.4 Cash Flow of FX Swap

Suppose that a calling party holds the following position about EUR/USD swap.

	Bid	Ask
Spot	1.1548	1.1552
12-month swap point	112	110
outright forward price under swap	1.1438	1.1440

If this calling party wants to sell 12-month swap for 10 million EUR at -112 point, that is, she longs EUR spot at $(1.1548+1.1552)\div 2=1.1550$ against shorts 12-month forward at $1.1550-0.0112=1.1438$.

The cash flow associates with this swap is shown in Figure 5-7.

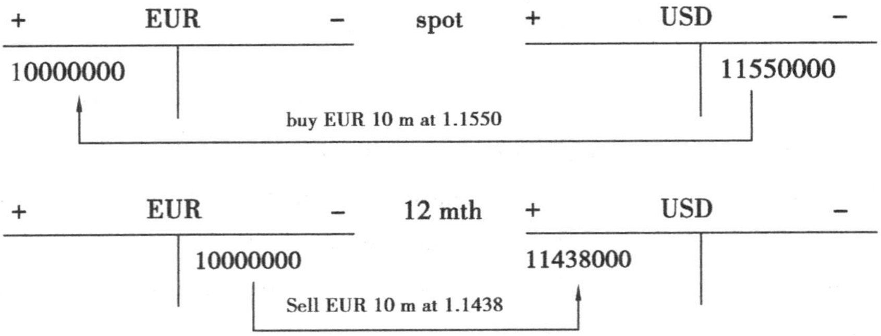

Figure 5-7 Cash Flow of a Calling Party Sells 12-month EUR Swap

1.5 Cost and Revenue of FX Swap

Given $S_{GBP/USD}=1.5020/30$ and 1-month swap point as 40/60

Swap	Bid	Ask
Spot	**1.5020**	**1.5030**
∵ in ascending order, ∴ +swap point	*40*	*60*
1-month forward in swap	**1.5070**	**1.5080**

This offer indicates a 60 pips' revenue with cost of 40 pips.

If a calling party longs spot and shorts forward for 1 million GBP, then the quoting party shorts spot at 1.5030 USD and longs forward at 1.5070 USD. Quoting party gets $(1.5030 \times 1$

million) USD in her short position and pays (1.5070 × 1 million) USD for her long position. In total, quoting party should pay calling party 4000 USD in this swap. This 4000 USD is the cost of quoting party in this FX swap.

If a calling party shorts spot and longs forward for 1 million GBP, then the quoting party longs spot at 1.5020 USD and shorts forward at 1.5080 USD. Quoting party pays (1.5020 × 1 million) USD for her long position and gets (1.5080×1 million) USD from her short position. Eventually quoting party gains 6000 USD from calling party. This 6000 USD is the revenue of quoting party in this FX swap.

Given $S_{USD/CAD}$ = 1.4060/70 and 3-month swap point as 45/40

Swap	Bid	Ask
Spot	**1.4060**	**1.4070**
∵ *in descending order*, ∴ *-swap point*	*45*	*40*
3-month forward in swap	**1.4025**	**1.4020**

Quoting party in this case has revenue of 45 pips and cost of 40 pips.

According to the IRP, the low interest rate currency usually trades at a premium to the high interest rate currency in the forward market. If base currency is at premium, the quote currency offers higher interest than the base currency. The bid of swap requires a short position in spot and a long position in forward. Exchanging base currency for quote currency can bring high interest gain. The revenue and cost derived here are not real profit or loss of quoting party, because that the swap cost in FX market would be compensated by interest gain in money market while the revenue of the swap in FX market suffers interest forgone in money market.

In general, between the two swap points, the smaller one is the pips that the quoting party should pay to the calling party and the bigger one is the pips that the quoting party gains from the calling party. Or, when base currency is at premium, the left-hand side point in swap is the cost of quoting party in shorting spot and longing forward; the right-hand side point in swap is the revenue of quoting party in longing spot and shorting forward. When base currency is at discount, the left-hand side point in swap is the revenue of quoting party in shorting spot and longing forward; the right-hand side point in swap is the cost of quoting party in longing spot and shorting forward.

In perspective of calling party, when long spot and short forward (Buy/Sell), it is the left-hand point that applies. If base currency is at premium, calling party profits; if base currency is at discount, calling party looses.

When calling party short spot and long forward (Sell/Buy), it is the right-hand point that applies. If base currency is at premium, calling party looses; if base currency is at premium, calling party profits.

Revenue and cost thus could be obtained by multiplying swap points with the base currency volume.

§2 FX Swap Price Determination

The difference between the forward rate and the spot rate for a particular currency pair when expressed in pips is typically known as the swap points.

Two methods are frequently applied to measure swap point, both based on interest rate difference.

2.1 IRP and Swap Point Limits

From the above explained swap quotation, one can see that swap points are in fact the cost/revenue for exchanging two currencies during one period of time. If the money market and FX market are liquid, then the cost/revenue is mainly determined by interest rates difference between base currency and quote currency. Interest rate parity, however, is not the only factor that determines swap points. Swap points are also affected by market demand and market supply. As a matter of fact, market forces may dominate swap point determination. Thus the following discussion constructs a range that swap points may possibly set in, and gives only part of the picture for swap points determination.

A very brief expression is swap points $=S\times(R-R^*)\times$swap days/360, where R is the annual interest rate of quote currency, R^* is the annual interest rate of base currency, S is the spot exchange rate in midpoint when swap is signed, swap days is the time length between near leg and far leg. Recall that the interest rate parity could be approximately expressed as $R-R^*=(F-S)/S \Rightarrow (R-R^*)S=F-S$, the swap points thus confirms with interest rate parity.

There is a simplified way to derive swap points from the perspective of quoting party. Suppose that one calling party is dealing with a swap of Buy/Sell, that is to long spot and short forward, then the counter party, quoting party, is trading a swap of Sell/Buy, that is to short spot and **long** forward. It means that quoting party is holding quote currency till far leg. During this period of time, this quoting party is earning quote currency interest R and paying base currency interest R^*, quoting party ends with interest earn as $R-R^*$. If denominated with quote currency, this interest rate difference could be expressed as $S(R-R^*)$. If $R>R^*$, then swap point is positive, base currency is therefore at premium (appreciation); if $R<R^*$, then swap point is negative, base currency is therefore at discount (depreciation).

Take transaction costs into swap point calculation, $R_a>R_b$, $R_a^*>R_b^*$, $S_a>S_b$, the cash-flows of money market profit/loss and swap points is presented in Table 5-5:

Table 5-5 Cash-flow Analysis of FX Swap

Calling Party Buy/Sell (Quoting Party Sell/**Buy**)		Calling Party Sell/Buy (Quoting Party Buy/**Sell**)	
Action	Cash Flow	Action	Cash Flow
borrow S_a units of quote currency, long spot	$-S_a$	borrow 1 unit of base currency, short spot	S_b
interest cost	$-R_a$	interest cost	$-R_a^*$
hold base currency till far leg, interest gain	R_b^*	hold quote currency till far leg, interest gain	R_b
money market profit/loss	$S_a(R_b^*-R_a)$	money market profit/loss	$S_b(R_b-R_a^*)$
short forward to repay loan	f_b	long forward	$-f_a$
sum (no-arbitrage principle)① ⇒	$f_b+S_a(R_b^*-R_a)-S_a<0$ ⇒ $f_b-S_a<S_a(R_a-R_b^*)$	sum (no-arbitrage principle) ⇒	$S_b+S_b(R_b-R_a^*)-f_a<0$ ⇒ $f_a-S_b>S_b(R_b-R_a^*)$
swap point bid<	$S_a(R_a-R_b^*)$	swap point ask>	$S_b(R_b-R_a^*)$

For FX swap, it is not important which spot price to be the spot basis. What really matters in a FX swap is the swap point. Take mid-point as spot basis, swap point bid<$S(R_a-R_b^*)$ and swap point ask>$S(R_b-R_a^*)$, where $S=(S_b+S_a)\div 2$. Make sure the time of interests matches with the swap.

Theoretically, $S_b(R_b-R_a^*)$ is the lowest possible bid price, and $S_a(R_a-R_b^*)$ is the highest possible ask price. Given $R_a>R_b$, $R_a^*>R_b^*$, $S_a>S_b$, any underlying swap must have at least one of its far leg prices be settled within the range $[S_b(R_b-R_a^*), S_a(R_a-R_b^*)]$.

Swap point limits could be quickly calculated by the above said short-cut method, however, it is only an approximation. More accurate methods to derive swap point limits need apply interest rate parity.

① according to no-arbitrage principle, FX premium/discount should be offset by money market profit/loss.

2.2 Outright Forward under a Swap Determined by Interest Rates Parity

Recall that in Chapter 4 interest rate parity implies that the hedged returns received after investing funds in two currencies should be equal. Using this theory, forward traders could determine the FX swap points for any given delivery date mathematically by considering the net cost or benefit involved when lending a currency and borrowing another against it during the period of time encompassed by the spot value date and the forward delivery date.

The fundamental equation used to compute the swap points is stated as follows:

Swap Points = Forward Price − Spot Price

Recall that the forward price calculation given in equation 4.5 as $F_n(q/b)=S(1+R)^n \div (1+R^*)^n$,

the swap points $=S\left[\left(\frac{1+R}{1+R^*}\right)^n-1\right]$

Take transaction cost into account, with B for base currency, Q for quote currency, given R_a, R_b, R_a, R_b^*, S_a, and S_b, the swap points are actually derived the same way as bid-ask price of forward: based on an assumption of no-arbitrage principle.

How a quoting party buys a swap is in fact the exact process of a calling party sells a swap: Table 5-6 presents the process to derive the bid of swap.

① Borrow quote currency loan for one period of time;

② Start swap, long spot and short forward (Buy/Sell), where forward has the same maturity as the quote currency loan;

③ Invest in base currency country, obtain principal and interest when due;

④ Execute far leg of swap for quote currency and repay the loan.

Table 5-6 Deriving Bid of Swap

Borrow $S_a\boldsymbol{Q}$			Repay $(1+R_a)S_a\boldsymbol{Q}$		
calling long spot ↓	quoting short spot		calling short forward ↑	quoting long forward	if $(1+R_b^*)f_b>(1+R_a)S_a$, calling party can apply covered interest arbitrage to gain arbitrage opportunity
1$\boldsymbol{B}$		invest in base currency for one time →	$(1+R_b^*)\,\boldsymbol{B}$		

Calling party is a price taker in the first 3 steps, and only becomes the price maker when quote swap point. More specifically, the corresponding cash flow is summed as follows.

	FX Market	Money Market	Base Currency	Quote Currency
near leg		① borrow S_a quote currency with R_a		$+S_a$
	② long spot at S_a		$+1$	$-S_a$
		③ lend base currency	-1	
	④ hedge by shorting forward at f_b		no cash flow	no cash flow
far leg		⑤ withdraw investment	$+(1+R_b^*)$	
	⑥ execute forward		$-(1+R_b^*)$	$(1+R_b^*)f_b$
		⑦ repay loan		$-S_a(1+R_a)$
Net Profit/Loss				$(1+R_b^*)f_b - S(1+R_a)$

According to no-arbitrage principle, the bid price of swap f_b quoting party offers should be no more than $S_a(1+R_a)/(1+R_b^*)$ or $f_b \leqslant S_a\dfrac{1+R_a}{1+R_b^*}$. On the left hand side, f_b is the price quoting party to buy a whole forward; the right hand side would be treated as the minimum cost a calling party spends on assembling a whole forward (buy 3 parts of the whole forward with the most disadvantage prices and assemble them up).

Recall that swap is a better offer than outright forward and the ask price of an outright forward is $F_a = \dfrac{1+R_a}{1+R_b^*}S_a$, then $f_b \leqslant F_a$.

The ask of swap is the price for a calling party to buy a swap (i.e. quoting party sells) is illustrated in Table 5-7.

① Borrow base currency loan for one period of time;

② Start swap, short spot and long forward (Sell/Buy), with the same maturity value and time as the base currency loan;

③ Invest in quote currency country, get revenue when due;

④ Execute far leg of swap for base currency and repay the loan.

Table 5-7 Deriving Ask of Swap

Borrow 1 **B**			Repay $(1+R_a^*)$ **B**		
calling short spot	quoting long spot		calling long forward	quoting short forward	if $(1+R_b)S_b/f_a > 1+R_a^*$, calling party can apply covered interest arbitrage to gain arbitrage opportunity
S_b**Q**		invest in quote currency for one time →	$(1+R_b)S_b$**Q**		

The corresponding cash flow of each step taken by calling party is listed below:

	FX Market	Money Market	Base Currency	Quote Currency
Near Leg		① borrow base currency with R_a^*	+1	
	② short spot at S_b		−1	$+S_b$
		③ lend quote currency		$-S_b$
	④ hedge by longing forward at f_a		no cash flow	no cash flow
Far Leg		⑤ withdraw investment		$+S_b(1+R_b)$
	⑥ execute forward		$S_b(1+R_b)/f_a$	$-S_b(1+R_b)$
		⑦ repay loan	$-(1+R_a^*)$	
Net Profit/Loss			$S_b(1+R_b)/f_a-(1+R_a^*)$	

For no-arbitrage principle, $S_b(1+R_b)/f_a-(1+R_a^*)\leqslant 0$

The ask price of swap f_a quoting party offers should be greater than $S_b(1+R_b)/(1+R_a^*)$ or $f_a\geqslant S_b\frac{1+R_b}{1+R_a^*}$. On the left hand side of the inequality, f_a is the price quoting party sells a whole forward; the right hand side could be treated as the maximum income a calling party gains from decomposing this whole forward (disassemble the whole forward into 3 parts and resale to the markets with the most disadvantage price).

Again, it has been proved that swap is a better offer than forward and the bid price of forward is $F_b=S_b\frac{1+R_b}{1+R_a^*}$, then $f_a\geqslant F_b$.

The no-arbitrage allows a range for forward price: $f_b\leqslant S_a\frac{1+R_b}{1+R_b^*}$ and $f_a\geqslant S_b\frac{1+R_b}{1+R_a^*}$. More specifically, f_b is the price quoting party to buy, this price should not be higher than calling party's cost $F_a\left(f_b\leqslant S_a\frac{1+R_a}{1+R_b^*}\right)$; f_a is the price quoting party to sell, this price should not be lower than calling party's gain $F_b\left(f_a\geqslant S_b\frac{1+R_b}{1+R_a^*}\right)$. Quoting party therefore should make sure the swap point offered overlap the theoretical outright forward price. Considering the result derived from the spread, as demonstrated in Figure 5-8 the no-arbitrage principle requires that at least one of the two legs of the swap locates within the theoretical outright forward spread, and the swap spread should not be greater than the underlying forward spread.

$F_a\geqslant f_b>F_b-(F_a-F_b)\Rightarrow F_a\geqslant f_b>(2F_b-F_a)$ or $(2F_b-F_a)<f_b\leqslant F_a$;

$F_a+(F_a-F_b)\geqslant f_a>F_b\Rightarrow(2F_a-F_b)>f_a\geqslant F_b$ *or* $F_b\leqslant f_a<(2F_a-F_b)$;

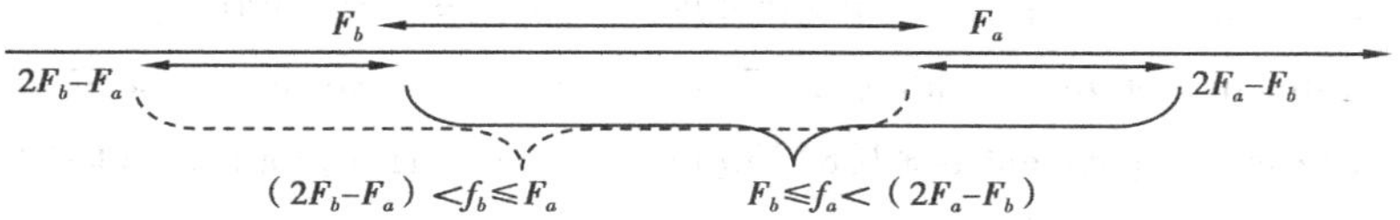

Figure 5-8 Swap Range

The above figure gives the range where the far leg of swap can lay. To derive a more accurate forward point under swap, at least 5 factors need to be taken into account:

① Spot exchange rate in the inter-bank market;

② Market conditions, for example, the degree of volatility in the spot exchange rate or forward exchange rate in the inter-bank market;

③ An allowance for quoting party's costs and risks;

④ The spread of swap is less than outright forward spread, $f_a - f_b < F_a - F_b$;

⑤ The size of the transaction, that is, the amounts of the relevant currency pair.

2.3 FX Swap Arbitrages

1) In FX Market

(1) A Numerical Example

If interest rate parity does not hold, FX swap can provide arbitrage opportunity. Suppose that a trader is facing the following quotes:

$S_{USD/JPY} = 88.40/50$;

USD interest rate $R_b^* = 8\%$ and $R_a^* = 8.125\%$ annually;

JPY interest rate $R_b = 10\%$ and $R_a = 10.125\%$ annually;

f_{12}(¥/$) = 40/50.

With the interest rates and spot prices one can work out the theoretical outright forward prices.

$F_b = S_b \dfrac{1 + R_b}{1 + R_a^*} = 89.93$ and $F_a = S_a \dfrac{1 + R_a}{1 + R_b^*} = 90.24$. Based on 40/50, however, the forward under this swap is $f_b = 88.85$ [(88.40+88.50)÷2+0.40] and $f_a = 88.95$[(88.40+88.50)÷2+0.50]. $f_a < F_b$, violates the no-arbitrage principle $f_a \geqslant F_b$. If interest rate parity be violated, arbitrage with FX swap can be obtained by the following 4 stpes.

① The trader borrows 1 million USD at 8.125%, so that at the end of 12 months the amount of the loan obligated reaches 1000000×(1+8.125%) = $1081250;

② The trader enters into a swap in the interbank market where 1 million USD are sold for JPY at 88.40. To obtain 88.4 million JPY, and to purchase the USD with JPY at $f_a = 88.95$ in one year, this trader should buy a swap (short spot and long forward);

③ The 88.4 million JPY are invested for one year obtaining 10% as rate of return, at maturity the value of the investment is 88400000×(1+10%)=￥97240000;

④ The investment matures, yielding ￥97240000, which is exchanged for 97240000 ÷88.95 = $1093198.43. The loan repayment is $1081250 only, producing a profit of $11948.43.

This, however, is not the final profit the trader can obtain (swap requires mark to market), and profit of this magnitude are rare if not non-existent. Modern communications and active tradings by banks, hedge funds, and other traders and speculators help to keep profit opportunities in check.

Nevertheless, any gap between quoting party forward spread and theoretical outright spread arises arbitrage opportunity. More specifically, recall that in chapter 4 the theoretical outright forward that meet interest rate parity are

$$F_b = S_b \frac{1 + R_b}{1 + R_a^*}$$

and

$$F_a = S_a \frac{1 + R_a}{1 + R_b^*}$$

the arbitrage arises when quoting party gives forward price of swap meet the inequalities as $f_a<F_b$ or $f_b>F_a$.

(2) when $f_a<F_b$

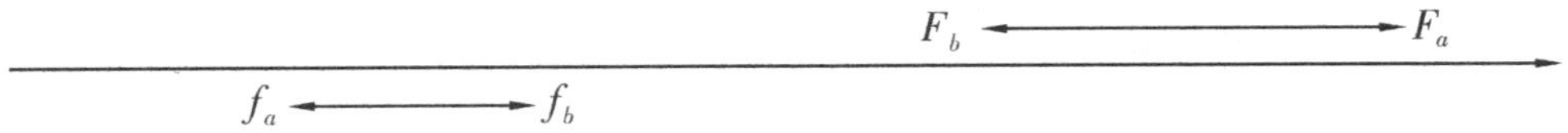

Under this circumstance, arbitrager can buy the whole forward from quoting party with the cost of f_a, then disassemble this whole forward into 3 parts and resale to markets for F_b, gaining profit of F_b-f_a.

The corresponding arbitrage process for calling party is ① borrow base currency; ② buy swap (short spot and long forward); ③ lend quote currency; ④ execute far leg of swap, pay up the loan and gain profit.

Borrow 1 $\boldsymbol{B}$			Repay $(1+R_a^*)$ $\boldsymbol{B}$		
calling short spot	quoting long spot	calling party buy swap	calling long forward	quoting short forward	$\because f_a<F_b$ $\therefore (1+R_b)S_b/f_a-(1+R_a^*)>0$ calling party gains risk-free profit with no initial investment
$S_b\boldsymbol{Q}$		invest in quote currency for one time	$(1+R_b)S_b\boldsymbol{Q}$		

(3) when $f_b>F_a$

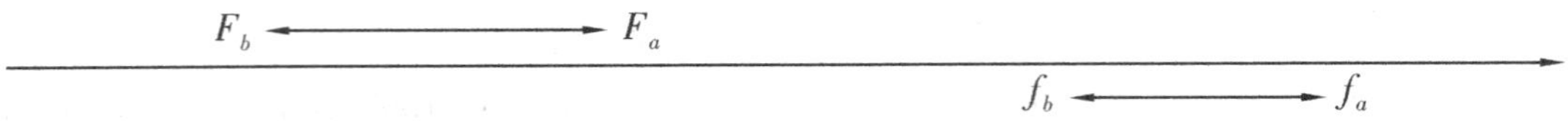

Under this circumstance, arbitrager is able to buy forward with low cost F_a, then assemble the parts into a whole forward and resale to quoting party for f_b gaining profit of $f_b - F_a$.

The corresponding arbitrage is ① borrow quote currency; ② sell swap (long spot and short forward); ③ lend base currency; ④ execute far leg of swap, pay up the loan and gain profit.

Borrow $S_a Q$		Repay $(1+R_a)S_a Q$	$\because f_b > F_a$ $\therefore (1+R_b^*)f_b - (1+R_a)S_a > 0$ calling party gains risk-free profit with no initial investment
calling long spot / quoting short spot	calling party sell swap	calling short forward / quoting long forward	
$1B$	invest in base currency for one time	$(1+R_b^*)B$	

To sum up: if swap is mispriced, calling party can arbitrage by purchasing swap when $f_a < F_b$ or selling swap when $f_b > F_a$.

2) Arbitrage in Money Market

Because that USD is the international vehicle currency, borrowers wishing to raise short-term USD have the option of borrowing directly in dollar money markets or raising funds in an alternative currency and exchanging these for USD in the foreign exchange market. In order to hedge the exchange rate risk that arises from borrowing in one currency and investing in another, investors will typically use a foreign exchange swap to exchange currencies. Under such a swap, two parties swap currencies in the beginning of the contract at the spot exchange rate and agree to reverse the swap at the forward rate when close the contract.

In essence, the FX swap is similar to a secured loan in the currency being received. Under normal circumstances, the forward rate is determined by the covered interest parity condition, which states that the cost of obtaining USD by borrowing another currency and swapping into USD (the implied USD interest rate) should be the same as borrowing directly in the dollar money market.

Figure 5-9 demonstrates the interest rate implied by FX swap and the interest rate prevailing in Libor market. During financial crisis, there is a significant difference between these two interest rates, i.e. it is more expensive to raise dollar in FX market than in money market. FX swap basis in Figure 5-9 is measured by comparing the cost of borrowing via the swap market with the cost to globally active banks of raising dollar deposits, typically proxied by dollar Libor given overnight interest is completely according to the interbank lending interest calculation. Historically, the basis measured in this way has been close to zero for most currency pairs, in line with the covered interest parity condition. A higher cost for obtaining dollars via the foreign exchange market is the evidence of a deviation from covered interest parity. One could take advantage of this deviation by borrowing from money market and lending to FX market if there is no capital control.

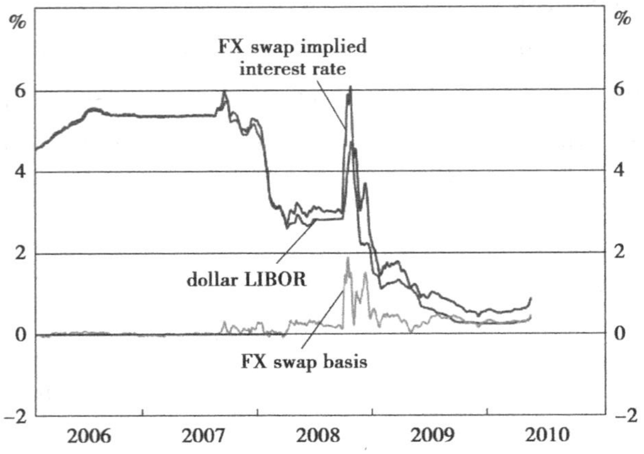

Figure 5-9 EUR/USD FX Swap Basis 3-Month Maturity, 5-Day-Centred Moving Average

sources: Bloomberg; RBA

§3 Other Calculations about FX Swaps

3.1 An Example of Mark to Market

The mark to market value of an FX swap is the sum of the present values of all cash flows which would occur if the swap were closed at the current market rate. An example will give a better explanation:

Given $S_{EUR/USD} = 1.1550$, 1 year (365 days) swap points are 112/110, annual interest rate of dollar is $R = 6\%$ and annual interest rate of euro is $R^* = 7\%$.

If a calling party buys a 1 year EUR swap 10million at −110. Some hours later interest rates are unchanged but EUR/USD surged to 1.2000. This leads to an increase in the swap rate to 114.30/112 (because she is longing forward, mark to market of this position is to calculate the p/l if she closed this position right now, i.e. short forward, thus she needs bid point of swap). Since this calling party bought at −110 (she spent 1.1550−110 pips = 1.1140 to long forward), she expects a loss of 4.3 pips (because her position is long forward, to close this position, she needs to short forward with bid price 1.2000−114.3 pips = 1.18857. In terms of far leg, she buys with 1.1140 and sells with 1.18857; in terms of near leg, she sells with 1.1550 but to close this position, she buys with 1.2000.) i.e. 10000000×0.00043 = $4300. The cash flow of the market to market at this swap of −114.30 is illustrated as follows

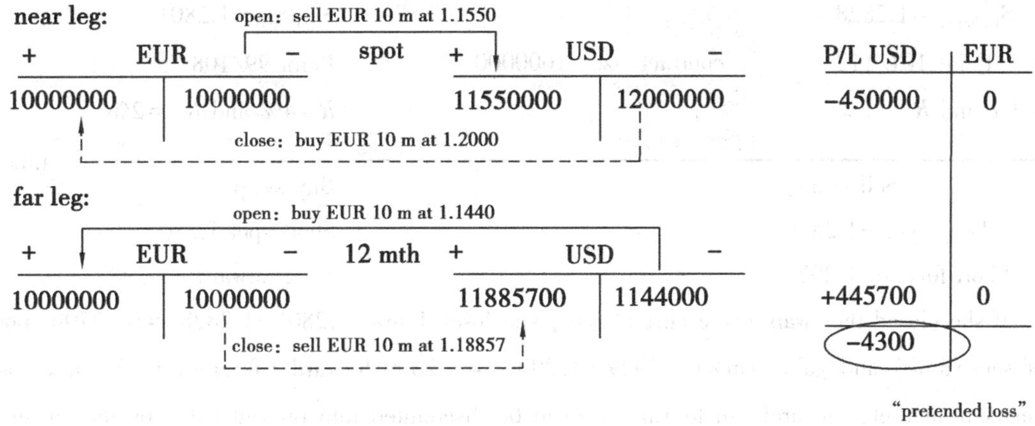

If she closed the swap at the current rates, she loses \$450000 spot and gains \$445700 forward. Marking to market requires present value. The profit in 1 year time thus should be discounted by the current dollar interest rate of 6%.

$$present\ value = \frac{Future\ Value}{1 + rate \times \dfrac{days}{basis}} = \frac{445700}{1 + 0.06 \times \dfrac{365}{360}} = 420141.40$$

Total loss of this calling party amounts to 420141.40−450000 = −\$29858.60 instead of the expected loss of \$4300.

buy swap at t_0	close swap at t_1	p/l in pips	p/l in \$	present \$ value	mark to market \$ value of swap
short spot 1.1550	long spot 1.2000	1.1550−1.2000 = −450 pips	−45000	−450000	420141.40−450000 = −29858.60
long forward 1.1550−110 pips = 1.1440	short forward 1.2000−114.3 pips = 1.18857	1.18857−1.1440 = 445.7 pips	445700	420141.40	

Let's illustrate another example.

At time t_0, $S_{GBP/USD}$ = 1.2828, 1 year (365 days) swap points are 101/112, annual interest rate of USD is $R = 4\%$ and annual interest rate of GBP is $R^* = 2\%$. If a calling party sells a 1−year GBP swap 1 million at 101 (she longs spot at 1.2828 and shorts forward at 1.2828+101pips = 1.2929). At time t_1, although interest rates are unchanged, $S_{GBP/USD}$ dropped to 1.2801. Accordingly, swap point changed to 99/108.

$S_{GBP/USD}=1.2828$ | contract size = 1000000 | $S_{GBP/USD}=1.2801$

Point 101/112 | | Point 99/108

$R=4\%$ and $R^*=2\%$ | | $R=4\%$ and $R^*=2\%$

→ time

Sell swap:

Long spot −1.2828

Short forward 1.2929

Buy swap:

Short spot 1.2801

Long forward −1.2909

If she closed the swap at the current rate, she loses 1 m×(1.2801−1.2828)=$−2700 spot (present value) and gains 1m×(1.2929−1.2909)=$2000 forward (future value). In terms of mark to market, the profit in forward need to be discounted into present value by the current dollar interest rate of 4%. She thus gains $\frac{2000}{1+4\%\times\frac{365}{360}}=\$1948.75$

Her total loss of selling swap amounts to 1948.75−2700=$−751.25 instead of pretended loss of 2000−2700=$−700. The mark to market dollar value of her swap therefore is $−751.25.

sell swap at t_0	close swap at t_1	p/l in pips	p/l in $	present $ value	mark to market $ value of swap
long spot 1.2828	short spot 1.2801	1.2801−1.2828 =−27pips	−2700	−2700	1948.75−2700 =−751.25
short forward 1.2828+101pips =1.2929	long forward 1.2801+108pips =1.2909	1.2929−1.2909 =20pips	2000	1948.75	

3.2 Residual FX Risk and Mismatched Principal FX Swap

At the very beginning of this chapter, the FX risk of the near leg is said to be offset by the reverse far leg. Strictly speaking, this is not quite true. The example above illustrates that the mark to market value of FX swaps may change along with the change in the spot rate even if interest rates remain unchanged. For simultaneous purchase and sell transactions there exist residual FX risk and interest rate risk.

Spot and forward transactions usually have the same nominal (matched principal swaps) quoted in the base currency. Buy and sell 1 million EUR for example means buy 1million EUR at the spot rate and sell 1million EUR at forward rate. If the nominal is the same, the residual FX risk is small but still exists.

Given, $S_{EUR/USD}=1.1200$, 1−year EUR/USD swap points = 102/112, 1−year USD interest rate is $R=2\%$, 1-year EUR interest rate is $R^*=1\%$. Recall that buying a swap includes short spot and long forward.

FX spot transaction is to short EUR for USD \$1120000;

In order to identify residual FX risk, the foreign currency should be discounted. FX forward gives $[(1.1200+0.0112)\times 1\text{m}]\div(1+0.02\times 365/360)=1131200\div 1.02027=-\$1108726$

Total net present value is what trader gains in spot deducted by the present value of what she receives in forward, it is also called USD exposure in this case: \$1120000 −\$1108726 = \$11274 or if exchanged into euro is 11274 ÷1.1200=€ 10066

Therefore, € 10066 should be bought in order to neutralize the FX residual exposure.

Generally, changes in the spot rate have two effects on an FX swap position:

① A change in the spot rate leads to swap value fluctuation at different points in time. Since future cash flows have to be funded, this may lead to additional profits or losses which is demonstrated in the example above.

② Since the spot rate is a part of the swap formula, a change in the spot rate will also cause a change in the forward points, even if interest rates do not change.

To cope with the residual FX risk, market follows a general rule: the FX position is the sum of the present value of all future cash flows in the quote currency.

One more example is helpful to illustrate how the residual FX risk of FX swap can be identified.

Given $S_{EUR/USD}=1.1550$, 1-year (365 days) swap points are 112/110, annual interest rate of USD is $R=6\%$ and annual interest rate of EUR is $R^*=7\%$, what is the residual FX risk or FX tail to buy 10 million euro swap at −110?

To identify the spot risk, one can first discount all cash flows of the foreign currency and then sum up the present values.

near leg: sell EUR 10 m at 1.1550

+ EUR −	spot	+ USD −	present value in USD
10000000		11550000	+ 11550000

far leg: buy EUR 10 m at 1.1440

+ EUR −	12 m	+ USD −	
10000000		1144000/ [1+ (0.06 × 365/360]	=-10783975
		spot exposure:	+ 766025

The given FX swap leads to an FX risk of USD766025 i.e. EUR−663225. In order to hedge against the risk, one should buy EUR663225 spot. The profit/loss on this hedge position offsets the profit/loss on the FX swap due to a spot change.

If one bought € 663225 at 1.1550 and $S_{EUR/USD}$ goes up to 1.2000, then profit on the hedge is $663225\times(1.2000-1.1550)=\$29,845$ which exactly offsets the loss suffered on the FX swap in the above example.

The open dollar FX position is then calculated as $\text{FX tail} = 11550000 + \frac{-11440000}{1+6\%\times\frac{365}{360}} = \$766025$

The FX position for this swap is \$766025 and can be hedged by longing EUR spot with this sum of money, \$766025.

The FX tail can be calculated with formula (5.1) and formula (5.2)

$$\text{To buy a swap, FX tail} = \text{volume spot} + \frac{Volume\ Forward}{1+R\,\frac{VaildDayNumberinSwap}{DaysOneYear}} \tag{5.1}$$

$$\text{To sell a swap, FX tail} = \text{volume spot} + \frac{Volume\ Forward}{1+R^{*}\,\frac{VaildDayNumberinSwap}{DaysOneYear}} \tag{5.2}$$

Although it is not important which spot price to be the spot basis when quoting a swap, the choice of the spot basis of matched principal swaps (FX swaps with the same principal amounts for the spot and forward transactions) does have a direct effect on the profit/loss of the position. When calculating mark to market swap value, spot basis does affect swap value.

Matched principal swaps have a FX risk which can be hedged with a spot transaction. If the rate of the spot hedge equals the agreed spot rate, the hedge will produce neither a profit nor a loss. If it differ from the agreed rate, there will be either a profit or loss.

More specifically, let's go back to the above example to explain the spot basis effect on profit/loss. Given $S_{EUR/USD} = 1.1545/55$, 1-year (365 days) swap points are 112/110, annual interest rate of USD is $R=6\%$ and annual interest rate of EUR is $R^{*}=7\%$, the profit/loss varies according to different spot basis in a buying 100 million EUR swap (matched principal) at −110.

The open USD FX position is calculated as $\text{FX tail} = -100000000 + \frac{100000000}{1+7\%\times\frac{365}{360}} = -€\,6626897$

To hedge, one needs to long spot EUR 6626897 against USD at the actual ask rate 1.1555.

The profit/loss on different spot basis is summed below:

spot basis	hedge rate	p/l in pips	p/l in dollars
bid 1.1545	1.1555	-10	$6627
midpoint 1.1550	1.1555	-5	$3313
ask 1.1555	1.1555	0	$0

To produce no loss nor profit, buying a swap need be hedged by longing spot at ask price S_a; selling a swap requires to be hedged by shorting spot at bid price S_b. The volume in hedge is called the FX tail.

Regular swaps as S/nM are usually matched principal swaps where the base currency is traded for the same volumes in the spot and in the forward transaction. There is mainly interest rate risks involved in such swaps, while the FX risk occurs as an unwanted side effect which is usually hedged by a FX spot trade.

Because that the present value of the forward transaction is always lower than the one of the spot transaction, to hedge FX tail, for a selling swap, one should short additionally in the spot market; to buy a swap, one should long additionally in the spot market. If the rate of the spot basis does not equal to the actual FX rate, there will be a possible loss. Therefore, to buy a swap, going long spot is needed to hedge the FX tail, take S_a as a spot basis would bring no loss; selling a swap, going short spot is needed to hedge the FX tail, take S_b as a spot basis would bring no loss.

The FX risk for both parties are exactly contrary, in order to hedge: one has to buy spot and the other has to sell spot. Thus both have the problem of potential risks if the hedge transaction can only be conducted with an unfavorable rate compared to the spot basis. It then became common practice to trade FX swaps with different principal amounts in the spot and forward transaction (mismatched principal FX swaps). If the forward volume equals the compounded spot volume, the present value of the forward transaction equals the volume of the spot transaction, the FX risk is zero.

Continue with the previous example, $S_{EUR/USD}=1.1545/55$, 1-year (365 days) swap points are 112/110, annual interest rate of USD is $R=6\%$ and annual interest rate of EUR is $R^*=7\%$, to eliminate FX tail, the amount of a mismatched principal selling a swap for 10 million EUR is calculated as follows:

Set FX tail = 0, then volume spot + $\dfrac{VolumeForward}{1+R^* \dfrac{ValidDayNumberinSwap}{DaysOneYear}} = 0 \Rightarrow -100000000 +$

$$\frac{VolumeForward}{1+7\%\times\frac{365}{360}} \Rightarrow \text{volume forward} = 100000000\times(1+0.07\times365\div360) = 107097222.22$$

The mismatched swap is composed of longing € 10 million EUR spot and short 107097222.22 EUR forward.

Interest rates changes, although are rare, can also affect swap value. Relevant calculation is left to readers.

3.3 Day-Count Convention

The day-count convention is the system used in mathematical finance when the next payment is less than a full period away. The day-count convention applies to swaps, mortgages and forward rate agreements as well as bonds. Many of the rules and definitions for applying the day-count convention are set forth by the International Swap Dealers Association, which provides documentation for a wide range of financial transactions.

Most money market calculate on an actual/360-day basis. The major exception is those denominated in the British pound, for which is on the actual/365 basis. Currencies that are or have been closely related to the British pound, such as currencies of Australia, New Zealand and Hong Kong region of China, also use 365 days.

The 30/360-day convention or 30/365 convention stipulates the month be treated as having 30 days in it, and the year will consistently be treated as having either 360 or 365 days. Swap markets using the 30/360 convention for the fixed rate of a swap include USD, EUR and CHF. Swaps in UK, Japan, Australia, New Zealand and Hong Kong Region of China use the 30/365 convention.

Actual/actual basis uses actual number of days in a month and actual number of days in a year for calculating interest payments. Date rolling (business date) conventions introduced in chapter 3 are a common practice to adjust non-business days into business days.

3.4 A FX Swap Case in Practice[①]

Company A plans to spend some CHF to buy a 3-month GBP from bank B. If bank B plans to take this trade with a profit margin of 35 pips, in order to hedge the position, what swap points is bank B supposed to quote given the following prices prevailing in interbank market?

$S_{GBP/USD} = 1.9010/20$

$S_{USD/CHF} = 1.6050/60$

① http://www.docin.com/p-332115484.html? docfrom=rrela.

3-month forward point of GBP/USD is 100/95

3-month forward point of USD/CHF is 50/45

As forward points are in descending order, outright forward is obtained by subtracting forward point from spot rate

$S_{GBP/USD}$	1.9010	1.9020	$S_{USD/CHF}$	1.6050	1.6060
Forward Point	100	95	Forward Point	50	45
$F_3(\$/£)$	1.8910	1.8925	$F_3(Fr/\$)$	1.6000	1.6015

Apply spot cross rate methods to work out forward cross rate

bid price of $F_3(£/Fr) = 1.8910 \times 1.6000 = 3.0256$

ask price of $F_3(£/Fr) = 1.8925 \times 1.6015 = 3.0308$

Bank B spends 3.0308 CHF to buy 1GBP and resales to company A. In order to gain 35 pips bank B should offer $3.0308 + 0.0035 = 3.0343$ to company A.

In 3 month, when forward is due, company A would like to extend this trade for another one month, given the following price, what would bank B offer?

$S_{GBP/USD} = 1.7310/20$

$S_{USD/CHF} = 1.5920/30$

1-month swap point of GBP/USD is 40/35

1-month swap point of USD/CHF is 15/10

An extension of forward makes a swap.

As swap points are in descending order, bid and ask price are obtained by subtracting swap point from midpoint of spot rate, $(1.7310+1.7320) \div 2 = 1.7315$ and $(1.5920+1.5930) \div 2 = 1.5925$

$S_{GBP/USD}$	1.7315		$S_{USD/CHF}$	1.5925	
Swap Point	40	35	Forward Point	15	10
$F_1(\$/£)$	1.7275	1.7280	$F_3(Fr/\$)$	1.5910	1.5915

Apply spot cross rate methods to work out forward cross rate

bid $= 1.7275 \times 1.5910 = 2.7485$

ask $= 1.7280 \times 1.5915 = 2.7501$

If company A closed up the previous 3-month forward, it will spent 3.0343 CHF to buy GBP and can resale GBP at spot, in swap, midpoint $1.7315 \times 1.5925 = 2.7574$ leading a loss of $100000 \times (2.7574 - 3.0343) = 27690$

§4 Forward Against Forward Swaps

4.1 Application in Practice

Suppose that one bank in Switzerland will receive 1 million USD in one month and it will pay 1 million USD in three month. Given $S_{USD/CHF}=1.6960/70$, $F_1(Fr/\$)=1.6868/80$ and $F_3(Fr/\$)=1.6729/42$, the receivable USD is at discount. To hedge against exchange rate exposure, this Swiss bank has 2 strategies:

- Strategy Ⅰ: spot+ outright forward

Notice that USD spot price is higher than forward, and bank has 1 million USD payable in 3 months, to hedge against payable appreciation, it can long this 1 million USD in forward market and short the same principal in spot market.

Short Spot	1.6960
Long F_3	1.6742
P/L	0.0218

To short USD in spot market this bank needs USD position. It may, at the same time, long USD in spot market. Besides, this bank has a 1 million USD receivable in 1 month, to hedge against receivable depreciation, it can short this 1 million USD receivable in forward market and long the same principal in spot market.

Short F_1	1.6868
Long Spot	1.6970
P/L	-0.0102

In total, this bank profits 1million×(0.0218−0.0102)= 11600 CHF from strategy I. This bank ends up longing $F_3(Fr/\$)$ and shorting $F_1(Fr/\$)$ to lock in 11600 CHF profit.

- Strategy Ⅱ: forward against forward swap

This bank could short $F_1(Fr/\$)$ to hedge exchange rate exposure of the receivable in one month and long $F_3(Fr/\$)$ to hedge exchange rate exposure of the payable in 3 months.

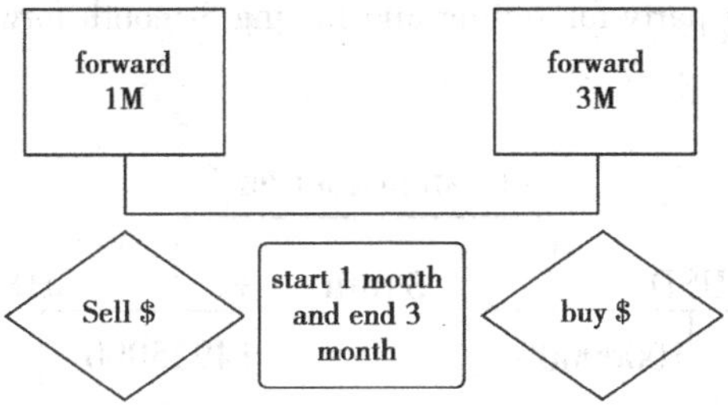

Short F_1	1.6868
Long F_3	1.6742
P/L	0.0126

In total, this bank gains 1 million×(1.6868−1.6742) = 12600 CHF from strategy Ⅱ. This bank ends up longing F_3(Fr/$) and shorting F_1(Fr/$) to lock in 12600 CHF profit, which in this case is better than strategy Ⅰ.

A forward against forward swap is an FX swap that both legs are in the future. That is, both FX transactions in this swap are forward transactions. It can be decomposed as two regular swaps with opposite spot transaction. For instance, a 1month/3month forward swap means two swaps: buy 1-month swap (short spot and long 1-month forward) and sell 3-months swap (long spot and short 3-month forward). As both spot transactions offset each other, the result of both transaction is to long 1-month forward and short 3-month forward.

Given $S_{USD/CHF}$ = 1.4995/05, 3-month swap points are 75/65 and 6-month swap points are 146/138. If the calling party intends to buy a forward swap, it is to short 3-month forward and to long 6-month forward, the calling party can have the following quotation:

	Bid	Ask
Spot	**1.4995**	**1.5005**
mid point	*1.5000*	
3-month point	*75*	*65*
6-month point	*146*	*138*
outright 3-month forward	**1.4925**	1.4935
outright 6-month forward	1.4854	**1.4862**

The cash flow of calling party for selling and buying 3-month forward against 6-month forward is shown below:

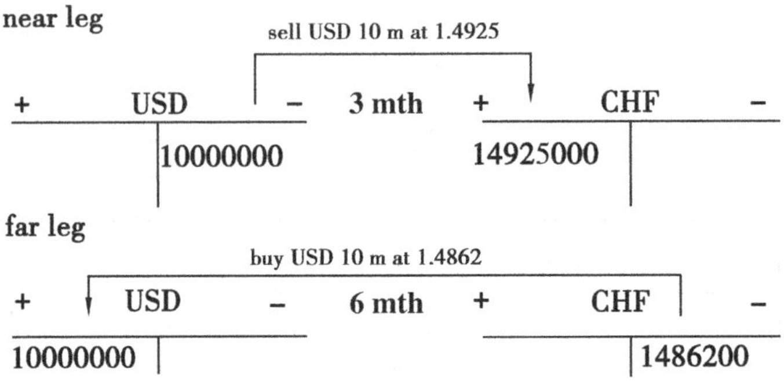

If the calling party plans to buy and sell 3-month forward against 6-month forward, it is to long 3-month forward and to short 6-month forward, the calling party thus has the following quotation:

	Bid	Ask
Spot	**1.4995**	**1.5005**
mid point	*1.5000*	
3-month point	*75*	*65*
6-month point	*146*	*138*
outright 3-month forward	1.4925	**1.4935**
outright 6-month forward	**1.4854**	1.4862

The bid price of the above forward swap is 1.4854 and the ask price of forward swap is 1.4935.

4.2 Construct a Forward Swap

Forward swap is composed by two forwards, its swap points are also calculated through two forward points. The forward swap points are the margin between the near forward transaction and the far forward transaction. The price can be derived by combining two regular swaps with reverse spot start. For example, given $S_{USD/CHF}$ = 1.4995/05 (mid-point is 1.5), 3-month swap points are 75/73, and 6-month swap points are 140/138. In perspective of a calling party, to buy a 3-6-month swap of 10 million USD is the same to effect the following 2 reverse spot start FX swaps: sell a 3-month swap at −75 and buy a 6-month swap at −138.

The spot transaction of the two regular swaps offset each other leaving the 3/6 forward swap, that is to sell 3-month at 1.4925 and to buy 6-month at 1.4862. The corresponding forward swap points are the margin between 1.4862 and 1.4925. The ask price of this 3-6-month swap is therefore 1.4862−1.4925=−0.0063.

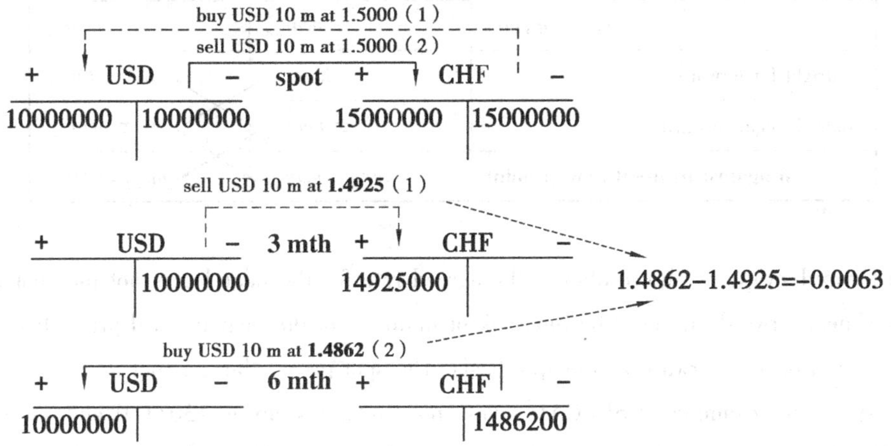

Similarly, the bid price of this 3 against 6 month swap is the calling party sells the swap. That is buy a 3-month swap at −73 and sell a 6-month swap at −140. The corresponding forward swap points are the margin between 1.4927 and 1.4860. The bid price of this 3-6-month swap is therefore 1.4860−1.4927=−67.

	Bid	Ask
Spot	1.4995	1.5005
mid point	*1.5000*	
6-month point	*140*	*138*
3-month point	*75*	*73*
outright 6-month forward	1.4860	1.4862
outright 3-month forward	1.4925	1.4927
3 against 6 month swap point	1.4860−1.4927	1.486 2−1.4925

To generalize, the n against m month forward swap point (m>n) could be derived as:

	Bid	Ask
Spot Price	S_b	S_a
mid point	S	
far leg point	far_{bid}	far_{ask}
near leg point	$near_{bid}$	$near_{ask}$
outright far forward:	$S \pm far_{bid}$	$S \pm far_{ask}$
outright near forward:	$S \pm near_{bid}$	$S \pm near_{ask}$
n against m month swap point	$far_{bid} - near_{ask}$	$far_{ask} - near_{bid}$

In a forward swap, as shown above, the agreed rate for the near leg is not the spot rate but the price of near forward, it could be bid, ask or midpoint of the near forward price. It is popular to take midpoint of near forward as the spot basis. The spot price, thus, is not necessary to derive a forward swap. For example, USD/CAD gives spot/1month swap as 130/140 and spot/3month swap as 200/240, then the bid point of 1/3 USD/CAD swap is 200−140=60 and the ask point of 1/3 USD/CAD swap is 240−130=110.

Forward swap point can be derived from the perspectives of both calling party and quoting party. Given $S_{USD/CHF}$=0.9743/52, spot/1month swap=60/50, spot/3month swap=160/150?

To achieve USD/CHF 1/3 bid price

	S=0.9743/52	Near Leg	Far Leg
	mid-point=0.97475	1month: 60/50	3month: 160/150
calling party intends		**long $**	**short $** → time
spot/forward1	short $ ↕ offset	long $	
spot/forward2	long $		short $
quoting party should		**short $**	**long $**
spot/forward1	long $ 0.97475 ↕ offset	short, swap ask=50 pips	
spot/forward2	short $ 0.97475		long, swap bid=160 pips
near leg sell=0.97475 −50 pips=0.96975; far leg buy=0.97475−160 pips=0.95875			
Take mid-point as spot base, forward swap bid point=160−50=110			

USD/CHF 1/3 ask price

	S=0.9743/52	Near Leg	Far Leg
	mid-point=0.97475	1month: 60/50	3month: 160/150
			→ time
calling party intends		**short $**	**long $**
spot/forward1	long $ ↕ offset	short $	
spot/forward2	short $		long $
quoting party should		**long $**	**short $**
spot/forward1	short $ 0.97475 ↕ offset	long, swap bid=60 pips	
spot/forward2	long $ 0.97475		short, swap ask=150 pips
near leg buy=0.97475−60 pips=0.96875; far leg sell=0.97475−150 pips=0.95975			
Take mid-point as spot base, forward swap ask point=150−60=90			

The above analysis can be summed as follows:

Bid point of forward swap=far leg bid point−near leg ask point

Ask point of forward swap=far leg ask point−near leg bid point

far leg point	far_{bid}	far_{ask}
near leg point	$near_{bid}$	$near_{ask}$
minus−		
forward swap point	bid	ask

§5 Short Dated Swaps

According to the classification in section 1.2, short-dated swaps include O/N, T/N, S/N and S/W. These are swaps with FX deals for value prior to spot. Take the most traded currency pair EUR/USD swap for instance, the short-dated swaps quoted by Reuters is shown below:

AIC	Bid	Ask	Srce	Time
EURON=	−0.385	−0.335	BAFX	12:46
EURTN=	−1.25	−1.21	RBSL	13:03
EURSN=	−0.41	−0.38	BOAF	12:46
EURSW=	−3.29	−3.24	RBSL	13:03

source: Reuters

5.1 T/N

This section elaborates more details on short-deted swaps applying similar method used for forward swap. Ordinary FX spot is settled in two business days after trading contract is signed, while T/N is short dated swap that starts tomorrow and ends the day after tomorrow, which is the spot settlement date. Let Q stand for quote currency, B for base currency, an example is illustrated to calculate T/N swap points.

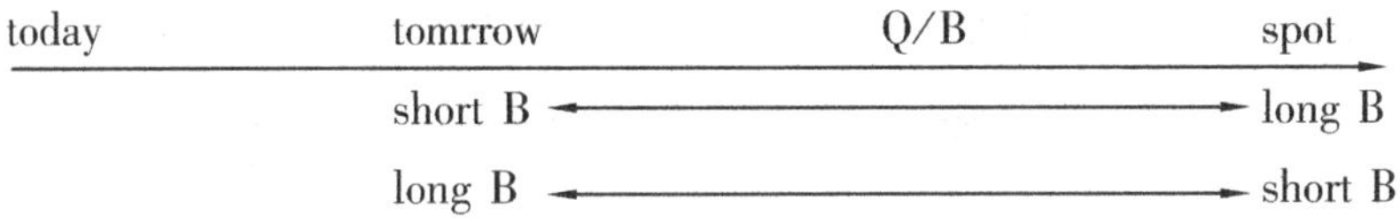

Given $S_{GDP/USD}$ = 1.5800/05, T/N as 1.5/1.4, the swap points to sell GBP/USD value tomorrow can be derived as follows:

Selling a T/N means that a trader sets a short position on spot settlement date and rolls back the settlement date one day earlier. In order to fulfill this short spot obligation, trader must first long the position so that she is able to short it tomorrow.

More specifically, selling a T/N involves the following deals

Sell GBP/USD spot at 1.5800 (choose 1.5800 as spot base) (1)

Sell/Buy GBP/USD T/N at −1.4 (2)

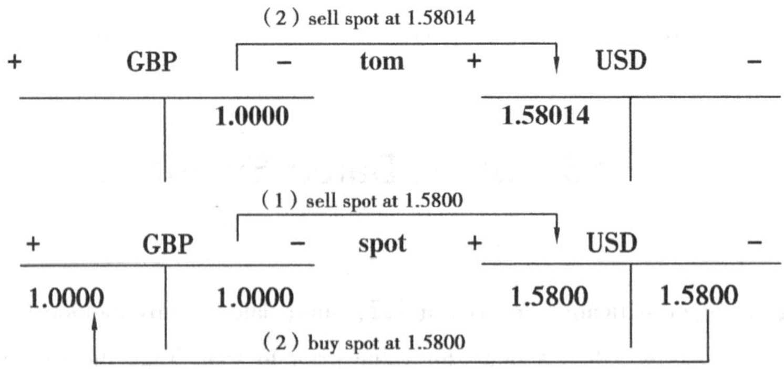

As the long leg of the T/N swap offsets the spot transaction, there is only one transaction left: short GBP value tomorrow. The rate of the resulting sale of GBP/USD T/N is 1.5800−(−0.00014)= 1.58014.

On the other hand, if a trader plans to buy GBP value tomorrow, she could long GBP spot and Buy/Sell GBP/USD T/N at −1.5. She ends up buying GBP settled tomorrow.

Generally, if traders plan to buy base currency settled tomorrow, then she could long spot and Buy/Sell a T/N rolling back settlement from 2 business days later to tomorrow; for selling base currency settled tomorrow, she could short spot and Sell/Buy a T/N rolling back settlement from 2 business days later to tomorrow.

The rate of GBP/USD T/N calculated below shows that to compute FX rates for T/N applies the following rule: reverse side and sign of T/N swap points and add them to the spot rate (value spot).

$S_{GBP/USD}=1.5802/05$, T/N is 1.6/1.3, the rate of GBP/USD value tomorrow is

	Bid	Ask
Spot	1.5802	1.5805
Reversed Swap, Ascending, +	1.3	1.6
GBP/USD Value Tomorrow	1.58033	1.58066

The result for value tomorrow is derived on the basis of the rate for value spot. For accuracy, the difference for value spot for one day should be discounted with the T/N interest rate of the foreign currency. In practice, however, this is disregarded.

Take another example: $S_{EUR/USD}=1.1231/36$, T/N = 2/1

The following tables presents the processes to derive the bid and ask.

Table 5-8 T/N Bid Price

		Near Leg	Far Leg S = 1.1231/36	
	Trade Today T+0	Value Tomorrow T+1	Value Spot, T+2	
			T/N = 2/1	time
Calling Party Intends		**short €**		
Spot			short €	offset
T/N		short €	long €	
Quoting Party Should		**long €**		
Spot			long € 1.1231	offset
T/N		long €	short €, swap ask = 1	
	descending order, € depreciates, T/N>spot>forward			
T/N Bid Price	1.1231+1pip = 1.1232			
Spot Bid Price	1.1231			

Table 5-9 T/N Ask Price

		Near Leg	Far Leg S=1.1231/36
	Trade Today T+0	Value Tomorrow T+1	Value Spot, T+2
			T/N=2/1 → time
Calling Party Intends		**long €**	
Spot			long € (offset)
T/N		long €	short €
Quoting Party Should		**short €**	
Spot			short €1.1236 (offset)
T/N		short €	long €, swap bid=2
	descending order, € depreciates, T/N>spot>forward		
T/N Ask Price	1.1236+2pips=1.1238		
Spot Ask Price	1.1236		

In conclusion, the swap points of T/N: can be calcuted according to the following rule

swap bid price = spot bid ±T/N ask point swap ask price = spot bid ±T/N bid point swap point in descending order, cross plus swap point in ascending order, cross minus	Spot Price	S_{bid}		S_{ask}
	Swap Point	T/N_{bid}		T/N_{ask}
	±			
	SWAP price	bid		ask

5.2 O/N

O/N is short dated swap that produces an FX transaction value today and ends tomorrow, i.e. O/N swap has the near leg on today and far leg on tomorrow. It lasts for one night.

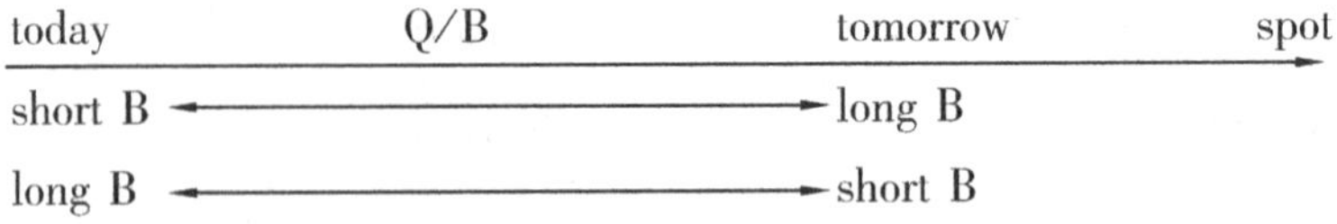

To derive the O/N swap price, T/N is applied.

For example, $S_{GBP/USD}$=1.5800/06, O/N=1.8/1.7, T/N=1.5/1.4. To produce a selling FX deal value today a calling party needs 3 deals:

short GBP/USD spot at 1.5800 (1)

sell-and-buy GBP/USD T/N at −1.4 (2)

sell-and-buy GBP/USD O/N at −1.7 (3)

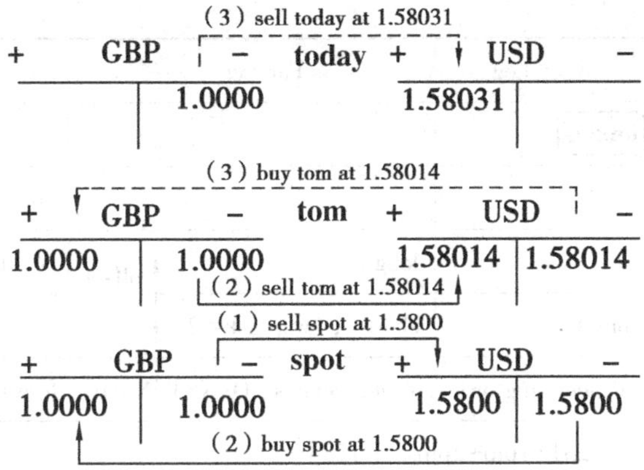

The far leg of the T/N swap offsets the spot transaction. The far leg of the O/N swap offsets the near leg of the T/N swap. The rate of the resulting sale of the GBP/USD value today is 1.5800−(−0.00014)−(−0.00017)= 1.58031, which is the bid price of O/N.

Similarly, the ask price of O/N is what a calling party should pay to buy such swap, which is composed by 3 deals: long GBP/USD spot at 1.5806, Buy/Sell GBP/USD T/N at −1.5, and Buy/Sell GBP/USD O/N at −1.8. The ask price is then 1.5806−(−0.00015)−(−0.00018)= 1.58093

	Bid	Ask
Spot	1.5800	1.5806
Reversed Swap O/N, Ascending, +	1.7	1.8
Reversed Swap T/N, Ascending, +	1.4	1.5
GBP/USD Value Tomorrow	1.58031	1.58093

Another example helps to confirm the calculation. Given $S_{EUR/USD}$ = 1.1231/36, T/N = 2/1, O/N = 3/2

The processes to derive the bid and ask are listed in the following tables:

Table 5-10 O/N Bid Price

	Near Leg	Far Leg	S = 1.1231/36
	Trade Today T+0	Value Tomorrow T+1	Value Spot, T+2
			O/N = 3/2, T/N = 2/1 → time
Calling Party Intends	**short €**		
Spot			short € ↕ offset
T/N		short € ↕ offset	long €
O/N	short €	long €	

Continued

	Near Leg	Far Leg	S=1.1231/36
Quoting Party Should	**long €**		
Spot			long € 1.1231 ↑ offset
T/N		long € ↑ offset	short €, swap ask=1 ↓
O/N	long €.	short €, swap ask=2 ↓	
	descending order, € depreciates, O/N>T/N>spot>forward		
O/N Bid Price	1.1231+1pip+2pips=1.1234		
T/N Bid Price	1.1231+1pip=1.1232		
Spot Bid Price	1.1231		

Table 5-11 O/N Ask Price

	Near Leg	Far Leg	S=1.1231/36	
	Trade Today T+0	Value Tomorrow T+1	Value Spot, T+2	
			O/N=3/2, T/N=2/1	→ time
Calling Party Intends	**long €**			
Spot			long € ↑	offset
T/N		long € ↑ offset	short € ↓	
O/N	long €	short € ↓		
Quoting Party Should	**short €**			
Spot			shot € 1.1236 ↑	offset
T/N		short € ↑ offset	long €, swap bid=2 ↓	
O/N	short €	long €, swap bid=3 ↓		
	descending order, € depreciates, O/N>T/N>spot>forward			
O/N Ask Price	1.1236+2pips+3pips=1.1241			
T/N Ask Price	1.1236+2pips=1.1238			
spot Ask Price	1.1236			

In conclusion, the swap points of O/N follows the following rule:

Rule	Spot Price	S_{bid}		S_{ask}
swap bid price = spot bid ±T/N ask point ±O/N ask point	T/N point	T/N_{bid}		T/N_{ask}
swap ask price = spot bid ±T/N bid point ±O/N bid point	O/N point	O/N_{bid}		O/N_{ask}
swap point in descending order, cross plus; swap point in ascending order, cross minus	±			
	SWAP price	bid		ask

5.3 Rollover Again

Rollover is first introduced in chapter 3 section 4. If a position was left open for the next trading day, the rollover is in fact an O/N swap, which is calculated on the basis of interest rates difference of two currencies in currency pair. In the trading terminal, "swap" is automatically converted into the deposit currency. The operation is conducted at 00.00 (Trading Server time, GMT+2) and can take several minutes.

For example, the swap points offer under the MT4 trading platform can be found by clicking "symbol properties".

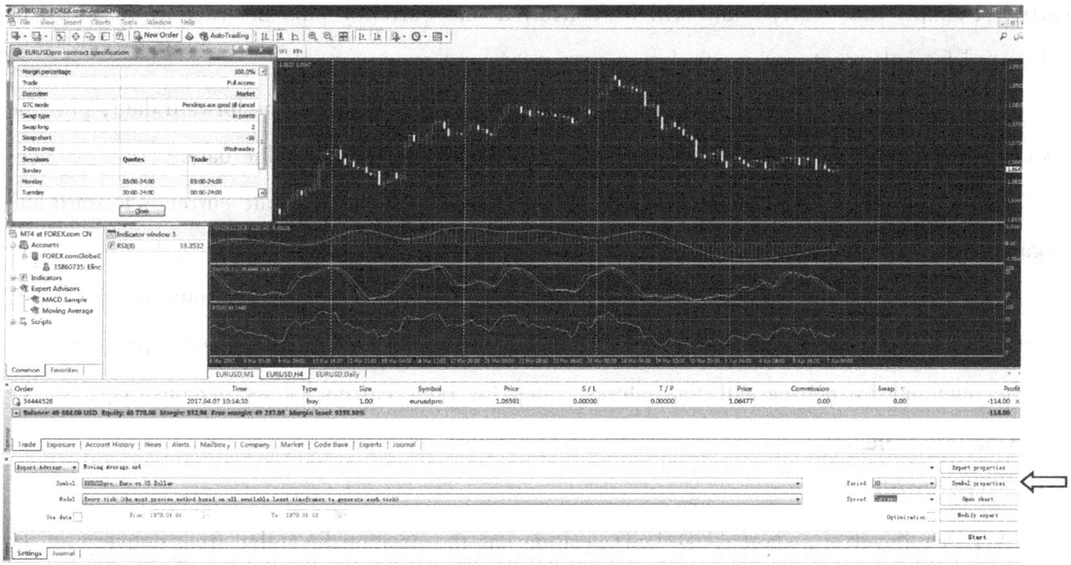

source: MT4 trading platform

The swap rate is indicative interest rates and subjects to change according to the volatility of the market. Holding long positions must pay interest and holding short positions can receive interest.

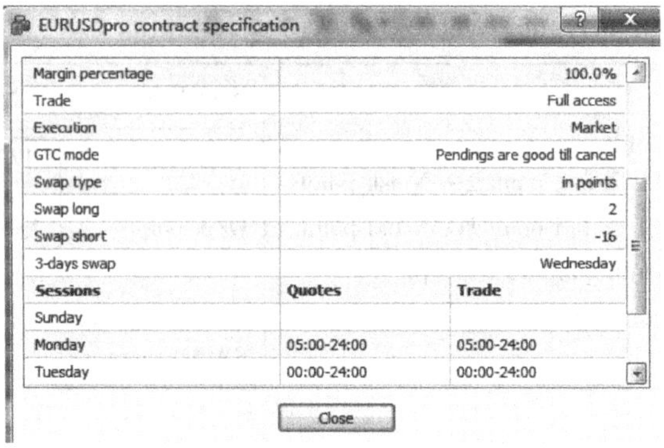

source: MT4 trading platform

Please note that the price after the transition of the weekend will be changed, the week will have a day that collects or pays 3 times overnight interest. Varieties of foreign exchange overnight interest every Wednesday adjust for differences in interbank lending interest rates.

Generally, short dated swap points to a particular value date will be determined mathematically from the overall cost involved when lending one currency and borrowing another during the time period stretching from the spot date until the value date. This is sometimes called the "cost of carry" or simply the "carry" and will be converted into currency pips in order to be added or subtracted from the spot rate.

The carry can be computed from the number of days from spot until the forward date, plus the prevailing interbank deposit rates for the two currencies to the forward value date.

The carry will be positive for the party who sells the higher interest rate currency forward and negative for the party who buys the higher interest rate currency forward.

To compute the fair value of a rollover swap, it is first necessary to determine the prevailing short term interbank deposit rates for each of the currencies involved in the currency pair. Rollover can be obtained by netting out the interest rates for both currencies as demonstrated by the following two examples.

1) Example Ⅰ

A T/N rollover of a short AUD/USD position has the position be rolled from delivery on the following business day from today until the next business day forward from that. Suppose that the short term interest rate for USD is $R = 0.25\%$ and the short term interest rate for AUD is $R^* = 4.5\%$. Because this trader is dealing with a T/N for short, which is equivalent "short AUD and long USD", she is gaining USD interest R and paying AUD interest R^*. This nets out to an annualized interest rate differential for the currency pair of $0.25\% - 4.5\% = -4.25\%$. Assuming a one day T/N rollover period and a 30/360 day count basis, the theoretical rollover fee on holding a short AUD/USD position overnight would cost the trader the annualized interest rate differential of 4.25% divided by 360. To get a currency quantity for the rollover fee, the resulting interest rate differential for the T/N period need be multiplied by the notional amount of the transaction and converted into AUD/USD pips (It is often charged by FX retail brokers in pips). Conversely, the trader would receive a similar amount to roll over a long position in AUD/USD. The amount received would generally be less since it would be adjusted downward by the FX broker's rollover bid/ask spread.

2) Example Ⅱ

Given the condition of FX swap as:

- Transaction volume of 1 lot (100000 AUD)
- Current exchange rate 0.9200.

Opening a long/short position is composed by a Buy/Sell of the base currency and a reverse operation with the quoted currency[①]. In case of rolling a position on the currency pair AUD/USD over to the next day, Libor/Libid overnight rates on the USD and Overnight Deposit/Lending Rate for AUD are used.

Libor/Libid is the average-weighted interest rates of interbank Lending/Deposit, daily fixed by the British Banking Association. From May 2013, the rates for different time periods are calculated on a daily basis for 5 major currencies, including CHF, EUR, GBP, JPY and USD.

Australian Dollar Overnight Lending/Deposit Rate is the interest rates of interbank financing in Australia, tied to the target overnight call rate of the Reserve Bank of Australia.

Suppose that overnight interest rates are as follows:

$R_a^* = 2.70\%$

$R_b^* = 2.50\%$

$R_a = 0.12\%$

$R_b^* = 0.00\%$

A long position of this swap is to roll a long position over to the next day, the client receives 2.50% annual interest from purchasing 100000 AUD, which is 2500 AUD per year or 6.94 AUD (6.38 USD) per day. At the same time, borrowing USD (at the current exchange rate 100000 AUD is equivalent to 92000 USD) implies an obligation for the client to pay 0.12% annual interest, which is equal to 110.4 USD per year or 0.31 USD per day.

Netting of mutual liabilities leads to a positive gain for the client of 6.1 USD, or if

① The U.K. Financial Conduct Authority (FCA) announced that it would no longer persuade or compel contributing banks to publish the London Interbank Offered Rate (LIBOR) after 2021. LIBOR is set to be phased out with the recommended replacement in the U.S. being the Secured Overnight Financing Rate (SOFR), which is set to replace LIBOR in 2023.

recalculated to swap points equals to 0.61.

When opening a short position and rolling it over, the client has to pay 2.70% annual interest for borrowing 100000 AUD, which equals to 2700 AUD per year or 7.5 AUD (6.9 USD) per day. At the same time, purchasing USD (at the current exchange rate 100000 AUD is equivalent to 92000 USD), the client does not get a reward, as the USD Libid rate is very close to zero.

Netting of mutual liabilities leads to a negative loss for the client of 6.9 USD, or if recalculated to swap points, equals to −0.69.

In practice, many banks or swap brokers, often move away from their original values adding their own interest, which may sometimes even exceed interbank rates. As a result, swap conditions become much worse for the clients, distorting the real parity of the money market.

Case Studies

Case 1 The Icelandic Carry Trade

https://wenku.baidu.com/view/7c76502758fb770bf78a5539.html? from=search.

In year 2008, market showed turmoil in the Icelandic foreign exchange market due to financial crisis triggered by sub-prime mortgage of the U.S.

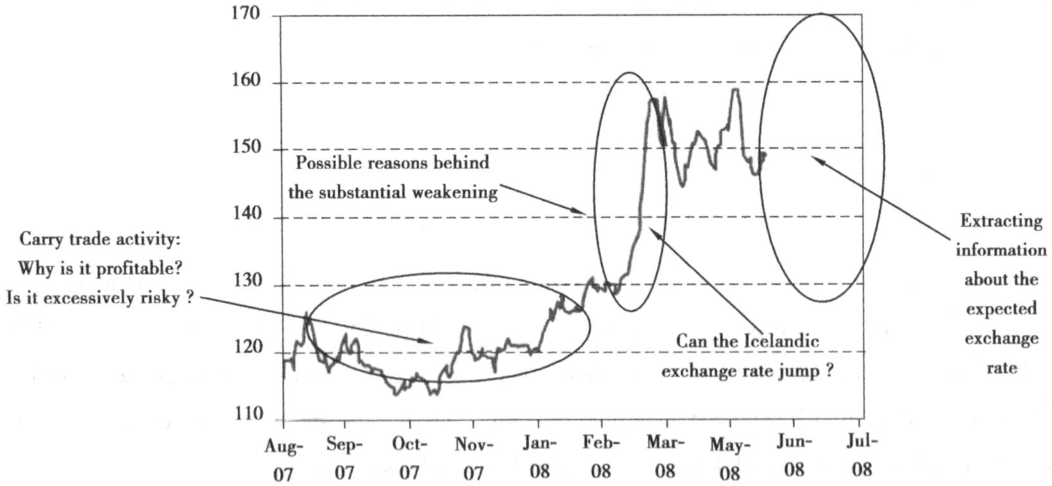

Icelandic Exchange Rate Index (Daily Data, Aug. 07-Mar. 08)

source: Bloomberg

Icelandic krona was depreciating against EUR since end of 2007 and the interest rate implied by interest rate parity deviated from Libor rate gradually.

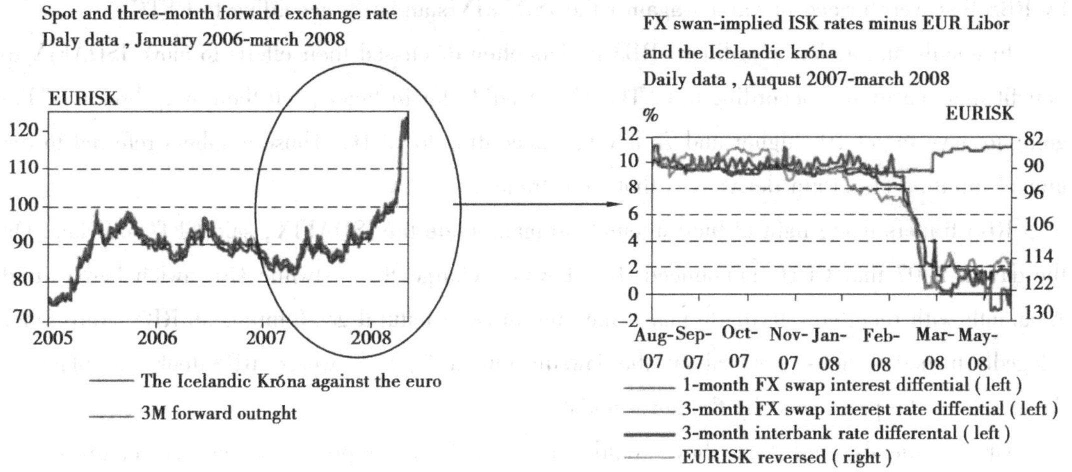

source: Bloomberg

Case 2 RBS Hit with $85 Million Fine for Alleged Stamford Trading Violations

By Paul Schott of Stamford Advocate

The U. S. Commodity Futures Trading Commission on Feb. 3, 2017 ordered Royal Bank of Scotland to pay an $85 million civil penalty to settle charges that traders at its Stamford complex allegedly tried to manipulate a benchmark for interest-rate products during a period spanning the global financial crisis.

CFTC's punishment of RBS for its purported attempts to rig the U. S. Dollar International Swaps and Derivatives Association Fix (ISDAFIX) represents the latest move in an ongoing campaign by the federal agency to tackle trading that allegedly abuses fiscal benchmarks. So far, CFTC has imposed more than $5.2 billion in penalties, in 19 cases, against banks and brokers for such violations.

RBS had twice incurred similar sanctions before Friday's announcement—a $325 million fine in 2013 for violations tied to the LIBOR interest rate benchmark and a $290 million penalty in 2014 linked to a foreign exchange rate case.

"People around the world rely on benchmark rates such as ISDAFIX," AitanGoelman, director of CFTC's enforcement division, said in a statement. "These actions and the CFTC's previous cases against those who sought to corrupt the LIBOR and foreign exchange benchmark rates make clear that the Commission takes very seriously its role in ensuring the integrity of any and all benchmarks used in our markets."

In a statement reported by MarketWatch, RBS CEO Ross McEwan said: "This is an example of past misconduct that has no place at RBS, and we strongly condemn these actions."

Between January 2007 and March 2012, a group of Stamford-based RBS traders tried to manipulate the ISDAFIX at a crucial 11 a.m. "fixing" time to benefit options for swap deals held by RBS that were priced or valued against the ISDAFIX standard, according to CFTC.

In emails and audio recordings, RBS traders often discussed their efforts to move ISDAFIX to benefit their positions, according to CFTC. They would, for instance, tell their swap broker, "I'm going to have to get 10s higher and 7s lower," according to CFTC. Those numbers referred to the annual duration of certain derivatives that were traded.

RBS traders made light of their attempts to manipulate the ISDAFIX, said CFTC officials. On the day in 2007 that CFTC announced that it would charge the erstwhile Greenwich hedge fund Amaranth with reportedly trying to manipulate the price of natural gas futures, an RBS swap trader allegedly turned a news story about the lawsuit into a "joke" where RBS took the place of Amaranth as the party sued by the government.

CFTC officials said that they would require RBS to improve its internal controls and procedures, measures that would include detecting and deterring trading that might try to manipulate yardsticks like the ISDAFIX.

RBS has faced major penalties for other practices during the time of the financial crisis.

Last October, state Attorney General George Jepsen announced a $120 million settlement with RBS tied to its oversight of mortgage-backed securities, representing the largest penalty against a company in the state's history. State officials described RBS' conduct in that case as "dishonest and/or unethical" and said that RBS made false statements about its securities products.

RBS' Americas headquarters are based at 600 Washington Blvd., in downtown Stamford. Since early 2016, RBS has laid off some 270 Stamford employees, as the firm has weathered major financial headwinds in the past year.

Case 3 Dialogue about Rollover for Individual Traders①

The conversation below explains the concept of rollover in the FX market, which is synonymous with the term swap.

Shaun: Ok, so we're going to go over rollover and what it is. It's really the interest that accrues for holding an open FX position. When we place a trade, you guys know that we're trading on leverage. When we trade one lot of the EURUSD, we are trading € 100000 and then we're selling whatever the equivalent is in USD at the time. Right now the rate is 1.30. That means that we are buying € 100000 and exchanging that for $130000. This is when EURUSD is equal to 1.3000.

Make sense so far? Unfortunately, everybody wants interest and they want their pound of flesh. You're not just paying it for the money in your account, you're actually owing interest and

---

① http://www.onestepremoved.com/FX-rollover-swap/

earning interest for the positions that you have open. If you again use a current example, interest rates are at historic lows. They use the overnight rate for setting the rollover and swap rate on a position. The euro overnight lending rate is set at 0.01%. It's basically free money.

The US dollar has an overnight lending rate of 0.15%. These are annual rates. It's pretty equivalent to what you're getting paid on a CD: almost nothing. But, that goes have a cost associated with it. When you look in Meta Trader, MT4 references it as the swap. In the industry, it's more commonly known as rollover.

You have to pay interest for the positions that you do have open because they have value. When we decide to buy the EURUSD, that means that we own Euros and we sold dollars. In interest terms, that means that we are owed interest on the Euros and we owe interest on the dollars.

Chris: That would be bad because the US dollar is more?

Shaun: Right. If you're buying the euro, and this is in magical fairy land where you earn and pay the exact same amount of rollover for buying and selling, and we'll get into exceptions in a minute, but in the "pure scenario", you're only earning 0.01% annual interest on your euro position. You're paying 0.15% interest on your dollar position. If you're buying EUR/USD and held that position for a year, you would expect to accrue a loss of 0.14%, which is the euro overnight interest rate (0.01%) minus the dollar overnight interest rate (0.15%).

If you did the exact opposite and sold EUR/USD, you only owe 0.01% overnight interest, but you make 0.15% percent interest.

Chris: Are you assuming that you have the position open for an entire year?

Shaun: Yes. Now, of course these rates change. These are overnight rates, which means that over night they change on a daily basis. The amount will fluctuate—slowly—but, it does fluctuate.

This is in the hypothetical example where you bought EURSD, the overnight rates never change and you held the position for precisely one year.

Chris: It's for one whole lot?

Shaun: Yes. It's precisely one lot. One lot is the equivalent of 100000 base currency units. Our base currency here is the euro. 100000 of the base currency is 100000 euros.

Let's go through and calculate the rollover in our scenario of buying one standard lot of EURUSD. Apply the 0.01% rate to the €100000 position. 0.0001 * €100000 = €10. Of course, you must put that back in dollar terms. €10 * $1.3000/€ (the current exchange rate) equals $13. The $13 is the credit for the holding the EURUSD position for an entire year.

The calculations are the same for the dollar, except for the fact that it's now a debit. The position of $130000 * −0.015 (this is a negative number because we owe it) equals... does anyone have a calculator on their phone? We all do; we're programmers.

Andy: $195

Shaun: We have a $13 credit and a $195 loss from the rollover. $182 is the amount of money that we're going to lose after one year in our hypothetical scenario with the EUR/USD exchange rate not fluctuating, the overnight interest rates not fluctuating and us holding our position for precisely one year.

The next thing is that we need to go over the mechanics of rollover and how it is charged. It's a little quirky. I'm stating the obvious, but there are seven days per week.

Chris: What's with MB Trading only giving 50∶1 leverage. What does that mean?

Shaun: It doesn't matter for the swap. If you have a position of € 100000, you owe interest on the € 100000.

Andy: You owe the interest on the leveraged amount?

Shaun: Yes. It's on the leveraged amount. When we opened that € 100000 position, we did that with $2000 on 50∶1 leverage or $1000 on 100∶1 leverage. You're not paying or receiving interest on your margin amount. You're paying or receiving it on the leveraged amount.

Chris: So if I were doing that with MB Trading, I'd have to do it with two lots?

Shaun: No. The interest is the same. You have a € 100000 position.

Chris: To leverage that much, don't I have to double my margin?

Shaun: Yes. Instead of using $1000, now you use $2000 to open the one lot trade.

Rollover is seven days a week, but we know that trading doesn't happen on the weekends. In FX, trading really happens from Sunday afternoon to Friday afternoon. This is more of a technicality. The only really important days are Monday, Tuesday, Wednesday, Thursday and Friday.They need to charge interest for seven days even though there are only five days that are important.

What they do is charge a single day of interest on Monday, Tuesday, Thursday and Friday. By convention and for no good reason, Wednesday's rollover carries the interest charges for Wednesday, Saturday and Sunday.

Chris: Why don't they do it on Monday?

Shaun: I don't know. Why don't they do it on Thursday?

Terry: Or why don't they spread it out across the week evenly?

Shaun: Why don't you pay 1.5 days? That's just the way it is.

This is referred to as triple rollover Wednesday.

Andy: That's the for the past weekend, correct?

Shaun: No. It has nothing to do with the weekends. Rollover occurs precisely at 5 pm ET. When you look at the charts of most brokers, they are mostly based on broker time. But in the FX industry by convention, 5 pm ET is the start of a new day. 5 pm ET on Sunday is actually the start of Monday. 5 pm ET on Monday is actually the start of Tuesday's trading day. Tuesday's trading day concludes at 4:59 pm on Tuesday.

Andy: But on Wednesday, you get charged for the past Saturday and Sunday?

Shaun: Even if you didn't have the trade open! If you decide—very poorly—at 4:59 pm on Wednesday that you're going to open a trade, and you close the trade two minues later at 5:01 pm on Wednesday, you are going to earn or pay triple rollover.

Andy: Oh, so it has nothing to do with the last weekend. They just charge you three times for whatever happens on that day.

Shaun: It's a market quirk. If you hold that position precisely at 5 pm, you owe interest. If you do not, you do not owe interest. If you had the trade open for 23 hours and 59 minutes, but you closed it before 5 pm, no triple rollover. But if you have it at 5 pm, then you pay triple rollover.

It's the same concept on Monday, Tuesday, Thursday and Friday, except it's only single rollover.

Chris: What's to keep people from finding a favorable currency comparison and just opening trades for two minutes every day?

Shaun: Lots of people try that and it doesn't work because of spread costs. Notice that the rollover rates are so tiny. We're talking about 0.01% per annum. Divide that per day and it's a silly amount. It's so negligible that you don't really care.

There are exceptions. There's Golden Week and this involves the yen. There are days where triple rollover Wednesday becomes nine times Wednesday. You earn the interest for two weeks of trading.

Andy: Do brokers do that to get people to trade with them or something? Is that a for fun thing or is there an actual reason:

Shaun: It's because Japan shuts down for two weeks.

Chris: It's only in yen pairs?

Shaun: Yes. Anything involving a yen pair in May has Golden Week where you have a monster rollover day. It's kind of the way it is.

People do try to take advantage of it. When interest rates were higher a couple of years ago, there was a big differential between the pound and the yen. The pound had an interest rate of 5.25% and the yen, as it is today, had an annual interest rate near zero at 0.25%. I think today that it's 0.1. The point is that there was a massive difference between the two of 5%. You could earn that on the leveraged position.

Chris: Does that make the price spike?

Shaun: Yeah, it does. People want to earn this money. This is what drives currency market, the shift in the interest rates. People chase yield. If I can open an account in GBP and I can earn 5.25%, if I'm holding yen, that's looking really attractive to me.

I might consider the idea of converting my yen into pounds so that I can the extra 5%. This is referred to as a carry trade. It's the idea of using leveraged money to earn the difference in the interest rates. It's possible and it can be lucrative. The problem is that it depends on your timing of exchange rates.

If you expect that... let me think of a scenario that applies to today. Let's say that the ECB decides to reverse course, and this is not likely to happen at all. Right now, they're trying to keep their interest almost at zero. Let's say they decided to stop intervening in the market and to charge a real interest rate. The EURO interest rate would go through the roof, which motivates people to put their money into Euros instead of dollars, yen, Australian dollars, whatever. If you expect that trend to continue for several years, that is a great motivation for buying that currency. Not only do you earn the increasing differential in the two currencies' interest rates, but more people are likely to follow the trade. The higher an interest rate is, the more likely people are to buy that currency.

That was the reason behind Brazil's hot market as of about two years ago. Interest rates were 13%~14% and everything was appreciating through the roof. You could sit back and know that you were going to make 14% in reals. The problem is that if you top the market like when the market yielded 14%, you earned 14% in reals and then the price plummeted by 30%. Timing is critical.

That's the fundamental reason that the market exists. That's why people trade currencies. Not just for exchanges of payments, but for speculation, that is entirely why people participate. It looks like free money. There are all sorts of examples.

Oddly enough, most of the mortgages in Poland are denominated in Swiss francs. The reason is that the Swiss had a very, very low interest rate compared to what the Polish zloty was charging at the time. If you could pay 0.5%, why are you going to pay 5% interest to have it denominated in zlotys?

Well, the reason is because the Swiss franc has been appreciating for several years. Now half of Polish homeowners are severely underwater because the value of their loans has appreciated by 20% or 30%. They only make their income in zlotys. That's the risk of the market. Those are the kind of real world examples of why people decide to participate and why rollover is really important.

This is the electronic form of how it applies to our traders and our customers speculating in markets. The real mechanics behind it are more tangible like in the mortgage example.

Andy: Is it common for strategies to keep track of I would make money, so I want to hold my trade until I hit my interest point for the day?

Shaun: You could, but it's a silly risk. If you think that it's dangerous to be in now, you're going to stay in risking an average of 120 pips of movement in the EURUSD so that you can capture the equivalent of 0.25 pips.

Andy: Ok, so it's pretty much worthless.

Shaun: Yeah.

Terry: Your current interest rate, is that something that a strategy has access to at the market level? Are we able to go out and query that?

Shaun: No.

Terry: So, it means that it has to be fed that values from some other source, which means...

Shaun: Nope. It has nothing to do with backtesting. It doesn't make assumptions about rollover. It isn't present in MetaTrader on a historical basis. It is available in real time and I can show you guys where to find that. It's not something that most people look at as part of a strategy. It is an important part, but it shouldn't be the maker or breaker. It should be a little bit of juice. You use it to pad the margins a little bit or it might be a drag on performance. It should not be the primary reason why you're entering a trade now at 4:59 pm so that you can capture the tenth of a pip in interest cost and pay 2.5 pips in the process.

The one thing that I wanted to point out, too, is that everything that I explained is kind of hypothetical. You either lose 0.14% or you make 0.14% on an annual basis. In reality, that's not how most brokers work. It's a good way that they pad their margins.

This is how they make a slight amount of money on traders that aren't trading, through the difference in the rollover rates that they charge. In the example that I sent you, and assuming that we opened MetaTrader and that it was a perfectly equal market, you would see that buying costs you. MetaTrader shows you in dollars, but I'm just going to put it in percentages. You expect a return of −0.14% for buying EURUSD and a return of +0.14% for selling EURUSD.

What happens most of the time is that everything gets skewed against you. The cost becomes a bigger number and the profit becomes a smaller number.

Chris: You're saying it's the broker that does this?

Shaun: Yes. It can be the broker or it can be the ultimate liquidity provider behind the broker, but yes, the interest rates are set and then they get shifted. Obviously, someone earns that differential.

Terry: So, obviously, these are within the bounds of legal priorities based on trading rules?

Shaun: Yes. It is a cost. I don't know of anybody that discloses it. I don't know who the ultimate beneficiary is to be honest.

Terry: It's the broker.

Shaun: That's my assumption that the broker is making the difference. If they net their trades, they should be capturing that difference. If you have 50000 clients and most of them are piled into the EURUSD, there's only going to be a certain amount of net exposure. Only say 10% of that difference is going to be net long or short. You can net out the difference between these two and keep all of it.

It's not super lucrative, but it's money sitting there and they take it.

Terry: A dime times 50000 is lucrative.

Shaun: Yes. It adds up.

Terry: Especially when it's all electronic.

Shaun. Yes.

Chris: Maybe I'm behind the times, but I thought they were pressuring the euro zone to ease.

Shaun: They are.

Chris: But they're already way below the dollar.

Shaun. Well, the target headline rate in the euro zone is 1.25%, which is the result of the central bank intervening. They're buying Spanish bonds, Italian bonds. Basically, the bonds that literally nobody wants. They're buying them so that the interest rates go down.

If I'm going to loan money, you have to make the call for your business or multinational corporation. You have to decide. Do you want to tie up money in junk debt for a year and get 6% in Spanish bonds? Or do you want to loan to the ECB directly at 0.01%. You get paid almost nothing, but at least you know you'll get your Euros back.

Terry: Well, it depends on how long you're planning on being in it and what you think the future is going to turn. If you think that's going to turn, then go ahead and camp on it now and get it for nothing.

Shaun: Right.

Terry: If you can afford to be in it that long.

Shaun: Yes, and that's why there are interest rate curves. That's a whole different subject.

If you lend for a day, and let's use the US Treasury as the simplest example, we start out with bills at the short end of the duration. Bills are anything about a 90 day coupon and out to a year. You can buy a treasury note for the one year, two year, five year and ten year. Each duration is supposed to get higher and higher, but the further out you go, you're supposed to get a higher rate of interest. It's rather negligible compared to the duration. The difference between the overnight and the 3 month is pretty substantial. The difference between the 10 year and 30 year is supposed to be more substantial, but obviously the time involved is almost beyond comparison.

That's why in the original EURUSD example I said that the overnight rate is this, because that's what we use in FX. What people are really looking at when they're deciding whether or not to take out mortgages or to loan money in different sovereign bonds, they're looking at one year yields, ten year yields.

Terry: It seems like it doesn't make sense to go past ten years. Three decades is a long time to tie something up.

Shaun: In that market I would agree, but there were people in the 1970s that caught the US Treasury in the height of the stagflation when interest rates in the US were at 17%. They loaned money when the short term rates were actually inverted. People were taking the easy money earning 17% annually over 3-6 months. The smart money locked up those interest rates at 14% for thirty years. They made 14% per annum.

Terry: Compounded.

Shaun: ... compounded for 30 years. They guys that made the thirty years made a killing and as close to risk free as you could get at the time.

Today, I would argue that's suicide. I don't think the dollar will be around in 30 years. But, that's a different story.

Andy: When do these costs get calculated? Every day at 5 o'clock, they say you gained two cents or whatever. When did that fee get charged.

Shaun: Interest rates are a really complicated subject. They're actually the result of a huge scandal right now that I know none of you know about, none of the people that I know know about, but that everyone should be up in arms about. It's called the LIBOR Scandal.

LIBOR is where overnight interest rates are set. It's not a free market. It's voted on by a group of 30 some-odd banks. It's all the normal culprits, the people that are despised and rightfully so: the Goldman Sachs of the world, Barclay's, RBS, Bank of America. Any bank that you've heard of that's international, they're probably one of the banks that set the LIBOR rates.

They all get to vote and decide what is tonight's interest rate for the US dollar. When they set the rate, that's what every bank in the world uses to set its overnight lending rate.

Chris: They just pull it out of thin air or they base it on something?

Shaun: They pull it out of thin air. They just vote. There's a formula where they throw out the most extreme votes and keep the average of the middle ones.

It's the most important market in the world because it affects everything that connects to money. It affects stocks, real companies, bonds, mortgages, currencies... it affects everything.

What happened this summer was that the Bank of England got caught encouraging Barclay's to manipulate the LIBOR rate. As you can image, banks have a strong interest in voting whether the

LIBOR goes up or down. It affects all sorts of things like how much they have to pay savers in their CDs. How much do they charge for a mortgage. They have all sorts of motivations to keep the interest rates as absolutely low as possible to benefit themselves. That's what happened.

LIBOR is set in London, but it really doesn't matter. All the banks are international. It's really just a committee.

Andy: With no government oversight?

Shaun: It was with the active collusion of the Bank of England and the Federal Reserve. They encouraged the banks to keep the interest rates low because it aligned with their policy objectives.

Exercises

Ⅰ. ***Multiple choice questions, choose all that apply.***

1. FX swap could be used to (　　).
   A. adjust cash flow dates or cash position
   B. hedge
   C. speculate
   D. finance international business expansion
2. One could get out of the FX swap before the pre-agreed termination date by (　　).
   A. buying out the counterparty
   B. selling on the swap contract
   C. using an offsetting swap
   D. using a swaption
3. Given spot EUR/USD as 1.2339/42 and 3-month swap points as 09/13, (　　).
   A. the bid price of swap is 1.2351
   B. the bid price of swap is 1.2348
   C. the ask price of swap is 1.2355
   D. the ask price of swap is 1.2352
4. (　　) are spot against spot FX swaps.
   A. O/N　　B. S/N　　C. T/N　　D. S/W
5. If a trader is to buy a swap, she will (　　).
   A. take a long position in near leg
   B. take a short position in near leg
   C. take a long position in far leg

D. take a short position in far leg

Ⅱ. ***Numerical works.***

1. $S_{EUR/USD}$ = *1.0646/52, 6-month swap point is 63/59, use mid-point to work out the outright forward prices and the forward prices under this 6-month swap.*

2. *Given* $S_{GBP/USD}$ = *1.5026/32 and 9-month swap point as 58/67, what is the cost and revenue of the quoting party for a £1 million trade of FX swap?*

3. *What is the mark to market value of the following swap?*

4. *Given* $S_{USD/JPY}$ = *109.89/95; annual USD interest rate* $R_b^* = 2.4\%$, $R_a^* = 2.7\%$; *annual JPY interest rate* $R_b = 0.3\%$, $R_a = 0.6\%$; *swap points* f_{12}(¥/\$) = *100/90. Take mid-point as spot basis,*
   (1) *Is there any arbitrage opportunity?*
   (2) *How to arbitrage?*
   (3) *Conclude the arbitrage rules.*

5. *Given* $S_{EUR/USD}$ = *1.1258/62, O/N = 0.25/0.5, T/N = 0.5/1, S/N = 1/2, S/W = 3/6, S/1M = 10/15, 1M/3M = 20/30,* (1) *work out swap bid price and ask price,* (2) *mark swap near leg and long leg price on time line.*

Chapter 6
Foreign Exchange Futures

Currency futures were created at the Chicago Mercantile Exchange (CME) in 1972. As the system of fixed exchange rates was abandoned along with the gold standard in the early 1970s, some commodity traders at the CME believed that significant changes were about to take place in the currency market, but they did not have access to the inter-bank exchange markets. They thus established the International Monetary Market (IMM) and launched trading in 7 currency futures on 16th May, 1972. (The IMM became a division of CME). The currency futures market has grown considerably since then. Although FX futures trading accounts for only 5% of the total FX daily volume, it is still an impressive number at \$173 billion per day with open interest as \$321 billion according to BIS 2023 Feb. record.

Before the rise of online retail FX trading in recent years, trading currency futures on the Chicago International Monetary Market (IMM) was one of the few ways that individuals could trade currencies in smaller amounts.

Nowadays North America took the lion's share (as shown in Figure 6-1) of FX futures trading.

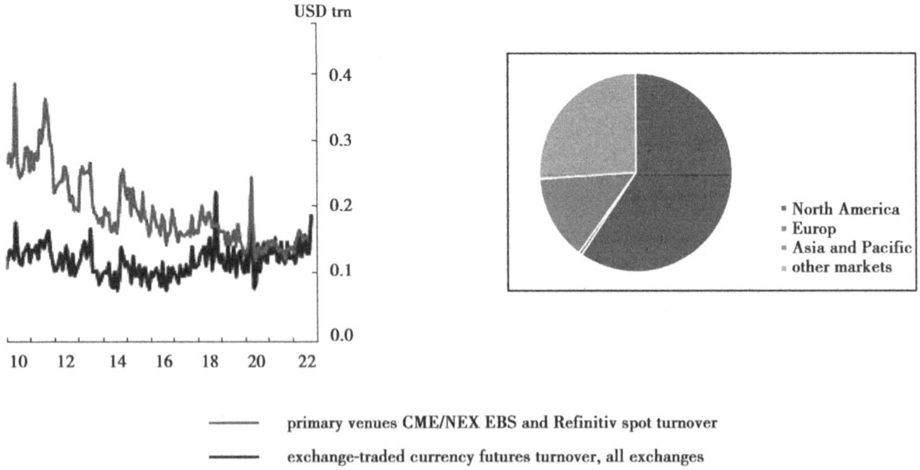

Figure 6-1 Trading Volumes of FX Futures

This chaper set the following knowledge sharing mainly based on IMM.

- FX futures definitions
- FX futures market and conventions
- Trading rules

§ 1 Conventions

1.1 Definition

Foreign exchange futures (FX futures), also called foreign futures or currency futures, are exchange-traded futures contracts to buy or sell a specified amount of a particular currency at a set price and date in the future.

While forwards as introduced in Chapter 4 are contracts that are individually negotiated and traded over the counter, FX futures are standardized contracts trading on organized exchanges. FX futures are essentially standardized forward contracts, trading on oranized exchanges with daily resettlement through a clearing house. Although most FX forwards are used for hedging exchange risk and are ended in the actual delivery of the currency, most positions in FX futures are closed out before the delivery date, because most FX futures are bought and sold purely for the potential profit.

FX futures by essential are standardized FX forward contracts, but the conventions about FX futures trade are different than that of the FX forward.

1.2 Exchange Traded vs. Over the Counter

In exchange trading market, transactions are taken through a centralized source, which acts as the mediator connecting buyers and sellers. This type of trading places great power on the mediator and solves the asymmetrical information and credit problems between sellers and buyers allowing for better transaction enforcement, and stricter security. The New York stock Exchange NYSE, for instance, is a typical centralized market where products traded are standardized and in compliance with the terms of trade.

Over-the-counter (OTC) markets, in contract with exchange-traded markets, are decentralized. There are many mediators in OTC market, who compete to match buyers with sellers for commission fee. The fierce competition among mediators ensures low costs for intermediary services. Although OTC markets are not easy to regulate and fraudulent mediators may find place to survive in such markets, OTC markets have overtaken exchange markets in terms of volumes traded daily, mainly due to the increase in electronic trading and the rise in alternative investing.

Generally, there is more counter party risk in OTC markets than in exchange markets. To ensure the delivery of currencies, the exchange acts as a counter-part to each trader. The central clearing and post-trade risk collateralisation in exchange markets keep counter party risk in check.

Trading in exchange markets is on a centralized system, which allows less chances of price manipulation; while in OTC markets, price manipulation is feasible given there are few dealers trading in a particular currency pair at a given time.

There are fewer traders in OTC markets than that in exchange markets, which explains higher level of liquidity in exchange markets. According to BIS Triennial Survey, the average daily turnover of OTC derivatives in Apr.2022 is about $7.5 trillion, the while by Mar.2023 exchange-traded derivatives is $ 197 billion per day. Although most FX instruments trading such as spot, forward and swap are traded in OTC market, there is also a quite vibrant and successful exchange-traded futures market.

In exchange markets, most FX futures trading do not end up as delivery. Traders close out FX futures position before its due and profit from the trading FX futures contract itself.

It is explained in chapter 3 that spot FX prices in OTC markets are usually for T + 2 settlements, while FX futures in exchange markets tend to have a maturity of 3-months and so are settled quarterly, normally in March, June, September and December. Although FX futures rates often look different from FX spot rates, they are highly correlated.

1.3 Quotations

Generally, USD is used to quote FX futures contract. For example, FX futures contracts for the JPY would be expressed as JPY/USD rather than the FX spot quote convention of USD/JPY. FX futures quotations mainly could be collected from 2 sources: newspaper or trading platform.

1) Newspaper

Because that FX futures are frequently traded in exchanges, FX futures prices are listed in daily newspapers and other media.

Following is a snapshot of a quote that appear in The Wall Street Journal, showing information of FX futures of previous day on the International Money Market (IMM) of the Chicago Mercantile Exchange (CME).

7 most commonly traded FX futures were quoted on Wall Street Journal. Take Japanese Yen for instance, the first line shows the size of the contract (12.5 million yen) and states that the prices of each 100 yen are quoted in dollars.

Newspapers only pick the two nearest contracts to post. In this case, the March contract has just expired, so the two contracts being traded on the previous day are the June and September contracts.

	Open	High	Low	settle	change	Open interest
Currency Futures						
Japanese Yen (CME)-¥12,500,000; $ per 100¥						
April	.9486	.9501	.9356	**.9368**	-.0121	856
June	.9531	.9542	.9393	**.9406**	-.0122	159,521
Canadian Dollar (CME)-CAD 100,000; $ per CAD						
April	.7764	.7770	.7741	**.7748**	-.0022	227
June	.7774	.7786	.7743	**.7756**	-.0022	120,670
British Pound (CME)-£62,500; $ per £						
April	1.4183	1.4200	1.4082	**1.4092**	-.0075	1,045
June	1.4219	1.4244	1.4113	**1.4127**	-.0074	173,671
Swiss Franc (CME)-CHF 125,000; $ per CHF						
June	1.0633	1.0639	1.0505	**1.0519**	-.0113	44,585
Australian Dollar (CME)-AUD 100,000; $ per AUD						
April	.7692	.7700 ▼	.7658	**.7662**	-.0026	1,377
May	.7693	.7696 ▼	.7660	**.7663**	-.0025	529
June	.7687	.7704 ▼	.7655	**.7663**	-.0026	101,836
Sept	.7698	.7702 ▼	.7664	**.7668**	-.0027	644
Dec	.7670	.7708 ▼	.7662	**.7675**	-.0026	370
Mexican Peso (CME)-MXN 500,000; $ per MXN						
June	.05371	.05429 ▲	.05357	**.05409**	.00028	199,946
Euro (CME)-€125,000; $ per €						
April	1.2425	1.2426	1.2315	**1.2325**	-.0096	1,589
June	1.2478	1.2492	1.2369	**1.2381**	-.0096	503,876

Figure 6-2 Futures Trade Summary

source: Wall Street Journal

In the top part of Figure 6-2 "open, high, low, settle, change, open interest" are different headers. Take June British pounds for instance:

(1) Open: the dollar price of June British pounds at the start of trading on the previous day is 1.4219.

(2) High: the highest transaction price on the previous day. June British pounds reached as high as 1.4244 on previous day.

(3) Low: the lowest transaction price on the previous day. June British pounds once dropped down to 1.4133 on previous day.

(4) Settle: the settlement price on the previous day. June British pounds closed at 1.4127 on previous day.

(5) Change: the change in the settlement price between the day before and the previous day. Comparing with the close rate on the day before, June British pounds dropped by 74 pips on previous day.

(6) Open interest (also known as open contracts or open commitments): the number of outstanding contracts. Trading on FX futures usually is concentrated in the nearest maturity contract. Open interest refers to the total number of the underlying FX futures that have not been settled in the immediately previous time period. A large open interest indicates more activity and liquidity for the FX futures. There were 173671 June British pounds contracts that have not been settled on previous day, comparing with other FX futures, it is pretty liquid.

2) Exchange Platform

It is easy to check current futures price through exchange websites, which provides a more detailed and updated FX futures quote. A snapshot of British Pound futures quotes from CME is shown below.

Quotes　Settlements　Volume　Time & Sales　Contract Specs　Margins　Calendar

Globex Futures　Globex Options　Open Outcry Options　　Auto Refresh Is ON

Market data is delayed by at least 10 minutes.

All market data contained within the CME Group website should be considered as a reference only and should not be used as validation against, nor as a complement to, real-time market data feeds. Settlement prices on instruments without open interest or volume are provided for web users only and are not published on Market Data Platform (MDP). These prices are not based on market activity.

Month	Options	Charts	Last	Change	Prior Settle	Open	High	Low	Volume	Hi / Low Limit	Updated
APR 2020	OPT		**1.2404**	**-0.0038**	1.2442	1.2404	1.2404	1.2404	1	1.2842 / 1.2042	21:06:58 CT 31 Mar 2020
MAY 2020	OPT		**1.2430**	**-0.0021**	1.2451	1.2429	1.2430	1.2429	3	1.2851 / 1.2051	21:06:58 CT 31 Mar 2020
JUN 2020	OPT		**1.2406**	**-0.0050**	1.2456	1.2439	1.2442	1.2378	6,852	1.2856 / 1.2056	00:35:10 CT 01 Apr 2020

Figure 6-3　A Snapshot of British Pound Futures Quotes

There is an increase of open interest of FX futures traded at CME as presented by the following charts.

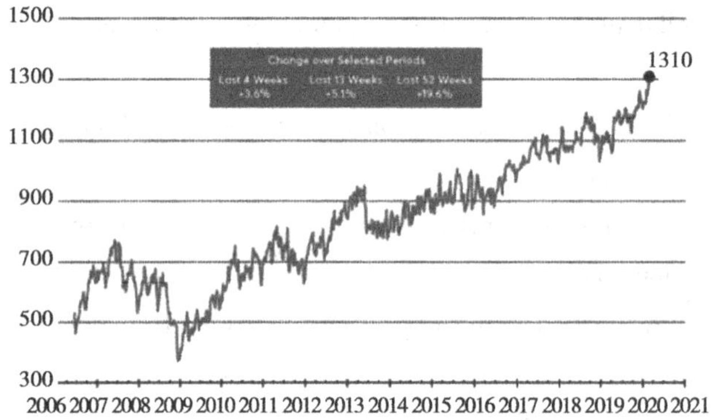

Figure 6-4　CME Group Foreign Exchange Futures Aggregate Number of Large Open Interest Holders①

source: CEM

Open insterest as stated before indicates the depth of the FX futures market, while the breadth of the market is how many different FX futures contracts are outstanding. Long term open interest holders are a measure of the diversity of marketplace and reflect shifts towards listed and cleared FX. CME long term open interest holders are up significantly since 2009.

① Large open interest holders are those have at least 400 open contracts in major foreign currency futures and at least 100 open contracts in other foreign currency futures.

§ 2 FX Futures Market

2.1 How FX Futures are Traded

Instead of be held to expiration, most FX futures contracts are either closed out or extended for profit. Usually, FX futures are traded through electronic or open outcry.

1) Electronic Trading

Electronic trading now is the predominant form of trading worldwide. This form of trading provides trading opportunities to not only main traders of FX market but also to smaller traders. Individual traders are now able to trade through internet, as visualised in the follow figure based on all kinds of data (such as the following candlestick chart) provided by their brokers.

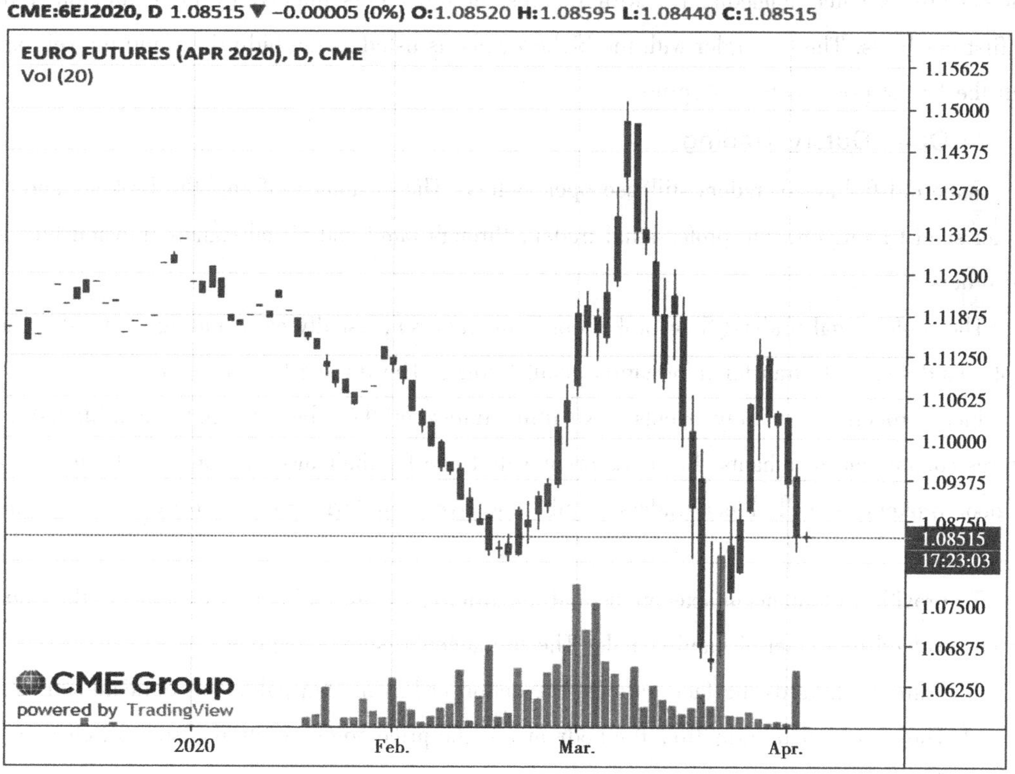

Figure 6-5 Candlestick Chart for Futures Price

source: CEM

During the 1980s and 1990s phone and electronic trading replaced physical floor trading in most exchanges around the world. The CME Globex was the first electronic market operational in

1992. The CME Globex is operational at all hours from Sunday evening to Friday afternoon except for 4PM to 5PM Central Standard Time.

Tradings on FX futures apply the following mechanism:

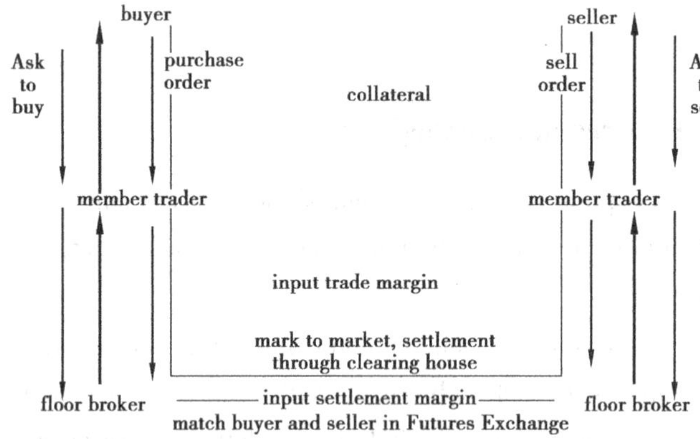

Buy and sell orders are matched or queued in computerized electronic trading systems. Any matches are executed immediately, with the rest of the orders queued by price and on a first in/first out basis. The buy order with the highest price is listed as the bid price, and the sell order with the lowest price as the ask price.

2) Open Outcry Trading

Some old-fashioned traders still use open outcry. The customer informs the broker, and this broker send trading order to professional trader, through hand and visual signals transmit buy and sell orders.

The professional traders(floor brokers or floor traders), usually on a trading floor, shout and apply hand signals to transfer information about trading. The trading floor is called pit.

Floor brokers are mainly agents, executing trades in their behalf, and are affiliated with futures commission merchants. Floor traders mostly trade for their own accounts, but can also act as floor brokers as well. Floor traders should not give their own orders priority over customers' orders.

To provide instantaneous executions and fair prices, the form of communication in the trading pit has evolved into a set of hand signals. The fundamental signals include:

① Palms in towards the face indicate the action of buying and palms out indicate selling;

② The arms' length away from the body means the price and quantity is displayed close to the face;

③ Vertical fingers are for numerical quantities of 1 to 5 and 6-9 are displayed with horizontal fingers;

④ Quantities of 1-9 are indicated at chin level whilst increments of 10s are indicated at the forehead.

Open outcry trading also uses electronic tickers and display boards, hand-held computers, and electronic entry and reporting of transactions. The display boards also show quotes from other futures exchanges.

3) Combination

Given fast trading speed of electronic trading, open outcry still exist because it offers more opportunity to improve the price of a FX futures.

Traders maintain the right to select the method they want to use. Because that electronic trading is faster, cheaper and provides for anonymity, the futures exchanges in the United States such as CME offer both traditional open outcry trading and electronic trading.

At CME, for example, some contracts designated as side-by-side are traded simultaneously on the floor and electronically; some contracts designated as after-hours electronic are traded on the floor during the exchange hours, then electronically other times.

2.2 Regulations

Not all currency exchanges offer trading platform for FX futures. So far, FX futures cannot be traded in China①. But the guidline released by the communist party of China Central Committee and the state council on 15th July 2021 said more international products will be launched at the Shanghai Futures Exchange, the China Foreigu Exchange Trade System, and the China Financial Futures Exchange. Other exchanges where FX futures are available are subject to different regulations, but the regulation of futures exchanges is generally overseen by the country in which the exchange is located. Exchanges offering FX futures in the U.S., for instance, must adhere to the rules set forth by the Commodity Futures Trading Commission, as well as the guidelines presented by the National Futures Association. The futures market is regulated by the Securities and Exchange Commission (SEC), the Commodity Futures Trading Commission (CFTC), the National Futures Association (NFA) and by the exchange themselves.

The exchanges must obtain approval for any regulatory changes, and for the introduction of any new futures or options on futures. All futures exchanges must have trading rules, contracts, and disciplinary procedures.

The exchanges have self regulations as well. They set their own departments to regulate and clear transactions. Exchanges have responsibility for auditing and enforcing compliance with industry rules, such as financial requirements, segregation of customers' funds, accounting procedures, sales activities, and floor trading practices.

① See http://www.chinamoney.com.cn/chinese/mgwhcphjy/

2.3 Clearinghouse

Clearinghouse as shown below operates in conjunction with the exchange. The main function of clearinghouse is the settling of and marking to market of the exchange members' accounts, guarantees the other side of all futures trades, and oversees contract performance. Well-capitalized members of the exchange entitle the membership of the clearing association. As Futures contracts are not initiated directly between clients, FX futures traders must clear their trades through a member of the clearing association.

With the clearing house, FX futures traders do not worry that any specific counterpart in the market will fail to honor an agreement. Moreover, the clearing house levies a small tax on all transactions, and thus has reserves that should cover losses from default.

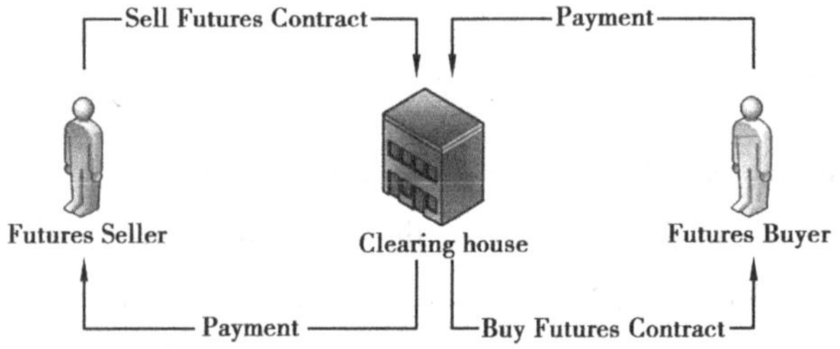

2.4 Staff Associate FX Futures Trading

1) Commission Merchant

An individual FX futures trader normally need a commission merchant to associate trading.

The futures commission merchant acts as a broker and as the custodian of the customers' funds by providing direct services to the public customers to trade futures. Services including:

① Holds and manages the customer's account;

② Executes the customer's trade orders;

③ Maintains all trading records, including keeping a record of all open positions in futures and the balance in the account;

④ Provides and receives the forms for opening an account to trade futures;

⑤ Collects the personal information of the customer, including customer income and net worth to determine whether the customer has sufficient assets to trade futures.

The customer should sign an account agreement, which identifies the ownership, and whether the account will be used for hedging or for speculating. This agreement also includes a transfer-of-funds authorization to allow the futures commission merchant to transfer funds from other accounts to maintain margin requirements, or to close out the futures positions.

2) Introducing Broker

An introducing broker is a firm or individual that accepts orders for an futures commission merchant, but does not hold the futures account for the customer. It is the futures commission merchant who opens and maintains the account, and executes the customer's trades. An independent introducing broker can use any futures commission merchant to service a customer's account and trades, but a guaranteed introducing broker works with an affiliated futures commission merchant.

3) Associated Person

An associated person is a salesperson for futures accounts, who works with an futures commission merchant or an introducing broker.

§3 Foreign Exchange Futures and Trading

3.1 Key Differences Between FX Futures and OTC FX Trades

Both FX futures and OTC foreign exchange (spot, forward, swap) are based on foreign exchange rates; however, there are 6 major differences between them:

1) Market Size

The OTC FX market is larger than FX futures market. The rise of electronic and automated trading made OTC markets larger and more diversified. In fact, FX futures trade at a fraction of the volume, with many FX futures contracts trading under high volume and good liquidity.

2) Delivery Dates

FX trading is done over an electronic and telephone network and FX spot typically has delivery date 2 business days from the transaction date; while FX futures contracts are exchange-traded, are regulated like other futures markets, and usually have quarterly delivery dates occurring on the 3rd Wed. of the month.

For example, a GBP/USD futures contract would be deliverable on the 3rd wed. of March, June, September and December.

3) Quote Currency

U.S. Dollars are applied to quote FX futures. This means that futures prices for currency pairs like EUR/USD, GBP/USD, AUD/USD are quoted the same way as in the FX spot market, but rates for pairs like USD/JPY, USD/CAD and USD/CHF are inverted.

4) Leverage

FX OTC trading can have higher leverage than FX futures.

The leverage allowed with FX futures is 5∶1 or 20% of the amount of the value of the futures contract. In contrast, the leverage on some retail FX OTC accounts can be as high as 500∶1.

5) Contract Size

Contracts are for minimum specified amounts or lot sizes. For example, the IMM GBP/USD futures contract is for 62500 pounds, while the IMM's USD/JPY contract is for 12500000 Yen.

FX spot on the other hand provides transactions for precise, specified amounts. OTC offers more flexibility.

6) Other

Other differences including tax, commissions and fees.

3.2 Trading FX Futures vs. Spot FX for Retail Traders

Electronic trading introduced more liquidity into FX futures, nevertheless, recent release of regulation put more attraction in FX spot trading while maintaining its flexibility. Retail traders now have more choices.

1) Benefit of Spot Trade①

When considering which market to actively trade, investors have a host of options from which to choose. As it pertains to the FX market, both futures and spot have their benefits for traders attempting to tap into the estimated $6.6 trillion daily FX volume according to data collected by BIS in Apr 2019. Closer examinations of the two options reveal benefits and flexibility for long/short-term, intra-day traders in the spot FX market.

Spot FX provides traders with highly leveraged accounts that allow them to trade multiple times their account size. While this works against the trader, leverage allows the average investor to effectively trade standard-sized lots while holding just a fraction the actual value traded. Whereas a typical FX brokerage will require the trader to hold just 2% of the value of the contract, futures traders must hold the CME Group's (or other FX futures exchanges') required margin, which on a standard lot of EUR/USD would be more than $5000. Comparatively, the margin required to hold one standard-lot of EUR in the spot market would be approximately $2800. Smaller contracts make it more appealing for new traders as the margin required for a single micro-lot can be as low as $20.

① by Michael Boutros, the currency analyst for Daily FX.com.

(1) Flexibility

Everyone trades differently. Whether a person is an active scalper or a longer-term fundamental trader, trading the proper size position becomes key when implementing various trading strategies. Spot FX brokerages allow for much more flexibility as many now offer mini-lots and even micro-lots to smaller traders looking to participate in FX OTC markets. The flexibility to trade various sized contracts also inherently gives investors more versatility with regard to their strategy and how much risk they would want to take on. The availability to trade smaller lots means an investor can participate in the market with less capital at risk while still being able to take advantage of intra-day market volatility.

While spot FX markets are open virtually 24 hours during the week, FX futures markets are closed one hour each day. Although markets are usually at their quietest during the break, it does mean traders will not be able to open/close positions or react to any unforeseen market moves. Once the FX futures market comes back online, there also may be gaps and/or slippage on orders as market liquidity spikes suddenly.

An important aspect of trading any market is transaction costs. While futures traders often are hitting the bid or lifting the offer and are charged a commission and clearing and exchange fees on every trade, spot FX traders usually pay only the spread. Spreads can widen dramatically under illiquid conditions that tend to happen more often in the FX futures market.

(2) Duration

Duration of the trade is another key aspect to consider when choosing the correct market. Execution is the single most important factor that can affect a trader's performance directly. Spot FX brokerages have fast and accurate execution, especially in light of the new ECNs (electronic communication network) now offered by various brokerages that match buyers and sellers at lightning speed. Although FX futures markets may provide traders more transparency in this regard, orders often can take a few seconds before confirmation of the trade is received by the trader as the order bounces from the broker to the exchange.

(3) Rollover

Rollovers are a process by which the settlement date of an open position is extended via the simultaneous closing and opening of a new value-dated contract. This process is needed because traders would be required to take delivery of the currency two days after transaction date. Another main function of rollovers is to take into account the different yields each currency offers. For example, if a trader is long a higher-yielding currency, she will receive a designated amount based on the interest rate differential of the counter-currency; whereas if a trader is long the lower-yielding currency in the pair, the position is charged on the rollover. In spot, this transition is seamless to the trader, and the exact amount of each roll is accessible on the trading platform or account history at the same time on every trading day. In the FX futures market, the value of the contract takes into account the differentials, and the actual exchange rate will reflect the diverging yields. It is not always as easy for a futures trader to identify the actual amount she is paying/gaining on a specific transaction, as the difference between the spot rate and futures rate dwindles as the futures contract reaches expiry.

This leads us to yet another important point for longer-term traders. As a futures contract reaches expiry, liquidity on that particular contact starts to dry up, requiring the futures trader to roll position (exiting position in the expiring contract and establishing it in the next delivery month, usually with a calendar spread). Spot traders never experience this problem. Traders can hold the same position for hours, months, days or even years without having to jump into a new, more active contract. All the while, the rollovers are accessible and readily available with most reputable brokerages.

(4) Broker

While futures traders will often argue the benefits of transparency in their respective market, a closer look reveals the importance of choosing the correct broker. While CME Group offers much more transparency for participants, does this really outweigh the other benefits? Choosing an FX brokerage should not be taken lightly and, with the proper research and due-diligence, traders can remain confident that they are doing business with the right firm. Some traders are not keen on having the broker trade against them, but there always is someone on the other side of a given trade; whether it is the broker or another trader is irrelevant. So long as the rates supplied are in line with broader markets, the counter-trader should be of no concern to a trader. More important is the reputation and track record of a broker. Most reputable FX brokerages are governed by a regulator that ensures fair business practices with clients. In the United States, this agency is the National Futures Association (NFA), while offshore brokerages are governed by their own respective agencies.

There are benefits for traders utilizing spot or futures FX. When deciding which market is best, trader needs to match her style of trading and risk tolerance to the platform that best serves her. For the average active trader looking to take advantage of market fluctuations with minimal transaction costs and ultra-flexibility with account and trade sizes, the spot market offers the most suitable trading environment.

2) Benefit of Futures①

There is no question that the FX OTC market continues to see tremendous growth. The continued uncertainty and market volatility caused by macroeconomic events such as the Eurozone

① By Scott Brusso and Dave Schulz, they are directors for FX products at CME Group.

sovereign debt crisis and the U.S. quantitative easing policy have been contributing factors to the spikes in volumes. But over the longer term, the FX OTC market has seen growth due in part to the marketplace's global nature, as well as the evolution of technology and electronic trading that allows a wide breadth of customers to participate.

(1) Equality

Everyone is on equal footing when it comes to pricing currency futures. Whether a large institution or individual trader, Best price wins. While in the fragmented OTC FX market, participants' credit ratings determine available executable prices. Outside of FX futures, there is less transparency with trade data in OTC FX. As a result, market participants can look only to Commodity Futures Trading Commission data. Because of the global financial crisis and regulation, the market is realizing how tremendously important transparency of market data is alongside central counterparty clearing.

The futures markets' equal access creates a diverse trading community in addition to access to a diverse FX product suite. Trading activity among market participants outside traditional commercial banks, especially proprietary firms, hedge funds, pension funds, mutual funds and insurance companies, is contributing to growth in the FX markets. Unlike some cash markets, these different customer groups all trade in one central trading system, which offers the same tradable prices with complete anonymity in all bids and offers.

(2) More Choices

There are more than 90 futures contracts based on major and emerging-market currencies, such as the Brazilian real, Chinese RMB, Korean won and the Turkish lira. On 27th Feb. 2017 CME group launched FX monthly futures, allowing invertors to hedge for 4 consecutive monthly periods. Market participants have the ability to mitigate risk with currency futures' longer dated currencies and benefit from the significant margin offsets available. The exchange-traded options quickly outpaced the OTC market as hedging tools, and customers also have benefited from trading the underlying futures of these options within the same platform. Furthermore, currency futures have seen strength with all 20 different currency pairs, while the spot market tends to provide strength in major currencies only.

E-micro FX contracts are one-tenth the size of standard FX futures with one-tenth the risk exposure. The contracts allow for exact offsets with corresponding standard-size FX futures.

CME's currency futures are traded on the CME Globex electronic trading system. These trades are executed and confirmed instantly, and traders can access Globex through approximately 1000 direct connections in more than 85 countries and foreign territories, providing fast, efficient trading on all our products.

(3) Safety and Security

Since the 2008 crisis, market participants have a greater appreciation of the counterparty and credit risk in cash markets. The importance of a guarantor and clearing method are key to today's FX markets. FX futures offer backing at clearinghouses and risk is shared among clearing members, protecting investors in the case of a default, guaranteeing every transaction and virtually eliminating counterparty risk.

The recent growth illustrates the need and desire for counterparty risk mitigation and the central counterparty clearing model that exchange trading offers.

The steady, strong growth of volume in FX and currency products at futures exchanges resulted from an increased desire, both on the sell-side and the buy-side, to mitigate counterparty risk.

FX futures have very competitive pricing, deep pools of liquidity, a diverse range of counterparties across all segments of the FX market and benefit from the diversity of product range at the exchange—such as fixed income and equities, alongside agricultural and commodity trades. These intriguing benefits have enabled FX futures to become an attractive alternative to spot FX.

Advantages over the cash FX market include open and transparent markets, cost-effectiveness and unrivaled security. To conclude, there are mainly 3 advantages to using FX futures:

- The futures exchange guarantees the transactions thus there is no such counterparty risk as in FX OTC market;
- The futures market is more heavily regulated, so brokers are less likely to engage in fraud or other unethical behavior;
- Because all futures are traded on organized exchanges, there is much more price competition for orders, whereas in foreign exchange OTC market, the number of participants is much more limited on the electronic communications network that is used to trade foreign exchange orders, and even more limited if the broker is a dealing desk broker①, where the foreign exchange traders are only trading with the broker, and no one else.

§4 FX Futures Contract Specifications

FX futures contract specifications are defined by the exchange on which they are traded. Below is a screenshot of EUR futures contract traded at CME. Based on information from CME, this section explains the essentials of FX futures contracts.

① The dealing desk broker acts as the only counterparty to the customer, and is free to set bid/ask prices. There is no price competition for a customer's order.

Contract Unit	125 000 euro
Trading Hours	Sunday–Friday 6:00 p.m. –5:00 p.m. (5:00 p.m. –4:00 p.m. Chicago Time/ CT) with a 60–minute break each day beginning at 5:00 p.m. (4:00 p.m. CT)
Minimum Price Fluctuation	Outrights: .00005 USD per EUR increments ($6.25 USD) Consecutive Month Spreads: (Globex only) 0.00001 USD per EUR (1.25 USD) All other Spread Combinations: 0.00005 USD per EUR (6.25 USD)
Product Code	CME Globex: 6E CME ClearPort: EC Clearing: EC
Losted Contracts	Contracts listed for the first 3 consecutive months and 20 months in the March quarterly cycle (Mar, Jun, Sep, Dec)
Settlement Method	Deliverable
Termination Of Trading	9:16 a.m. Central Time (CT) on the second business day immediately preceding the third Wednesday of the contract month (usually Monday)
Settlement Procedures	Physical Delivery EUR/USD Futures Settlement Procedures
Position Limits	CME Position Limits
Exchange Rulebook	CME 261
Block Minimum	Block Minimum Thresholds
Price Limit Or Circuit	Price Limits
Vendor Codes	Quote Vendor Symbols Listing

Figure 6-6 EUR Futures Contract Specification

4.1 Some Terms to Start a FX Futures Trade

1) Definitions

The futures business has a language all its own. Following is a list of some of the key terms and concepts that may be helpful for FX futures trading:

① **Contract size**: the amount or quantity of the currency represented by each FX futures contract. Each exchange publishes contract size for all listed FX futures contracts on its web site.

② **Contract value**: the current dollar price of the FX futures contract multiplied by the contract size.

③ **Tick size**: the minimum price fluctuation for a FX futures contract. Different FX futures contracts have different tick sizes.

④ **Tick value**: tick value is tick size multiplied by the contract size for a particular FX futures contract.

⑤ **Limit move**: the exchange imposes a circuit breaker for very volatile periods for purposes of controlling price risk and margin flows.

Each FX futures contract has a different contract size and each tick value or minimum price fluctuation.

⑥ **Contract month**: futures trade for a variety of months.

The exchange sets the months for each contract. Normally, one letter is employed to represent each month when citing the futures contract:

Jan.	Feb.	Mar.	Apr.	May	Jun.	Jul.	Aug.	Sep.	Oct.	Nov.	Dec.
F	G	H	J	K	M	N	Q	U	V	X	Z

⑦ **First notice day**: although most FX futures do not come to the settlement section, FX futures contracts still have a physical delivery mechanism, this is the first day in which the owner of a futures contract may be required to take physical delivery of the underlying currency.

⑧ **Pit trading hours**: Pit is a specific area of a trading floor that is designated for the trading of an individual futures or option contract. Pit trading hours are the times that the exchange is open for active business. Nowadays very few futures trade in pits.

⑨ **Electronic trading hours**: Electronic trading hours are the times that the contracts are available for buyers and sellers to transact on that platform. Most trading takes place on the exchange's electronic platform.

⑩ **Basis**: basis is the differential between the spot rate and its nearby futures price (f-S).

⑪ **Convergence**: convergence is the process of futures prices gravitating to the same level as spot rate when the futures contract moves through first notice day into the delivery period. The success of futures markets depends on the effective convergence of futures prices and the spot.

⑫ **Daily settlement**: most of exchanges provide FX futures daily settlement report for reference only. Those report data should not be used as validation against, nor as a complement to, the exchange real time feed.

2) A CME Example

Take the following daily settlement report of CME as an example:

Month	Open	High	Low	Last	Change	Settle	Estimated Volume	Prior Day Open Interest
APR 20	1.09420	1.09630	1.08255A	1.08635B	-.00800	1.08520	1046	4216
MAY 20	1.09415	1.09765B	1.08380A	1.08760B	-.00825	1.08640	276	2047
JUN 20	1.09790	1.090905	1.08440	1.08810	-.00840	1.08730	170439	538833
JLY 20	—	1.09950B	1.08570A	1.08915A	-.00850	1.08815	0	1
SEP 20	1.09910	1.10155B	1.08745A	1.09095A	-.00865	1.08995	404	3666
DEC 20	1.09445	1.10380B	1.09030A	1.09365A	-.00880	1.09265	79	1815
MAR 21	1.09670	1.10645B	1.09330A	1.09620B	-.00910	1.09545	55	240
JUN 21	1.09910	1.10800B	1.09500	1.09750B	-.00925	1.09795	28	150
SEP 21	1.10300	1.10300	1.09900A	1.09900A	-.00945	1.10035	4	1
DEC 21	1.10450	1.10450	1.10450	1.10450	-.00960	1.10275	5	3

Figure 6-7 Daily Settlement Report

① The Month column designates the month and year of the contract.

② The Open column represents the first price at which the contract traded after opening, on either Globex or Open Outcry.

③ The High column displays the highest price at which the contract traded during the trading day, in either Globex or the Open Outcry session. If the price is followed by a "B", this indicates a bid price that was higher than the highest traded price.

④ The Low column displays the lowest price at which the contract traded during the trading day, in either Globex or the Open Outcry session. If the price is followed by an "A", this indicates an ask price that was lower than the lowest traded price.

⑤ The Last column displays the last price traded in Open Outcry. If the last price is followed by a "B" or an "A", this indicates that the last price was a bid or an ask.

⑥ The Change column displays the change in price between the trade date settlement price and the previous day's settlement price. If the current day's settlement price is the same as the previous day's price, or if the previous trading day was the first day the product was settled, "UNCH" is displayed.

⑦ The Settle column displays the settlement price calculated at the end of the trading day for the contract. Settlement prices on instruments without open interest or volume are provided for web users only and are not published on Market Data Platform (MDP). These prices are not based on market activity.

⑧ The Volume column displays the total number of contracts traded during the trading day, in both Globex and the Open Outcry session. A dash in this column indicates that the contract did not trade on the trade date.

⑨ The Open Interest column displays the total number of contracts long or short in the respective month, during both Globex and the Open Outcry session. Each open transaction has both a buyer and seller, but only one side of the transaction is counted when calculating open interest. The Settlement page always displays the previous trading day's open interest. For example, preliminary and final reports for a Wednesday trade date will include estimated volume for Wednesday, but Open Interest from Tuesday.

4.2 Main Features of FX Futures Contract

Like other FX trade, FX Futures trading is a zero sum game. The adjustments made to one investors' long futures position are mirrored by similar (but oppositely signed) adjustments to another investor that has taken out a short position in the same futures contract.

FX Futures contracts have a zero initial market value: neither the buyer nor the seller has to pay anything when a contract is initiated at the going market rate.

In fact, FX futures market is a complete market, i.e. there is no direct trade fees, no bid and ask spread between interest rates, nor mechanism such as sell short in spot market that apply in FX futures market.

4.3 Main Contents of a FX Futures Contract

FX futures contracts are listed on exchange website. Table 6-1 demonstrates most frequntly traded FX futures in CME.

Table 6-1 Main Contents of FX Futures Contracts

CME FX Futures Specifications	AUD	GBP	CAD	EUR	CHF	JPY
Contract Size in Base Currency	100000	62500	100000	125000	125000	12500000
Tick Size①	1 pip	1 pip	0.5 pip	0.5 pip	1 pip	0.005 pip
Tick Value②	10	6.25	5	6.25	12.5	6.25
Months Traded	Jan., Mar., Apr., Jun., Jul., Sep., Oct., Dec. and spot month					
Last Day of Trading	The 2nd business day immediately preceding the 3rd Wed. of the delivery month					
Trading Hours	07:20—14:00 central time					

source: CME

① minimum price fluctuation

② tick value = tick size × the contract size

CME also provide E-mini on EUR and JPY futures, as shown in Table 6-2.

Table 6-2 E-mini FX Futures Contracts

E-mini	EUR	JPY
Contract Size	€ 62500	¥ 6250000
Tick Size	1 pip	0.01 pip
Tick Value	6.25 $	6.25 $
Listed Contracts	2 months in the March quarterly cycle (Mar., Jun., Sep., Dec.)	
Settlement Method	deliverable	
Termination of Trading	09:16 central time on the 2nd business day immediately preceding the 3rd Wed. of the contract month	

FX futures contract may vary in different exchanges. No matter how different, there are 8 major features that must be standardized and included in the FX futures contract:

1) A Specific Contract Size

FX futures have 3 standard contract sizes in CME. For the British pound is 62500 pounds, for other currencies a full-size contract represents 100000 to 125000 units of currency. Mini-contracts are 1/2 of the standard, and E-micro futures are 1/10 of the original futures contract size. The notional principal is that trading in each currency must be done in an even multiple of currency units. For example, at CME, contract sizes are required as in Table 6-3.

Table 6-3 FX Futures Contract Size

Currency	AUD	GBP	EUR	JPY	CHF	CAD	CNY
Contract size	100000	62500	125000	12500000	125000	100000	1000000
E-mini	50000	31250	62500	6250000	62500	20000	500000
E-micro	10000	6250	12500	1250000	12500	10000	100000

E-micro contracts are fungible with the standard contract. For example, a 10-contract long E-Micro position will offset 1 short standard contract if both positions are held in the same account. When combined with standard contracts, E-Micros can help customers create more accurate hedges by allowing customers to better manage tail risks.

2) A Standard Method of Stating Exchange Rates

Almost all FX futures, except some E-micro futures and some lesser volume contracts, use the USD as the quote currency.

The tick, expressed in dollars, is the minimum change in value of a futures contract. (tick = the contract size × the pip value of the currency) What a tick is worth in USD is calculated by multiplying the number of ticks by a constant multiplier, it is also the price changes in FX futures. The tick value for FX futures contracts varies according to contract sizes. The EUR, CHF, JPY futures have the same tick value of \$12.5, but the GBP futures tick value is \$6.25. For example, the spot exchange rate of EUR appreciated from $S_0 = 1.0935$ to $S_1 = 1.0936$, this one tick's change costs loss of \$12.5 to the short trader which is in turn a gain of \$12.5 to the long trader.

EUR and CHF futures contracts each represent 125000 units of the underlying currency, but the JPY futures contract represents 12500000 units. The JPY futures contract quote of 0.89 would mean that each ¥100 cost \$0.89.

The CME has amended the minimum price increment for JPY/USD futures since 21st Jun. 2015. The minimum tick changed from 0.000001 to 0.0000005; the minimum tick for EUR futures changed from 0.0001 to 0.00005 since 10th Jan. 2016.

3) A Standard Delivery Date

The delivery date of FX futures contract is the 3rd Wednesday of the contract month (March, June, September and December). If that day is not a business day, then delivery is postponed to the coming business day.

4) A Specified Last Trading Day

Last trading day is the final day that a FX futures contract may trade or be closed out. As most investors use FX futures as a method to hedge or speculate, delivery of the specific currency underlying the futures contract seldom occur.

Each futures exchange gives detailed explanation on last trading and delivery dates. Take CME for instance, detailed actively traded FX futures calendar on relevant dates is offered. Figure 6-8 is the screenshot of EUR futures posted at CME, the data elements are:

① First Trade Date: The date on which the contract will start trading.

② Last Trade Date: The date on which the contract will cease trading.

③ Settlement Date: The date on which the final settlement price for the contract will be determined.

④ First Holding Date: The date when CME Clearing will begin accepting position dates, where applicable, for deliverable contracts.

⑤ Last Holding Date: The date when CME Clearing will no longer require position dates, where applicable, for deliverable contracts.

⑥ First Position Date: The first date on which CME Clearing will accept intents and run assignments for deliverable contracts.

⑦ Last Position Date: The last date on which CME Clearing will accept intents and run assignments for deliverable contracts.

⑧ First Notice Date: The first date that users will get notified that they have been assigned a delivery.

⑨ Last Notice Date: The last date that users will get notified that they have been assigned a delivery.

⑩ First Delivery Date: The first date that users will complete delivery.

⑪ Last Delivery Date: The last date that users will complete delivery.

Contract Month	Product Code	First Trade Last Trade	Settlement	First Holding Last Holding	First Position Last Position	First Notice Last Notice	First Delivery Last Delivery
Apr 2020	ECL20	19 Nov 2019 13 Apr 2020	13 Apr 2020	- -	13 Apr 2020 13 Apr 2020	- -	15 Apr 2020 15 Apr 2020
May 2020	ECK20	14 Jan 2020 18 May 2020	18 May 2020	- -	18 May 2020 18 May 2020	- -	20 May 2020 20 May 2020
Jun 2020	ECM20	16 Jun 2015 15 Jun 2020	15 Jun 2020	- -	15 Jun 2020 15 Jun 2020	- -	17 Jun 2020 17 Jun 2020
Jul 2020	ECN20	18 Feb 2020 13 Jul 2020	13 Jul 2020	- -	13 Jul 2020 13 Jul 2020	- -	15 Jul 2020 15 Jul 2020
Aug 2020	ECQ20	14 Apr 2020 17 Aug 2020	17 Aug 2020	- -	17 Aug 2020 17 Aug 2020	- -	19 Aug 2020 19 Aug 2020
Sep 2020	ECU20	15 Sep 2015 14 Sep 2020	14 Sep 2020	- -	14 Sep 2020 14 Sep 2020	- -	16 Sep 2020 16 Sep 2020
Dec 2020	ECZ20	15 Dec 2015 14 Dec 2020	14 Dec 2020	- -	14 Dec 2020 14 Dec 2020	- -	16 Dec 2020 16 Dec 2020
Mar 2021	ECH21	15 Mar 2016 15 Mar 2021	15 Mar 2021	- -	15 Mar 2021 15 Mar 2021	- -	17 Mar 2021 17 Mar 2021

Figure 6-8 Screenshot of EUR Futures

For more information on FX futures dates, one may check http://www.eurexchange.com/exchange-en/trading/trading-calendar

5) Margins: Initial Margin and Maintenance Margin

Like spot, FX futures require margins as well. Margins are deposits held at clearinghouse to ensure that clearing members can meet their obligations to their customers. Most FX trading platforms automatically liquidate customer holdings as soon as their account balances drop below the margin requirements. Previous discussed FX spot has only one margin requirement that applies to everyone at all times. In FX futures, however, there are two margins: initial margin and maintenance margin.

When one enters into a FX futures trade, initial margin is required as a collateral. The value of the contract is marked-to-market daily, and all changes in value are paid in cash daily. The net value of each FX futures account is calculated at the end of the trading session. If a FX futures account increases in value, then margin is increased for that account. Any loss is also taken directly from this initial margin. When the loss is accumulated to a certain amount, the margin is reduced below the level of maintenance margin, this trader is facing a margin call. When a margin call is issued, the margin must be brought back up to the initial margin requirement. Margin can be restored by liquidating positions, depositing more funds, or using option hedges. Traders usually have 2 to 3 days to eliminate a margin call.

The margin requirements in FX futures markets are determined by the exchanges. Brokers usually have more restrictive requirements. Brokers can adjust margin requirements according to market conditions. During fast-moving markets, margin requirements may increase significantly.

Note that different exchanges may have different margin requirement, traders should make sure to check out before being involved in any FX futures trading.

Table 6-4 summarises initial margin and maintenance margin of the most traded FX futures at CME (in $)

Table 6-4 Margins Required by CME

FX Futures	EUR	GBP	AUD	NZD	CAD	JPY	CHF
Initial	3685	3960	1980	2090	1595	4510	3960
Maintenance	3350	3600	1800	1900	1450	4100	3600
Since	29Jul.16	27Jun.16	30Oct.15	24Apr.15	15Apr.16	1Jul.16	6May16

source: CME

Different from CME, NASDAQ has its own margin requirement as Table 6-5 below.

Table 6-5 Margins Required by NASDAQ Futures

FX Futures	Initial margin	Maintenance margin
AUD	1350	1000
GBP	1823	1350
CAD	1350	1000
EUR	2400	1100
JPY	1755	1300
CHF	1800	1300

source: NASDAQ Futures, Inc.

6) Settlement

Few FX futures contracts are settled by the physical delivery of foreign exchange between the buyer and seller. Most often, buyers and sellers offset their original position prior to delivery date by taking an opposite position. That is, if one had bought a futures contract, that position would be closed out by selling a futures contract for the same delivery date. The complete buy/sell or sell/buy is called a round turn.

If the FX futures contracts are held on the expiration date, then the short seller must make delivery and the long holder must take delivery of the underlying currency.

7) Commissions

Customers pay a commission to their broker to execute a round turn and only a single price is quoted. This practice differs from that of the interbank market, where dealers quote a bid and an ask and do not charge a commission.

Table 6-6 below features the fees Eurex charges members for proprietary and customer business. Brokers may charge additional fees for their services.

Table 6-6 Fees for FX Futures at Eurex

Contracts	Currency	Order book Standard fee	Order book Reduced fee	Eurex TES Standard fee	Eurex TES Reduced fee
FX Futures(A-and M-accounts)	USD	0.30	n.a.	0.45	n.a.
FX Futures(P-accounts)	USD	0.15	n.a.	0.225	n.a.

source: Eurex

8) Clearinghouse as Counterparty

All FX futures contracts are agreements between the client and the exchange clearing house, rather than between the two clients. Consequently, clients need not worry that a specific counterparty in the FX futures market will fail to honor an agreement. All trades, for instance, at CME are backed by CME Clearing and executed instantly on CME Globex virtually 24 hours a day.

§ 5 The Profit and Loss of FX Futures and Mark to Market

5.1 The Profit and Loss Profile of FX Futures Positions

1) A Profit and Loss Graph

A profit and loss (*P/L*) graph of FX futures position (payoff diagrams) gives an intuitive summary of profit or loss on holding one FX futures. P/l graphs help visualize how a certain futures may perform over a variety of prices and help replicate various positions with futures.

Set horizontal line as spot exchange rate which is the price of base currency, and vertical line as profit and loss in U.S. dollars. Anything on the vertical axis above the horizontal axis represents a gain; anything on the vertical axis below the horizontal axis represents a loss. Because the spot rate cannot be negative, horizontal axis (theoretically) ends at zero on the vertical axis.

The graph is visualised in Figure 6-9.

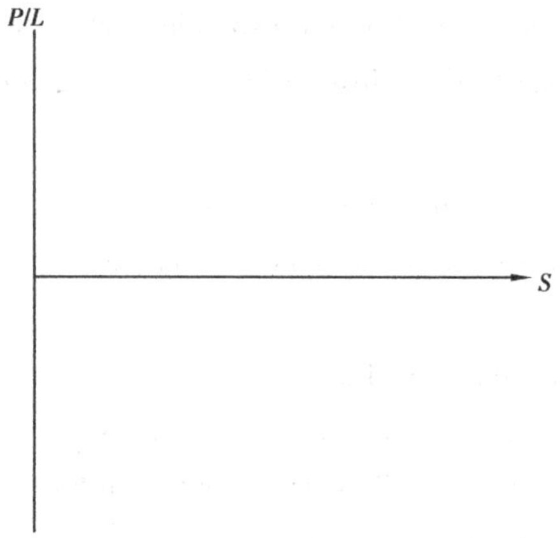

Figure 6-9 Profit and Loss (*P/L*) Quadrants

2) Payoff for Holding a Long Position

Recall that the buyer of a FX futures contract agrees to purchase a certain quantity of base currency at a specified price and time. The value of this FX futures to the buyer therefore increases as the spot exchange rate of the base currency appreciates.

Figure 6-10 tells that as the base currency appreciates, the payoff to the buyer of the futures contract rises. More specifically, one pip increase in the exchange rate of base currency raises the payoff to the long position by one pip. As the exchange rate falls below the settlement price, the value of the long position falls. Once the exchange rate of the base currency rises above the settlement price, the payoff to the futures contract buyer goes up one for one. In fact, the payoff from longing spot the underlying base currency is exactly the same as the payoff from longing a futures, since arbitrage forces the futures price to move with the spot exchange rate. The difference between longing spot and buying futures is that futures buyer only need to pay margin to get into a futures position but has to face greater risk.

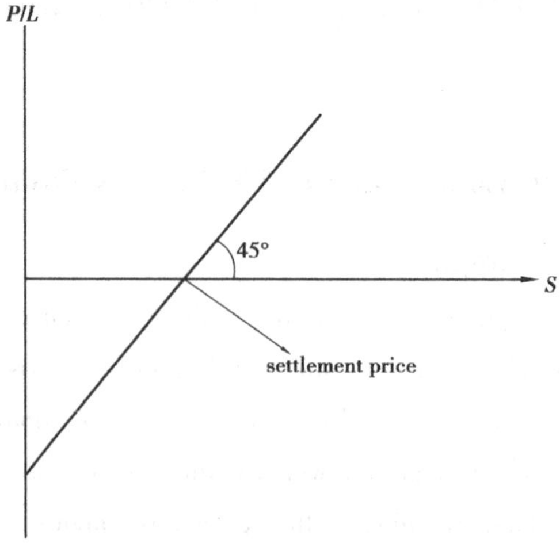

Figure 6-10 *P/L* for a Long Position

3) Payoff for Holding a Short Position

Selling a futures contract, or taking the short position, bears the payoff as the following figure. Because that buyer's gains are the seller's losses, short position payoff is a mirror image of long position payoff. The payoff to the short position rises and falls one-for-one with the price of the underlying base currency. As the exchange rate of the base currency drops below the settlement price, the payoff to the FX futures seller goes up.

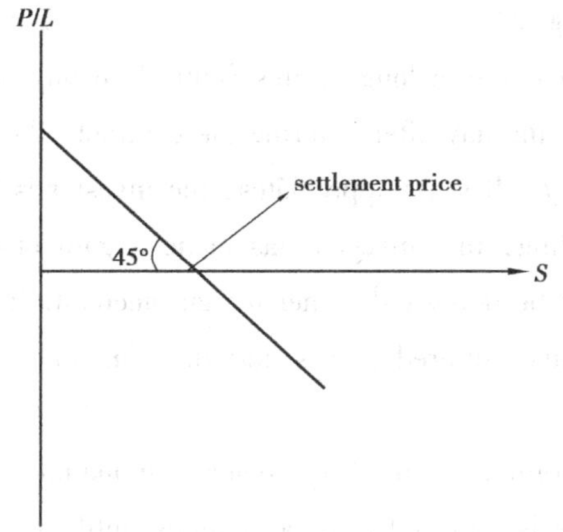

Figure 6-11 *P/L* for a Short Position

4) Profit or Loss Calculation

Generally, to buy a FX futures means that buy at the futures price and sell at the ending spot price (traders can make profit if the futures price is less than the ending spot price). To sell a futures means that buy at the ending spot price and sell at the futures price (traders can make profit if the futures price is greater than the ending spot price). FX futures follows the same rule as forward: It is profitable for a long position, if the base currency go appreciate; and short position if the base currency go depreciate.

Equations to calculate the payoff to traders of FX futures or the P/L of holding a futures position are given as follows.

Long position: notional×(spot-futures)×contracts

Short position: notional×(futures-spot)×contracts

5.2 Mark to Market

1) Equations for Mark to Market

As FX futures contracts are traded in exchange, to avoid the counter party risk, one investor is required to post initial margin to clearinghouse as collateral before entering into any FX future contract. At the end of each trading day, as the margin account is adjusted to reflect the investor's gain or loss from the futures during the day, the futures contract is revalued as well.

To post the intermediate gains or losses of one futures contract is called marking to market.

To further explain the practice of marking to market, a bit of notation is required.

Set S_0 as the exchange rate stipulated in the futures contract, it is the spot rate specified when enter into one futures and will be executed when the futures contract is due.

The futures exchange rate at any time is noted as $f_t(t=1,\ 2,\ 3\cdots)$.

The payoff of FX futures contract is $f_t\text{-}S_0$, it can either represent a gain or a loss for the investor at the end of a trading day depending on the investors position when entering the currency futures contract (short or long).

Suppose that an investor enters a long futures contract to buy one CAD at an exchange rate of S_0, the end of the first trading day after entering the contract, the futures exchange rate on the same contract turns out to be f_1. If CAD appreciates, the investor is in a favorable position.

On the first day of trading, this investor has made a gain of notional① × $(f_t\text{-}S_0)$ × number of contracts, this amount will be deposited in her margin account. If the FX futures rate, f_t, had fallen, the investor would have suffered a loss and that amount is withdrawn from her margin account.

When the investor's margin account drops below the maintenance margin, the investor is facing a margin call, and she is required to deposit funds until the account is back to the initial margin.

For the following days, take day t for example, mark to market is derived by:

long position, p/l = notional × $(f_t\text{-}f_{t-1})$ × number of contracts;

short position, p/l = notional × $(f_{t-1}\text{-}f_t)$ × number of contracts.

long position		$f_1\text{-}S_0$		$f_2\text{-}f_1$	…		$f_t\text{-}f_{t-1}$	
short position		$S_0\text{-}f_1$		$f_1\text{-}f_2$	…		$f_{t-1}\text{-}f_t$	
exchange rates	S_0		f_1	f_2	…	f_{t-1}		f_t **time**
day		**Day 1**		**Day 2**	…		**Day** t	

This investor need not hold this FX futures till its due, she can close out her position (enter into the same futures contract but with the opposite position) whenever the payoff suits her. Even she closed out her position, the futures contract is still trading on the exchange. For example, an investor holding a long position on a currency futures contract expiring in 3 months can close out her position by entering into the same contract but with a short position. Their total gain or loss will be the sum of their daily gains or losses recorded in her margin account minus the funds used to top up the margin account.

2) Mark to Market Calculations: Daily Settlement Examples

(1) An Example for Holding a Short Position

Given that one trader entered into 1 EUR futures contracts on Fri. in Jan. to sell EUR in June at the price of \$1.2546 for one EUR.

The contract size is € 125000 per contract. Suppose that the initial margin is set at \$3240 and the maintenance margin is \$2400. As the spot rate changes, the daily settlement prices are given

① contract size

in the table below:

Table 6-7 EUR Futures Daily Settlement (Short Position)

1. Date	2. Settlement Price	3. Daily P/L	4. Cumulative P/L	5. A/C Without Margin Calls	6. A/C	7. Margin Call	8. Margin A/C Balance
Fri.	1.2546			3685	3685		3685
Mon.	1.2621	-937.5	-937.5	2747.5	*2747.5*	937.5	3685
Tue.	1.2708	-1087.5	-2025	1660	*2597.5*	1087.5	3685
Wed.	1.2593	1437.5	-587.5	3097.5	5122.5		5122.5
Thu.	1.271	-1462.5	-2050	1635	3660		3660
Fri.	1.2789	-987.5	-3037.5	647.5	*2672.5*	1012.5	3685
Mon.	1.27	1112.5	-1925	1760	4797.5		4797.5
Tue.	1.2699	12.5	-1912.5	1772.5	4810		4810
Wed.	1.2617	1025	-887.5	2797.5	5835		5835
Thu.	1.2529	1100	212.5	3897.5	6935		6935
Fri.	1.2328	2512.5	**2725**	**6410**	**9447.5**	**3037.5**	**9447.5**

① The 1st column is the trading date;

② The 2nd column is the futures price at the end of the trading day collected from the exchange;

③ The 3rd column is the profit or loss by the end of the day. For long position, p/l = notional× $(f_t - f_{t-1})$ ×contracts, and for short position, p/l = notional× $(f_{t-1} - f_t)$ ×contracts. In this case 125000×($\text{column2}_t - \text{column2}_{t+1}$)×1 = $\text{column } 3_{t+1}$;

④ The 4th column is the total sum of money this trader gains or loses after netting out profit or loss. Because of the mark to market regulation, each day's gain or loss is added or subtracted from trader's account, her daily gain or loss is calculated and realized by the end of each day. $\text{column4}_t + \text{column3}_{t+1} = \text{column4}_{t+1}$. In this case, the futures price did not go with this trader's favorite direction all the time. In fact, as this trader is holding short position, futures appreciation damages her account. She has suffered loss for 4 days that led to margin call 3 times. But futures dropped dramatically in the last two days, this trader has profited $2725 in the end;

⑤ The 5th column starts with the initial margin, each day take account in the daily profit or loss, $column5_t + column3_{t+1} = column5_{t+1}$;

⑥ The 6th column shows the money in this trader's account, there are 3 times that this trader confronted a margin call, i.e. her account is less than \$3350, which calls for refilling her account to meet the initial margin requirement;

⑦ The 7th column keeps a record of margin call. Once trader's account is below the maintenance margin requirement, she should top up her account back to its initial margin, \$3685 (column6+column7=column8). During these days, she has refilled her account 3 times, a sum of \$ 3037.5 has been input into her account to meet the initial margin requirement;

⑧ The 8th column provides account money after refilling according to the initial margin requirement($column8_t + column3_{t+1} = column6_{t+1}$);

⑨ In the end, initial margin \$3685+accumulative p/l \$2725 = account without margin call \$6410, account without margin call \$6410+total margin call \$3037.5=account \$94475= margin account balance \$9447.5. This trader has input \$3685+ \$3037.5 =\$6722.5 and has \$9447.5 in her account by the end, gaining \$2725 as profit.

(2) An Example for Holding a Long Position

Other things equal, suppose the trader in the previous case is holding a long position, can she get the result opposite to the short position? Her situation is analyzed in the following table.

Table 6-8 EUR Futures Daily Settlement (Long Position)

1. Date	2. Settlement Price	3. Daily P/L	4. Cumulative P/L	5. A/C Without Margin Calls	6. A/C	7. Margin Call	8. Margin A/C Balance
Fri.	1.2546			3685	3685		3685
Mon.	1.2621	937.5	937.5	4622.5	4622.5		4622.5
Tue.	1.2708	1087.5	2025	5710	5710		5710
Wed.	1.2593	-1437.5	587.5	4272.5	4272.5		4272.5
Thu.	1.271	1462.5	2050	5735	5735		5735
Fri.	1.2789	987.5	3037.5	6722.5	6722.5		6722.5
Mon.	1.27	-1112.5	1925	5610	5610		5610
Tue.	1.2699	-12.5	1912.5	5597.5	5597.5		5597.5
Wed.	1.2617	-1025	887.5	4572.5	4572.5		4572.5
Thu.	1.2529	-1100	-212.5	3472.5	3472.5		3472.5
Fri.	1.2328	-2512.5	**-2725**	**960**	**960**		**960**

On the first trading day, this trader bought one futures at the price of $1.2546. On the 2nd trading day, the settlement price was $1.2621. As the price is higher than before, this long position holder made a gain of (1.2621-1.2546)×125000=$937.5 per contract. Considering the contract size, she bought €125000 with 1.2546×125000=$156825, and on the 2nd trading day the same amount of EUR was worth 1.2621×125000=$157762.5. So this trader profited 157,762.5-156,825=$937.5 per contract. This profit contributes an increase in her account, which will be deducted when futures price drop down on the 4th trading day as well as the last 5 trading days.

All the columns follow the same calculation except column 3. As for long position, p/l = notional×(f_t-f_{t-1})×contracts, thus 125000×(column 2_{t+1}-column 2_t)×1=column 3_{t+1}. In this long position, the futures price did not go with this trader's favorite direction all the time. In fact, as this trader is holding long position, futures depreciation damages her account. As futures drop dramatically in the last two days, this trader has lost $2725 in the end. To sum up, initial margin+accumulative p/l=$3685-$2725 = account without margin call $960, account without margin call $960+total margin call $0=account $960=margin account balance $960. This trader has input $3685, and for the whole process there is no margin call happened. She has $960 in her account by the end, if she closed out this account immediately, she would not need to refill her account back to its initial margin, but she must shoulder a loss of 3685-960=$2725, which is exactly the profit of the opposition position.

From the above two cases one can see that opposite position of the same FX futures have exactly opposite gain and loss. FX futures is thus a zero-sum game. Margin call, however, does not necessarily to be opposite due to the mark to market feature.

§6 Pricing FX Futures

6.1 Patterns of Futures Prices

In a normal market, FX futures prices may increase as time to maturity increases; in a inverted market, the futures prices decreases as time to maturity increases. Futures prices thus may perform as an increase function of maturity or sometimes a decrease function of maturity. Interest rates are the main forces to determine futures prices. FX futures, by its essential, is kind of FX forward. The main forces that drive its fluctuations are interest rate of base currency and interest of quote currency. Given most FX futures are quoted in dollars, Fed interest rate is the key interest rate all FX futures trader would pay attention to.

6.2 Evolution Paths of FX Futures

Figure 6-12 gives an comparison of EUR spot and Apr. 2020 Euro futures from 19th Nov. 2019 to 5th Apr. 2020. One may find that the two prices are quite close to each other.

Spot	Futures
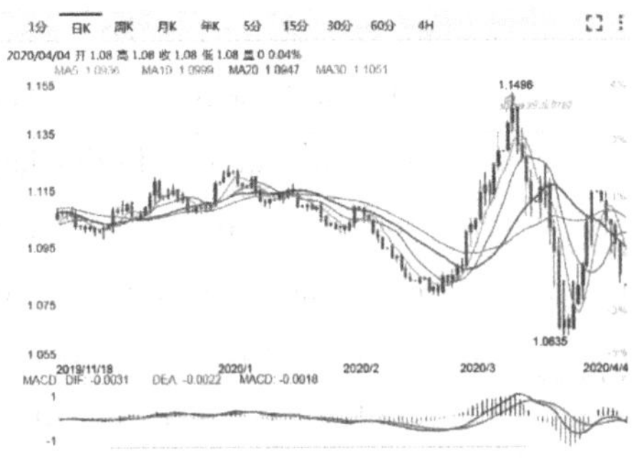	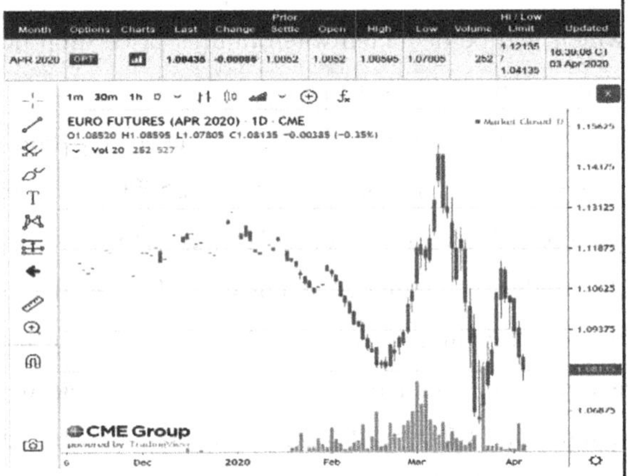

Figure 6-12 EUR Spot and Futures

When a futures is about to mature, it converges to the spot exchange rate. When the delivery day is reached, the futures price goes very close to spot rate and even equals to spot rate. Otherwise, there arises an arbitrage opportunity.

To prove the convergence of futures price to spot exchange rate, suppose that the futures price is higher than the spot rate when mature. One trader can take the following 3 steps to achieve the arbitrage opportunity:

step 1: take a short position in futures

step 2: long spot

step 3: make delivery

This trader can make a profit equal to the amount of the futures price over the spot rate. When many traders notice this arbitrage opportunity, their arbitrage activities push the futures price down.

If the futures price is lower than the spot rate during the delivery period, traders can enter into a long futures contract and then wait for delivery to be made. Their arbitrage activities, again, drive up the futures price and the arbitrage opportunity is erased.

Although FX futures converges to the spot exchange rate, according to interest rate parity, a FX futures may locate up or below the spot rate before its due.

If USD offers higher interest rate than base currency does, FX futures price would be higher than spot rate; if Fed cuts dollar interest rate, FX futures price would be lower than spot rate. Thus the futures prices, as visualised in the follow figure, may increase or decrease when it converges to the spot rate making it an increase function of maturity or a decrease function of maturity.

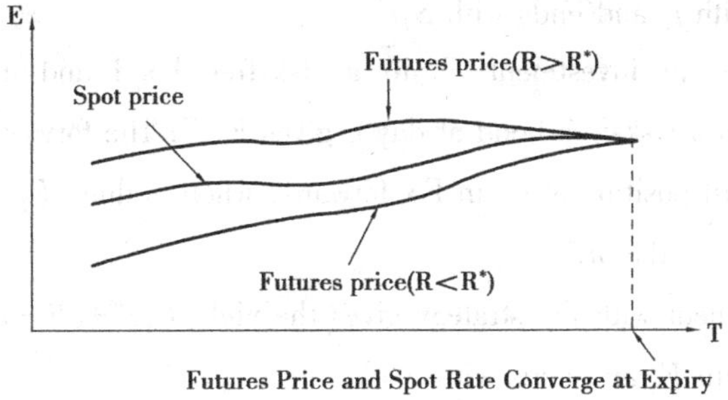

Figure 6-13 FX Fulures and Spot

6.3 FX Futures Valuation

Futures and forward share many calculations in common. Forward rates and futures prices have been found to be approximately equal. A futures contract is in essential a standard forward that requires mark to market. When interest rates are constant, forward and futures prices should be equal.

Portfolio A is constructed to prove the above claim. This portfolio includes an investment f_0 in a risk-free bond that provides rate of return as r, and a strategy involves a sequence of investments in FX futures. Suppose that there are n days left for this FX futures to be delivered. At the end of day i, futures price is f_i. Quote currency provides a fixed daily interest rate r. The strategy about FX futures is:

at the end of day 0, take a long position of e^r;

increase the long position to e^{2r} at the end of day 1;

increase the long position to e^{3r} at the end of day 2;

...

Day	0	1	2	…	$n-1$	n
Futures Price	f_0	f_1	f_2	…	f_{n-1}	f_n
Position	e^r	e^{2r}	e^{3r}	…	e^{nr}	delivered
P/L	0	$(f_1-f_0)e^r$	$(f_2-f_1)e^{2r}$	…	$(f_{n-1}-f_{n-2})e^{(n-1)r}$	$(f_n-f_{n-1})e^{nr}$
P/L Compounded to day n	0	$(f_1-f_0)e^{nr}$	$(f_2-f_1)e^{nr}$	…	$(f_{n-1}-f_{n-2})e^{nr}$	$(f_n-f_{n-1})e^{nr}$

At the beginning of day i, the trader holds a long position of e^{ir}, the p/l from her position is $(f_i-f_{i-1})e^{ir}$, if compounded to the delivery day, this profit/loss becomes $(f_i-f_{i-1})e^{ir}e^{(n-i)r}=(f_i-f_{i-1})e^{nr}$. Then value of entire strategy is $\sum_{i=1}^{n}(f_i-f_{i-1})e^{nr}$. Unfold this sum gives $[(f_1-f_0)+(f_2-f_1)+\cdots+(f_{n-1}-f_{n-2})+(f_n-f_{n-1})]e^{nr}=(f_n-f_0)e^{nr}$. Considering the convergence of futures price f_n to spot exchange rate S_T, the above terminal value of the strategy can be expressed as $(S_T-f_0)e^{nr}$.

In the end, portfolio A gives a value as $f_0e^{nr}+(S_T-f_0)e^{nr}=S_Te^{nr}$.

Portfolio A starts with f_0 and ends with S_Te^{nr}.

Portfolio B involves an investment F_0 in a risk-free bond and a long position of a FX forward. Investment F_0 in a risk-free bond at day n gives F_0e^{nr}. The forward rate at the end of day 0 is F_0. Take a long forward position of e^{nr} in FX forward, when is due, $F_T=S_T$. The forward value is $(F_T-F_0)e^{nr}=(S_T-F_0)e^{nr}$ at day n.

Combine the investment with the strategy gives the yield $F_0e^{nr}+(S_T-F_0)e^{nr}=S_Te^{nr}$.

Portfolio B starts with F_0 and ends with S_Te^{nr}.

Both portfolios end with the same value, yet each has initial outlay of f_0 and F_0. In the absence of arbitrage opportunity, $f_0=F_0$ i.e. the forward rate and the futures rate are identical given that interest rates are constant over the life of the futures contract.

When interest rates change, forward and futures prices are no longer the same. For example, when interest rate of base currency increases, the base currency appreciates accordingly. The investor who holds a long position of FX futures makes immediate profit by the end of the day because of the mark to market of futures. This gain, again, benefits from higher interest rate that caused the appreciation. On the other hand, when there is interest cut in base currency, it depreciates. Investor who is holding long position suffers from an immediate loss in the daily settlement procedure of futures. In fact, when there is an increase in base currency interest rate, futures price will tend to be higher than forward rate; when there is a cut in base currency interest rate, futures price will tend to be lower than forward rate.

Case Studies

Case 1　Major Exchanges to Trade FX Futures

Futures markets remove credit risk from buyers and sellers. Upon execution of a futures trade, the exchange clearing house becomes the buyer for the seller and the seller for the buyer. The exchange manages performance risk by the use of margin. It requires each market participant to post margin for each transaction.

The futures exchange usually owned by its members, determines what contracts will be traded, what the terms of the contracts will be, the trading hours, and how and when futures can be traded. The exchange also is the main regulator of the futures business conducted at the exchange. It houses the trading floor for floor trading and the computers used for electronic trading.

The major futures exchanges that provide FX futures trading are:

(1) CME Group

Founded in 1898, CME Group FX claims to be the largest regulated FX market in the world. CME Group is said to be the world's leading and most diverse derivatives marketplace, handling 3 billion contracts worth approximately $1 quadrillion annually (on average). The company provides a marketplace for FX futures buyers and sellers, bringing together individuals, companies and institutions that need to manage risk or that want to profit by accepting risk.

The company is comprised of four Designated Contract Markets (DCMs): CME, CBOT, NYMEX and COMEX, that offer the widest range of global benchmark products across all major asset classes, including futures and options based on interest rates, equity indexes, foreign exchange, energy, agricultural commodities, metals, weather and real estate. To provide innovative risk-management solutions to the marketplace, CME Group also offers a growing slate of cleared OTC products and services.

Through CME Globex electronic trading platform, users worldwide are able to access the broadest array of the most liquid financial derivatives markets available anywhere. Additionally, CME Group operates CME Clearing, one of the world's leading central counterparty clearing providers. By serving as the counterparty to every trade that happens in markets, CME protects the integrity of the markets, virtually eliminating third-party credit risk. CME clearing offers clearing and settlement services across asset classes for both exchange-traded contracts and OTC derivatives transactions.

From the earliest rice markets of Osaka, Japan, to the Chicago Board of Trade's first "forward" contract on 3000 bushels of corn in 1851, agricultural products are the historic core of trading. Volumes in grain trading continue to grow, elevating the role of the futures industry. However, when the U.S. Congress passes the Onion Futures Act in 1958, the exchanges are faced for the first time with a specific commodity being banned from trading. This moment of uncertainty spurs one of the earliest commodity innovations. In 1961, CME develops contracts on pork bellies (bacon), the first contracts based on frozen meat. The new contract gains momentum and, soon after, the exchange follows with live commodities—cattle and hogs. Diversification into live commodities opens the door to revolutionary new risk management vehicles for the nation's meat industry.

From its roots as an agricultural commodities exchange, CME Group makes a revolutionary leap into the realm of financial futures with the launch of FX futures on 16th May 1972. One of the most important market for foreign currency futures is the International Money Market (IMM) of Chicago, a division of the Chicago Mercantile Exchange.

Beginning with the introduction of the first financial futures products based on foreign currencies, CME Group revolutionizes the futures markets with decades of innovative financial products. Driven by these innovations, CME Group becomes the leading financial marketplace in the world. By mitigating the risk of currency fluctuations, CME Group foreign exchange (FX) products help facilitate cross-border commerce. CME FX currently offers platform access for 59 futures, 30 options on 23 currencies. The IMM is continually experimenting with new contracts. Those that meet the minimum volume requirements are added and those that do not are dropped.

Companies, banks, governments and individuals convert currencies to pay for products and services bought in other countries. For example, an international company may see its profits from global commerce evaporate due to swings in currency exchange rates. Similarly, companies with investments in international stocks or hard assets, such as factories or real estate, face risks related to currency fluctuations in the countries where their holdings are based. These companies can use FX futures to protect the value of their portfolio against currency risks.

While financial futures trading influences the world at a macro level, it also impacts individuals on a daily basis. FX products traded in CME, for instance, shape the exchange rate families pay on a European vacation.

Through trading in these FX futures, CME therefore provides price discovery, transparency, liquidity and opportunities to investors and consumers.

Individual traders can also trade CME FX Futures through partner brokers, including Infinity Futures, Vision, eTrade, ADM, Phillip Futures, and Interactive Brokers. There are incentive programs and memberships available that affect the fees one pays, and how much one starts with. In many cases, traders expect to need at least $10000 to open an account (as with eTrade), and be able to maintain capital requirements for margin accounts.

Since 1985, FX futures contracts traded on the IMM CME have been interchangeable with those traded on the Singapore International Monetary Exchange (SIMEX).

As shown in the following figure, CME provide a huge exchange platform for FX futures. In Mar. 2017 FX futures average daily volume hits 905719, $87 billion notional.

CME FX futures: average daily volume and open interest

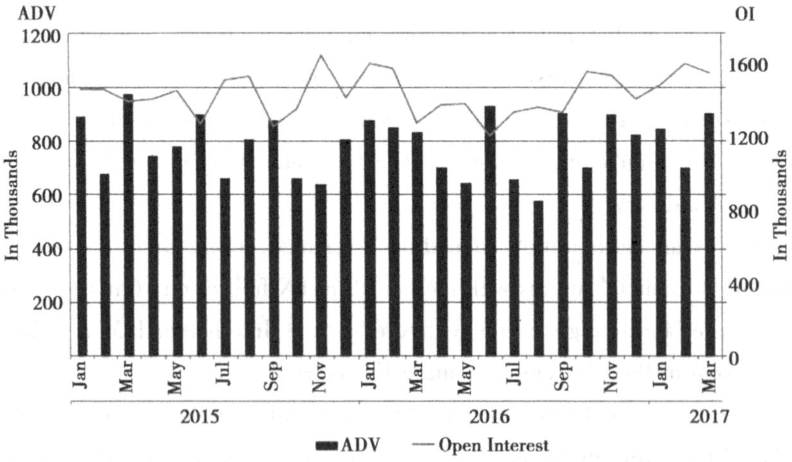

source: CME

(2) Intercontinental Exchange (ICE)

In Sep. 1982, London International Financial Futures and Options Exchanges (LIFFE) started FX futures.

In 2000 by building a link between Liffe Connect and Globex2, the Liffe and CME enabled their members to use a single terminal to execute transactions for the exchanges' full complement of electronically traded products. The interface put an end to Liffe's trading technology isolation.

Through an in-house-built application programming interface to the internally developed Liffe Connect, Liffe has supplied its members with a multitude of front-end software options for accessing its trading platform.

But in 2002 LIFFE was acquired by Euronext, which was formed from the merger of the Amsterdam, Brussels, Paris and Portugal stock exchanges to support growth of the European Union financial markets.

In 2007 NYSE Group merged with Euronext, creating NYSE Euronext, the first trans-Atlantic stock exchange group. It then acquired the American Stock Exchange and in 2013 it was acquired by Inter-continental Exchange to create the premier financial markets operator. In 2014 ICE acquired Singapore Mercantile Exchange, expanding network of futures exchanges to Asia. After acquiring National Stock Exchange in 2017, ICE now becomes a leading operator of global exchanges and clearinghouses and a leading provider of data and listings services. It has 12 exchanges to support more than 12000 listed contracts and securities trading with 5.2 million futures traded each day.

This exchange makes use of nearly 60 contracts on heavily traded currencies, doing more than \$3 billion in notional value daily. ICE features a low exchange and clearing fee of \$0.30 per side in emerging market contracts. ICE works with thousands of trading firms in more than 70 countries. To trade ICE products, one must meet the requirements of the broker, or sign up to be a member under the required regulations of the region in which one lives.

(3) Eurexchange

Eurex is a public company wholly owned by Deutsche Börse AG. Eurex operates the Eurex Exchanges, Eurex Clearing and the ECNs (Electronic Communication Networks) Eurex Bonds and Eurex Repo. Eurex is one of the world's leading derivatives exchanges offering a broad range of international benchmark products, operating the most liquid fixed income markets in the world and featuring open and low-cost electronic access.

With market participants connected from 700 locations worldwide, trading volume at Eurex exceeds 1.5 billion contracts a year.

Eurex enables trading of FX Derivatives and more than 2000 products across nine asset classes on one single platform. All cleared via Eurex Clearing and for FX Derivatives physically delivered through the Continuous Linked Settlement (CLS) system.

FX Futures and Options are now fully integrated into Eurex Clearing Prisma, a portfolio-based margining approach. Eurex Clearing Prisma calculates combined risks across all markets cleared by

Eurex Clearing and enables cross margining between products as well as across markets.

On 12 September 2016, Eurex extended its listed FX Futures and Options portfolio to include six new currency pairs—while the overall minimum block trade sizes has been reduced across all currency pairs to further improve hedging opportunities. There are currently 12 currency pairs traded at Eurex: EUR/USD, USD/CHF, EUR/GBP, GBP/CHF, EUR/CHF, GBP/USD, EUR/AUD, AUD/USD, EUR/JPY, AUD/JPY, USD/JPY, NZD/USD. Those are also FX futures provided by Eurex. FX futures contracts at Eurex are all 100000 of the base currency, and minimum price movement is half a pip. FX futures are quoted in OTC convention. Eurex offers FX futures with tenors of 3 serial, 3 quarterly and 4 semi-annual expirations, maturities of up to 3 years.

(4) Hone Kong Futures Exchange (HKFE)

Mainland China has started FX futures trade on 1st June 1992, but has officially closed FX futures trading in June 1994. Although there is no FX futures traded in mainland China so far, on 15th Aug. 2005, FX forward that featured with FX futures has been launched in China Foreign Exchange Trade System. In April 2006, CFETS has achieved an agreement with CME that enables members of CFETS take part in FX trading in IMM.

To trade FX futures, one may choose HKFE, which is a world-leading capital raising venue for Hong Kong, Mainland Chinese and international issuers. It provides a wide range of products including equities, ETFs, REITs, bonds, structured equity products, equity index and single stock derivatives, currency futures and commodity derivatives. It is also a clearing house for on-exchange and OTC transactions. In 2016, there were 188 million futures contracts traded in HKEX, entitled it the top futures exchange for RMB FX futures trading.

Established in 1976, the Hong Kong Commodity Exchange (the predecessor of Hong Kong Futures Exchange Limited) is a derivatives leader in the Asia-Pacific region. The main products traded on the commodity exchange were cotton futures, sugar futures, soybean futures and gold futures. The Hong Kong Commodity Exchange was renamed the Hong Kong Futures Exchange (HKFE) on 7th May 1985.

HKFE launched on 6th May 1986 its flagship product, the HSI Futures, which is still among its most popular futures products in HKEX's derivatives markets today. HKFE provides efficient and diversified markets for trading futures and options contracts by its more than 160 participant organizations, including many that are affiliated to international financial institutions. The derivatives market under HKEX trades a broad range of products, including equity index, stock, FX and interest rate.

HKEX and its subsidiary companies, HKFE Clearing Corporation Limited and SEHK Options Clearing House Limited, operate rigorous risk management system which enables participants and their clients to meet their investment and hedging needs in a liquid and well-regulated market place.

Other well-known futures exchanges that offer currency futures contracts include:

(5) MICEX: This Russian exchange includes contracts with maturities ranging from one week to one year. The MICEX is merged with the RTS Stock Exchange. One can engage in FX swaps, and it's possible to trade in U.S. dollar, Euro, and Chinese yuan, as well as with the Ukrainian hryvnia, Kazakh tenge, and Belarusian ruble. It's possible to participate according to the unified trading session system, as well as participate in off-book trades. MICEX features a list of general principles and trading requirements. In 2012, MICEX was the 33rd largest derivatives exchange by volume, with close to 32 million contracts.

(6) TFX: Tokyo Financial Exchange claims to offer the world's first listed FX margin contracts, with the margin requirement figured based on a formula that takes into account open interest, swap points, and profit/loss in addition to the reference amount. For 2012, the USD/JPY Exchange FX Margin Contracts saw a volume of more than $9 million. TFX offers a variety of yen pairs with other major currencies, as well as crosses.

(7) TURKDEX: Futures contracts are fairly limited on this exchange, offering TRY with USD or EUR, as well as EUR/USD cross futures contract. TURKDEX is regulated by the Capital Markets Board of Turkey, and traders must comply with the rules and regulations of TURKDEX.

(8) JSE/SAFEX: The Johannesburg Stock Exchange offers currency derivatives including futures contracts. The JSE owns SAFEX, and the financial derivatives portion includes currency derivatives. JSE is the largest exchange in Africa, and is more than 125 years old. However, the listed contracts are rather limited, including Dollar/Rand, Euro/Rand, Aussie/Rand, and Yen/Rand. In order to trade currency derivatives on this exchange, one need to meet the requirements associated with clients.

(9) ROFEX: Argentina's exchange includes futures contracts in the dollar and futures contracts in the Euro and the real. In 2011, ROFEX ranked 30th out of the top 81 derivatives exchanges listed by the Futures Industry Association as largest by volume, trading more than 55 million contracts.

Case 2 CNH Futures in CME

CME's CNH futures contract launched at the end of Feb. 2013 is a young and growing contract, which illustrates hedging trends in CNH, distinguished from hedging trades of other currencies. The plurality of open interest held is in contracts extending out some 6 to 12 months from the present. This distinguished CNH futures from most other FX futures where the bulk of open interest is typically held in the front month.

USD/CNH open interest

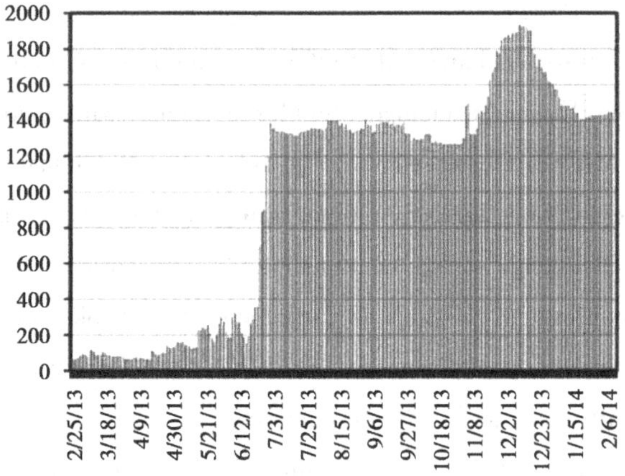

source: CME

Pricing differentials observed in the various RMB markets are a reflection of the comparative difficulties associated with cross-border transfers. Ultimately, the market valuation differentials should converge to zero once the flows are fully convertible between onshore and offshore markets.

CME provides both USD/CNY futures and CNY/USD futures. Check the following snapshot for contract specifications.

USD/CNY	CNY/USD
Contract Size 100,000 U.S. dollars	**Contract Size** 1,000,000 Chinese renminbi (CNY)
Settlement Cash-settled	**Settlement** Cash-settled
Position Accountability/Position Limits: Position Accountability Trigger Levels: 6,000 contracts; Position Limit: 2,000 contracts for Spot month**	**Position Accountability/Position Limits:** Position Accountability Trigger Levels: 6,000 contracts; Position Limit: 2,000 contracts for Spot month**
Ticker Symbol CME Globex Electronic Markets: **CNY** CME ClearPort: **CNY**	**Ticker Symbol** CME Globex Electronic Markets: **RMB** CME ClearPort: **RMB**
Minimum Price Fluctuation (Tick) Trading can occur in .0001 Chinese renminbi per U.S. dollar increments (10 RMB/contract). Also, trades can occur in .00005 Chinese renminbi per U.S. dollar increments (5 RMB/contract) for USD/CNY futures intra-currency spreads executed electronically.	**Minimum Price Fluctuation (Tick)** Trading can occur in $.00001 per Chinese renminbi increments ($10.00/contract). Also, trades can occur in $.000005 per Chinese renminbi increments ($5.00/contract) for CNY/USD futures intra-currency spreads executed electronically.
Contract Month Listings Thirteen consecutive calendar months plus eight deferred March quarterly cycle contract months.	**Contract Month Listings** Thirteen consecutive calendar months plus eight deferred March quarterly cycle contract months.
Last Trading Day Trading ceases at 9:00 a.m. Beijing time on 2nd Beijing business day intermediately preceding 3rd Wednesday of the contract month (i.e., in Chicago, 7:00 p.m. CT on Sunday night during the winter and 8:00 p.m. CT on Sunday night during the summer.	**Last Trading Day** Trading ceases at 9:00 a.m. Beijing time on 2nd Beijing business day intermediately preceding 3rd Wednesday of the contract month (i.e., in Chicago, 7:00 p.m. CT on Sunday night during the winter and 8:00 p.m. CT on Sunday night during the summer.

Case 3 How FX Futures Contracts are Settled an example from CME

At CME, FX futures has daily settlement and final settlement. The related procedures are as follows.

(1) Daily settlement price procedures

① Normal daily settlements up until "rollover date"

• Tier 1: For the actively-traded, nearby futures contract month, volume-weighted average price (VWAP) which utilizes CME Globex "sales", that is, "traded volumes at price" information, is calculated over a 30-second interval (1:59:30 to 1:59:59), which ends at 2:00 p.m. Central Time. Tier 1 applies if 3 or more "sales" occur in the 30-secondinterval. This VWAP is used as the settlement price for the nearby futures contract month.

• Tier 2: If less than 3 sales (either zero, one or two sales) occur in the 30-second closing range, then no VWAP is used to determine settlement prices (as described under "Tier1"). In such case, the nearby contract month settlement price is determined by the average (midpoint) of the CME Globex bid and ask prices over the 30-second closing range ("Tier 2").

• Tier 3: If no CME Globex bid and offer midpoint is available, then CME Group Operations staff uses quote vendor spot rates and forward points to IMM dates to determine the nearby contract synthetic daily settlements.

• For all deferred contract months, CME Group Operations staff settles these contract months based on traded/quoted spread relationships, if available. If these traded/quoted spread relationships are unavailable, then deferred contract months are settled on spot market information taking into account the forward rate.

• For the less liquid foreign exchange futures contracts (minor FX futures contracts), daily settlement prices are based upon spot market or other relevant information taking into account the forward rate.

② Normal daily settlements from "rollover date" up to Termination of Trading Day(usually a five-day interval)

• Tiers 1 through 3 as described above apply, except that instead of using the now less liquid nearby contract month as the reference for prices, the more liquid first deferred contract month (next contract month in expiration cycle from the nearby) is used in either the VWAP Tier 1 or bid and ask Tier 2 calculation. Then forward points to the nearby contract month IMM date are applied to determine the nearby daily settlement prices.

• For all other deferred contract months, CME Group Operations staff settles these contract months based on traded/quoted spread relationships, if available. If these traded/quoted spread relationships are unavailable, then deferred contract months are settled on spot market information taking into account the forward rate.

(2) Last day of trading settlement price procedures (termination of trading day)

The settlement price on the last day of trading of the expiring contract is determined at 9:16 a.m. Central Time. An expiring contract settlement price is derived from the more actively traded, next deferred contract month by applying the "appropriate spread differential" between the first and the second expiring contracts to the VWAP of sales in the next deferred contract month during the closing range (defined as between 9:15:30 to 9:15:59 a.m. CT).

To determine the "appropriate spread differential" at termination of trading for the nearby FX futures contract month, CME Group Operations staff looks first at the CME Globex prices (sales or bids and offers) for both contract months during the time period before the 9:16 AM Central Time expiration (for example, between 8:30 AM and 9:15 AM CT) and calculates the typical spread differential between the two contract months as the "appropriate spread differential." If there are no CME Globex prices available, then for the major seven currency pairs, CME uses the differential from the previous day's settlement prices for the two contract months to determine an appropriate spread differential.

Exercises

Ⅰ. ***Multiple Choice Questions, Choose all that apply.***

1. (　　) are traded in exchange.

   A. option　　B. forward　　C. swap　　D. futures

2. A GBP/USD futures contract would be deliverable in the months of (　　).

   A. March　　B. June　　C. September　　D. December

3. (　　) are financial derivatives.

   A. FX spot　　B. FX forward　　C. FX futures　　D. FX option

4. (　　) are true regarding FX futures contracts and forward.

   A. a futures contract is a standardized amount per currency whereas the forward contract is for any size desired.

   B. the counterparty to the futures participant is unknown with the clearinghouse stepping into each transaction whereas the forward contract participants are in direct contact setting the forward specifications.

   C. futures contracts trade on organized exchanges whereas forwards take place between individuals and banks with other banks via telecom linkages.

   D. the futures contract is marketed to market daily whereas the forward contract is only due to be settled at maturity.

5. (   ) affect FX futures price.

A. spot rate　　B. interest rate of base currency

C. market expectation　　D. interest rate of quote currency

Ⅱ. ***Numerical Works.***

1. *Should the basis strengthens unexpectedly, comment a short hedger's position.*

2. *One trader uses the following futures quotes on the British pound to speculate on the value of the British pound.*

British Pound Futures, U.S. $/pound(CME)				*Contract = 62500 pounds*			
maturity	*open*	*high*	*low*	*settle*	*change*	*high*	*open interest*
March	*1.4246*	*1.4268*	*1.4214*	*1.4228*	*0.0032*	*1.4700*	*25605*
June	*1.4164*	*1.4188*	*1.4146*	*1.4162*	*0.0030*	*1.4550*	*809*

(1) *if this trader buys 5 June pound futures, and the spot rate at maturity is $1.3980/pound, what is the value of trader's position?*

(2) *if this trader sells 12 March pound futures, and the spot rate at maturity is $1.4560/pound, what is the value of trader's position?*

(3) *if this trader buys 3 March pound futures, and the spot rate at maturity is $1.4560/pound, what is the value of trader's position?*

(4) *if this trader sells 12 June pound futures, and the spot rate at maturity is $1.3980/pound, what is the value of trader's position?*

Assumptions	**Values**	**Values**	**Values**	**Values**
Pounds(£) per futures contract	**£ 62500**	**£ 62500**	**£ 62500**	**£ 62500**
Maturity month	**June**	**March**	**March**	**Juns**
Number of contracts	**5**	**12**	**3**	**12**
Did he buy or sell the futures?	**buys**	**sells**	**buys**	**sells**
Ending spot rate($/£)	**$1.3980**	**$1.4560**	**$1.4560**	**$1.3980**
Pound futures contract, settle price($	**$1.4162**	**$1.4228**	**$1.4228**	**$1.4162**
Spot-Futures	**($0.0182)**	**$0.0332**	**$0.0332**	**($0.0182)**
Value of position at maturity($)	**($5687.50)**	**($24900.00)**	**$ 6225.00**	**$ 13650.00**

3. *You expect to receive a payment of 1 million British pounds after six months for your business. The pound is currently worth $1.60 (i.e., £1 =$1.60), but the six-month futures price is $1.56. You expect the price of pound to decline. If this expectation is fulfilled, you will suffer a loss when the pounds are converted into dollars when you receive them six months in the future.*

(1) *Given the current price, what is the expected payment in dollars?*

(2) *Given the futures price, how much would you receive in dollars?*

(3) *If, after six months, the pound is worth $1.35, what is your loss from the decline in the value*

of the pound?

(4) To avoid this potential loss, you decide to hedge and sell a contract for the future delivery of pounds at the going futures price of \$1.56. What is the cost to you of this protection from the possible decline in the value of the pound?

(5) If, after the hedging, the price of the pound falls to \$1.35, what is the maximum amount that you lose?

(6) If, after the hedging, the price of the pound rises to \$1.80, how much do you gain from your position?

(7) How would your answer be different to part (6) if you had not hedged and the price of the pound had risen to \$1.80?

4. *Your company sells 10 machines to a Swiss company. The sale price is 100000 Swiss Francs each and payment is to be made at the end of the calendar year. The December futures price for Swiss Francs is 0.6915. You are worried that the Swiss Franc will depreciate against the U.S. Dollar between now and the end of the year. How can you hedge this exchange rate risk?*

5. *Answer questions according to the following diagram. The middle line is the spot exchange rate, the two lines stand for FX futures. Given interest rate of base currency as R^* and interest rate of quote currency as R. Which line stands for $R>R^*$ Why?*

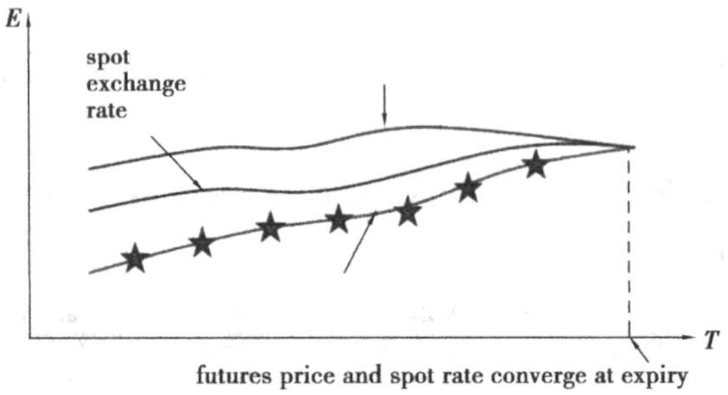

6. *Assume that at the beginning of the day you have taken a short position on a CME EUR futures with a settlement price as \$1.3140/€, one EUR contract size is EUR 125000. By the end of the day, settlement price ends at \$ 1.3126. Calculate the profit or loss according to daily mark-to-market.*

Chapter 7 Foreign Exchange Option Basics

The earliest option in record could be sourced back to the Bible. In Genesis, Jacob made an option-like contract with Laban. In order to marry Laban's younger daughter, Rachel, Jacob agreed to exchange his 7-years-labor for the right, but not the obligation to marry her. In the jargon of option, this 7-years-labor is the premium Jacob paid for this right, which is to choose marrying or not marrying Rachel.

Nowadays Dongguan city, for another instance, in China is dubbed the "world's factory" as this city is home to more than 28000 industry firms producing footwear, cloths, and IT products to sell all over the world. For each order, the export-oriented companies in Dongguan usually sign sales contract in advance, produce goods, then deliver. Usually, it costs at least 2 months before the payment is made.

Suppose that one firm signed a contract on 19th Jul.19, payment receivable will be made in USD (5 million dollars) on 19th Sep. 19. Meanwhile, this firm is going to make the payment on wool imported from Australia on 19th Sep. 19. It would like to exchange USD for AUD to fulfill the payment. Figure 7-1 shows that ever since 19th Jul. AUD has been depreciating continually against USD.

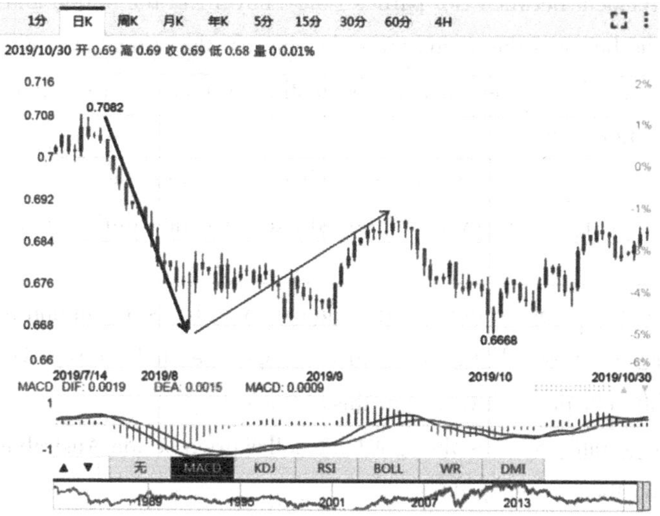

Figure 7-1 Exchange Rate Movement

If this firm believed that AUD will continue to depreciate against USD, it has no need to hedge exchange rate risk. This decision may cause loss in the coming months: AUD rallied back. To avoid the potential loss, the firm can apply forward or futures. But both forward and futures are one-direction protection. If AUD depreciates against USD, futures or forward contract will make this firm forgo the profit. If this firm is very risk averse, FX options would be an ideal instrument to hedge against exchange risk for allowing the option buyer to benefit from favorable exchange rate movements. People thus use FX options as an insurance to hedge when there is no specific trend in exchange rate movement or to profit from favorable exchange rate changes when the exchanfe rates vibrate wildly.

In this chapter, you may find fundamental knowledge about

- FX option definition
- Basic FX option positions and their profit/loss
- Calculations and basic valuation of FX option

§ 1 Conventions

1.1 Definition

One of the important classes of financial instruments is option. Option holders are entitled to buy or sell some underlying asset with agreed price and trading time stated in option contract. A FX option is an agreement between two parties (the 'buyer' of the option and 'the seller' of the option) that gives the buyer of the option the right, but not the obligation, to exchange a specified amount ('the face value') of one currency for another currency at a nominated foreign exchange rate on a nominated future date.

In short, a FX option is a contract that gives the option holder the right (but not the obligation) to buy or sell a currency at an agreed exchange rate during a specified period or on some day.

The firm in the above case could spend some money to buy a FX option that entitles this firm the right to exchange USD for AUD at an ideal exchange rate on 19th Sep. 19.

There are 3 different prices involved in this option:

- Spot exchange rate, S_t. It is the spot U.S. dollar price of one Australian dollar at the close of trading on the preceding day;
- Exercise exchange rate/strike price, E. It is the exchange rate agreed in the option contract for how much USD this firm needs to pay for each AUD if the option is exercised. For

example, E=$0.6700;

- Premium, c. It is the cost to buy the option, the price of the option or the market value of the option. The firm in the above case can spend some money to buy the right (but not the obligation) to sell USD for AUD. The sum of money cost to buy the option is called the option premium.

The firm paid c to buy a call option on AUD, which offers the firm the right to buy AUD on 19th Sep. 19 with the strike exchange rate of $E=0.67$ USD. Then the foreign market did see that the AUD spot exchange has rallied to almost 0.7 USD. This firm thus could exercise the option by spending only 0.67 USD to buy each AUD. The option saved this firm (0.7-0.67) USD for each AUD.

The mechanics of FX option could be demonstrated as follows:

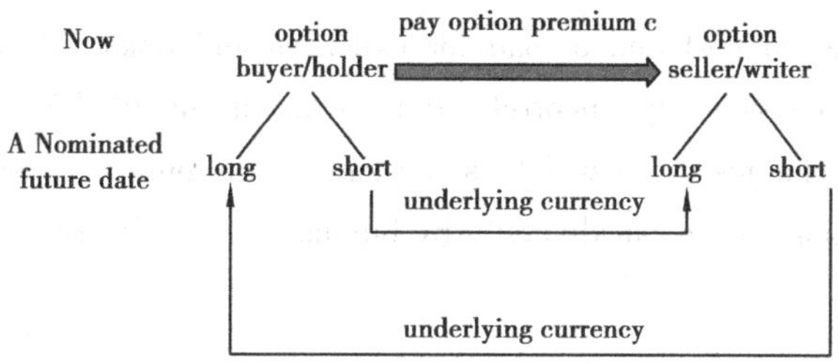

1.2 Comparison

FX option, as a fundamental derivative, has much in common with other derivatives, such as futures, forward, insurance. etc.

1) FX option vs. FX futures/forward

A FX option, is one-way bet on the forward rate, at a premium reflecting the market's forecast of the volatility of that rate. Futures and forward contracts are obligations on both the buyer and the seller. Whereas options are binding on only the option seller. A FX forward or futures contract locks in the exchange rate for a future transaction, while a FX option provides a type of insurance against the exchange rate fluctuation. For example, the holder of a long FX futures or FX forward contract is committed to buy a currency with a certain exchange rate at a certain time in the future. The buyer of a FX call option, however, has a choice as to whether to buy the currency at a certain exchange rate at a certain time in the future. Because FX option provides extra flexibility, it requires a premium c (the cost), to be paid upfront whereas it costs nothing to enter into a forward transaction.

2) FX Option vs. Insurance

Borrowers and lenders are main participants of financial market. Borrowers are in debt and are obligated to repay. Appreciation of debt is what borrowers try to avoid. For anyone who has borrowed foreign currency, the appreciation of foreign currency is unwanted. Lenders are creditors and are receiving money. Lenders do not want the depreciation of their receivables.

For borrowers, a FX call option can be used to "insure" this foreign currency debt against a high spot exchange rate in the future; for lenders, a FX put can be used to "insure" foreign exchange risk against currency depreciation.

Both borrower and lender can apply FX option to hedge any unwanted exchange rate movement.

parties	borrower	lender
avoid	debt appreciaton	credit depreciation
hedge	long call	long put

This process is quite similar to insurance. An insurance company charges a fee which is the sum of discounted expected cost and a load for expenses and risks. Insurance companies make money by diversifying across many uncorrelated risks according to the Law of Large Numbers. While an option writer charges a fee which is the sum of discounted expected cost corrected for exchange rate risk. Option writer can diversify by buying assets that are negatively correlated with the option.

1.3 Types

Forwards, swaps and options are plain vanilla instruments that are traded in generally liquid markets according to more or less standard contracts and market conventions. Option is more complicated than forward and swap. It is diverse in many ways as follows:

1) Basic Types

A call is an option to buy foreign currency; it gives the buyer the right, but not the obligation to buy a foreign currency at a predetermined price. A put is an option to sell foreign currency; it gives the buyer the right, but not the obligation to sell a foreign currency at a predetermined price.

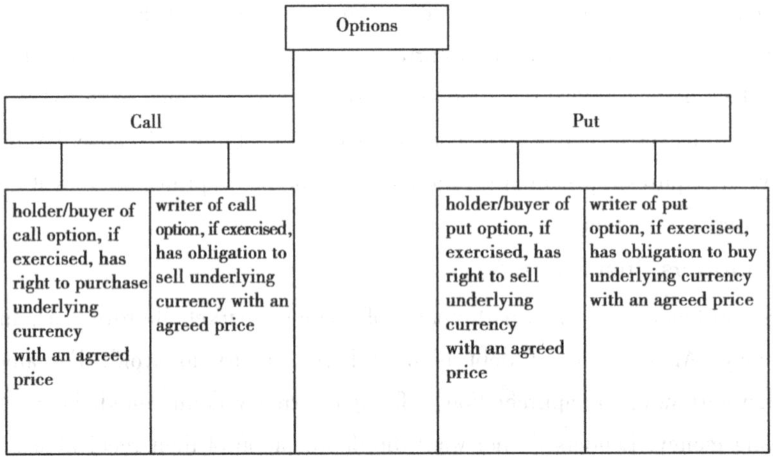

Based on the above types, there are two basic combined options.

A straddle is to buy a call and a put (long straddle) or to sell a call and a put (short straddle) with the same strike price.

A strangle is to buy a call and a put (long strangle) or to sell a call and a put (short strangle) with different strike prices.

2) Other Types

(1) Classified by the Characteristics

If categorized by the characteristics of exercising, there are two types of options, vanilla option and exotic option.

① Vanilla Option

In foreign exchange market, vanilla options are standardized options. There are two types of vanilla option: European option and American option. The options' names have nothing to do with the continents where they are traded but rather to their exercise characteristics. A European option can be exercised only at the maturity or expiration date of the option contract. An American option can be exercised at any time during the contract. Not every option is physically exercised. Those options that are offset before expiration are called non-deliverable options (NDO). As China has not fully opened its financial market and CNY is not freely exchanged, considering China's heavier weight in world economy, its currency gains importance in foreign exchange market. Thus on 20th Jun. 2006, Chicago Mercantile Exchange announced the listing of 3 American options contracts that are NDOs: CNY/USD, CNY/EUR and CNY/JPY. Those NDO were launched on 28th Aug. 2006, with each size of 1 million CNY. On 1st April 2011, China has launched FX option, individval traders can buy options from banks. Individual traders are not allowed to sell FX option yet.

② Exotic Option

Combinations of the basic options can be used to construct tailor-made exotic options.

Take a swaption for instance. Trader A has EUR deposit which offers fixed interest rate. Euro rate is low and constant.

Trader B has USD deposit which offers floating interest rate. Dollar rate is high but is not going to last.

Both EUR and USD deposits are even in present value.

B hates risk while A believes FED may raise interest rate to quench inflation. They can engage in a swaption: B gets fixed cash flows from the EUR deposit and A gets the variable USD interest rate. In addition to swaption, the following exotic options are frequently traded in FX.

- Asian option: an option whose exercise price is determined by taking the average exchange rate over a pre-determined period and applying a fixed discount to it.

- Look-back option: an option whose payoff is based on the maximum that the underlying exchange rate attains over some interval of time prior to expiration.
- A ratchet option: an option, also called a reset option, is a series of consecutive forward start options. The first is active immediately. The second becomes active when the first expires, etc. Each option is struck at-the-money when it becomes active. Each successive forward start option becomes active when the previous one expires. The effect of the entire instrument is of an option that periodically "locks in" profits in a manner somewhat analogues to a mechanical ratchet.
- Barrier option: the value of this option depends on the underlying exchange rate passing (or not) a particular level. Knock-out and knock-in options are the commonest types of barrier option. A knock-out option is canceled if the exchange rate passes a particular level. Once the rate barrier has been breached, the option cannot be exercised regardless of what subsequently happens to the exchange rate. A knock-in option can only be exercised if the rate has passed (above or below, depending on the option) a certain level over the life of the option. Once the barrier is breached the option may then be exercised regardless of what the exchange rate does subsequently.

Exotic options are much harder to price than vanilla options, and no type of option is entirely easy to price despite the existence of well established formulas.

This chapter focuses on basic knowledge on vanilla options.

(2) Categorized by the Underlying Asset

① Currency option/FX option: If an option gives the option buyer the right to buy or sell a currency at a given price during a given period is called currency option;

② Currency futures option: If the underlying asset of an option is not a physical currency but a futures contract on the foreign currency, it is called currency futures option. Currency futures options can only be American options;

③ Futures-style option: If the underlying asset is the option premium, it is called futures-style option;

④ Compound option: If the underlying asset is an option, it is called compound option, which is simply an option on an option.

This chapter focuses on currency options/FX options.

(3) Categorized by the Trading Venue

①Exchange-traded options: Some FX options are traded on organized exchanges, such as the NASDAQ OMX PHLX and the Chicago Mercantile Exchange (CME). These FX options, like FX futures, are usually standardized financial instruments and are marked to market every day. Exchange-traded options are cleared and settled through official clearing houses such as the New York Clearing Corporation, which guarantees that contracts are honored.

② Over-the-counter (OTC) options: A larger volume of FX options are tailor-made, like FX forward, according to the specifications of the buyer in terms of maturity length, exercise price and the amount of the underlying currency.

Usually, American options are traded anonymously on recognized exchanges like the CME, Nybot and Finex, with quarterly expiry dates in March, June, September and December. The underlying currency pair is usually a "major", such as a pairing with USD, although some crosses are available. Over-the-counter (OTC) options are flexible arrangements negotiated between parties known to one another and conducted and settled outside the exchanges without the safeguards of the official clearing houses.

1.4 FX Option Markets

The foreign exchange option market is the largest and most liquid market for options of any kind. Most trading is over the counter, with a fraction is traded on exchanges like the International Securities Exchange, Philadelphia Stock Exchange, or the Chicago Mercantile Exchange for options on FX futures contracts. The daily average turnover of OTC FX option trade has reached $304 billion in 2022 by "net-net" basis; the global market for exchange-traded currency options was notionally valued by the Bank for International Settlements at $152 billion in 2022.

1) OTC Market for FX Options

Prior to 1982, all FX option contracts were OTC options. The largest market for FX option trading is the interbank market where options traded were written by international banks, investment banks, and brokerage houses for USD against GBP, CHF, JPY, CAD and EUR. Each OTC option contract is written for large amounts, called "face value of an option". At least one million U.S. dollars of the currency serving as the underlying asset. Up to year 2019, the OTC market volume still dominated the whole option market, according to the triennial survey by BIS. Many banks and other financial institutions are prepared to sell or buy foreign currency options that have strike prices, exercise dates, and other features tailored to meet the needs of their corporate clients. The OTC thus is home to a wide variety of exotic FX options. The OTC market has grown to such proportions that it is able to offer quite good liquidity despite the large minimum accessing assets—one million U.S. dollars. Although OTC options dominant the option market, buyers of such options are facing counterparty risk, because the fulfillment of the option contract is not always guaranteed by option writers. Counterparty risk can be reduced by having an organized exchange with extremely good credit acts as an intermediary between option writer and option holder.

2) Organized Exchanges for FX Options

Listed FX options are mostly traded on the NASDAQ OMX PHLX and listed FX futures options, mostly on the Chicago Mercantile Exchange (CME).

In Dec.1982, the PHLX[①] began trading European options and American options on foreign currency. Nowadays, PHLX offers dollar-settled options on 11 currencies (*AUD*, *GBP*, *CAD*, *EUR*, *JPY*, *CHF*, *NZD*, Mexican pesos *MXN*, Norwegian krones *NOK*, South African rands *ZAR*, Swedish krona *SEK*), covering both major world currencies and emerging markets.

Another main exchange is the Chicago Mercantile Exchange (CME). It trades American options on the currency futures contracts. On 26th Aug. 2006, CME offered options on CNY/USD currency futures.

In addition to the PHLX and the CME, there are some limited exchange-traded currency options trading at:

① Intercontinental Exchange (ICE)

② International Securities Exchange(ISE)

③ London International Financial Futures and Options Exchange (LIFFE)

④ Hong Kong Futures Exchange (HKFE)

⑤ NYSE Euronext (Deutsche Börse and NYSE Euronext have formally unveiled their plan to create what would be the largest stock and derivatives exchange run from dual headquarters in Frankfurt and New York)

⑥ Marche a Terme International de France (MATIF)

⑦ Financial Instrument Exchange (FINEX)

⑧ Malaysia Monetary Exchange (MME)

⑨ the BM&F Exchange in Brazil

⑩ the Tel-Aviv Stock Exchange in Israel

⑪ China Foreign Exchange Trade System (CFETS)

On 1st Apr. 2011 China launched an option market for CNY. China Foreign Exchange System started CNY-foreign currency option trading on the national interbank foreign exchange market. The CNY exchange rate options are European-style options. The premium under a currency option is denominated in CNY.

① On 24th July 08, PHLX has been purchased by NASDAQ Group, becoming NASDAQ OMX PHLX (PHLX). More information could be found on www.nasdaqtrader.com.

3) Comparison

Generally, the exchange-traded option and OTC are different in 9 aspects summarised in the following table.

Table 7-1 A Comparison Between exchange-traded and OTC Option

Characteristics	Organized Exchanges	OTC
Pricing	Published online	Not publically available
Location	Trading occurs on an organized exchange	Trading by telecom linkages or through brokers
Contract Articles	Standard contract	By negotiation
Settlement	Easily offset position	Position cannot be easily offset
Delivery	Rarely delivered upon	Most have been held and delivered
Risk	Fulfillment guaranteed by clearing house	Counterparty risk
Counterparties	Unknown to each other	Parties contact directly
Trading Hours & Regulation	fixed business hour and strict regulation	Trade 24 hours, less regulated
Liquidity	Liquid and small in total volume and value	Liquid and large in volume

1.5 Quotation

This section introduces quotation conventions on vanilla option, more specifically dollar-settled foreign currency option, traded on the NASDAQ OMX PHLX (PHLX). The call and put strike price are usually specified in terms of pip (a specific dollar amount rounded to the nearest one hundredth of a dollar) for most of the currency options other than the Japanese yen currency option. Options on the Japanese yen are specified in terms of a specific dollar amount rounded to the nearest ten thousandth of a dollar.

1) Closing Prices Quoted on Newspapers

PHLX World Currency Option quotes are available on all quote vendor services. Typical quotes could be collected from The Wall Street Journal. Table 7-2 illustrates the closing prices of some of the main currency options traded on 15th Mar. (Newspaper issued on 16th Mar. Saterday).

The beginning of each section of the table gives the sizes of option contracts.

The expiration date of each foreign currency option used to be the Sat. preceding the 3rd Wed. of the expiration month.

The option prices for the Japanese yen are in hundredths of a cent (ten thousandth of a dollar). For the other currencies, they are in cents (one hundredth of a dollar).

Table 7-2 Currency Options Quotations

PHILADELPHIA EXCHANGE OPTIONS

	CALLS VOL.	CALLS LAST	PUT VOL.	PUT LAST
ADtlr				54.26
50,000 Australian Dollar EOM-European.				
51 Apr	4	0.44	...	...
ADollr				54.26
50,000 Australian Dollars-European Style.				
52 Mar	...	...	4	2.71
ADollr				54.26
50,000 Australian Dollars-cents per unit.				
53 Jun	1	0.41	...	...
CDollr				66.48
50,000 Canadian Dollars-European Style.				
66 Mar	...	...	20	1.76
67^{50} Mar	...	...	20	3.35
67^{50} Sep	...	...	20	3.37
CDollr				66.48
50,000 Canadian Dollars-cents per unit.				
71^{50} Mar	...	...	20	7.90
72^{50} Mar	...	...	20	8.40
74^{50} Mar	...	...	20	10.42
75 Mar	...	...	20	10.86
CDollr				66.48
50,000 Canadian Dollars-cents per unit.				
64 Jun	8	0.85	...	...

	CALLS VOL.	CALLS LAST	PUT VOL.	PUT LAST
JYen				93.49
6,250,000 J.Yen EOM-European style.				
87^{50} Mar	...	...	30	5.55
JYen				93.15
6,250,000 J.Yen-100ths of a cent per unit.				
81^{50} Mar	...	...	5	0.30
82^{50} Apr	2	1.10	2	1.44
83 Apr	...	...	5	1.51
JYen				92.53
6,250,000 J.Yen-European Style.				
77 Mar	110	5.80	...	...
79 Sep	110	6.40	...	...
82 Mar	22	0.93	...	...
84 Jun	22	1.95	...	...
Euro				88.15
62,500 Euro-European Style.				
88 Mar	...	...	8	0.25
94 Jun	...	...	10	4.40
98 Jun	...	...	5	7.48
104 Mar	8	0.55	...	...
Euro				88.15
62,500 Euro-European Style.				
92 Apr	2	0.73.	...	...

	CALLS VOL.	CALLS LAST	PUT VOL.	PUT LAST
96 Mar	...	...	5	5.38
Euro				88.15
62,500 Euro-cents per unit.				
88 Apr	...	...	10	0.43
90 Jun	22	2.34	1	2.35
94 Mar	...	...	3	3.65
114 Mar	...	...	2	23.55
SFranc				57.83
62,500 Swiss Franc EOM-European style.				
59 Apr	2	1.00	...	...
SFranc				57.83
62,500 Swiss Francs-European style.				
58 Apr	16	1.30	...	...
60 Apr	16	0.34	...	...
SFranc				57.83
62,500 Swiss Francs-cents per unit.				
58 Apr	6	1.38	...	...
60 Sep	2	1.90	...	...
Call Vol. 1,221		Open Int. 12,520		
Put Vol. 3,926		Open Int. 12,955		

Data source: the Wall Street Journal

Take Euro Options from Table 7-2 for instance, contract size is 62500 Euros.

		Calls		Put	
		VOL	LAST	VOL	LAST
Euro				88.15	
62500 Euro-cents per unit					
88	Apr	—	—	10	0.43
90	Jun	22	2.34	1	2.35
94	Mar	—	—	3	3.65
114	Mar	—	—	2	23.55

(1) Call Option

① Spot Rate $S_t = \$0.8815$. The spot exchange rate on 15th Mar. closed at 88.15 cents per Euro (middle point).

② Exercise Price $E = \$0.9$. One call option contract on the Euro with exercise price 90 cents and exercise month June would give the option buyer the right to buy 62500 Euros for $0.90 \times 62500 = \$56250$.

③ Premium c=\$0.0234, The indicated price of the contract is 2.34 cents so that one contract would cost 62500×0.0234=\$1462.50.

④ 22 call options have been traded, on 15th Mar..

(2) Put Option

① Spot Rate S_t=\$0.8815. The spot exchange rate is 88.15 cents per Euro(middle point).

② Exercise Price E=\$0.9. "The Jun. put option on Euro of 90" means the price to sell per Euro is 90 cents.

③ Premium c=0.0235. The price of "The Jun. put option on Euro of 90" is 2.35 cents per Euro. Since one option contract on the PHLX consists of 62500 Euros, the total cost for the put is 62500×0.0235=\$1468.75.

④ one put option has been traded, on 15th Mar..

2) Quotes in Exchanges

This section applies dollar-settled options on major currencies (AUD, GBP, CAD, EUR, CHF, NZD, JPY) traded in Nasdag options Market (NOM). Some explanation on dollar-settled foreign currency option could be found on its website: nasdagtrader.com.

Generally, there are 13 aspects that one FX option contract should include.

① Contract Size: 10000 units of underlying currency (AUD, GBP, CAD, EUR, CHF, NZD) or 1000000 JPY.

② Exercise Style: European.

③ Expiration Date: the 3rd Friday of the expiration month.

④ Expiration Cycle: Quarterly on the March cycle plus two additional near-term months (six months at all times).

⑤ Settlement: U.S. dollars.

⑥ Settlement Value for Expiring Contracts: The spot price at 12:00:00 Eastern Time (noon) on the expiration date. The settlement value is disseminated under the symbol JQL. Consult PHLX Rule 1057 for further information.

⑦ Last Trading Day for Expiring Contracts: The third Friday of the expiration month.

⑧ Contract Point Value: \$100 (i.e., .01 x 10000).

⑨ Exercise (Strike) Price Intervals: The Exchange shall determine fixed-point intervals of exercise prices. Generally, the exercise (strike) price interval shall be set at half-cent intervals. Consult PHLX Rule 1012 for further information.

⑩ Premium Quotation: One point = \$ 100. Thus a premium quote of 2.13 is \$ 213. The minimum change in a premium is .01=\$1.00.

⑪ Position Limits: 600000 contracts on the same side of the market. Hedge exemptions are available. For more information consult PHLX Rules 1001 and 1002.

⑫ Trading Hours: 9:30 a.m. to 4:00 p.m. Eastern Time.

⑬ Issuer and Guarantor: The Options Clearing Corporation (OCC).

There are many websites that provide on-time FX option prices:

http://www.cmegroup.com/trading/products/#pageNumber=1&sortAsc=true&sortField=cleared&group=3&page=1

https://www.investing.com/currencies/forex-options

https://sentryderivatives.com/#home

https://www.nasdaq.com/markets/currency-options.aspx

online FX option trading platforms such as www.saxotrader.com, are provided by banks. http://www.fxoptions.com/site/OptionsQuotesand Calculator.aspx

future options are traded on CME as well.

3) Quotes in OTC

In OTC market, FX options are quoted in terms of exchange rate volatility. Take quotes page for instance, one can find charting of 50 & 200 day moving average, candlestick indicators with open, high, low and closing values, intraday implied and historical volatility data and a full display of strike prices. The options calculator helps traders forecast the theoretical value, calculate the implied volatility and option contract pricing, and sensitivities (Greeks) based on the volatility.

The skew tab displays the implied volatility skew across various strike prices and expiration months for the FX options symbol.

The skew chart allows traders to recognize where and when the market is expecting movement (variance) in the underlying instrument.

§2 Basic FX Option Strategies

An option has two parties: option seller (writer) and option buyer (holder). The action that an option writer sells the right to the option holder is called short an option. As each trade includes selling and buying, the counter-action of short is called long. Generally, when someone buys an option, she is said to hold a "long" position. If someone sells an option, then she is said to hold a "short" position. Option strategies involve taking position in options, the underlying currency, and borrowing or lending.

Because purchase of one currency entails the simultaneous sale of another, it follows that each currency option involves one call and one put.

2.1 Definitions

Take option on EUR/USD as an example.

1) A long call option on EUR/USD

Option holder has bought the right, but not the obligation, to buy EUR from option writer at the strike rate in USD. The mirror transaction is a long put option: option holder has bought the right, but not the obligation, to sell.

2) A short call on EUR/USD

Option writer has sold option holder the right (but not the obligation) to buy EUR from option writer at the strike rate in USD. The mirror transaction is a short put option: option writer has sold the right (but not the obligation) to option holder to sell.

3) A long put on EUR/USD

Option holder has bought the right, but not the obligation, to sell EUR to option writer at the strike rate in USD. The mirror transaction is a long call: option holder has bought the right, but not the obligation, to buy.

4) A short put on EUR/USD

Option writer has sold option holder the right (but not the obligation) to sell EUR to option writer at the strike rate in USD. The mirror transaction is a short call: option writer has sold the right (but not the obligation) to option holder to buy.

2.2 Trading Actions

1) Long an Option

Long an option is to buy a FX option, which means no commitment to buy or sell the underlying currency. There are three ways for option holders to deal with options. Following examples demonstrate when each method might be appropriate:

(1) Hold the Option till Maturity

Hold until maturity then trade: hold options contracts until the end of the contract period, and then exercise the option at the strike price. This applies when exchange rate moves as forecasted.

(2) Trade Before the Expiration Date

Many traders do not really need the underlying currency, they trade options for profit. If forecast exchange rate right, the option value increases. One can sell her option with capital gain without spending big sum of money as the contract size required.

(3) Let the Option Expire

If exchange rate goes against option holder's interest, option holder simply do nothing. At expiration, option holder will have no profit and the option will expire worthless. Option holder's loss is limited to the premium she paid for the option and commissions.

2) Short an Option

"Selling" options is often referred to as "writing" options. In contrast to buying options, selling FX options comes with an obligation: the obligation to sell or buy the underlying currency with strike price to option holder if that option holder decides to exercise the option. Option writer gets option premium and is assigned the obligation.

To short an option, one may choose covered or uncovered type, both will be funther discussed next section.

2.3 Position Payoff

There are four basic option positions, which can be adopted singly or in combination for strategic purposes. Take option on GBP/USD for instance.

1) Long Call (option holder)

A currency investor who is bullish about spot sterling vis-a-vis the U.S. dollar can choose to buy the right to purchase GBP/USD at the strike price. The cost of this right is the "premium".

A long call is profitable or in-the-money when the spot rate is greater than the strike rate. The deeper into the money, the greater the profit from exercising the option.

A long call is unprofitable or out-of-the-money if the spot rate is lower than the strike rate. If the situation remains unchanged until expiry then the option will expire unexercised and the buyer will lose the option premium. The maximum loss is limited to the premium even if the spot rate goes to zero.

When the strike and spot exchange rates are equal, the option is said to be at-the-money.

More specifically, given that:

- C_{aT} be the value of the American call at expiration;
- C_{eT} be the value of the European call at expiration;
- E be the strike dollar price per GBP;
- S_T be the spot exchange rate at time T;
- c be the cost of the premium.

Shown in Figure 7-2 the value of a call at expiration is $C_{aT}=C_{eT}=\text{Max}[S_T-E,\ 0]$, and the buyer of a call could have profit as $\text{Max}[S_T-E-c,\ 0]$ on the call option.

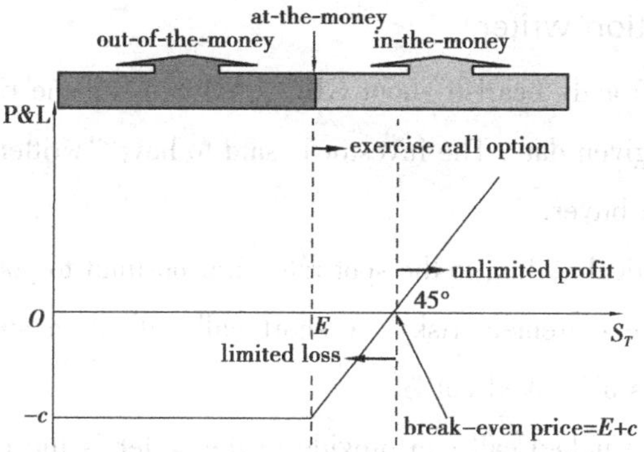

Figure 7-2 Long Call Option

① If $S_T<E$, this call option is out-of-the-money, because it brings loss to the buyer and will not be exercised; option buyer bares loss limited to premium, c.

② If $S_T=E$, this call option expires at-the-money. Option is worthless for the buyer. Option buyer may not exercise the call option in practice, considering the transaction cost. In the case, option buyer bares loss limited to its premium, c.

③ If $S_T>E$, this call option is said in-the-money and will be exercised by option buyer. If $S_T-c\leqslant E$, this call option is not profitable, but as long as $S_T>E$, the buyer of the call will still exercise the option to recoup part of the premium. If $S_T-c>E$, this call option is profitable for option buyer.

An option holder of a call benefits from base currency appreciation. The more base currency appreciates against quote currency, the higher gain for a call option holder.

The current GBP/USD spot exchange rate $S=1.5770/75$. An investor thinks that GBP/USD is going to rise over the next three months, and she buys one three-month call option on GBP/USD with a strike rate of E = 1.6000, expiring in the third week of March.

Assume that the call option premium is quoted at $c=\$0.0233/0.0235$[①]. The option contract size for sterling is £ 125000.

- This call option costs option holder 125000×0.0235 =$2938, which represents investor's margin requirement;
- If at expiry, the closing spot rate is 1.6350, option holder gains profit (1.6350−1.6000)× 125000−2938 =$1437, then rate of return is 1437÷2938×100% =48.91%. A profit of $1437 on an outlay of $2938 gives this option holder 48.91% return on margin.
- Had the closing price at expiry been $S_T=1.5650$, this option holder would not exercise the option and would have a loss of $2938, 100% of the margin requirement.

① in foreign exchange market any underlying asset is quoted both in selling price and buying price. The "bid low ask high" principle also applies here.

2) Short Call (option writer)

An investor who is strongly bearish about GBP/USD can sell the right to buy GBP/USD at a strike rate on or before a given date. The investor is said to have "written" a call for which she has taken a premium from the buyer.

As there is no theoretical ceiling to the spot rate, i.e. no limit to potential losses for the seller, writing options is therefore extremely risky. A short call without a simultaneous holding in the currency itself is known as a "naked call".

The maximum profit a naked call can provide to the seller is the premium, even if spot rate falls to zero.

Naked calls are considered inefficient, because they offer limited upside and potentially unlimited downside to the seller.

When option is due, as shown in Figure 7-3:

① If $S_T<E$, the option brings loss to the buyer, and it will not be exercised. The option writer then can earn the full premium c.

② If $S_T=E$, this call option expires at-the-money. As option buyer would not choose to exercise, the option writer earns the full premium c.

③ If $S_T>E$, option buyer will exercise option. When $S_T-c\leqslant E$ this call option is not profitable for the buyer, but as long as $S_T>E$, the buyer of the call will still exercise the option to recoup the premium. The writer thus could only earn part of the option premium. If $S_T-c>E$, this call is profitable for the buyer. If the writer wrote the option "naked", that is, the writer wrote the option without owning the currency, the writer has to buy the currency at spot and resales to the buyer with the strike exchange rate. The loss the writer suffers increases as the price of the underlying currency rises, and it is unlimited. Even if the writer already owns the underlying base currency, the writer will still suffer an opportunity loss: surrendering against the option the same base currency that could have been sold for more in the open market.

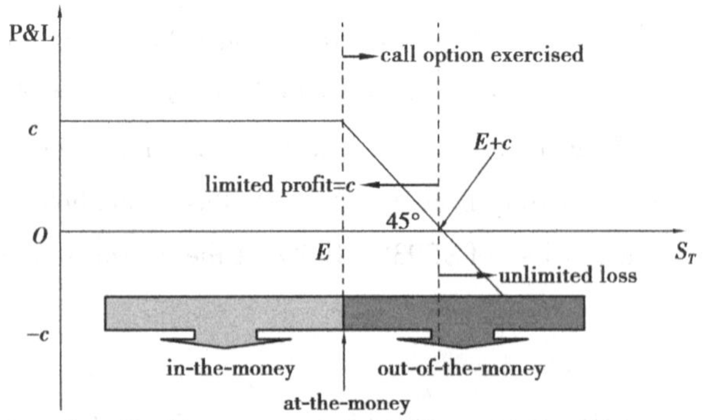

Figure 7-3 Selling a Call Option Naked

With limited profit and unlimited loss, the writer of a "naked" call has a rather unattractive combination of potential outcomes. But if the writer has owned the underlying currency of the option before writing, it is a "covered" call. The writer of "covered" call experiences an opportunity loss which is subjected to the underlying currency owned by the writer.

An option writer of a call benefits from base currency depreciation. Following is an example of a short call held by an investor to expiry.

An investor is strongly bearish about GBP/USD which is trading at 1.5750/55. Attracted by the prospect of taking in a premium. She writes one March GBP/USD call option contract at a strike of 1.5500, The option premium is quoted as 0.0446/0.0493.

- The premium the option writer takes in is 0.0446×125000=$5575;
- If the settlement price is 1.5400 at expiry, this short call finishes out-of-the-money for the option holder. As this FX option is not exercised, option writer can keep the premium of $5575;
- If GBP/USD has risen to 1.60 at expiry, the option holder would exercise the option. This option writer, would have to buy a GBP/USD at around 1.6000 and deliver it at 1.5500. Netting out the option premium, option writer ends up with a loss as (1.6000−1.5500)×125000−5575=$675;
- Note that there is no ceiling on GBP/USD, option writer's losses are potentially unlimited with maximum possible gain as 5575 USD.

3) Long Put (option holder)

The currency investor who is bearish about GBP/USD would buys the right to sell at a strike rate. The option will be in-the-money when the spot rate is below the strike rate and out-of-the-money when the spot rate exceeds the strike rate.

An option that expires out-of-the-money will not be exercised. The option holder will take a loss equal to the premium paid.

More specifically, given the following notations:

- P_{aT} be the value of the American put at expiration;
- P_{eT} be the value of the European put at expiration;
- E be the exercise price per unit of FC;
- S_T be the spot exchange rate at time T;
- c be the cost of the premium.

The value of a put at expiration is given by $P_{aT}=P_{eT}=\text{Max}[E-S_T, 0]$, then the buyer of a put could have a profit as $\text{Max}[E-S_T-c, 0]$ from the put option.

Upon expiration as shown in Figure 7-4:

① If $S_T<E$, this put option is said in-the-money for holder and will be exercised. If $S_T+c\geqslant E$, this put option is not profitable, the option holder will still exercise the option to recoup some

premium; if $S_T+c<E$ put option is profitable for the option holder.

② If $S_T=E$, this put option expires at-the-money. In practice, the option holder may not choose to exercise the put option considering the transaction cost. Option holder thus bares loss limited to premium.

③ If $S_T>E$, the option is said out-of-money for holder, because it brings loss to the option holder and will not be exercised. Option holder thus bares loss limited to premium, and writer keeps premium as gain.

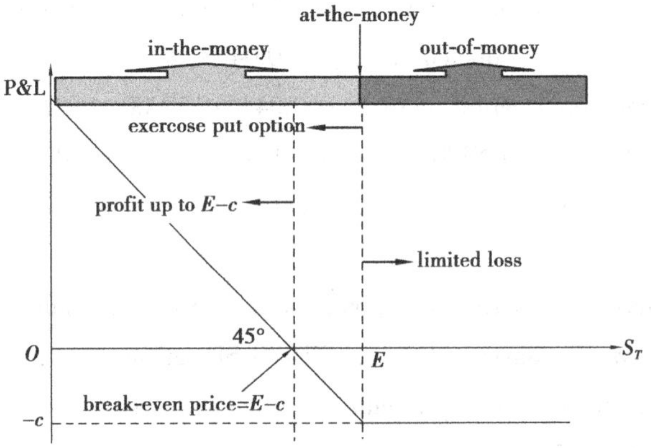

Figure 7-4 Buying a Put Option

An option holder of a put benefits from base currency depreciation. The more base currency depreciates against quote currency, the more a put option holder gains.

Suppose the current spot rate for GBP/USD is 1.5770/75, and an investor is bearish about sterling. She buys one three-month put option contract in GBP/USD at a strike price of 1.5500. The option is quoted at 0.0295/0.0298. This purchase brings the following facts:

- The option holder pays $0.0298\times125000=\$3725$ to buy a put;
- If at expiry GBP/USD falls to $S_T=1.5150$, the profit option holder gains is $(1.5500-1.5150)\times125000-3725=\$650$, and rate of return is $650\div3725\times100\%=17.4\%$;
- If the closing price for GBP/USD is $S_T=1.6000$, option holder would not exercise the option and forgos the $3725 premium.

4) Short Put (option writer)

An investor who is strongly bullish about GBP/USD can write a put.

The maximum possible profit to the option writer is the premium taken in, even if spot goes to infinity. Maximum loss occurs when spot hits zero, which is most unlikely.

Figure 7-5 illustrates when option is alue:

① If $S_T<E$, this option will be exercised. But if $S_T+c\geqslant E$, the writer could still earn part of the option premium. If $S_T+c<E$, the writer has to buy the currency at the strike price. The loss the writer's loss increases as the price of the base currency falls.

② If $S_T = E$, this put option expires at-the-money. As option buyer would not choose to exercise, the option writer earns the full premium c.

③ If $S_T > E$, the put option brings loss to the buyer, and it will not be exercised. The option writer earns the full premium c.

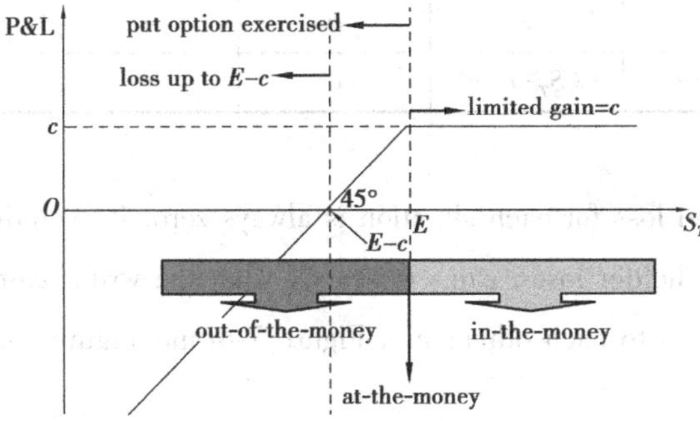

Figure 7-5 Selling a Put Option Naked

To confirm the theory, see the following short put held to expiry example.

An investor is strongly bullish about GBP/USD (trading at S_t = 1.5770/75 in the spot market). She sells one three-month March GBP/USD put at a strike price of E=1.6000. The put option premium is 0.0567/0.0571.

- She takes in 0.056 7×125000=$7088 for option premium;
- If the settlement price at expiry is S_T=1.5100, then option will be exercised, and writer loses (1.6000−1.5100)×125000−7088=$4162;
- If the settlement price is above 1.6000, option writer would not exercise and option writer retains the $7088 premium.

The following table gives a brief description on the basic option strategies.

Table 7-3 FX Option Strategies

Type	Long	Short
Call	buy the right from option seller to buy the currency from this option seller at the strike exchange rate on or before expiry of the option	sell option buyer the right to buy the currency from herself at the strike rate on or before expiry of the option
Put	buy the right from option seller to sell the currency to this option seller at the strike exchange rate on or before expiry of the option	sell option buyer the right to sell the currency to herself at the strike rate on or before expiry of the option

The profit or loss for the option/holder and the option/writer of the above strategies is summed in Table 7-4:

Table 7-4 The profit/loss for the Option Holder and the Option Writer

Situation	Call			Put		
	Buyer	Writer	Sum	Buyer	Writer	Sum
$S_T<E$	$-c$	c	0	$E-S_T-c$	$-(E-S_T-c)$	0
$S_T=E$	$-c$	c	0	$-c$	c	0
$S_T>E$	S_T-E-c	$-(S_T-E-c)$	0	$-c$	c	0

The sum of profit and loss for each situation is always zero. If excluding costs, an option is a zero-sum game. What the holder loses/gains is exactly what the writer gains/loses. Figure 7-2 and figure 7-3 are mirror images to each other; and Figure 7-4 and Figure 7-5 also are mirror-images of one another.

2.4 Exercise Mechanics

Upon exercise, a currency option turns into a spot foreign exchange deal done at the option strike for settlement on the spot value date. Suppose that a European option is cited as follows:

		Calls		Put	
		VOL	LAST	VOL	LAST
Euro					
188.15					
62500 Euro-European Style					
192	Apr	2	0.73	—	—
196	Mar	—	—	5	5.38

The precise expiration date of foreign currency option is the last trading day in the 3rd Wed. of the maturity month. In this case, it was on 17th Mar. If $S>\$1.92$, then the call option was exercised. The option holder had the right to deliver $1.92\times62500=\$120000$ dollars into the option writer's account, and in return, the option writer had to deliver 62500 Euros into the buyer's account. The holder then made $(S-1.92-0.0073)\times62500$ \$ of income. The holder of Mar. 196 put option on Euro would be rational to exercise the put option if $S<\$1.96$. Upon exercising, the holder delivered 62500 Euros into writer's account, and received $1.96\times62500=\$122500$ in return, making income of $(1.96-S-0.0538)\times62500$ \$.

In practice, buyers and sellers tend to close out their positions before expiry by adopting equal and opposite new positions that exactly cancel out the original positions.

If an investor has a long/short call position in GBP/USD, she can close it out by selling/buying the identical call option at the respective bid/offer rate. Likewise, if an investor has a long/short put position in GBP/USD, she can close it down before exercising by selling/buying the identical put option at the bid/offer rate.

For example GBP/USD spot is $S_t = 1.5770/75$. An investor is bullish about GBP/USD and decides to buy two 3-month call option contracts at a strike price of $E = 1.6000$. The GBP/USD long call premium is quoted at $c_t = 0.0233/0.0235$.

- Investor buys in 2 call options at 0.0235 USD and becomes an option holder, putting up margin of $0.0235 \times 125000 \times 2 = 5875$ USD;
- Sterling duly appreciates to $S_t = 1.6400/05$ after one month and holder decides to close out without waiting for expiry. Meanwhile, the option premium has risen to $c_t = 0.0503/0.0507$. Investor's profit is $(0.0503-0.0235) \times 125000 \times 2 - 5875 = \$6700$;
- Had GBP/USD fallen instead to $S_t = 1.5600/50$ and the option price to $c_t = 0.0206/0.0208$, investor's loss would have been $(0.0235-0.0206) \times 125000 \times 2 = \$725$.

§ 3 Basic Theories on Option Pricing

The value of each option, the premium, is composed by two parts: intrinsic value and time value (extrinsic value). premium = intrinsic value + time value

3.1 Option Premium Components

1) Intrinsic Value

Intrinsic value is the financial gain for option holder if the option is exercised immediately. For a call option, the intrinsic value is Max $[S_T - E, 0]$; for a put option, the intrinsic value is Max $[E - S_T, 0]$.

Intrinsic value is zero when option is at or out-of-the-money; intrinsic value is positive if the option is in-the-money; at maturity, an option will have a value equal to its intrinsic value.

The foreign currency option premium, c, is supposed to be greater than the intrinsic value (call $c \geqslant S_T - E$; put $c \geqslant E - S_T$), otherwise there arise arbitrage opportunities. For example, an American call option has exercise price as $E = \$1.5216/£$, the spot exchange rate is $S_t = \$1.5227/£$, then the intrinsic value = Max$[S_t - E, 0] = \$0.0011/£$. If the option premium is $\$0.0008/£$, the arbitrage process is:

Arbitrage process	Cash flow (denominated in $)	
1. At time T borrow $	$E+c$	1.5216+0.0008
2. Long call option	$-c$	−0.0008
3. Exercise call option for £	$-E$	−1.5216
4. Sell out £ in spot market	S_t	1.5227
5. Repay loan at time T, no interest occurs	$-(E+c)$	−(1.5216+0.0008)
Sum:	S_t-E-c	0.0003

Arbitrages trigger option premium c adjustment, and option premium soon is restored. The economic adjustment for option premium restore is left to readers.

2) Time Value (extrinsic value)

The difference between the option premium and the option's intrinsic value is nonnegative, and referred to as the option's time value (extrinsic value). Investors are willing to pay more than the immediate exercise value as the option can potentially move further into the money between today and maturity. Time value is this extra money other an intrinsic value for potential profit. The time value is positively correlated with the time to maturity.

The rationale for time value is the unbalance risk exposure for option holder and option writer. While the option holder entitles the right to choose exercise option or not, the option writer has to shoulder a potential loss if the option turned out to be in-the-money for holder. This unbalance risk exposure brings potential loss for option writer. To compensate this risk exposure, option writer asks for time value in addition to the intrinsic value.

Not every option can be exercised when due. Those out-of-the-money options that be expired without exercising are wasting assets. As an option approaches its expiry date without being in-the-money, its time value declines since the probability of that option being profitable is reduced.

Foreign currency option is quite liquid, it is tradable before it's due. In terms of American option, though option writer can exercise option before expiration date, few of them choose to do so. If exercised, the profit of an option is subject to intrinsic value only; if hold the option and trade it in market, traders could earn time value in addition. Option holder, thus, choose trading options in market instead of exercising options. This explains why the price of American option is quite close to that of European option.

3) Strike Exchange Rate (Exercise Price)

The strike exchange rate is the exchange rate the option holder of a call has the right to long the base currency, or the holder of a put has the right to short the base currency. This is also referred to as the exercise price. The strike exchange rate is not only the factor built into the supply and demand equation of the option, it is but also a factor of determining both the extrinsic value and intrinsic value of an option. Figure 7-6 shows that the closer the strike exchange rate to the current exchange rate, the more expensive the option is, even if there is no intrinsic value. Because the closer the strike exchange rate to the current exchange rate, the higher possibility that the option will expire in-the-money and the higher the demand will be for the option.

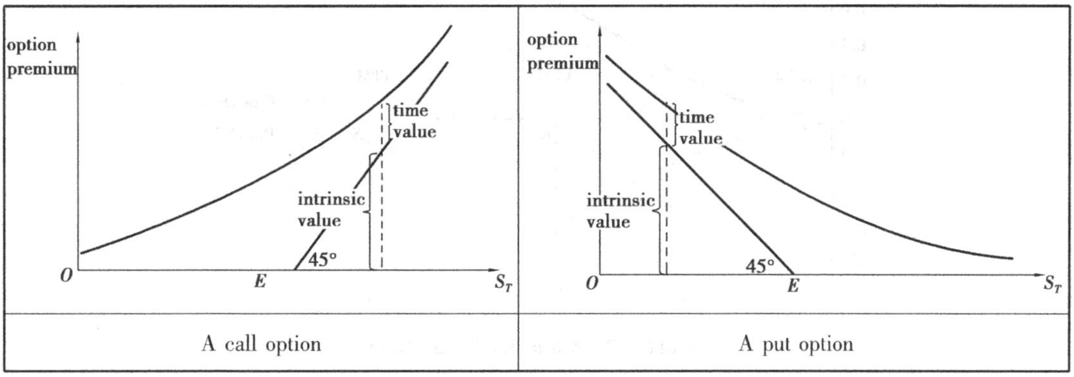

Figure 7-6 Premium Comparison

When spot rate moves benefit option holder, time value decreases as the intrinsic value increases. Option holder scarifies less time value if exercises option when spot rate is good.

A FX option can be described by its strike exchange rate's proximity to the current exchange rate. The pricing of any currency option premium c combines 6 elements: ① current spot rate S_t, ② time to maturity T, ③ forward rate for matching maturity F_t, ④ dollar interest rate R (or continuous interest rate i), ⑤ base currency interest rate R^* (or continuous interest rate i^*), ⑥ volatility σ (the standard deviation of daily spot exchange rate movement in annual percentage). Option pricing is based on an expected distribution of possible outcomes around the forward rate. Distribution is determined by volatility, i.e. standard deviation of daily spot exchange rate movement. Option premium is positively related with exchange rate's volatility. Volatility, unfortunately, is unobservable. It is the only judgmental component in the option pricing formula. It is determined subjectively by the trader.

3.2 Sensitivity Measures of FX Options

Options function quite like insurance: the more uncertainty the foreign exchange market is, the more valuable options cost. Sensitivity measures how the value of FX option changes relative to changes in a given parameter. Option Greeks are applied for sensitivity measures.

1) Option Delta, $\delta = c_S$(Partial Differentiate the Option Premium c with S)

Option delta is a ratio estimates to which extend the value of the option change as the exchange rate changes and measures the probability of the option expiring in/out-of-the-money. It is the slop of the curve that relates the option premium to the spot exchange rate, i.e. it is the first order partial derivative of option premium with respect to spot exchange rate. Figure 7-7 shows that calls and puts have opposite deltas. Call delta values are positive and put delta values are negative.

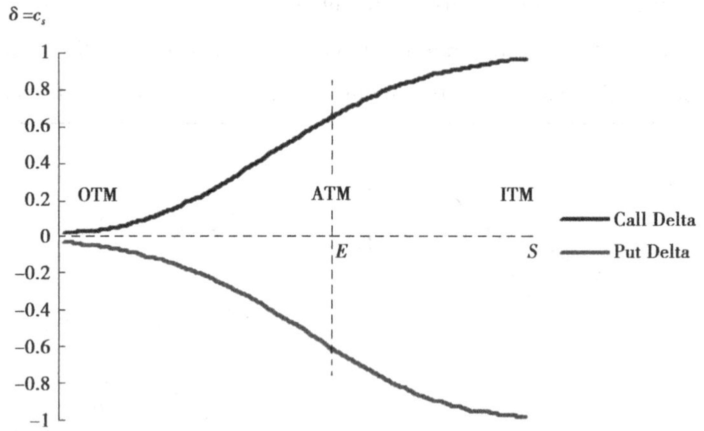

Figure 7-7 δ and Exchange Rate

Option delta values range from −100 to 0 for put options, and from 0 to 100 for calls, or −1 to 0 and 0 to 1, if use expression in decimals. For example, an option with a delta of 0.5 will move half a cent for every full cent movement in the exchange rate.

Delta is often used for hedging. Suppose that current exchange rate $S=2$, the option price $c=0.2$, and option size is 100000. Given $\delta=0.6$, an investor who has sold 2 call options would hedge her position by purchasing $0.6\times200000 = 120000$ units of base currency. If the base currency appreciated by 1 pip against quote currency, this investor would have a gain of $0.0001\times120000=12$ from the base currency she holds. But the call option she has sold will tend to go up by 0.0001×0.60, producing a loss to the option writer by $0.0001\times0.60\times100000\times2=12$. The gain from spot trading can offset the loss from option. If the base currency depreciated by 1 pip against quote currency, this investor would have a loss of $0.0001\times120000 = 12$ from the base currency she holds. But the call option she has sold will tend to go down by 0.0001×0.60, producing a gain to the option writer by $0.0001\times0.60\times100000\times2=12$, which is canceled by her spot loss. Option writer of a call/put should long/short spot $\delta\times$contract size unites of base currency for hedging.

Delta would change from time to time, thus the above investor's position remains delta hedged for only a short period of time. The hedge has to be adjusted periodically. How often should the rebalance be? Option gamma provides some solution.

2) Option Gamma $\gamma = c_{ss}$ (Partial Differentiate δ with S)

The Gamma shows the option delta's sensitivity to spot rate changes, i.e. γ shows how large the position risk changes. It is the second order partial derivative of option premium with respect to spot exchange rate. Small gamma indicates that delta changes slowly, and means relatively infrequently adjustment to keep a portfolio delta hedged. Put γ as the vertical line, S the horizontal line, the following graph shows how sensitive option premium changes are to the strike prices. Gamma is the same value for calls and puts.

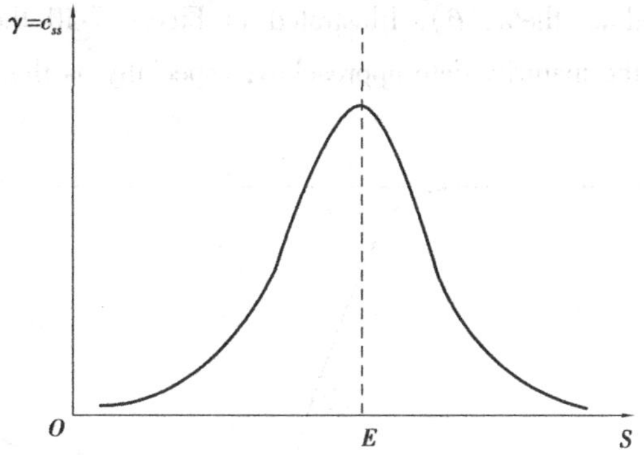

Figure 7-8 γ and Exchange Rate

Option gamma reaches the highest value when option is at-the-money; gamma drops to the lowest value when an option is deeply in-the-money or completely out-of-the-money. Options with short term to expiration have higher gamma than long term options. Option gamma and option delta are the two most commonly analyzed Greek letters related to option's sensitivity to changes in the underlying spot rate.

3) Option Vega $v = c_\sigma$ (Partial Differentiate c with σ)

Option vega estimates the effect a change in the exchange rate volatility on the option value. Option vega is the first derivation of the option's value function by volatility.

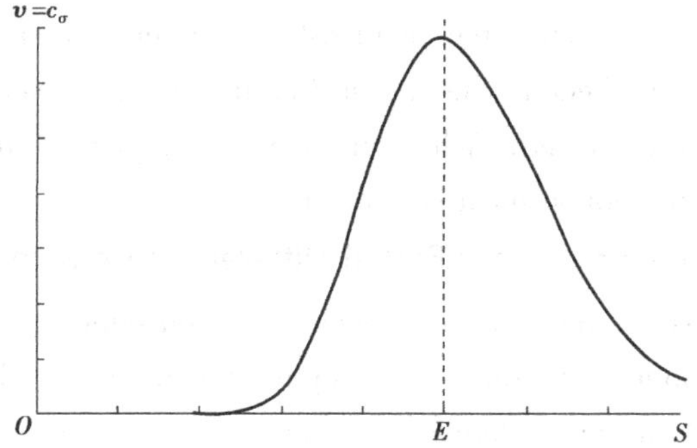

Figure 7-9 v and Exchange Rate

Let v be the verticle line and S as horizontal line, Figure 7-9 shows that if the FX option is worthless, it does not matter much how volatile the underlying exchange rate is, because the chance that the option suddenly flips into in-the-money is relatively small.

If the option is deep in-the-money, the chance that the option suddenly becomes worthless with increased volatility is also relatively slim.

Option vega reaches the peak when $S = E$. Because the option is at-the-money (i.e. on the verge of being worthless or valuable), even a relatively small change in the volatility in the excharge rate can change the position.

4) Option Theta $\theta = c_t$ (Partial Differentiate c with t)

The ratio of the change in an option price to the decrease in time to expiration is called Time-Value Decay (denominated as theta, θ). Illustrated in Figure 7-10 the time value of an option decreases exponentially as the maturity date approaches; especially as the time to maturity passes the 30 day mark.

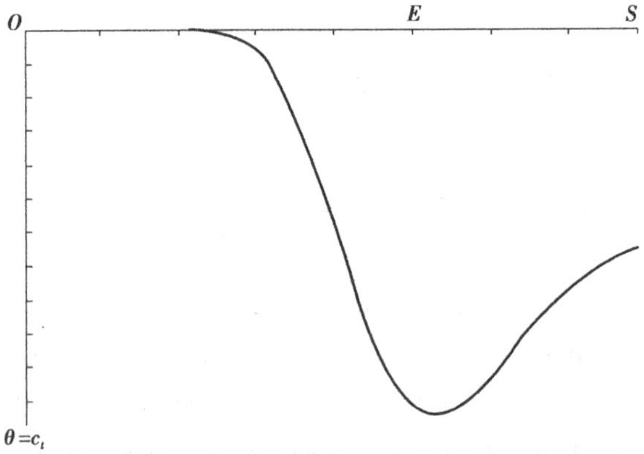

Figure 7-10 θ and Exchange Rate

For those options that are deep in-the-money, time value decays more rapidly. The market finds these options too expensive compared to other strike prices. The holders of deep in-the-money options nearing expiry will have to discount the time value to attract buyers in order to realize the intrinsic value. The greater the certainty about an option's expiry value, the lower the time value. The greater the uncertainty about an option's expiry value, the greater the time value.

Option theta is negative because the relationship between option's value and the time to expiration is inversed. Option theta is the lowest (or the highest when looking at its absolute value) when an option is at-the-money. When an option is completely worthless or very valuable, then the absolute value of the option theta is minimal.

5) Option Rho $\rho = c_i$; or $\rho^* = c_{i*}$ (Partial Differentiate c with Interest Rate i or i^*)

This Greek letter measures the impact of interest rate on option premium. As there are two interest rates under a FX option, the quote currency interest rate i and the base currency interest rate i^*, and there are call and put difference, pho may have different performances.

Although interest rate is of essential for central banks' monetary policy and can affect economy dramatically, changes in interest rates are infrequent and in small magnitudes. Thus rho has less impact compared with other Greek letters, if rho is not negligible.

The way interest affects option price is mainly depends on the profit interest rate brings. For example, one trader plans to buy some base currency. She can either long spot or long call. Call option in this case provides her cheaper cost. She pays option premium, which costs much less money than literally buying the same sum of base currency, and becomes option holder. While waiting for base currency appreciates, this trader can use the saved money for other investment or simply deposit. Thus if there is an increase in quote currency interest rate, call option brings extra profit. This profit should be reflected in call option price. An increase in interest rate can raise call option price. On the other hand, put option prices are impacted negatively by increasing interest rates.

3.3 Basic Principles for Option Pricing

The following notations are applied for option pricing:

- S_0 the spot exchange rate at time 0, S_t is the spot exchange rate at time t, and S_T is the spot exchange rate at option maturity
- E exercise/strike price
- τ time to expiration, $\tau = T-t$ (suppose that the current time is t, because option expiration occurs at time T, the remaining time, denoted as τ, is then $T-t$)
- r is the continuously compounded risk-free quote currency interest rate during time 0 to time T
- r^* is the continuously compounded risk-free base currency interest rate during time 0 to time T
- C_{aT} is the value of the American call at expiration
- C_{eT} is the value of the European call at expiration
- P_{aT} is the value of the American put at expiration
- P_{eT} is the value of the European put at expiration

To simplify analysis, start with a two-country world: domestic country and foreign country. Take base currency as foreign currency (FC), quote currency as domestic currency (DC).

1) Basic Rules

(1) European currency option values at expiration and immediate exercise value for American currency options

The European option values at expiration are intrinsic values.

$$C_{eT} = \text{Max}[S_T - E,\ 0] \text{ and } P_{eT} = \text{Max}[E - S_T,\ 0]$$

As American option holds more flexibility, it costs more than European option if other things are equal.

The minimum value of an in-the-money American option is the intrinsic value, which is the value of immediate exercise.

$$C_{at} \geqslant S_t - E,\ P_{at} \geqslant E - S_t,\ \text{where } 0 \leqslant t \leqslant T$$

(2) Option prices are non-negative

Because the option is the right but not the obligation, it has non-negative value all the time.

$$C_e \geqslant 0 \text{ and } P_e \geqslant 0;\ C_a \geqslant 0 \text{ and } P_a \geqslant 0$$

2) Boundaries and Parities for European Currency Options

(1) Upper Boundaries

$$C_{et} \leqslant S_t \text{ and } P_{et} \leqslant Ee^{-r*\tau}$$

① $C_{et} \leqslant S_t$

At any time, the value of call option cannot be greater than the spot exchange rate S_t; otherwise, an arbitrage will arise. For example, if $C_{et} > S_t$, then one arbitrager can write a covered call option. That is writing a call and at the same time longing the underlying base currency at spot market, achieving risk-free profit $C_{et} - S_t$.

② $P_{et} \leqslant Ee^{-r*\tau}$

For a European put option, before expiration, the maximum possible price cannot exceed the present value of the exercise price①$Ee^{-r*\tau}$, (where the term $e^{-r*\tau}$ represents the continuous time present value operators for the foreign interest rates) because the buyer must wait until expiration to exercise. For example, if $P_{et} > Ee^{-r*\tau}$, then one arbitrager can write a put option, obtaining premium P_{et}, and invest the premium into foreign market. At maturity, the investment provides $P_{et}e^{r*\tau}$ in return. Even if option holder requires delivery, option writer gains arbitrage profit as $P_{et}e^{r*\tau} - E > 0$. (because $P_{et} > Ee^{-r*\tau}$, $P_{et}e^{r*\tau} > Ee^{-r*\tau}e^{r*\tau}$, i.e. $P_{et}e^{r*\tau} > E$)

(2) Lower Boundaries

Consider the following two portfolios:

Portfolio Ⅰ is to long a currency call, which entitles the right to purchase 1 unite of FC with E unit of DC; and to purchase domestic zero coupon bond with the same expiration as the call option. The bond pays E at expiration.

Portfolio Ⅱ is to purchase a foreign zero coupon bond, which gives 1 unit of FC at expiration.

Suppose that holding domestic bond offers a continuous interest r, the present value of portfolio Ⅰ is $C_{et} + e^{-r\tau}E$.

If the foreign bond offers a continuous interest r^*, then the present value for portfolio Ⅱ, denominated in domestic currency, is $e^{-r*\tau}S_T$.

The future value for portfolio Ⅰ depends on the comparison between E and S_T: if $S_T \leqslant E$, then the call option brings no return, the total future value is the return of domestic bond, E; if $S_T > E$, then the call option brings return of $S_T - E$, plus the domestic bond return E, the total future value for portfolio Ⅰ is S_T.

---

① The term $e^{-r*\tau}$ represents the continuous time present value operators for the foreign interest rates. Similarly, the term $e^{-r\tau}$ represents the continuous time present value operators for the domestic interest rates. The rationale is: The interest rate r is the instantaneous rate at which a sum of money accumulates. r is a force of interest, it is a constant. Let $A(0)$ be the present value, $A(t)$ be the future value, then $r = \dfrac{\frac{dA(t)}{dt}}{A(t)} = \dfrac{d\ln A(t)}{dt}$. Take integral equation on both sides, $\because \int_0^\tau r_t dt = \int_0^\tau \dfrac{d\ln A(\tau)}{dt} dt = \ln A(t)\Big|_0^\tau = \ln\dfrac{A(\tau)}{A(0)} \therefore e^{\int_0^\tau r_t dt} = e^{\ln\frac{A(\tau)}{A(0)}}$ and $\because \dfrac{A(\tau)}{A(0)} = e\int_0^1 r_1 dt\, e\int_1^2 r_2 dt \cdots e\int_{\tau-1}^\tau r_t dt = e^{r+r+\cdots+r} = e^{\tau r} \therefore A(0) = A(\tau)e^{-\tau r}$, where $A(\tau) = A(T) = 1$.

Portfolio Ⅰ	Present Value	Future Value	
		$S_T \leq E$	$S_T > E$
Long Call	C_{et}	0	$S_T - E$
Long Domestic Bond	$e^{-r\tau}E$	E	E
Sum	$C_{et} + e^{-r\tau}E$	E	S_T

The future value for portfolio Ⅱ is S_T. The following table gives the comparison between portfolio Ⅰ and portfolio Ⅱ:

Table 7-5 Compare Portfolio Ⅰ with Portfolio Ⅱ

Portfolios	Present Value	Future Value	
		$S_T \leq E$	$S_T > E$
Ⅰ	$C_{et} + e^{-r\tau}E$	E	S_T
Ⅱ	$e^{-r^*\tau}S_T$	S_T	S_T

In either situation, portfolio Ⅰ offers return not less than portfolio Ⅱ. The no-arbitrage rule then requires the present value of portfolio I to be greater than or equal to that of portfolio Ⅱ: $C_{et} + e^{-r\tau}E \geq e^{-r^*\tau}S_T$. If rearranged, the greater lower boundary for currency calls is achieved as: $C_{et} \geq e^{-r^*\tau}S_T - e^{-r\tau}E$. The greater lower boundary for European puts is given by: $P_{et} \geq e^{-r\tau}E - e^{-r^*\tau}S_T$.

It is left to the readers to construct the proof for European puts lower boundary.

(3) Put-Call Parity

Put-call parity is an arbitrage linkage between the prices of put and call options. Consider two portfolios:

Portfolio Ⅰ is to long a European put and to short a European call, both options have the same strike price and expiration. The present value and future value for this portfolio is summed below.

Portfolio Ⅰ	Present Value	Future Value	
		$S_T < E$	$S_T \geq E$
Long Put (Holder)	P_{et}	$E - S_T$	0
Short Call (Writer)	$-C_{et}$	0	$E - S_T$
Sum	$P_{et} - C_{et}$	$E - S_T$	$E - S_T$

Portfolio Ⅱ is to long a domestic zero coupon bond, which will be worth E at expiration and to short a foreign zero coupon bond, which will be worth S_T at expiration. The present value and future value for this portfolio is summed below.

Portfolio Ⅱ	Present Value	Future Value	
		$S_T<E$	$S_T \geqslant E$
Long Domestic Bond	$e^{-r\tau}E$	E	E
Short Foreign Bond	$-e^{-r*\tau}S_T$	$-S_T$	$-S_T$
Sum	$e^{-r\tau}E-e^{-r*\tau}S_T$	$E-S_T$	$E-S_T$

Because at expiration two portfolios offer the same payoff, $E-S_T$, their present value, must be equal.

$$P_{et} - C_{et} = e^{-r\tau}E - e^{-r*\tau}S_T$$

The above is the put-call parity. It states that at any time t before expiration, the difference between the price of a European put (P_{et}) and a European call (C_{et}) having the same strike and the same expiration must be equal to the difference between the present value ($e^{-r\tau}$) of the deliverable quantity of DC, E, and the present value ($e^{-r*\tau}$) of the deliverable quantity of FC, S_T.

3) Boundaries and Parities for American Currency Options

(1) Time Value for American Currency Options

Let $T \geqslant t_1 > t_0$, $T-t_0$ and $T-t_1$ be times to expiration. Other things equal, then

$$C_a(T - t_0) \geqslant C_a(T - t_1) \text{ and } P_a(T - t_0) \geqslant P_a(T - t_1)$$

The rationale is that a reduction in the remaining time to expiration reduces the value of C_a and P_a.

(2) Lower Boundaries

Because an American option could be exercised before expiration, it costs more than a European option. The minimum value of an American option at any time t is a European option, $C_{at} \geqslant C_{et}$ and $P_{at} \geqslant P_{et}$. Combining immediate exercise value with the lower boundaries for European option gives the lower boundaries for American option:

$$C_{at} \geqslant \text{Max}[0,\ S_t - E,\ e^{-r*\tau}S_T - e^{-r\tau}E] \text{ and } P_a \geqslant \text{Max}[0,\ E - S_t,\ e^{-r\tau}E - e^{-r*\tau}S_T]$$

(3) Put-Call Parity

Considering longing one portfolio and shorting one put American option, let $T \geqslant t_1 > t$, $t_1 - t = \tau$, the portfolio gives the following combination:

① Long an American call;

② Spend E to long a domestic zero coupon bond, which matures at option expiration, at time t_1 its value is $e^{r\tau}E$;

③ Short one foreign zero coupon bond, which pays one unit of FC when matured.

The present value and future value are summed below:

	Present Value	Future Value	
		$S_{t1}>E$	$S_{t1}<E$
Long a Call	C_{at}	$S_{t1}-E$	0
Long Domestic Bond	E	$e^{r\tau}E$	$e^{r\tau}E$
Short Foreign Bond	$-e^{-r*\tau}S_t$	$-S_{t1}$	$-S_{t1}$
Short a Put	$-P_{at}$	0	$-(E-S_{t1})$
	$C_{at}+E-e^{-r*\tau}S_t-P_{at}$	$e^{r\tau}E-E$	$e^{r\tau}E-E$

$$\because e^{r\tau}E - E \geqslant 0 \therefore C_{at} + E - e^{-r*\tau}S_t - P_{at} \geqslant 0 \Rightarrow C_{at} + E - e^{-r*\tau}S_t \geqslant P_{at}$$

Considering shorting one portfolio and longing one put American option, let $T \geqslant t_1 > t$, $t_1 - t = \tau$, the portfolio gives the following combination:

① Short an American call;

② Short a domestic zero coupon bond, which matures at option expiration, with the maturity value of E;

③ Long one foreign zero coupon bond with present value of 1 unit FC.

The present value and future value are:

	Present Value	Future Value	
		$S_{t1}>E$	$S_{t1}<E$
Short a Call	$-C_{at}$	$-(S_{t1}-E)$	0
Short Domestic Bond	$-e^{-r\tau}E$	$-E$	$-E$
Long Foreign Bond	S_t	$e^{r*\tau}S_{t1}$	$e^{r*\tau}S_{t1}$
Long a Put	P_{at}	0	$E-S_{t1}$
	$P_{at}-C_{at}-e^{-r\tau}E+S_t$	$e^{r*\tau}S_{t1}-S_{t1}$	$e^{r*\tau}S_{t1}-S_{t1}$

$$\because e^{r*\tau}S_{t1} - S_{t1} \geqslant 0 \therefore P_{at} - C_{at} - e^{-r\tau}E + S_t \geqslant 0 \Rightarrow P_{at} \geqslant C_{at} + e^{-r\tau}E - S_t$$

The put-call parity for American currency options is: $C_{at}+E-e^{-r*\tau}S_t \geqslant P_{at} \geqslant C_{at}+e^{-r\tau}E-S_t$

§ 4 The Black-Scholes Model for European Currency Options

Black-Scholes (1973) developed a model for European call option on shares of a common stock that does not pay dividends. Merton (1973) extended this model to the theoretical case of an option on a share of stock that pays dividends continuously. Garman and Kohlhagen (1983) adapted the Black-Scholes-Merton model for European options on foreign currencies.

This section introduces some basic knowledge on European option pricing.

4.1 Assumptions

The Black-Scholes Model makes certain assumptions:

① No market frictions: no transaction cost, no margin requirements, no short sales restrictions, no wash sales restrictions, no taxes. All market participants are price takers.

② All interest rates are riskless continuously compounded rates, and do not change over the term of the option. Holding any currency would earn riskless interest rate, either i or i^*.

③ The performance of the spot exchange rate follows the weak form market efficiency. This assumption indicates that the instantaneous changes of the exchange rate, dS_t/S_t, meet a diffusion stochastic process. An Ito process (also known as Geometric Brownian motion), thus, could be applied to generate the exchange rate changes.

4.2 Ito Process

1) Definition

Ito process is a stochastic differential equation (SDE). It takes the form as $dS_t = \mu_t S_t dt + \sigma S_t dz_t$, where μ is the instantaneous drift or drift coefficient, which stands for the risk premium on the spot exchange rate;

dt is an instant in time;

σ is the standard deviation or diffusion coefficient, also known as theoretical volatility. (Do not confused with the option delta) This σ is assumed to be a constant that is greater than 0, it measures the volatility of exchange rate;

dz_t is the differential of a stochastic variable. It represents the infinitesimal change in a Brownian motion over the next instant of time. z_t is called a Brownian path, it is also a standard Wiener process. Given ε as the random number from a standard normal distribution set, when $\Delta t \to 0$, $dz_t = \varepsilon\sqrt{dt}$. It has the following 3 features:

① The expected mean of Δz is $E(\Delta z) = 0$; the variance of Δz is $\mathrm{Var}(\Delta z) = \Delta t$. Δz is a stochastic term, which is positively related with time t.

② The expected mean of Δz^2 is $E(\Delta z^2) = \Delta t$[①]; the variance of Δz^2 is $\mathrm{Var}(\Delta z^2) = E(\Delta z^4) -$

---

① $\mathrm{Var}(\Delta z) = E(\Delta z^2) - E^2(\Delta z) = E(\Delta z^2) - 0 = \Delta t$

$E^2(\Delta z^2)=3\Delta t^2-\Delta t^2=0$①; $\Delta z^2=\Delta t$. Δz^2 is a deterministic term.

③ The expected mean of $\Delta z\Delta t$ is $E(\Delta z\Delta t)=\Delta tE(\Delta z)=0$; because $\text{Var}(\Delta z)=0$, $\text{Var}(\Delta z\Delta t)=\Delta t^2=0$; $\Delta z\Delta t=0$. $\Delta z\Delta t$ is a deterministic term.

Brown motion dz_t is a continuous stochastic process, $dz_t\equiv\lim_{\Delta t\to 0}(z_{t+\Delta t}-z_t)$. The rule could then be summed as:

	Δz	Δt			dz	dt
Δz	Δt	0	⟹	dz	dt	0
Δt	0	0		dt	0	0

2) Ito's Lemma

Suppose that the value of a European call option, C_{et}, is a function of S_t and t: $C_{et}=f(S_t,t)$. Its Taylor series expansion is $df=f_s ds+f_t dt+1/2f_{ss}ds^2+f_{st}dsdt+1/2f_{tt}dt^2+\cdots$

f_s is to partial differentiate function $f(S,t)$ with S.

f_t is to partial differentiate function $f(S,t)$ with t.

According to the features of Brown motion dz_t, $dtdt=0$, $dtdz_t=0$.

$ds^2=(\mu S_t dt+\sigma S_t dz_t)^2=(\mu S_t dt)^2+2\mu S_t\sigma S_t dtdz_t+(\sigma S_t dz_t)^2$

where $dsdt=(\mu S_t dt+\sigma S_t dz_t)dt=\mu S_t dtdt+\sigma S_t dz_t dt=0$ and

$dt^2=0$

$ds^2=0+0+\sigma^2 S_t^2 dt=0+0+\sigma^2 S_t^2 dt$

Higher central moments, with zero variance, could be eliminated because they are all deterministic terms.

The Taylor series expansion could be simplified as

$df=f_s ds+f_t dt+1/2f_{ss}ds^2$

$df=f_s ds+f_t dt+1/2f_{ss}\sigma^2 S_t^2 dt$

$df=f_s(\mu S_t dt+\sigma S_t dz_t)+(f_t+1/2f_{ss}\sigma^2 S_t^2)dt$

$df=(f_s\mu S_t+f_t+1/2f_{ss}\sigma^2 S_t^2)dt+\sigma S_t f_s dz_t$

The Ito lemma indicates that the stochastic differential equation of an option value can be derived from the stochastic differential equation of the underlying foreign currency's price, i.e. exchange rate.

Let $G=\ln S_t$, then $G_s=1/S_t$, $G_t=0$, $G_{ss}=-1/S_t^2$, $dG=(G_s\mu S_t+G_t+1/2G_{ss}\sigma^2 S_t^2)dt+\sigma S_t G_s dz_t\Rightarrow$

① The mean of the 4th central moment of a normal distribution, Kurtosis $E(\Delta z^4)$, is 3 times the square of the 2nd central moment, $3\text{Var}^2(\Delta z)$, then $E(\Delta z^4)=3\text{Var}^2(\Delta z)=3\Delta t^2$

$$dG=\left[\frac{1}{S_t}\mu S_t+0+\frac{1}{2}\left(-\frac{1}{S_t^2}\right)\sigma^2 S_t^2\right]d_t+\sigma S_t\frac{1}{S_t}dz_t=\left(\mu-\frac{\sigma^2}{2}\right)dt+\sigma dz_t$$

It shows that $\ln S_t$ follows a normal distribution, and S_t follows a log-normal distribution.

If take integral from t to T on both side, gives $\int_t^T d\ln S_t=\int_t^T\left(\mu-\frac{\sigma^2}{2}\right)dt+\sigma\int_t^T dz$

$$\ln S_T-\ln S_t=\left(\mu-\frac{\sigma^2}{2}\right)(T-t)+\sigma(z_T-z_t)$$

$$\ln S_T=\ln S_t+\left(\mu-\frac{\sigma^2}{2}\right)(T-t)+\sigma\varepsilon\sqrt{T-t}$$

i.e. given S_t, $\ln S_T\sim N\left(\ln S_t+\left(\mu-\frac{\sigma^2}{2}\right)(T-t),\ \sigma^2(T-t)\right)$

$$e^{\ln S_T}=e^{\ln S_t+\left(\mu-\frac{\sigma^2}{2}\right)(T-t)+\sigma\varepsilon\sqrt{T-t}}$$

$S_T=S_te^{\left(\mu-\frac{\sigma^2}{2}\right)(T-t)+\sigma\varepsilon\sqrt{T-t}}$, $E(S_T)=S_te^{\mu(T-t)}$, $\mathrm{Var}(S_T)=S_t^2e^{2\mu(T-t)}[e^{\sigma^2(T-t)}-1]$, note that the variance of exchange rate is an infinite variance, which is positively related with $T-t$; also is positively related with spot exchange rate S_t. The mean $E(S_T)=S_te^{\mu(T-t)}$ is actually the theoretical value for forward exchange rate.

4.3 Derive the B-S Model

Let $f(S_t,t)$ be the value of a European call option with the Taylor series expansion as $df=(f_s\mu S_t+f_t+1/2f_{ss}\sigma^2S_t^2)dt+\sigma S_tf_sdz_t$, then the corresponding discrete form is $\Delta f=(f_s\mu S_t+f_t+1/2f_{ss}\sigma^2S_t^2)\Delta t+\sigma S_tf_s\Delta z$.

Given that the exchange rate follows Ito process as $dS_t=\mu S_tdt+\sigma S_tdz_t$, the corresponding discrete form is $\Delta S=\mu S_t\Delta t+\sigma S_t\Delta z$.

Both f and S_t follow the same Wiener process, thus both have stochastic term Δz. In order to eliminate the Wiener process, (i.e. Δz be eliminated) take the following portfolio:

At time t, short a European call option with option value of f (this call option costs f), the expiration date is at time T. In order to delta hedge the risk, long f_s units of FC in spot exchange market. The present value of this portfolio is $\Pi=f_sS_t-f$. After time Δt, the change of this portfolio value is $\Delta\Pi=f_s\Delta S-\Delta f$. Note that holding FC for $T-t=\tau$, gives the value of $e^{r^*\tau}f_sS_t$ in the end. To simplify the calculation, ignore foreign interest rate for now.

$$\Delta\Pi=f_s(\mu S_t\Delta t+\sigma S_t\Delta z)-(f_s\mu S_t+f_t+1/2f_{ss}\sigma^2S_t^2)\Delta t-\sigma S_tf_s\Delta z$$

$$\Delta\Pi=-(f_t+1/2f_{ss}\sigma^2S_t^2)\Delta t$$

There is no Δz. This portfolio, within Δt, is riskless. According to the no-arbitrage rule, given the same period of time, Δt, the change value of this portfolio, $\Delta\Pi$, must equal to the gain of the same initial invest value, Π, on riskless bond, which offers return as $e^{r\tau}$.

$\Delta\Pi = e^{r\tau}\Pi\Delta t \Rightarrow -(f_t + 1/2f_{ss}\sigma^2 S_t^2)\Delta t = e^{r\tau}(f_s S_t - f)\Delta t \Rightarrow f_t + 1/2\sigma^2 S_t^2 f_{ss} + e^{r\tau}S_t f_s = e^{r\tau}f$. Thus, $f_t + 1/2\sigma^2 S_t^2 f_{ss} + e^{r\tau}S_t f_s = e^{r\tau}f$ is the Black-Scholes differential equation.

This equation does not have the risk premium μ, which agrees with the principle of risk-neutral valuation. Under risk-neutral condition, all securities and financial derivatives offer the same return as the risk-free rate of return, $e^{r\tau}$. That is, no extra return is required to cover risk, risk-free rate is enough to attract risk-neutral investors, i.e. the risk premium on the spot exchange rate $\mu = e^{r\tau}$.

4.4 Solution to the B-S Model

Let $g(S)$ be the probability density function, recall that S_T is a log-normal distribution, general formula for the probability density function is $g(S_T) = \dfrac{e^{-\frac{[S_T - E(S_T)]^2}{2\sigma^2}}}{\sqrt{2\pi}\sigma} C_{et} = e^{-r\tau}\int_E^{\infty}(S_T - E)g(S_T)\mathrm{d}s$

Impose the present value, $C_{et} = e^{-r\tau}\,\mathrm{Max}[S_T - E, 0]$ as the boundary condition into the Black-Scholes differential equation, the B-S Model value for C_{et} is solved as:

$$\begin{cases} f_t + 1/2\sigma^2 S_t^2 f_{ss} + e^{r\tau}S_t f_s = e^{r\tau}f \\ C_{et} = f = e^{-r\tau}\int_E^{\infty}(S_T - E)g(S_T)\mathrm{d}s \end{cases}$$

Let, $d_1 = \dfrac{\ln\dfrac{S_t}{E} + \left(r + \dfrac{\sigma^2}{2}\right)(T-t)}{\sigma\sqrt{T-t}}$, $d_2 = d_1 - \sigma\sqrt{T-t} = \dfrac{\ln\dfrac{S_t}{E} + \left(r - \dfrac{\sigma^2}{2}\right)(T-t)}{\sigma\sqrt{T-t}}$, and $N(\cdot)$ be the cumulative standard normal distribution,① the value of the European call option is $C_{et} = S_t N(d_1) - e^{-r\tau}EN(d_2)$.

Where $N(d_2)$② is the probability that $S_T > E$, (the call option will be exercised)

$EN(d_2)$ is the strike price times the probability that the call option will be exercised.

$e^{-r\tau}EN(d_2)$ is the expected present value of exercised price E under risk-neutral.

$S_t N(d_1) = e^{-r*\tau}S_T N(d_1)$ is the expected present value of S_T under risk-neutral.

Summing them up gives the present value of income this European call option could provide, i.e. the present value of the European call option, C_{et}.

Apply the theory of Mellin transformation and Fourier transformation, the European call option has the value as $C_{et} = S_T e^{-r*\tau}N(d_1) - Ee^{-r\tau}N(d_2)$

According to the put-call parity, $P_e - C_e = e^{-r\tau}E - e^{-r*\tau}S_T$

the European put option has the value as $P_{et} = Ee^{-r\tau}N(-d_2) - S_T e^{-r*\tau}N(-d_1)$

---

① According to the symmetry of the distribution, $N(-x) = 1 - N(x)$.

② $N(x) = \dfrac{1}{2\pi}\int_{-\infty}^{x} e^{-\frac{u^2}{2}}\mathrm{d}u$

where again $d_1=\dfrac{\ln\dfrac{s_t}{E}+\left(r+\dfrac{\sigma^2}{2}\right)(T-t)}{\sigma\sqrt{T-t}}$, $d_2=d_1-\sigma\sqrt{T-t}=\dfrac{\ln\dfrac{S_t}{E}+\left(r-\dfrac{\sigma^2}{2}\right)(T-t)}{\sigma\sqrt{T-t}}$

§5 Binomial Option Pricing Model

There are many ways to price options, among which binomial option pricing is a mathematically straightforward and powerful method. Based on no arbitrage principle it is an iterative solution that models the exchange rate evolution over the whole option validity period. Binomial option pricing model is applicable for both American options and European options.

There are 7 assumptions in binomial option pricing:

① No market frictions: no transaction cost, no margin requirements, no short sales restrictions, no taxes;

② Default free: all counterparties perform on an obligation;

③ Competitive market: all market participants are price takers. No bubbles, trade has no impact on exchange rate;

④ No arbitrage opportunities: interest rate parity holds;

⑤ Interest rates are constant;

⑥ No intermediate cash flows;

⑦ Exchange rate evolves according to binomial process as shown by Figure 7-11: at the very beginning, current exchange rate is S_0, over some time Δt, it has a probability p of appreciation by a factor "u", and a probability $1-p$ of depreciation in exchange rate by a factor "d". That is, the exchange rate either rises to "uS_0" or drops down at "dS_0".

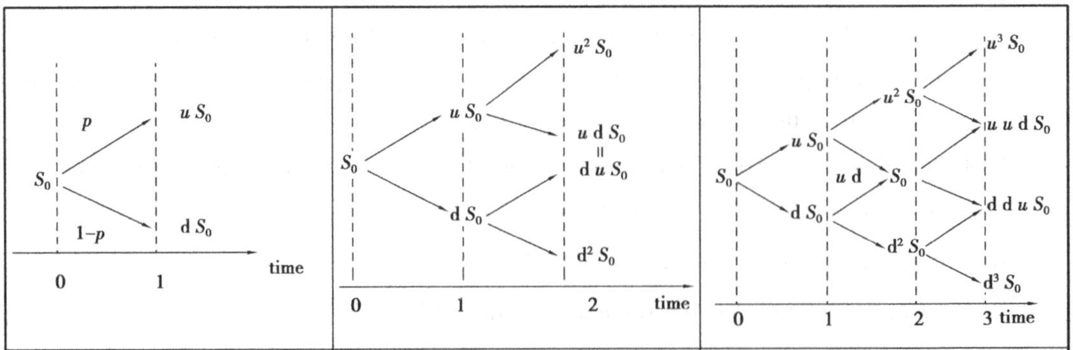

one step binomial model	two steps binomial model	three steps binomial model

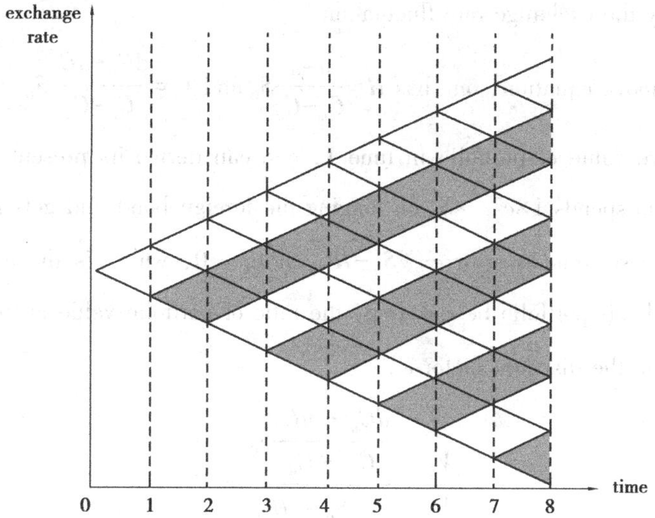

Figure 7-11 Exchange Rate Binomial Process

5.1 One-Step Option Premium

Option-cover IRP is applied to evaluate option premium. The mechanism starts with one step binomial model, given the possibility of exchange rate as p and 1-p, the call premium and put premium are shown as following:

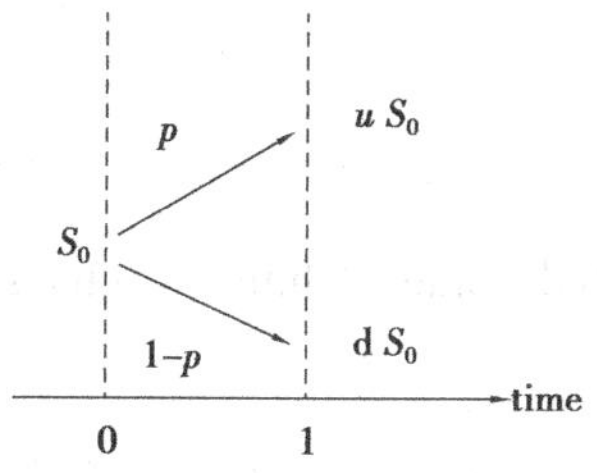	Possibility	Call	Put
	p	$C_u = \max[0, uS_0 - E]$	$P_u = \max[0,\ E - uS_0]$
	$1-p$	$C_d = \max[0, \mathrm{d}S_0 - E]$	$P_d = \max[0,\ E - \mathrm{d}S_0]$

By the end of the stage, at time 1, one risk-free portfolio that is constructed by H units of short position in call and one unit of foreign bond offers the value as follows:

S_1	One Unit of Foreign Bond	Short Position in Call	Value of Portfolio
$S_1 = uS_0$	$1 \times uS_0$	$-HC_u$	$uS_0 - HC_u$
$S_1 = \mathrm{d}S_0$	$1 \times \mathrm{d}S_0$	$-HC_d$	$\mathrm{d}S_0 - HC_d$

Construct a delta-neutral portfolio by letting $V_1 = uS_0 - HC_u = \mathrm{d}S_0 - HC_d$, the value of portfolio is thus not affected by the exchange rate fluctuation.

To solve the above equation, one has $H=\frac{u-d}{C_u-C_d}S_0$ and $V_t=\frac{dC_u-uC_d}{C_u-C_d}S_0$

With the above value of portfolio in time 1, one can derive its present value. The investor holding this portfolio spends $1\times e^{-r^*}\times S_0$ on longing the foreign bond and gets $H\times C_0$ by shorting a call. The portfolio costs this investor $e^{-r^*}S_0-HC_0$ at time 0, which is the present value of this portfolio V_0. Should this portfolio be risk-free, the ratio of portfolio value at time 1 to its value at time 0 must equal to the discount factor e^r.

$$\frac{V_1}{V_0}=\frac{\frac{dC_u-uC_d}{C_u-C_d}S_0}{e^{-r^*}S_0-HC_0}=e^r$$

Substitute $H=\frac{u-d}{C_u-C_d}S_0$ into the above equation: $C_0=\frac{C_u(e^{r-r^*}-d)+C_d(u-e^{r-r^*})}{u-d}e^{-r}$.

Let $\varphi=\frac{e^{r-r^*}-d}{u-d}$, then the call premium $C_0=[\varphi C_u+(1-\varphi)C_d]e^{-r}$. Put premium can be derived by call-put parity.

If the interest rate parity holds, then forward rate due in time 1 is the future value of current exchange rate, $F_1=S_0e^{r-r^*}$, thus $e^{r-r^*}=F_1/S_0$ and $\varphi=\frac{\frac{F_1}{S_0}-d}{u-d}$.

Under the interest rate parity, as the forward rate is the expected value of future exchange rate, then $dS_0\leqslant F_1\leqslant uS_0$, hence $0\leqslant\varphi\leqslant 1$.

If the exchange rate follows a Bernoulli experiment, then one can take φ as the possibility of appreciation ($p=\varphi$), S_0 *to* uS_0; while $1-\varphi$ as the possibility of depreciation, S_0 to dS_0 when $\varphi=\frac{\frac{F_1}{S_0}-d}{u-d}$. As spot rate S changes, however, the hedging ratio H changes as well. Because neutral δ requires that different weight be assigned to portfolio assets in order to keep portfolio risk-free.

5.2 General Expression of Option Premium

Suppose that one option lasts from time 0 to time T, and that it takes n steps of exchange rate to go up and down. Let each step last τ, then $\tau=T/n$.

The forward rate and spot rate of each step would have the relationship as $F = Se^{(r-r*)\tau}$.

The spot rate of each step and the corresponding call premium follow the following path:

					u^nS	C_{un}=max[$0, u^nS-E$]
			q	u^2S	$u^{n-1}dS$	C_{un-1d}=max[$0, u^{n-1}dS-E$]
	q	uS			…	
S			$1-q$	udS	$u^jd^{n-j}S$	C_{ujdn-j}=max[$0, u^jd^{n-j}S-E$]
	$1-q$	dS	q		…	
				d^2S	$ud^{n-1}S$	C_{udn-j}=max[$0, ud^{n-1}S-E$]
			$1-q$		d^nS	C_{dn}=max[$0, d^nS-E$]
	step 1		step 2		step n	$j=0,1,\cdots,n$

Where j could be regarded as the number of spot rate's up moves.

After n steps the spot rate has a possibility of $q^j(1-q)^{n-j}$ to change from S to $u^jd^{n-j}S$. This change may take a number of paths to achieve. Take a 5-step-change for instance, any combination of 4 up and 1 down moves ($n=5$ and $j=4$) could be achieved with 5 possible paths: uuuud, uuudu, uuduu, uduuu, duuuu. To derive the number of possible path, by essential, is to work out a combination: $combination_n^j = \frac{permutation_n^j}{permutation_j} = \frac{n!}{j!\ (n-j)!}$. Generally, for any n steps exchange rate that has experienced j ups, there are $\frac{n!}{j!\ (n-j)!}$ paths, and the probability of any one path is $q^j(1-q)^{n-j}$.

The probability of an up move, denoted as q, $q = \frac{e^{(r-r*)\tau} - d}{u-d}$.

The present value of call option is then

$$C_0 = e^{-r\tau} \sum \frac{n!}{j!\ (n-j)!} q^j (1-q)^{n-j} \max[0,\ u^jd^{n-j}S - E]$$

In order to obtain a more recognizable form, define the variable "a" as the minimum number of up moves that would be required to make the option end up in-the-money. That means only $j \geqslant a$ $\max[0,\ u^jd^{n-j}S-E] = u^jd^{n-j}S-E$, then $C_0 = e^{-r\tau} \sum \frac{n!}{j!\ (n-j)!} q^j(1-q)^{n-j}(u^jd^{n-j}S - E)$.

Let $q' = ue^{-(r-r*)\tau} q \Rightarrow q = q'e^{(r-r*)\tau}/u$,

then $C_0 = e^{-r*\tau} S \sum_{j=a}^{n} \frac{n!}{j!\ (n-j)!} q'^j (1-q')^{n-j} - e^{-r\tau} E \sum_{j=a}^{n} \frac{n!}{j!\ (n-j)!} q^j (1-q)^{n-j}$.

If the exchange rate follows a Bernoulli experiment, then within n steps the accumulated possibility of up moves that lay in the range of a to n is $B(a,\ n,\ q) = \sum_{j=a}^{n} \frac{n!}{j!\ (n-j)!} q^j(1-q)^{n-j}$. To simplify the call premium equation, $C_0=e^{-r^*\tau} S \sum_{j=a}^{n} \frac{n!}{j!\,(n-j)!} q'^j (1-q')^{n-j} - e^{-r\tau} E \sum_{j=a}^{n} \frac{n!}{j!\,(n-j)!} q^j (1-q)^{n-j}$, let $B'(a, n, q') = \sum_{j=a}^{n} \frac{n!}{j!\,(n-j)!} q'^j (1-q')^{n-j}$ and $B(a, n, q) = \sum_{j=a}^{n} \frac{n!}{j!\,(n-j)!} q^j (1-q)^{n-j}$, then $C_0=e^{-r^*\tau} SB'(a, n, q') - e^{-r\tau} EB(a, n, q)$. Put premium can be derived by call-put parity.

When $n \to \infty$, the binomial distribution converges at the limit on the log-normal distribution. Suppose that this log-normal distribution follows a Wiener-Levy process, the binomial solution for European options will closely approximate the B-S model, i.e. parameters of binomial option pricing model can be chosen to approximate B-S.

§6 Controlling FX Option Risks

Risk may be controlled by setting stop losses, otherwise known as barriers, or by combining put and call positions to create limited risk/limited profit and risk-averse volatility strategies. This section introdues briefly 3 types of strategy to control FX option risks:

6.1 Barriers

1. Out-of-the-money knock out: an order to cancel a position by taking an equal and opposite position if spot moves through a set rate. The trigger rate is set below the strike rate for long calls and short puts, and above the strike rate for short calls and long puts.

2. In-the-money knock out: An order to cancel out a position if spot moves past a pre-set "in-the-money" rate. The trigger rate is set above the strike rate for long calls and short puts, and below the strike rate for short calls and long puts.

3. Double knock out: An order to cancel out a position if spot moves through one of two pre-set levels, one in-the-money and one out-of-the-money.

6.2 Limited Risk Limited Profit Trades

Currency option traders can combine the basic four option positions to manage risk:

1. Long call spread: A long call (lower strike rate) + short call (upper strike rate) yielding capped profit (when spot rises) and loss (when spot falls).

2. Short call spread: A short call (lower strike) + long call (upper strike) yielding capped

profit (when spot falls) and loss (when spot rises).

3. Long put spread: A short put (lower strike) +long put (upper strike) yielding capped profit (when spot falls) and loss (when spot rises).

4. Short put spread: A long put (lower strike) +short put (upper strike) yielding capped profit (when spot rises) and loss (when spot falls).

6.3 Risk-Averse Volatility Trades

With volatility trades, the direction in which the spot price moves does not matter. Investors are merely concerned with the magnitude of the movement.

① Long Straddle: A long call+a long put at the same strike rate. Unlimited profit when spot is rising. significant but limited profit when spot is falling. Maximum loss is limited to the sum of the premiums. To be profitable, the spot rate must deviate from the strike rate by more than the sum of the premiums (market neutral and bullish volatility).

② Long Strangle: A long put (lower strike) +a long call (upper strike). Unlimited profit when spot is rising. Significant but limited profit when spot is falling. Maximum loss is the sum of the premiums. To be profitable the spot must rise beyond the upper strike rate or fall below the lower strike rate by at least the sum of the premiums (market neutral and bullish volatility)

Straddles and strangles may be combined to produce other risk-reducing combinations, for example:

3. Long iron butterfly: A long straddle financed by a short strangle with strike prices above and below the long straddle strike rates (neutral direction and bullish volatility).
4. Short iron butterfly: A long strangle financed by a short straddle and the inverse of the long iron butterfly (Neutral direction and bearish volatility).
5. Long iron condor: A long strangle+a short strangle with strike rates above and below the long strangle strike rates (neutral direction and bullish volatility).
6. Short iron condor: A short strangle+a long strangle with strike rates above and below those of the short strangle (neutral direction and bearish volatility).

Case Studies

Case 1 Hand Signals in Open Outcry①

(1) Basic Signals

In the old time, CME brokers trading in pit usually applied the following hand signals.

buy		A trader signals a purchase by pulling his open hands toward his body. Numerals relating to a buy are made with the palm facing in.
sell		A trader signals a sale by pushing his open hands away from his body. Numerals relating to a sell are made with the palm facing out.

(2) Call and Put

For call option, fingers are arched to form the letter "C" ("C" for call);

For put option, thumb and index finger are formed into a circle with other fingers extended upward, so hand forms an upside-down "P".

Call Put (CME hand signals)

(3) Numerical Hand Signals

Numerical hand signals are generally constant throughout all trading floors but slight variations are made with figures greater than 99. Generally price is displayed before quantity ("price on quantity") to buy and it's the opposite to sell ("quantity at price").

① Quantity

Quantity is displayed close to the face. Numerical quantities of 1-5 are displayed with vertical fingers and 6-9 are displayed with horizontal fingers. Quantities of 1-9 are indicated at chin level whilst increments of 10s are indicated at the forehead.

The following table demonstrates some examples of the quantity:

① This case is the regulation from CME.

One	
Two	
Three	
Four	
Five	
Six	
Seven	
Eight	
Nine	
Even	

One	
Ten	
Seven	
Ninsty	
One Hundred	
Five Hundred	
Seven Hundred	

One: Index finger is pointed upward at chin level.

Two: Index and middle fingers are pointed upward at chin level.

Three: Middle, ring and pinky fingers are pointed upward at chin level. Thumb holds down index finger.

Four: Index, middle, ring and pinky fingers are pointed upward at chin level. Thumb is folded against palm.

Five: All five fingers are pointed upward at chin level.

Six: Index finger is extended horizontally at chin level.

Seven: Index and middle fingers are extended horizontally at chin level.

Eight: Middle, ring and pinky fingers are extended horizontally at chin level. Thumb holds down index finger.

Nine: Index, middle, ring and pinky fingers are extended horizontally at chin level. Thumb is folded against palm.

Ten: Index finger is pointed upward at forehead level.

Twenty: Index and middle fingers are pointed upward at forehead level.

Thirty: Middle, ring and pinky fingers are pointed upward at forehead level.

Forty: Index, middle, ring and pinky fingers are pointed upward at forehead level. Thumb is folded against palm.

Fifty: All five fingers are pointed upward at forehead level.

Sixty: Index finger is pointed horizontally at forehead level.

Seventy: Index and middle fingers are pointed horizontally at forehead level.

Eighty: Middle, ring and pinky fingers are pointed horizontally at forehead level. Thumb holds down index finger.

Ninety: Index, middle, ring and pinky fingers are pointed horizontally at forehead level. Thumb is folded against palm.

100: Index finger is extended upward at forehead level to indicate the multiple of hundred. Hand is formed into a fist held at forehead level.

200: Index and middle fingers are extended upward at forehead level to indicate the multiple of hundred. Hand transitions from multiple of hundred into fist.

1000: Hand on vertical arm signals quantity "one." Other arm is held horizontally.

2000: Hand on vertical arm signals quantity "two." Other arm is held horizontally.

② Price

Price is indicated at arms' length away from the body. When contracts are quoted in increments of 10ths, generally the signals used will be 1-9 and rather than increments of 10s.

One: Index finger is pointed upward at arm's length.

Two: Index and middle fingers are pointed upward at arm's length.

Three: Middle, ring and pinky fingers are pointed upward at arm's length. Thumb holds down index finger.

Four: Index, middle, ring and pinky fingers are pointed upward at arm's length. Thumb is folded against palm.

Five: All five fingers are pointed upward at arm's length.

Six: Index finger is extended horizontally at arm's length.

Seven: Index and middle fingers are extended horizontally at arm's length.

Eight: Middle, ring and pinky fingers are extended horizontally at arm's length. Thumb holds down index finger.

Nine: Index, middle, ring and pinky fingers are extended horizontally at arm's length. Thumb is folded against palm.

Even/zero: Fist is held at arm's length.

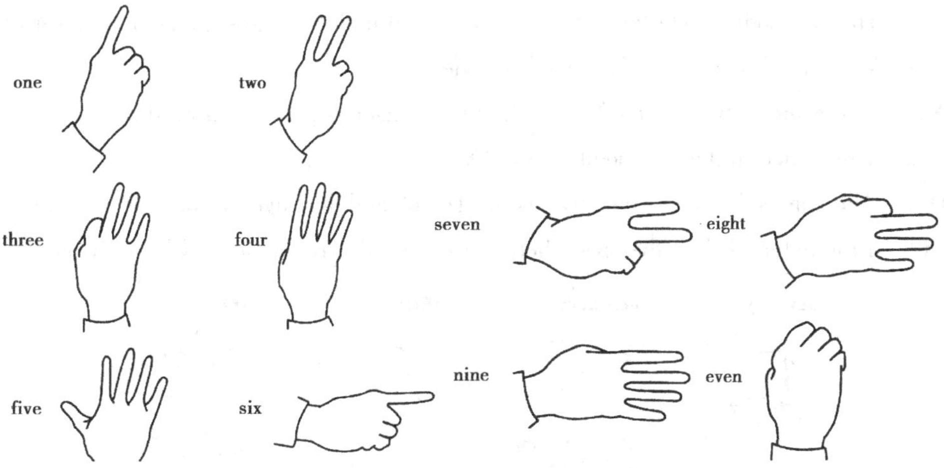

③ Time

Futures and options contracts are standardized for monthly expiration cycles and different hand signals evolved to signify each month. Like most signals, the monthly signals were developed based upon simplicity and sometimes based upon the letter of the alphabet which serves as an industry code for each month. For instance, the commodity codes are F-January, G-February, H-March, J-April, K-May, M-June, N-July, Q-August, U-September, V-October, X-November, Z-December.

Jan.: The commodity code for Jan. is F. Hand holds throat between thumb and index finger, representing the scarf around neck for the cold.

Feb.: The commodity code for Feb. is G. With hand facing away from body, middle finger, index finger and thumb form the letter "F."

Mar.: The commodity code for Mar. is H. Hand signals as index, middle, ring and pinky fingers are pointed away from body and wiggled. It looks like matching, representing for the first letter of March, “M”.

Apr.: The commodity code for Apr. is J. Fingers are pointed outward and wiggled while hand is lowered, representing April rainfall.

May: The commodity code for May is K. Hand grabs lapel of trading jacket.

Jun.: The commodity code for Jun. is M. Index and pinky fingers pointed downward. Reference to the commodity code “M”.

Jul.: The commodity code for Jul. is N. Because that eye rhymes with July, hand signals as index finger is pointed at eye.

Aug.: The commodity code for Aug. is Q. Hand is held flat against the forehead and moved laterally, as if wiping sweat from brow in August heat.

Sep.: The commodity code for Sep. is U. All fingers are pointed upward to form the letter “U.”, a reference to the commodity code “U”.

Oct.: The commodity code for Oct. is V. Index and middle fingers are angled upward to form the letter “V.”, a reference to the commodity code “V”.

Nov.: The commodity code for Nov. is X. Index finger is pointed outward and draws an “X” in the air, a reference to the commodity code “X”.

Dec.: The commodity code for Dec. is Z. Tip of middle finger is pressed to index finger. Fingers form the letter “D” in the space between them. Also resembles “X” for Xmas.

Case 2 Excursion: Fin-tech and FX

Now that basic FX theories and models have been shared, empirical evidence, unfortunately, is often lacking. Because that traditional FX theories and models have been developed on the basis of simplifying mathematical assumptions such as normally distributed returns for FX instruments and linear relationships between quantities of interest. The rational research on FX should start with data and moves on to hypotheses and theories that are then tested against the data. When data was scarce, theories and models have been formulated, proven, and published first and have only later been tested empirically. Poor empirical evidence is thus due to the lack of financial data when those fundamental FX theories and models formulated.

As technology developed since 1990's, tremendous historical FX data down to the tick level as well as real-time tick data via streaming services are available making science research progress feasible. Technological advances increase the speed and frequency FX transactions. Data are available not only on ever-smaller time scales, but also with huge volumes. When speeds, frequencies, and data volumes of FX increase at a rapid pace, technology with capabilities for large amounts of data in real time is addressed by. Financial institutions nowadays are applying software and technology in combination with algorithms and methods to gather, process, and analyze FX data in order to gain insights, to make decisions, or to fulfill regulatory requirements. FX participants that are slow in picking-up fin-tech will be kicked out, and traders with advanced fin-tech in FX market drive the competition level further up.

Quantitative methods dominant FX. Trading floors have been substituted by machine trading, where 300-400 models running for professional FX trading. Machine learning is applied to find out the weak pattern hides in financial market. Professional traders usually write software and code themselves. Financial institutions create environment to hire top programmers to stay head of the industry. The availability of large amounts of financial data via application programming interface for different machine learning algorithms functions reshaped financial market. FX market is thus more diversify. Traders are in a riskier environment than the last 20 years. Although financial transactions address to quantitative analyse, core factors persist. Momentum such as time series momentum still applied. Empirical research shows that it is easier to predict risk than returns. Correlation between returns is about 0 while there is high predictibility among volatility: 0 correlation of volatility is around 40% in currency markets and time series correlation is found in volatility. FX option, with its insurance feature, becomes more and more attractive.

Case 3 The Python Code for FX Option Pricing

Given current spot for EUR/USD $S_0 = 1.1373$, exercise rate $E = 1.1398$, 3-month U.S. interest rate r=0.75%, 3-month euro interest rate rf=0.45%, 3-month volatility $\sigma=8\%$

```
In [1]: import math
        import numpy as np
In [2]: SO=1.1373
        E=1.1398
        T=0.25
        r=0.0075
        rf=0.0045
        Sigma=0.08
In [3]: I=100000
In [4]: np.random.seed(10000)
In [5]: z=np.random.standard_normal(I)
In [6]: ST=SO * np.exp((r-rf-0.5 * sigma * * 2) * T+sigma * math.sqrt(T) * z)
In [7]: hT=np.maximum(ST-K, 0)
In [8]: C0=math.exp(-r * T) * np.mean(hT)
In [9]: print('3-month European call on EUR cost: '. CO)
```

Case 4　A Sample Interbank Option Confirmation

ABC Bank

New York, New York

March 1, 2018

XYZ

Greenwich, CT

To Whom it May Concern:

The purpose of this confirmation is to confirm the terms and conditions of the Foreign-Exchange Option entered into between ABC Bank and XYZ.

General Terms

Trade date: March 1, 2018

Buyer: XYZ

Seller: ABC Bank

Call Currency: JPY

Put Currency: USD

Option Style: European

Notional Amount USD: $1000000

Notional Amount JPY: 89336700

Expiration Date: June 8, 2018

Strike Price: 89.3367

Premium: $27389

For a premium of 27389 USD, receipt of which is due on 8th June 2018, you may call on the undersigned for up to 89336700 yen, at a JPY per USD rate of 89.3367. You may exercise this European Style option up to 10:00 A.M. New York time only on 8th June 2018 (the "Expiration Date") by telephone notice to the undersigned, confirmed in writing, indicating the amount of the currency you have elected to purchase, whereupon delivery and settlement shall be made on 10th June 2018. If the Expiration Date is not a New York business day, the Expiration Date shall be the next succeeding business day.

This option may not be assigned by either party and any such assignment shall be void and of no force or effect.

Unless you instruct us otherwise by 10:00 A.M. New York time on the Expiration Date, this option shall be deemed to be automatically exercised if at such time on such date it is in-the-money.

Acceptance by you of the premium constitutes your representation that you have substantial assets and/or liabilities denominated in the currency underlying this option, are in the business of trading or investing in such currency, in options in such currency or in assets and/or liabilities denominated in such currency or are otherwise a commercial user of such currency, and that you will be entering into such transaction for purposes related to your business in such currency.

The parties hereby consent to the jurisdiction of a state or federal court situation in New York City, New York in connection with any dispute arising hereunder. This option shall be governed and construed in accordance with the laws of the State of New York with regard to the principles of conflict of laws.

Very truly yours,

ABC Bank

Case 5 RMB Option Innovations Prepare Chinese Corps for Complex FX Hedging[①]

by Carrie Hong

8th Aug. 2014

China's State Administration of Foreign Exchange (SAFE) has put in place a new framework through which banks can offer corporate customers a greater variety of RMB FX option hedging products—although only on the basis of genuine corporate needs—allowing them to better guard against currency volatility.

The development is potentially the biggest in the sector since the offshore RMB derivatives market began in 2010.

---

① https://www.globalcapital.com/asia/rmb

A handful of Chinese and international banks, including ICBC, Citic Bank, HSBC, Standard Chartered, Deutsche Bank and DBS Bank have announced their first transactions for corporate clients based in China.

FX specialists said that the new regime—with one of its biggest changes being giving corporations the ability to sell options to other counterparties—complemented China's existing FX options market well.

"With the new tools, the onshore FX market has got almost every hedging derivative that is being used in the international market," said an FX banker with a big Chinese bank based in Beijing.

- Important Changes

Safe announced in late June that the new rules would apply from August 1. Previously, corporations in China were almost always unable to sell options, and could trade only limited types of simple RMB option structures with banks, such as plain vanilla forwards, buy options or zero premium risk reversals.

Also, options had to be fully settled: net settlement was not permitted.

The new rules enable corporations to buy or sell options, or use a combination of options—and they can be either fully settled or net settled.

The innovations also extend to cross currency swaps, where corporations are allowed to decide, on an actual-needs basis, whether to exchange principal either on the effective date or at maturity. With very limited exceptions, principal exchange was previously compulsory.

"The most important feature of the new rules is the availability of a wider range of tools and instruments," Jacky Tai, managing director and head of treasury and markets at DBS Bank (China), told Global RMB.

"These new instruments will allow Chinese companies greater flexibility to better manage their currency risks as the exchange rate of the RMB becomes more volatile," Tai added. "It will also allow corporations to hedge more effectively and significantly reduce the cost of hedging."

Others agree. Beng-Hong Lee, head of markets, China, at Deutsche Bank, noted that in a market where the RMB is at last showing two-way volatility, Chinese corporations needed effective tools to help them reduce their overall currency risk.

"The relaxation of these restrictions enables companies to choose from a variety of more straightforward hedging structures to appropriately manage risk, and contributes to a more efficient currency market in China," said Lee.

- Increasing Volatility

Market participants see the changes as a critical step in the ongoing evolution of China's FX and capital markets, especially after the Chinese currency began to show two-way exchange rate fluctuation this year, in a departure from its traditional one-way appreciation.

The recent depreciation of the RMB began in mid February and was widely seen as having been engineered by the People's Bank of China (PBOC) to prepare the market for more exchange rate flexibility. Later, on March 17, the PBOC doubled the trading band of onshore RMB against the U.S. dollar to 2% either side of each day's official fixing.

"The new rulings have come on the back of the development of RMB internationalization, where two-way RMB fluctuation has become the new normal and companies need effective tools to help lower overall currency risks," said DBS's Tai.

Deutsche Bank's Lee added that change was being implemented at the correct pace.

"Given that China is a very complex economy, I think the regulator has been taking the right approach to introduce new solutions to clients on an incremental basis," he said. "Corporateions also benefit from the measured introduction of new products, as it is equally important to give them the chance to learn about the difference between products and to understand how to use them effectively."

"It also helps the regulator to more effectively monitor the new market risks that come with the new derivative combinations."

DBS's Tai also pointed out that deregulation done step by step with conditions put in place, such as allowing the changes only on an actual-needs basis, would help ensure the orderly development of the market and prevent speculation.

- Corporations Go Global

As for which clients will stand to gain most, bankers said that for now it would be those corporations involved in import and export trade with a currency mismatch between their receivables and payables, or corporations that have overseas investments or activities.

But they also said it was essential corporations be properly informed of product features to ensure they have adequate understanding of the risks involved.

HSBC said that it had conducted several transactions featuring combined buy and sell options with corporate clients on August 1, and Ryan Song, head of global markets at HSBC Bank (China) said in a statement that the bank had received strong interest from many customers since the changes were first announced in June.

DBS, meanwhile, said it had executed several transactions including European-style options for clients in eastern and southern China, as well as a RMB cross currency swap for a northern China client. Standard Chartered also said it had carried out deals using a combination of vanilla European-style RMB FX options.

Deutsche Bank went somewhat further, naming one of its clients. It said that it had conducted several trades for Mengniu Dairy and other corporations on 1st August, using instruments including FX call spreads to construct FX option strategies for the first time.

A call spread would usually involve the corporate simultaneously buying and selling call options at different strike prices (with the sell being either higher or lower than the buy, depending on the corporations' view of the currency's direction). Selling one call helps to finance the purchase of the other, and so reduces cost, but its existence also effectively sets a cap on the profit (or saving) that can be achieved from having the option in the first place.

Mengniu Dairy issued a statement saying that it had worked "with Deutsche Bank to complete our first RMB call spread under the new Safe regulation to more effectively hedge currency fluctuation".

Bankers are now hoping that other developments—such as American-style options or digital options—will gradually be allowed.

Exercises

Ⅰ. *For the following questions, consider each of the choices seperately and select all that apply.*

1. FX options can be traded at (　　).

A. super market　　B. OTC

C. flee market　　D. exchanges

2. (　　) are plain vanilla instruments in foreign exchange market.

A. Forwards　　B. Swaps

C. Spot　　D. Options

3. A strangle option is (　　).

A. to sell a call and a put with the same strike price

B. to buy a call and a put with different strike prices

C. to sell a call and a put with different strike prices

D. to buy a call and a put with the same strike price

4. Investors with the (　　) option position bearish about the base currency.

A. long call　　B. short call

C. long put　　D. short put

5. Option holder (　　).

A. pays the premium

B. receives the premium

C. has the right but no obligation in the option

D. has the obligation to execute the option

6. ( ) are essential prices in a FX option.

A. spot exchange rate S_t B. strike price E

C. tuition fee X D. premium c

7. Option writers suffer loss when ( ).

A. a call expiries, and $S_T>E$

B. a put expiries, and $S_T>E$

C. a call expiries, and $S_T<E$

D. a put expiries, and $S_T<E$

8. It costs nothing to enter into a FX ( ) transaction.

A. swap B. futures

C. forward D. option

9. Investors with the ( ) option position bullish about the base currency.

A. long call B. short call

C. long put D. short put

10. FX option premium is the sum of ( ).

A. base currency interest rate

B. quote currency interest rate

C. intrinsic value

D. extrinsic value

Ⅱ. ***Short answer questions.***

1. *What is the main difference between an FX option and an insurance in terms of risk diversification?*

2. *What is the quotation for Apr. call option on Swiss Franc?*

		Calls		*Put*	
		VOL	*LAST*	*VOL*	*LAST*
SFranc				*57.83*	
62500 Swiss Francs-cents per unit					
58	*Apr*	*6*	*1.38*	—	—
60	*Sep*	*2*	*1.90*	—	—

3. *What is the quotation for March put option on Japanese yen?*

		Calls		*Put*	
		VOL	*LAST*	*VOL*	*LAST*
Japanese yen				*93.15*	
6250000 J.yen-100 ths of a cent per unit					
81^{50}	*Mar*	—	—	5	0.30
82^{50}	*Apr*	2	1.10	2	1.44
83	*Apr*	—	—	5	1.51

4. *An American put option has exercise price as* $E=\$1.5227/£$, *the spot exchange rate is* $S_t=\$1.5216/£$, *then the intrinsic value* $= Max[E\text{-}S_t,\ 0]=\$0.0011/£$. *If the option premium is* $\$0.0008/£$, *how to arbitrage from this misprice?*

5. *American option holders can exercise option before expiration date, why few of them choose to do so?*

6. *Answer questions according to the following diagrams.*

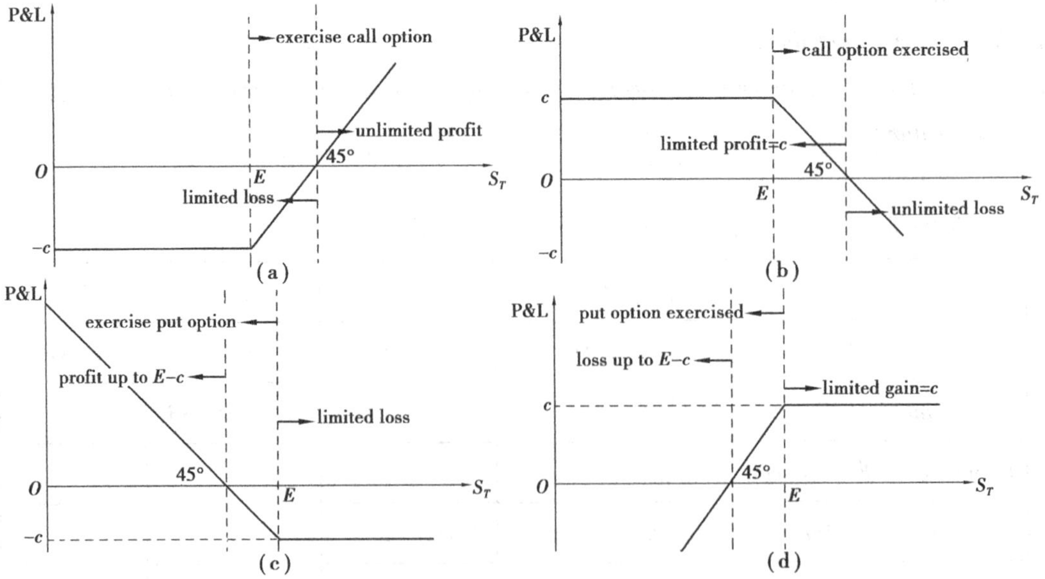

(1) *What are the profit-loss diagrams for option writer?*

(2) *What is the break-even exchange rate for option holder?*

(3) *What is the break-even exchange rate for option writer?*

(4) *Other things equal, given the underlying spot exchange rate performance as above, which FX option asks higher option premium?*

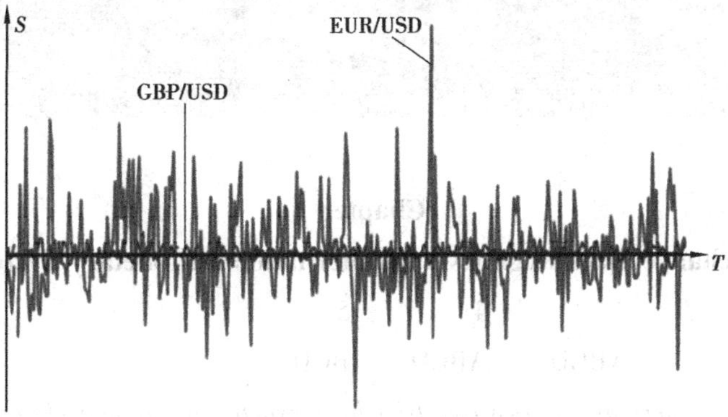

Answers

Chapter 1

Exchange Rate Regimes and International Monetary Systems

1	2	3	4	5
ABCD	BD	ABCD	ABCD	BCD

1. *Why in reality there are no two countries have exactly the same exchange rate regime?*

Because that the exchange rate regimes have many subtle virilities in between, countries with the same exchange rate regimes may differ widely if central banks have different international reserves and interest rates. Central banks need to find the most suitable one for their countries by balancing between the monetary autonomy and exchange rate stability. Meanwhile, the choice of foreign exchange rate regimes can influence or determine how the exchange rate between two currencies' moves and fluctuates on foreign exchange market. This explains why in reality there are no two countries have exactly the same exchange rate regime.

2. *How do international monetary systems fulfill the transaction function?*

By inspiring confidence, providing sufficient liquidity for fluctuating levels of trade and offering means to correct global imbalances, international monetary systems give acceptable means of payment to buyers and sellers of different nationality, including deferred payment.

3. *Has the modern international monetary system successfully facilitated the exchange of goods, services and capital among countries?*

No.

(1) Exchange Rate Regimes

It is desirable that exchange rates should move stably in reflection of economic fundamentals, however the floating exchange rates introduced by recent international monetary system has brought greater volatility since the collapse of the Bretton Woods system. This volatility failed exchange rates to reflect fundamentals between countries.

(2) International Payment and Transfer

Increased free flow of capital has unfortunately not brought the expected benefits to the global economy. On the contrary, it enlarged the volatility of exchange rates, destabilized the economies' growth and encouraged speculations.

(3) International Capital Movements

As financial markets get more integrated and cross border financial transactions become freer, capital flow are enhanced and their volatilities are heightened. Financial crises are more contagious and fatal since the rise of shadow banking system.

(4) International Reserves

The birth of Euro has tested the role of the U. S. dollar as the global economy's reserve currency. However the currency composition of allocated reserves is still concentrated in U. S. dollars.

Emerging economies have dominated the surge of reserve accumulation, especially Asian's share that accounts for more than half of the reserve. Again, it shows that international monetary system has not succeeded in its key objective of growth with stability in the global economy in the post-Bretton Woods regime.

Chapter 2
The Foreign Exchange Market

1	2	3	4	5
ABCD	ACD	BCD	ABCD	ABCD

1. *What are orders that commonly used in foreign exchange market?*

The Market Order instructs the broker to buy at the current market rate. This order type is usually executed immediately, at the price displayed in the trading platform at the time the order is placed. The Limit Order instructs the broker to execute a trade to enter a trade at a specific price. The trade could be either to buy currency when it reaches a specific price below the present market price, or to sell the currency pair when it reaches a specific price above the present market price. Because the Limit Order automates the process, traders save a lot of time from waiting for their target entry price, but this kind of order is only effective at the price input before, it cannot meet much flexibility requirement.

The Stop Order is used to exit an existing trade by liquidating a position when the market price changes against the expectations of the trader. This order is thus used to limit losses.

2. *What is short position and short selling?*

A short position in FX can be realized by short selling just like that in stock market. In stock market the investor borrows the stock, sells it, and uses the proceeds to make some other investment. The owner of the stock keeps all the rights to it, including receive any dividends due and can sell the stock at any time. By the end the investor should close the short position by repurchasing the stock and return it to the owner. In foreign exchange market, the trader can place an order to sell a currency pair that she does not "own". She needs to borrow this currency and pay the interest to the owner. To exit that "short trade", the trader simply places an order to buy the currency pair later on. A trader thus exits a position when she executes the opposite trade by which she started.

3. *What are factors that can significantly affect the fluctuation of foreign exchange rates?*

(1) Inflation Rates

Market inflation causes change in currency rates. The value of currency appreciates when a country is experiencing low inflation rates. When the inflation rate is low, good and services price will increase at a low rate. When a country is experiencing high inflation rates, the currency value depreciates and this leads to very high interest rates.

(2) Interest Rates

Varying interest rates affect the value of a currency and also affects the rate of dollar exchange. When a country has high interest rates, its currency value appreciates because lenders make more profit, this results to increased foreign capital and high exchange rates.

(3) Country's Balance of Payments

When a country has loss on its current account because of earning less money from its exports and spending more on imports, this leads to depreciation. Balance of payments can lead to unstable domestic currency rates.

(4) Government Debts

When a country has a lot of debts, it cannot acquire foreign capital which makes it experience inflation. Foreigners do research and if they foresee a debt in a certain country, they sell all their bonds in an open market not escape the consequences they might face in future. As a result, the exchange rate value of this country goes down.

(5) Terms of Trade

Terms of trade are the ratio of price between imports and exports. A country has better terms of trade of the prices of exports are greater than prices of imports. This country will experience a high revenue, high currency demand and increased currency value.

(6) Political Stability and Performance

Political and economic stability of a country determines the strength of its currency. Foreign investors are always attracted to countries that are stable both economically and politically. Countries that experience political and economic turmoil often miss a lot of investment from foreign investors. High inflow of foreign capital causes a country's currency value to appreciate while countries facing political and economic crisis experience low currency value.

(7) Recession

When countries experience recession, their interest rates fall drastically making it impossible to attract foreign investors. The currency values of such countries become weak leading to low exchange rates.

(8) Speculation

Foreign investor will invest more in countries that have a possibility of experiencing high currency values in future to plough back more profits. This leads to a high demand on that currency and the currency value rises up.

Chapter 3
Foreign Exchange Spots

1	2	3	4	5
ABD	ABCD	BD	AC	AB

1. *Cross exchange rates with no transaction costs: suppose that $S_{EUR/USD}=1.5$ and $S_{GBP/USD}=2$, work out $S_{EUR/GBP}$.*

$S_{EUR/GBP}=S_{EUR/USD}\div S_{GBP/USD}=1.5\div 2=0.75$

2. *Fill in how far to the right of the decimal point for the following currency pairs*

EUR/USD: 4

USD/JPY: 2

USD/CNY: 4

3. *Given rates found on the following currency pairs EUR/USD = 1.1325, EUR/GBP = 0.7805, GBP/USD = 1.4528, work out possible way for triangular arbitrage and explain potential risk.*

In the first step, the trader buys € 10000 at 1.1325 to obtain the equivalent of U.S. $11325. In the second portion of the trade, the trader sells € 10000 at 0.7805 to obtain £ 7805. Finally, the trader uses the British pounds to buy dollars at a rate of 1.4528, yielding U.S. $11339.

Subtracting the amount obtained from the initial trade from the final amount (US $11339−US $11325) would produce a positive difference of U.S. $14 per trade.

As with other trades, however, attempts at arbitrage can be subject to risks. This includes execution risk, where the amount quoted is unable to be filled by a broker. If in the above trade, for example, the Euro had moved to 0.7795 against the pound before the trader locked in a price, the action would produce a loss (US $11324.58−US $11335) of about U.S. $10.42 per trade.

4. *Is there any triangular arbitrage? (round to 4 decimal places)*

Barclays: GBP/USD = 1.8400/27

Deutsche: GBP/EUR = 1.5085/109

Citibank: EUR/USD = 1.2211/33

No arbitrage. Borrow $1 from Citibank, exchange with Barclays for £(1/1.8427), sell £ to

Deutsche for €(1.5085/1.8427), then go back to Citibank for \$0.9996 (1.2211×1.5085÷1.8427). Start with \$1, end with \$0.9996.

5. *Given a 10:1 leverage ratio, what is the corresponding margin? If the margin is 0.02, what is the corresponding leverage?*

1÷10=0.1=10%

1÷0.02=50

6. *calculating margin requirements for a trade and the remaining account equity. You have \$3000 in your account. You want to buy 100000 EUR with a current price of 1.0621 USD, and your broker requires a 2% margin. What is the required margin? How many more Euros could you buy after commit the margin?*

required margin=100000×1.0621×0.02=\$2124.2

After paying margin you have 3000−2124.2=\$875.8 left in your account, with leverage of 1÷2%=50, you can buy an additional \$875.8×50=\$43790 worth of Euros, that is 43790÷1.0621=€41229.64

7. *How much should one trader to pay to buy 10 lots USD with an account that its leverage is 50:1?*

\$100000×10÷50=\$20000, this trader should pay \$20000 to buy 10 lots.

8. *Suppose that one trader has a \$10000 account and she has some open positions with the total margin of \$900 and her positions are \$400 in profit. What is her equity and how much left for her free margin?*

equity=\$10000+ \$400=\$10400

free margin=\$10400− \$900=\$9500

9. *Solve for cross rates with two sided quotes.*

(1) *USD/CHF=1.6545/50 and NZD/USD=0.6195/0.6200, NZD/CHF=?*

(2) *USD/CHF=1.6545/50 and USD/JPY=115.05/07. CHF/JPY=?*

(1) USD/CHF=1.6545/50 and NZD/USD=0.6195/0.6200, NZD/CHF=?

- Bid price of NZD/CHF

① Sell 1 NZD for USD. 1 NZD sells for 0.6195 USD.

② Use 1 USD to buy CHF. 1 USD buys 1.6545 CHF. Stated differently, we can sell1 USD for 1.6545 CHF.

③ Calculate the CHF amount received for 1 NZD. Since 1 USD buys 1.6545 CHF, 0.6195

USD buys 0.6195×1.6545 CHF, or about 1.0250 CHF. Therefore, the bid price in CHF for 1 NZD is 1.0250.

- Ask price of NZD/CHF

① Use CHF to buy 1 USD. It takes 1.6550 CHF to buy 1 USD.

② Use the 1 USD to buy NZD. Traders can buy 0.6200 NZD for 1 USD (which is the same as selling 1 USD for 0.6200 NZD). Selling a USD is the same as buying a NZD. The 1 USD obtained in step 1 can buy 1.6129 NZD, which is obtained from solving(1/0.6200).

③ Calculate the offer rate in CHF for NZD. 1.6550 CHF buys 1.6129 NZD, so that 1.6129 NZD/1.6550 CHF. Dividing by 1.6129 and rearranging gives the ask price in CHF for 1 NZD is 1.0261.

Combining the above results gives NZD/CHF = 1.0250/61

(2) USD/CHF = 1.6545/50 and USD/JPY = 115.05/07. CHF/JPY = ?

$\because$

$$USD/X = bid_X/ask_X$$
$$USD/Y = bid_Y/ask_Y$$
$$X/Y = \frac{bid_X}{ask_Y} \Big/ \frac{ask_X}{bid_Y}$$

$\therefore$

$bid_{CHF/JPY} = 115.05 \div 1.6550 = 69.52$

$ask_{CHF/JPY} = 115.07 \div 1.6545 = 69.54$

CHF/JPY = 69.52/54

10. *A German student plans a trip to St. Petersburg, Russia. She leaves Berlin with €1000 in her money pouch, wanting to exchange all of these for Russian rubles. She obtain the following quotes:* $S_{EUR/USD} = 1.0792/98$, *and* $S_{USD/RUB} = 54.45/56$. *How much rubles will she obtain from her Euros?*

$\because$

$$X/USD = bid_X/ask_X$$
$$USD/Y = bid_Y/ask_Y$$
$$X/Y = bid_X \times bid_Y / ask_X \times ask_Y$$

$\therefore$

$bid_{EUR/RUB} = 1.0792 \times 54.45 = 58.76$

$ask_{EUR/RUB} = 1.0798 \times 54.56 = 58.91$

she can have 1000×58.76 = 58 760 rubles

11. *If* $S_{USD/JPY} = 109.86/93$ *and* $S_{USD/CAD} = 1.3556/62$, *solve for* $S_{CAD/JPY}$.

$$USD/X = bid_X/ask_X$$
$$USD/Y = bid_Y/ask_Y$$
$$X/Y = \frac{bid_Y}{ask_X} \Big/ \frac{ask_Y}{bid_X}$$

take CAD as X, JPY as Y

bid price of $S_{CAD/JPY}$ is $109.86 \div 1.3562 = 81.01$

ask price of $S_{CAD/JPY}$ is $109.93 \div 1.355\,6 = 81.09$

$S_{CAD/JPY} = 81.01/09$

12. *If* $S_{GBP/USD} = 1.277\,8/82$ *and* $S_{USD/MXN} = 18.8068/73$, *solve for* $S_{GBP/MNX}$.

$$X/USD = bid_X/ask_X$$
$$USD/Y = bid_Y/ask_Y$$
$$X/Y = bid_X \times bid_Y/ask_X \times ask_Y$$

take GBP as X, MNX as Y

bid price of $S_{GBP/MNX}$ is $1.2778 \times 18.8068 = 24.0313$

ask price of $S_{GBP/MNX}$ is $1.2782 \times 18.8073 = 24.0395$

$S_{GBP/MNX} = 24.0313/95$

13. *If* $S_{OMR/USD} = 2.5988/07$ *and* $S_{BHD/USD} = 2.6568/92$, *solve for* $S_{BHD/OMR}$.

$$X/USD = bid_X/ask_X$$
$$Y/USD = bid_Y/ask_Y$$
$$X/Y = \frac{bid_X}{ask_Y} \Big/ \frac{ask_X}{bid_Y}$$

take BHD as X, OMR as Y

bid price of $S_{BHD/OMR}$ is $2.6568 \div 2.6007 = 1.0216$

ask price of $S_{BHD/OMR}$ is $2.6592 \div 2.5988 = 1.0232$

$S_{BHD/OMR} = 1.0216/32$

14. *On 31st Dec 2015*, $S_{USD/JPY} = 120.21$, *while one year later on 30th Dec. 2016*, $S_{USD/JPY} = 116.95$. *Calculate the magnitude of percentage appreciation or depreciation for the base currency USD.*

percentage change in USD exchange rate is $(116.95 - 120.21) \div 120.21 \times 100\% = -2.71\%$

the negative value indicates that for the past one year USD has depreciated against JPY by 2.71%.

15. *Given rates found on the following currency pairs EUR/USD = 1.0798, EUR/JPY =*

119.53, USD/JPY = 110.07, work out possible way for triangular arbitrage if there is any.

1 € ⇒1×119.53 = 119.53 ¥ ⇒119.53÷110.07 = 1.0859 $ ⇒1.0859÷1.0798 = 1.0057 €, or

1 $ ⇒1÷1.0798 = 0.9261 € ⇒0.9261×119.53 = 110.70 ¥ ⇒110.70÷110.07 = 1.0057 $, or

100 ¥ ⇒100÷110.07 = 0.9085 $ ⇒0.9085÷1.0798 = 0.8414 € ⇒0.8414×119.53 = 100.57 ¥

16. *How is the central parity of RMB against USD determined?*

The CFETS first enquires prices from all market makers before the opening of the market on each business day. Market makers should refer to the closing rate of the inter-bank foreign exchange market on the previous day, in conjunction with demand and supply condition in the foreign exchange market and exchange rate movement of the major currencies. CFETS excludes the highest and lowest offers, and then calculates the weighted average of the remaining prices in the sample as the central parity of RMB against USD for the day. The weights are determined by the CFETS in line with the transaction volumes of the respective market makers in the market as well as other indicators such as the performance of market-making.

17. *Explain the dialogue of FX spot transaction between bank A and bank B.*

A: GBP 5 Mio.

B: 1.4131/1.4137.

A: My risk.

B: 1.4134 *Choice.*

A: Sell PLS. My USD To ANY.

B: OK, done. At 1.4134 *We Buy GBP* 5 *Mio AG USD Val March*-26 *GBP To My London, TKS for deal, BIBI.*

A wants B offer price for 5 million pounds, however, A does not tell if it is buying or selling.

The prices B offers is $GBP/USD_{bid} = 1.4131$ and $GBP/USD_{ask} = 1.4137$.

A is not satisfied with the prices and it encourages B to give better prices.

This time, B offers just one price: GBP/USD = 1.4134, leaving A choose to sell or to buy.

With GBP/USD = 1.4134, A would like to sell GBP to B. A requires that dollars go to its New York account.

B should sum this contract up by stating that at GBP/USD = 1.4134, B purchase GBP from A, and the value date is 26th March. B also requires that pounds go to its London account.

18. *For currency pair EUR/USD, bank A offers prices as EUR/USD = 1.2445/51 and bank B offers prices as EUR/USD = 1.2454/60. There is a two-currency arbitrage. Give two ways to exploit*

the arbitrage.

borrow \$ from A	long € A	short € B	repay A and gain positive rate of return
1 \$	(1÷1.2451) €	(1.2454÷1.2451) \$	0.03%

or

borrow € from B	short € B	long € A	repay B and gain positive rate of return
1 €	1.2454 \$	(1.2454÷1.2451) €	0.03%

Both ways provide the same positive rate of return.

19. *What does the quote USD/CHF = 0.961 8/23 indicate?*

A market maker normally quotes a two-way price. She is obliged to make a bid and an ask for dollars against the Swiss franc. Market makers always quote to their advantage and to the other person's disadvantage. A market maker quotes spot Swiss Franc against the dollar expressing as: "dollar/Swiss franc is 0.9618 - 0.9623." The bid is at Sfr 0.9618/ \$ and the ask is at Sfr 0.9623/ \$. It indicates that the client will sell 1 \$ for Sfr 0.9618 which is the market maker's bid. Conversely, the client buys at the market maker's offer, 0.9623.

Chapter 4
Foreign Exchange Forwards

1	2	3	4	5
ABCD	AB	BC	AD	BC

1. *In the London FX market,* $S_{USD/JPY}$ *= 130.47/57, the points of 1-month USD is 40/50;* $S_{EUR/USD}$ *= 1.8252/62, the points of 1-month EUR is 30/20. work out* F_1(¥/ \$) *and* F_1(\$/€).

points of USD/JPY is quoted as "smaller-bigger", so the forward rate equals to spot plus point

1-month forward rate of USD/JPY

bid = 130.47+0.4 = 130.87

ask = 130.57+0.5 = 131.07

points of USD/EUR is quoted as "bigger-smaller", so the forward rate equals to spot minus point

1-month forward rate of EUR/USD

bid = 1.8252−0.003 = 1.8222

ask = 1.8262−0.002 = 1.8240

2. *Company A expects to receive* €*100 million 6 months from now and enters into a cash*

settlement currency forward to exchange these Euros for U. S. dollars at \$ 1. 0613/€. If market exchange rate is \$1.0615/€ at settlement, what is the amount of the payment to be received or paid by company A?

Under the terms of the contract Company A would receive:

€ 100 million×\$1.0613/€=\$106.13million

Without the forward contract, company A would receive:

€ 100 million×\$1.0615/€=\$106.15million

The counter party would be disadvantaged by difference between contract rate and market rate in an amount equal to the advantage that would have occurred to company A had not entered into the currency forward.

Company A must make a payment of \$20000 to the counterparty.

3. *$R=5\%$, $R^*=8\%$, $F_{GBP/USD}=1.458333$ and $S_{GBP/USD}=1.50$. If round to two decimals, is there any arbitrage opportunity?*

IRP holds if $1+R=F\div S(1+R^*)$

$1+R=1+5\%=1.05$, $F\div S(1+R^*)=(1.4583/1.50)\times(1+8\%)\approx 1.05$

Investing \$1000 in U.S. gains 1000×1.05=\$1050

Investing \$1000 in U.K. gains 1000÷1.50×1.08=720×1.4583333=\$1050

In this case, investor does not mind which currency to hold, because IRP holds and both currencies offer the same return.

4. *Read the following news on 27th Mar. 2015, explain the relationship among onshore RMB rate, offshore RMB rate and NDF.*

HONG KONG, Mar 27 2015: China's yuan edged down against the dollar on Friday after the central bank set a weaker midpoint and is heading for its first weekly loss in a month. The People's Bank of China set the midpoint rate at 6.1397 per dollar prior to market open, lower than the previous fix at 6.1375.

The spot yuan opened at 6.2150 per dollar and was changing hands at 6.2171 at midday, 47 pips weaker than the previous close and 1.26% below the midpoint. It traded within a tight 6.2190 and 6.2130 range in morning trade. The spot rate is currently allowed to trade with a range 2% above or below the official fixing on any given day. A sudden turnaround in the dollar's fortunes overnight saw the currency trading broadly higher early in Asia on Friday, underpinned by a set of encouraging data on Thursday and a rise in U.S. Treasury yields.

Analysts remain cautious on the outlook for the yuan as the world's second-largest economy saw its manufacturing activity slowing to a 11-month low in March. The dollar is also expected to strengthen as the U.S. Federal Reserve moves closer to the day when it embarks on tightening policy rates. The offshore yuan was trading 0.07% weaker than the onshore spot at 6.2215 per dollar.

Offshore one-year non-deliverable forwards contracts (NDFs), considered the best available proxy for forward-looking market expectations of the yuan's value, traded at 6.3705, or 3.62% weaker than the midpoint.

One-year NDFs are settled against the midpoint, not the spot rate, and now that the trading band has been widened to 2% in either direction, corporates have become much more cautious when using the NDF to hedge given the basis risk inherent in them.

As a result the market has lost liquidity in recent years and has frequently proven an unreliable measure of market sentiment.

5. *Convert forward quotations expressed on a points basis into an outright forward quotation: Given* $S_{USD/CHF}=1.6557/68$ *and the forward points as 25/15, solve for the outright forward.*

The forward points are given in descending order, thus should be subtracted from its associated spot quote. Outright forward is 1.6532/53.

6. *Convert forward quotations expressed in percentage terms into an outright forward quotation: Swiss franc is selling forward at a 3.96%per annum premium over the dollar at the 3-month forward rate,* $S_{USD/CHF}=1.4800$*, what is the 3-month outright forward quotation,* $F_3(Fr/\$)=?$

Under European terms, that USD is the base currency, the formula for the percent-per-annum premium or discount is given as

$$F_n(q/\$)=\frac{S-F}{F}\times\frac{\text{days in year}}{\text{number of forwad valid days}}\times 100\%$$

then $3.96\%=(1.48-F)\div F\times 360\div 90\times 100\%\Rightarrow F_3(Fr/\$)=1.4655$

7. *Given* $S_{GBP/USD}=1.2543/46$*, suppose that annual interest rate of dollars is 3% and 6%, annual interest rate of pounds is 1% and 4%. What is the 9-month forward outright that a bank would offer?*

According to convention, base currency is British pound and quote currency is U.S. dollar. It is 9-month forward bank is offering, thus interest rates need to be adjusted into 9 months. $R_b=3\%\times 9\div 12=2.25\%$, $R_a=6\times 9\div 12=4.5\%$, $R_b^*=1\%\times 9\div 12=0.75\%$, $R_a^*=4\%\times 9\div 12=3\%$

$$F_{bid}=S_b\frac{1+R_b}{1+R_a^*}=1.2543\times\frac{1+2.25\%}{1+3\%}\approx 1.2452$$

$$F_{ask}=S_a\frac{1+R_a}{1+R_b^*}=1.2546\times\frac{1+4.5\%}{1+0.75\%}\approx 1.3013$$

8. $S_{EUR/USD}=1.0681/83$*, 6-month forward points are 97/99, 9-month forward points are 151/156. One trader plans to buy EUR 8-month forward. What is the forward rate?*

Trader intends to buy EUR 8-month forward, bank should offer ask price of 8-month EUR forward.

Assume that forward goes in linear pattern, then each month worth (156-99)÷3=19 pips.

As the forward point is in ascending order, and 8-month is 2 months greater than 6-month, bank should offer 1.0683+0.0099+0.0019×2=1.0721, i.e. F_8(€/ $)= 1.082

9. *Given $S_{USD/CHF}$ = 1.5000/10, annual interest rate of dollars is 5.875% and 6% while annual interest rate of Swiss Franc is 2% and 2.125%, considering bid and ask, what are the 6-month forward points and outright rates?*

According to the FX convention, base currency is USD and quote currency is CHF.

∵ premium/discoun $t_{bid} = S\left(\frac{1+R_b}{1+R_a^*}-1\right)$ and premium/discoun $t_{ask} = S\left(\frac{1+R_a}{1+R_b^*}-1\right)$

$S=(S_a+S_b)\div 2=(1.5000+1.5010)\div 2=1.5005$

interest rates need to be adjusted into 6 months. $R_b=2\%\times 6\div 12=1\%$, $R_a=2.125\%\times 6\div 12=1.0625\%$, $R_b^*=5.875\%\times 6\div 12=2.9375\%$, $R_a^*=6\%\times 6\div 12=3\%$

bid point is $1.5005\times\left(\frac{1+1\%}{1+3\%}-1\right)\times 10000\approx -291$; outright forward bid price is thus 1.5000−0.029 1=1.4709

ask point is $1.5005\times\left(\frac{1+1.0625\%}{1+2.9375\%}-1\right)\times 10000\approx -273$; outright forward ask price is thus 1.5010−0.0273=1.4737

forward points are negative thus USD is at discount, F_6(*Fr*/ $)= 1.4709/37

10. *$S_{EUR/USD}$ = 1.0645/53, 3-month forward points are 62/63, 6-month forward points are 97/99. What are the rates for an optional forward from 3 to 6 months?*

	bid	ask
spot	1.0645	1.0653
3-month	62 ⇒**1.0707**	63 ⇒1.0716
6-month	97 ⇒1.0742	99 ⇒**1.0752**

optional forward from 3 to 6 months are 1.0707/52.

11. *$S_{GBP/USD}$ = 1.2778/84, 1-month forward points are 43/42, 3-month forward points are 69/67. What are the rates for an optional forward from 1 to 3 months?*

	bid	ask
spot	1.2778	1.2784

1-month	43 ⇒1.2735	42 ⇒**1.2742**
3-month	69 ⇒**1.2709**	67 ⇒1.2717

optional forward from 1 to 3 months are 1.2709/42.

12. $S_{USD/CAD}$ = *1.3500/06, annual interest rates of Canadian dollar are 5.98% and 6.02%, annual interest rates of U.S dollar are 3.92% and 3.98%. If one Canadian company needs USD in 90 days, what forward price it could have should the IRP holds? If one U.S. company needs CAD in 90 days, what forward price it could have should the IRP holds?*

According to FX conventions, USD is base currency, CAD is quote currency.

$R_b = 5.98\%$, $R_a = 6.02\%$, $R_b^* = 3.92\%$, $R_a^* = 3.98\%$, $S_b = 1.3500$, $S_a = 1.3506$

To meet currency position requirement, this Canadian company has two strategies, but if IRP holds, two strategies are break-even.

It could either long USD forward or pursue borrow CAD—long spot—invest in USD for 90 days.

Strategy Ⅰ needs the forward ask price of the USD: long 3-month USD forward cost this company F_a CAD;

Strategy Ⅱ borrow CAD—long spot—invest in USD for 90 days strategy leads both cost and income:

cost: $S_a[1+R_a\times(90\div365)] = 1.3506\times[1+6.02\%\times(90\div365)] = 1.3706$CAD

income: $1+R_b^*\times(90\div360) = 1+3.92\%\times(90\div360) = 1.0098$USD

The forward price F_a required for the two strategies to break-even (i.e. no arbitrage) would be 1.3706÷1.0098 = 1.3575.

To meet currency position requirement, this U.S. company has two strategies, but if IRP holds, two strategies are break-even.

It could either short USD forward or pursue borrow USD—short spot—invest in CAD for 90 days.

Strategy Ⅰ needs the forward bid price of the USD: short 3-month USD forward brings this company F_b CAD;

borrow USD—short spot—invest in CAD for 90 days strategy leads both cost and income:

cost: $[1+R_a^*\times(90\div360)]\div S_b = [1+3.98\%\times(90\div360)]\div1.3500 = 0.7481$USD

income: $1+R_b\times(90\div365) = 1+5.98\%\times(90\div365) = 1.01475$CAD

The forward price F_b required for the two strategies to break-even, i.e. no arbitrage would be 1.01475÷0.7481 = 1.3564.

If IRP holds, 3-month forward price should be 1.3564/75

Chapter 5
Foreign Exchange Swaps

1	2	3	4	5
ABCD	ABCD	AD	AC	BC

1. *$S_{EUR/USD}$ = 1.0646/52, 6-month swap point is 63/59, use mid-point to work out the outright forward prices and the forward prices under this 6-month swap.*

		bid	ask
		1.0649	1.0652
spot	mid point	1.0649	
	∵ in descending order, ∴ −swap point	63	59
6-month forward in swap		1.0586	1.0590
outright 6-month forward		1.0583	1.0593

2. *Given $S_{GBP/USD}$ = 1.5026/32 and 9-month swap point as 58/67, what is the cost and revenue of the quoting party for a £1 million trade of FX swap?*

cost: 1 million×0.005 8 = 5800

revenue: 1 million×0.0067 = 6700

3. *Given $S_{AUD/USD}$ = 0.7527/33, annual interest rate in Australia is 3%~5% and annual interest rate in U.S. is 1%~2%. What is the 6-month swap points implied by interest rate difference? Explain the meaning of swap point sign. (what does it mean when it is positive, what does it mean when it is negative)*

$S=(0.7527+0.7533)\div 2=0.7530$

With annual interest rates as above, 6-month interest rate should be $R_b^*=1.5\%$, $R_a^*=2.5\%$, $R_b=0.5\%$, $R_a=1\%$

bid point of swap $=S(R_b-R_a^*)=0.7530\times(0.5\%-2.5\%)=-0.01506$, -150.6 pips

ask point of swap $=S(R_a-R_b^*)=0.7530\times(1\%-1.5\%)=-0.003765$, -37.65 pips

∵ $R<R^*$ ∴ swap point is negative, base currency AUD is at discount.

4. *What is the mark to market value of the following swap?*

At time t_0, $S_{GBP/USD}=1.2828$, 1 year (365 days) swap points are 101/102, annual interest rate of dollar is R = 4% and annual interest rate of British Sterling is $R^*=2\%$. If a calling party expects that sterling is going to depreciate in one year, she buys a 1-y GBP swap 1 million at 102. At time t_1, interest rates are unchanged, $S_{GBP/USD}$ dropped to 1.2801. Accordingly, swap point changed to 105/108.

buy swap at t_0	close swap at t_1	*P/L* in pips	*P/L* in $	present $ value	mark to market $ value of swap
short spot 1.2828	long spot 1.2801	1.2828−1.2801 = 27pips	2700	2700	2700−2786.97 = −86.97
long forward	short forward	1.2906−1.2935 = −29pips	−2900	−2786.97	

1.2828+102pips = 1.2935 1.2801+105pips = 1.2906

The mark to market \$ value of her swap therefore is \$ −86.97.

5. *Given* $S_{USD/JPY}$ = *109.89/95*; *annual USD interest rate* $R_b^* = 2.4\%$, $R_a^* = 2.7\%$; *annual JPY interest rate* $R_b = 0.3\%$, $R_a = 0.6\%$; *swap points* f_{12}(¥/ \$) = *100/90. Take mid-point as spot basis.*

(1) *Is there any arbitrage opportunity?*

(2) *How to arbitrage?*

(3) *Conclude the arbitrage rules.*

(1) With the given condition, the indicate forward exchange rates should be $F_b = \frac{1+R_b}{1+R_a^*}S_b$ and $F_a = \frac{1+R_a}{1+R_b^*}S_a$.

F_b = 109.89×(1+0.3%)÷(1+2.7%) = 107.32

F_a = 109.95×(1+0.6%)÷(1+2.4%) = 108.02

mid-point of spot exchange rate is (109.89+109.95)÷2 = 109.92

forward points under swap are

f_b = 109.92−1.00 = 108.92

f_a = 109.92−0.9 = 109.02

$f_b > F_a$, swap is mis-priced, there is arbitrage opportunity.

(2) More specifically, she can borrow 1 million ¥.

sell swap, long spot at 109.95, gets 1 million ¥÷109.95 = \$ 9095.04, and short forward at 108.92

lend \$ and in the end she obtains \$ 9095.04×(1+2.4%) = \$ 9313.32

execute far of swap by taking a short position of forward \$ 9313.32×108.92 = ¥ 1014406.9

repay the loan and she gains profit of 1014406.9−1 million(1+0.6%) = ¥ 8406.9

(3) Notice that $f_b > F_a$, one may arbitrage by the following steps:

①borrow quote currency;

②sell swap (long spot and short forward);

③lend base currency;

④execute far leg of swap, pay up the loan and gain profit.

Chapter 6
Foreign Exchange Futures

1	2	3	4	5
AD	ABCD	BCD	ABCD	ABCD

1. *Should the basis strengthens unexpectedly, comment a short hedger's position.*

Let F_1 be initial futures rate, F_2 be final futures rate, and S_2 be final spot exchange rate; then one hedge the future sale of base currency by entering into a short futures contract, this short hedger's position would be improved because that $S_2+(F_1-F_2)=F_1$+basis.

2. *One trader uses the following futures quotes on the British pound to speculate on the value of the British pound.*

British Pound Futures, U.S. \$/pound(CME) *Contract = 62500pounds*

maturity	*open*	*high*	*low*	*settle*	*change*	*high*	*open interest*
March	*1.4246*	*1.4268*	*1.4214*	*1.4228*	*0.0032*	*1.4700*	*25605*
June	*1.4164*	*1.4188*	*1.4146*	*1.4162*	*0.0030*	*1.4550*	*809*

(1) *if this trader buys 5 June pound futures, and the spot rate at maturity is \$1.3980/pound, what is the value of trader's position?*

(2) *if this trader sells 12 March pound futures, and the spot rate at maturity is \$1.4560/pound, what is the value of trader's position?*

(3) *if this trader buys 3 March pound futures, and the spot rate at maturity is \$1.4560/pound, what is the value of trader's position?*

(4) *if this trader sells 12 June pound futures, and the spot rate at maturity is \$1.3980/pound, what is the value of trader's position?*

Assumptions	Values	Values	Values	Values
Pounds(£) per futures contract	£ 62500	£ 62500	£ 62500	£ 62500
Maturity month	June	March	March	June
Number of contracts	5	12	3	12
Did he buy or sell the futures?	buys	sells	buys	sells
Ending spot rate($/£)	$1.3980	$1.4560	$1.4560	$1.3980
Pound futures contract, settle price($	$1.4162	$1.4228	$1.4228	$1.4162
Spot-Futures	($0.0182)	$0.0332	$0.0332	($0.0182)
Value of position at maturity($)	($5687.50)	($24900.00)	$6225.00	$13650.00

3. *You expect to receive a payment of 1 million British pounds after six months for your business. The pound is currently worth \$1.60 (i.e., £1 = \$1.60), but the six-month futures price is \$1.56. You expect the price of pound to decline. If this expectation is fulfilled, you will suffer a loss when the pounds are converted into dollars when you receive them six months in the future.*

(1) *Given the current price, what is the expected payment in dollars?*

(2) *Given the futures price, how much would you receive in dollars?*

(3) *If, after six months, the pound is worth $1.35, what is your loss from the decline in the value of the pound?*

(4) *To avoid this potential loss, you decide to hedge and sell a contract for the future delivery of pounds at the going futures price of $1.56. What is the cost to you of this protection from the possible decline in the value of the pound?*

(5) *If, after the hedging, the price of the pound falls to $1.35, what is the maximum amount that you lose?*

(6) *If, after the hedging, the price of the pound rises to $1.80, how much do you gain from your position?*

(7) *How would your answer be different to part (6) if you had not hedged and the price of the pound had risen to $1.80?*

Futures and forwards are nearly identical in their ability to hedge risk

(1) Given the current price, what is the expected payment in dollars?

Payment in terms of the spot price: 1000000×$1.60=$1600000

(2) Given the futures price, how much would you receive in dollars?

Payment in terms of the futures price: 1000000=$1560000

(3) If, after six months, the pound is worth $1.35, what is your loss from the decline in the value of the pound?

If the price of the pound declines to $1.35, the recipient receives pounds worth $1350000. The loss from the decline in the value of the pound form $1.60 to $1.35 is $250000 (i.e., $1350000−$1600000).

(4) To avoid this potential loss, you decide to hedge and sell a contract for the future delivery of pounds at the going futures price of $1.56. What is the cost to you of this protection from the possible decline in the value of the pound?

To hedge, you sell (shorts) a contract for the future delivery of pounds. The value of that contract is $1560000 based on the future price of $1.56. When you receive the pounds after six months, you can deliver the pounds at the price specified in the contract. The cost of the hedge is the difference between the spot and futures prices times the number of pounds: (1.60−1.56)×1000000=$40000.

(5) If, after the hedging, the price of the pound falls to $1.35, what is the maximum amount that you lose?

Since the investor has a contract to sell pounds at $1.56, the price decline is irrelevant. The loss (the cost in (4)) remains $40000 because the investor hedged. In (3) you did not hedge and, therefore, were exposed to the larger loss.

(6) If, after the hedging, the price of the pound rises to $1.80, how much do you gain from

your position?

Since the investor has a contract to sell pounds at 1.56, the price increase is irrelevant. By hedging, the investor has foregone the opportunity for profit that would result from an increase in the value of the pound.

(7) How would your answer be different to part (6) if you had not hedged and the price of the pound had risen to $1.80?

If the investor had not hedged, £1000000 would be worth $1800000. The investor earns a $200000 profit on the increase in the value of the pound from $1.60 to $1.80. However, the intent of the hedge is to reduce the risk of loss from a price decline. To achieve risk reduction, the hedger must forgo the opportunity for profit. Any profit goes to the speculator who buys the contracts and bears the risk.

4. *Your company sells 10 machines to a Swiss company. The sale price is 100000 Swiss Francs each and payment is to be made at the end of the calendar year. The December futures price for Swiss Francs is 0.6915. You are worried that the Swiss Franc will depreciate against the U.S. Dollar between now and the end of the year. How can you hedge this exchange rate risk?*

Note that since (1) the total exposure is one million Swiss Francs and (2) each futures contract is for 125000 Francs, eight contracts are required to hedge the exposure. Further, since (1) the company stands to lose if the Swiss Franc depreciates (each Swiss Franc can be converted back into a smaller number of Dollars) and (2) the futures contracts decrease in value if the Swiss Franc depreciates (since the basis of the contract is Swiss Francs per Dollar), the contracts should be sold. To illustrate that selling eight futures contracts provides an adequate hedge, first suppose that the value of the Swiss Franc is 0.30 at the end of December. In this case, the U.S. Dollar value of the payment for the machines will be 0.30(10)(100000) = $300000. The gain on the futures position will be −8(125000)(0.30 − 0.6915) = $391500. Hence the total income is $691500, which equals the un-hedged income in dollars if the exchange rate does not fluctuate.

5. *Answer questions according to the following diagram. The middle line is the spot exchange rate, the two lines stand for FX futures. Given interest rate of base currency as R^* and interest rate of quote currency as R. Which line stands for $R>R^*$ Why?*

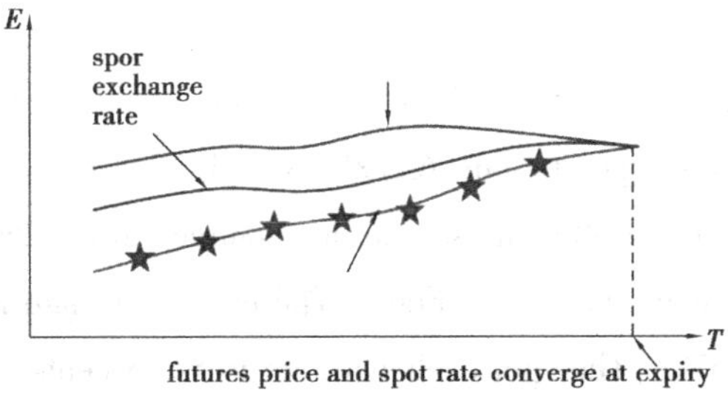

According to interest rate parity, a currency is at forward premium (discount) by as much as its interest rate is lower (higher) than interest rate in the other country. Base currency provides lower interest rate, then it will be appreciate in the future, thus the upper line stands for $R>R^*$.

6. *Assume that at the beginning of the day you have taken a short position on a CME EUR futures with a settlement price as \$1.3140/€, one EUR contract size is EUR 125000. By the end of the day, settlement price ends at \$1.3126. Calculate the profit or loss according to daily mark-to-market.*

Short position: p/l = notional×$(f_{t-1}-f_t)$×contracts

125000×(\$1.3140−\$1.3126)×1 =\$175 for profit

Chapter 7

Foreign Exchange Option Basics

1	2	3	4	5	6	7	8	9	10
BD	ABD	BC	BC	AC	ABD	AD	ABC	AD	CD

1. *What is the main difference between a FX option and an insurance in terms of risk diversification?*

Insurance companies diversify across many uncorrelated risks according to the Law of Large Numbers, and make money. While for an option writer, she charges a fee which is the sum of discounted expected cost corrected for exchange rate risk. She diversifies by buying assets that are negatively correlated with the option.

2. *What is the quotation for Apr. call option on Swiss Franc?*

		Calls		*Put*	
		VOL	*LAST*	*VOL*	*LAST*
SFranc				*57.83*	
62500 Swiss Francs-cents per unit					
58	*Apr*	*6*	*1.38*	—	—
60	*Sep*	*2*	*1.90*	—	—

One call option contract on the Swiss Franc with exercise price 58 cents and exercise month Apr. would give the buyer the right to buy 62500 Swiss Francs for 0.58×62500 = \$ 36250. The indicated price of the contract is 1.38 cents so that one contract costs 62500×0.013 8=\$862.50. The spot exchange rate is 57.83 cents per Swiss Franc. The expiration date is 14th Apr. 01.

(1) Spot Rate S_t=\$0.5783. The spot exchange rate is 57.83 cents per CHF (middlepoint).

(2) Exercise Price E=\$0.58. One call option contract on the CHF with exercise price 58 cents and exercise month Apr. would give the option buyer the right to buy 62500 CHF for U.S. 0.58×62500=\$36250.

(3) Premium c=\$0.0138. The indicated price of the contract is 1.38 cents so that one contract would cost 62500×0.0138=\$862.50.

(4) The expiration date of Apr. 58 call option is 14th Apr. 01.

3. *What is the quotation for March put option on Japanese yen?*

		Calls		*Put*	
		VOL	*LAST*	*VOL*	*LAST*
Japanese yen				*93.15*	
6250000 J.yen-100ths of a cent per unit					
81^{50}	*Mar*	—	—	*5*	*0.30*
82^{50}	*Apr*	*2*	*1.10*	*2*	*1.44*
83	*Apr*	—	—	*5*	*1.51*

One put contract on the Japanese yen with exercise price 81.50/100 cents and exercise month Mar. would give the buyer the right to sell 6250000 Japanese yen for 81.50/100÷100×6250000=\$50937.50. The indicated price of the contract is 0.3/100 cents, so that one contract would cost 6250000×0.3/100÷100=\$187.50. The spot exchange rate is shown as 93.15/100 per Japanese yen.

(1) Spot Rate S_t=\$93.15/10000. The spot exchange rate is 93.15/100 cents per JPY (middlepoint).

(2) Exercise Price E=\$81.50/10000. *The Mar. put option on JPY of 81.50* means the price to sell per JPY is 81.50/100 cents U.S. dollars.

(3) Premium c=\$0.30/10000. The price of *the Mar. 81.50 put option on JPY* is 0.3/100 cents per JPY. Since one option contract on the PHLX consists of 6250000 JPY, the total cost for the put is 6250000×0.3/100÷100=\$187.50.

(4) The expiration date of this Mar. 81.50 put option is 17th Mar. 01.

4. *An American put option has exercise price as* E=\$1.5227/£, *the spot exchange rate is* S_t=\$1.5216/£, *then the intrinsic value* = Max[E-S_t, 0]=\$0.0011/£. *If the option premium is* \$0.0008/£, *how to arbitrage from this misprice?*

Arbitrage Process	Cash Flow (Denominated in $)	
1. At time T borrow £	$E+c$	1.5227+0.0008
2. Long put option	$-c$	−0.0008
3. Exercise put option (short £ for $)	E	1.5227
4. Long £ in spot market	$-S_t$	1.5216
5. Repay loan at time T, no interest occurs	$-(E+c)$	−(1.5227+0.0008)
Sum:	$E-S_t-c$	0.0003

5. *American option writer can exercise option before expiration date, why few of them choose to do so?*

If exercised, the profit of an American option is subject to intrinsic value only; if hold this American option and trade it in market, option buyer could earn time value in addition. American option buyers, thus, choose trading options in market instead of exercising options. This also explains why the price of American option is quite close to that of a European option.

6. *Answer questions according to the following diagrams.*

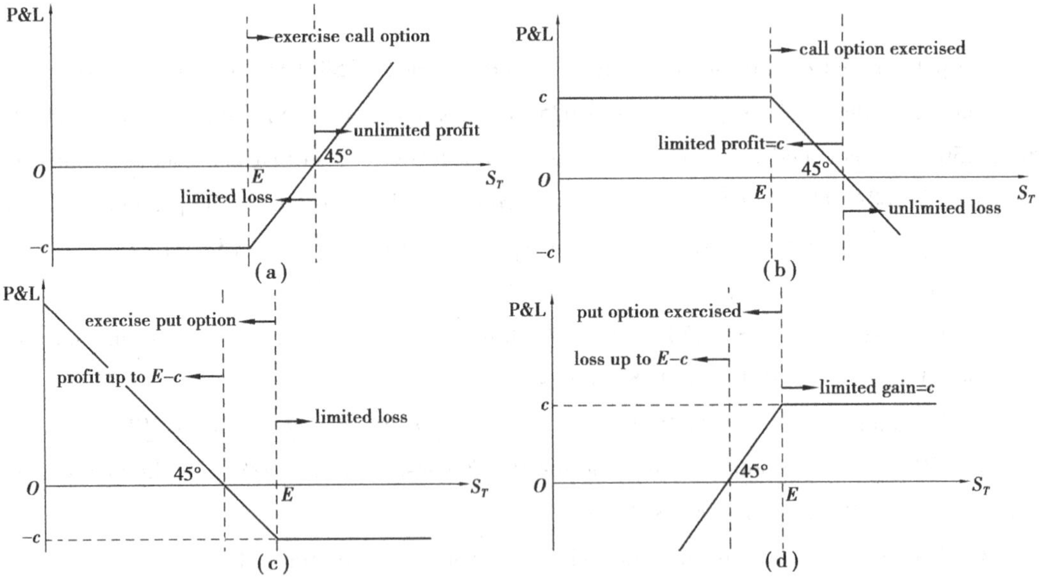

(1) *What are the profit-loss diagrams for option writer?*

diagram (b) and (d)

(2) *What is the break-even exchange rate for option holder?*

holder of a call starts to gain when $S>E+c$

holder of a put starts to gain when $S<E-c$

(3) *What is the break-even exchange rate for option writer?*

writer of a call gains when $S \leqslant E+c$

writer of a put gains when $S \geqslant E-c$

(4) *Other things equal, given the underlying spot exchange rate performance as above, which FX option asks higher option premium?*

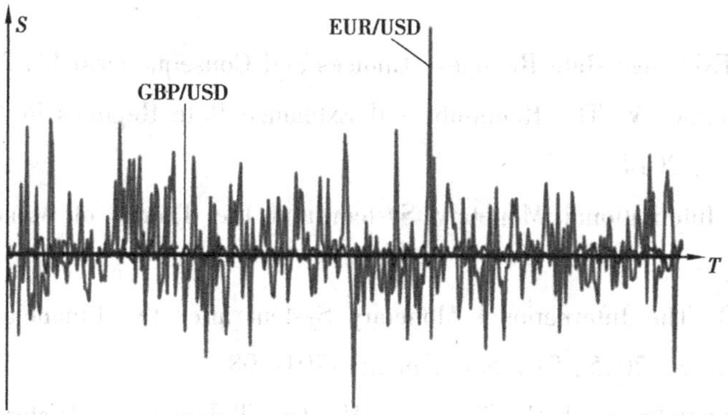

FX option is to insure against the uncertainty of exchange rate fluctuation. Because that currency pair EUR/USD shows wider variance than currency pair GBP/USD, EUR/USD asks higher option premium.

References

[1] Vidaković N. Exchange Rate Regimes: Choices and Consequences[J]. 2014.

[2] Kawai M, Pontines V. The Renminbi and Exchange Rate Regimes in East Asia[J]. Adbi Working Papers, 2014.

[3] Salin P. The International Monetary System and the Theory of Monetary Systems [J]. Books, 2016.

[4] Eichengreen B. The International Monetary System after the Financial Crisis [J]. Open Economies Review, 2015, 9(1 Supplement):701-708.

[5] Obstfeld M, Shambaugh J C, Taylor A M. The Trilemma in History: Tradeoffs among Exchange Rates, Monetary Policies, and Capital Mobility [J]. Review of Economics & Statistics, 2005, 87(3):423-438.

[6] Triennial Central Bank Survey. Basel, Switzerland: Bank for International Settlements, Septermber 2016.

[7] Moore M, Schrimpf A, Sushko V. Downsized FX Markets: Causes and Implications[J]. Bis Quarterly Review, 2016.

[8] Foundation C D. China's Exchange Rate Regime[J]. Asia Pacific Business Review, 2016: 1-2.

[9] Treepongkaruna S. Explaining the Bid-Ask Spread in the Foreign Exchange Market: A Test of Alternate Models[J]. Australian Journal of Management, 2014, 39(4):573-591.

[10] Bollerslev T, Melvin M. Bid-Ask Spreads and Volatility in the Foreign Exchange Market: An Empirical Analysis[J]. 1994, 36(3-4):355-372.

[11] Liang D. Bid-Ask Spread and Order Size in the Foreign Exchange Market: An Empirical Investigation[J]. International Journal of Finance & Economics, 2009, 14(1):98-105.

[12] Huang R D, Masulis R W. FX Spreads and Dealer Competition across the 24-Hour Trading Day[J]. Social Science Electronic Publishing, 1999, 12(1):61-93.

[13] Pasquariello P. The Microstructure of Currency Markets: An Empirical Model of Intra-day Return and Bid-Ask Spread Behavior[J]. Social Science Electronic Publishing, 2000.

[14] Osler C, Wang X. The Microstructure of Currency Markets[J]. Market Microstructure in Emerging and Developed Markets. 2013:79-97.

[15] Aiba Y, Hatano N, Takayasu H, et al. Triangular Arbitrage as an Interaction among Foreign Exchange Rates[J]. Physica a Statistical Mechanics & Its Applications, 2002, 310(3-4):

467-479.

[16] Pasquariello P. Financial Market Dislocations[J]. Ssrn Electronic Journal, 2012, 27(6): 1868-1914.

[17] Villanueva O M. Spot-forward Cointegration, Structural Breaks and FX Market Unbiasedness [J]. Journal of International Financial Markets Institutions & Money, 2007, 17(1): 58-78.

[18] Wang Y D. Convertibility Restriction in China's Foreign Exchange Market and Its Impact on Forward Pricing[J]. Journal of Banking & Finance, 2010, 50(8):616-631.

[19] Li K F, Hui C H, Chung T K. Determinants and Dynamics of Price Disparity in Onshore and Offshore Renminbi Forward Exchange Rate Markets [J]. Ssrn Electronic Journal, 2012.

[20] Otani, Ichiro, and Siddharth Tiwari. Capital Controls and Interest Rate Parity: The Japanese Experience, 1978-81[J]. International Monetary Fund Staff Papers, 28(1981): 793-815.

[21] Burnside C, Eichenbaum M, Rebelo S. Carry Trade and Momentum in Currency Markets [J]. International Journal of Urban & Regional Research, 2011, 3(1):460-481.

[22] Huszar Z R, Zhang W, Tan R S K. Efficiency of Regulated and Unregulated FOREX Markets: An Analysis of Onshore and Offshore Renminbi Forward Markets [M] // The Political Economy of Chinese Finance, 2016.

[23] Otani I, Tiwari S. Capital Controls and Interest Rate Parity: The Japanese Experience, 1978-81[J]. IMF Economic Review, 1981, 28(4):793-815.

[24] Otani I, Fukumoto T, Tsuyuguchi Y. China's Capital Controls and Interest Rate Parity: Experience during 1999-2010 and Future Agenda for Reforms[J]. Bank of Japan Working Paper, 2011.

[25] Zhang W, Yang J. An Empirical Analysis of RMB Exchange Rate Misalignment of RMB NDF-9 Relations[J]. Journal of International Finance Research, 2005 (10): 49-54.

[26] Polito E. Is the Forward Exchange Rate a Useful Indicator of the Future Exchange Rate? [J]. 2000.

[27] Ando M. Recent Developments in U.S. Dollar Funding Costs through FX Swaps[J]. Bank of Japan Review, 2012.

[28] Baba N, F Packer. From Turmoil to Crisis: Dislocations in the FX Swap Market Before and After the Failure of Lehman Brothers [J]. Journal of International Money and Finance, 2009, 28(8): 1350-1374.

[29] Baba N, F Packer, T Nagano. The Spillover of Money Market Turbulence to FX Swap and Cross-Currency Swap Markets[J]. BIS Quarterly Review, 2008 (3): 73-86.

[30] Finch, Gavin, Elliott Gotkine. LIBOR Banks Misstated Rates, Bond at Barclays Says,

Bloomberg News, 2008, May 29.

[31] Chen and Gau. News Announcements and Price Discovery in Foreign Exchange spot and Futures Markets[J]. Journal of Banking & Finance, 2010, 34(7):1628-1636.

[32] Butler K C. 5. Currency Futures and Futures Markets [M] // Multinational Finance: Evaluating Opportunities, Costs, and Risks of Operations. 5th Ed. John Wiley & Sons, Inc., 2015:107-134.

[33] Röthig A, Chiarella C. Small Traders in Currency Futures Markets[J]. Journal of Futures Markets, 2011, 31(9):898-914.

[34] Friedman M. The Need for Futures Markets in Currencies[J]. Cato Journal, 2011, 31: 635-641.

[35] Tornell A, Yuan C. Speculation and Hedging in the Currency Futures Markets: Are They Informative to the Spot Exchange Rates[J]. Journal of Futures Markets, 2012, 32(2): 122-151.

[36] Rodriguez M, Wu T. The Effect of Capital Controls and Prudential FX Measures on Options-Implied Exchange Rate Stability[J]. Ssrn Electronic Journal, 2013.

[37] Black, Fischer, and Myron Scholes. The Pricing of Options and Corporate Liabilities [J]. Journal of Political Economy, 1973, 81 (May-June): 637-659.

[38] Merton, Robert C. Theory of Rational Option Pricing[J]. Bell Journal of Economics and Management Science, 1973, 4 (Spring): 141-183.

[39] Garman Mark B, and Steven V Kohlhagen. Foreign Currency Option Values[J]. Journal of International Money and Finance, 1983 (December): 231-237.

[40] Clark I J. Foreign Exchange Option Pricing: A Practitioner's Guide [M]. New York: Wiley, 2015.